THEY FOLLOWED THE PLUME

Maj. Gen. James Ewell Brown Stuart

THEY FOLLOWED THE PLUME

The Story
of J. E. B. Stuart
and His Staff

ROBERT J. TROUT

STACKPOLE
BOOKS

First published in paperback in 2003 by
STACKPOLE BOOKS
5067 Ritter Road
Mechanicsburg, PA 17055
www.stackpolebooks.com

Maps by Robert E. Lee Trout

Cover design by Caroline M. Stover

Cover illustration: "Gen. J. E. B. Stuart's Raid around McClellan. June 1862" by Henry A. Ogden (Library of Congress)

Printed in the United States of America

10 9 8 7 6 5 4 3 2 1

FIRST EDITION

Library of Congress Cataloging-in-Publication Data

Trout, Robert J., 1947–
    They followed the plume : the story of J. E. B. Stuart and his staff/
by Robert J. Trout.—1st ed.
        p.   cm.
    Includes bibliographical references and index.
    ISBN 0-8117-2904-4
    1. Confederate States of America. Army. Virginia Cavalry
Regiment, 1st. 2. Confederate States of America. Army. Virginia
Cavalry Regiment 1st—Officers—Biography. 3. Stuart, Jeb.
1833–1864. 4. Virginia—History—Civil War, 1861–1865—
Regimental Histories. 5. United States—History—Civil War,
1861–1865—Regimental Histories. I. Title.
E581.6 1st T76   1993   92-41004
973.7'455—dc20   CIP

To those who followed the plume
and
to those who follow it still

Maj. Gen. "Jeb" Stuart

CONTENTS

FOREWORD

THIS BOOK PROVIDES important information regarding most of the men who served at General Stuart's cavalry headquarters and is a most valuable contribution to the literature of the War Between the States. It also serves as a tribute to those men who contributed so much to our heritage.

Life at Stuart's Headquarters has been fully documented in the postwar memoirs and books of such well-known members of his staff as McClellan, Boteler, Blackford, Cooke, and von Borcke. Additional information is contained in numerous letters written by Channing Price, and of course General Stuart's own voluminous correspondence provides additional insights.

The men of intellect, culture, and refinement who served on Stuart's staff were noted for their devotion to him and to each other. When occasional differences occurred, Stuart, with his tact and charisma, quickly resolved the issue and harmony reigned. During the brief respites from the vicissitudes of war, their beloved general arranged for recreational and morale-building events such as boating, charades, dancing, serenades, and dramatic presentations.

The superb leadership qualities of General Stuart inspired his men, and they followed wherever he led. Col. John Singleton Mosby, the Confederacy's most famous guerrilla fighter, wrote, "My only desire was to serve him." Channing Price once wrote his sister, "We are having a very dull time lately, as indeed we always do when the General is absent, he seeming to take all its life from Headquarters when he goes." As the war continued, there was great sorrow at headquarters as many of these gallant men gave their lives for the cause. Finally Stuart himself made the supreme sacrifice. Those who survived the war and Reconstruction in the South became well known as successful diplomats, judges, lawyers, ministers, educators, and businessmen. They richly deserve to be remembered for their contributions in war and peace.

In addition, there were numerous other men who faithfully served Stuart in one capacity or another at headquarters. These men were not so well known, but they too should be remembered. To locate information about them, Mr. Trout spent several years in extensive and diligent research. With sometimes scarcely more than a surname to guide him, he managed to discover pertinent information about their lives, their service records, and photographs. Most rewarding of all, he located a number of descendants who were proud of their ancestors who "rode with 'Jeb' Stuart."

This book is a very valuable reference tool for present and future writers who have an interest in researching the history of the Cavalry Corps of the Army of Northern Virginia.

ADELE H. MITCHELL, EDITOR
SOUTHERN CAVALRY REVIEW

PREFACE

CIVIL WAR LITERATURE is filled with the names of the men who commanded the armies, corps, divisions, and brigades of the Northern and Southern military forces. Entire books have been devoted to the lives and careers of many of these general officers. Other works recounting the campaigns and battles give significant space to these men. Whether they were viewed as heroes or villains, the responsibility of leadership on the drill ground or battlefield was in their hands. Some proved capable; others failed. The stories of their successes and failures fill library shelves.

Virtually lost, however, are the names of others who rode beside these men. The duties of the staff officers, scouts, couriers, clerks, and escort troops varied according to the whims of their commanders-in-chief, but without them, the generals would not have been able to lead effectively.

A small number of the men who served on the generals' staffs rose to attain generalship themselves, but most labored in anonymity. A few gained some measure of fame by authoring books after the war. These works, however, invariably focused on the men they served. As a result, no record of an entire staff in either army has appeared in print. The only mark that many of these men left was a signature at the bottom of an order or requisition.

This book is an attempt to place in the spotlight, if only briefly, a few of those thousands who served on the staffs of generals both blue and gray. It delves into the careers of the men who served one of the most celebrated generals of the war, Major General James Ewell Brown Stuart.

ACKNOWLEDGMENTS

THE ACCUMULATION OF the facts, quotations, excerpts, obituaries, articles, and letters included in this volume would have been an impossibility without the assistance of dozens of individuals, either privately or through the institutions for which they work. To say the writer is indebted to them is a gross understatement; without them the story of the men who "followed the plume" could not have been told.

To the descendants of a few staff officers and headquarters personnel or their families, the writer owes a special debt of gratitude. Their willingness and enthusiasm to share material about their ancestors permitted a closer look at Stuart and the men who rode by his side.

Finally, to Mrs. Adele Mitchell; Ms. Jennifer Young; my son, Robert E. Lee Trout; my daughter, Desirée K. Trout; and last but not least, my wife, Judy: Thank you for your time, help, advice, patience, and understanding over the past six years.

The following descendants of Stuart's staff provided valuable assistance or documents: Mrs. Sally-Bruce B. McClatchey (W. W. Blackford), Mr. Staige D. Blackford (W. W. Blackford), Mr. Talcott Eliason, III (T. Eliason), Mr. William A. Eliason (T. Eliason), Mrs. Isabel Smith Stewart (W. D. & H. S. Farley), Capt. R. Scott Sayre (G. Freed), Mrs. Maria Hood (T. S. Garnett), Mr. Theodore S. Garnett, Jr. (T. S. Garnett), Mr. Charles R. Goldsborough (R. H. Goldsborough), Mr. George J. Goldsborough (R. H. Goldsborough), Mr. George Grattan Weston (C. Grattan), Mrs. George G. Grattan, IV (C. Grattan), Mr. C. Grattan Price, Jr. (C. Grattan), Judge Peter W. Hairston (P. W. Hairston), Mrs. Aldine West (L. Levy), Mrs. Robert E. Osth (P. H. Powers), Mr. Philip H. Powers, Jr. (P. H. Powers), Mrs. Virginia N. Pillsbury (P. H. Powers), Mr. James S. Patton (F. S. Robertson), Mr. Samuel Hopkins (C. M. Smith), Mr. Edwin M. Wilson (S. G. Staples), and Mr. Robert deT. Lawrence, IV (T. Turner).

The following individuals also provided assistance or materials: Ms. Mary Emma Allen, Mr. L.C. Angle, Jr., Mrs. Nancy C. Baird, Mrs. Shirley B. Bassett, Mr. Keith Bohannon, Mrs. Mildred Brownlee, Mrs. William Bushman, Mr. Frank A. Christian, Ms. Eileen Conklin, Mr. John Divine, Mr. Robert Driver, Mr. David Dubble, Mr. Thomas Evans, Ms. Myrtle Hanger, Mr. David D. Hartzler, Mrs. Marie Hays, Mr. Michael F. Howell, Mrs. Mary Anne Jackson, Mrs. Edward J. Jones, Mrs. Junius W. Jones, Mrs. Lucy B. Jones, Mr. Robert K. Krick, Mrs. Betty L.

Krimminger, Mr. Thomas Lehman, Mr. Lewis Leigh, Jr., Mrs. John D. Lowe, Jr., Mr. David R. Lowther, Ms. Linda Manwiller, Mr. Scott C. Mauger, Mr. C. E. May, Mr. F. Lawrence McFall, Jr., Mr. James Miller, Mrs. June Mitchell, Dr. Ray Moreland, Mr. Martin Morris, Mr. George I. Mulholland, Mr. Michael Musik, Mrs. Mary Beirne Nutt, Mr. Thad Patterson, Mr. Harry Roach, Mr. Eugene Scheel, Ms. Mary Elizabeth Sergent, Mr. Richard F. S. Starr, Col. W. D. Swank, Mr. William Turner, Mr. Adrian H. von Borcke, Ms. Peggy Votsberger, Mr. Ronald Waddell, Mr. Lee A. Wallace, Jr., Mr. Robert Walls, Mrs. James Madison Weaver, Jr., Ms. Donna J. Williams, and Mr. Charles Young.

The following institutions and organizations and the people who work for them were also of great help: Ms. Sandra O'Keefe, Alexandria Library; Ms. J. West, Amelia Historical Committee; Mr. Robert A. Buerlein, American Historical Foundation; Ms. Betty Ammons, Baltimore Conference—United Methodist Historical Society; Ms. Linda Chancey, Bartow Public Library; Mr. Barry Reynolds, Blue Ridge Regional Library; Ms. Julie Sandidge, Brunswick-Greensville Regional Library; Ms. Jeri Fahrenbach, CEL Regional Library; Mrs. Barbara P. Willis, Central Rappahannock Regional Library; Mr. Steven Roehling, Charleston County Library; Ms. Patricia G. Bennett, Charleston Library Society; Peggy A. Haile, City of Norfolk—Department of Libraries; Ms. Anne T. Richardson, City of Virginia Beach—Department of Public Libraries; Ms. Mary T. Morris, Clarke County Historical Association; Mr. G. Elliott Cummings, Col. Harry W. Gilmor Camp #1388 Sons of Confederate Veterans; Ms. Laura Francis Parrish, The College of William and Mary in Virginia; Mr. Bernard Crystal, Columbia University in the City of New York; Mr. John B. Thomas, Davidson County Community College; Mr. Kenneth T. Jones and Ms. Theresa M. Gazaleh, Department of Health and Rehabilitative Services—State of Florida; Ms. Marie Booth Ferré, Dickinson College; Ms. Linda McCurdy, Duke University; Mr. William E. Sleeman and Ms. Anna Curry, Enoch Pratt Free Library; Mr. Richard L. Mueller, The Evergreen Cemetery Association (Jacksonville, Florida); Mrs. Barbara M. Jenner, Fannie Bayly King Staunton Public Library; Mr. James J. Holmberg, The Filson Club; Ms. Nadine Doty-Tessel, Florida State Archives; Ms. Kathryn Flynn, Frederick County Public Libraries; Ms. Carolyn Ocheltree, Mr. Michael Minch, and Ms. Mary-Louise Mussell, General Commission on Archives and History—The United Methodist Church; Ms. Mary Pitt, Georgia Historical Society; Ms. Nancy J. Fallgren, Georgetown University; Ms. M. Stoner, The Greensburg Library; Ms. Catherine B. Pollari, Hampden-Sidney College; Miss Mary E. Pugh, Hampshire County Public Library; Ms. Rebecca A. Ebert, The Handley Library; Mrs. Faye A. Witters, Harrisonburg-Rockingham

Historical Society; Mr. William G. Willmann, The Historical Society of Frederick County; Mr. L. C. Angle, Jr., The Historical Society of Washington County, Virginia; Brother James Sommers, Holy Cross Abbey; Ms. Harriet McLoone and Mr. Bryant M. Duffy, The Huntington; C. H. Harris, Jacksonville Public Library; Mr. John Ingalls, Jefferson County Museum; Miss Elaine Martin, Laurens County Library; Ms. Martha H. LeStourgeon, Longwood College; Ms. Carolyn Neault, Lowndes County Library; Mr. Keith E. Hammersla, Martinsburg-Berkeley County Public Library; Mr. Raymond B. Clark, Jr., The Maryland and Delaware Genealogist; Mr. Michael Hennen, Mississippi Department of Archives and History; Ms. Renita Lane, Mississippi Library Commission; Mr. Charles T. Jacobs, The Montgomery County Historical Society; Mrs. Netty Bryant, Mount Olivet Cemetery; Ms. Corrine P. Hudgins, The Museum of the Confederacy; Ms. Cynthia Barnes, Norfolk Public Library; Ms. Roberta Y. Arminio, Ossining Historical Society; Mrs. Lucille C. Payne, Pittsylvania Historical Society; Ms. Wendy K. Davies, Polk County Historical and Genealogical Library; Ms. Janice S. Mahaffey, Putnam County Archives & History; Ms. Anna Roberts Ware, The Queen Anne's County Historical Society; Mr. Henry O. Robertson, Randolph-Macon College; Mr. William S. Simpson, Jr., Richmond Public Library; Ms. Alice Carol Tuckwiller, Roanoke City Public Library; Mr. Nick Whitmer, Rockingham Public Library; Mrs. W. E. Martinsons and Ms. Jacqueline Fretwell, St. Augustine Historical Society; Mr. David T. Newlin and Ms. Jean A. Elliott, Shepherd College; Mrs. Ralph Mitchell and Mrs. Carol Terry, Stuart-Mosby Historical Society; Ms. Scotti Oliver and Mr. William Bodenstein, The Talbot County Free Library; Mr. Jonathan Walters, The University of Chicago Library; Ms. Sharon Eve Sarthou, The University of Mississippi; Ms. Judith A. Robins, Thomas Jefferson University; Mr. John White, University of North Carolina at Chapel Hill; Mr. Ervin L. Jordan, Jr. (Technical Services Archivist), University of Virginia; Mr. Michael J. Winey (Special Collections Branch) and Dr. Richard J. Sommers (Archivist-Historian), U.S. Army Military History Institute (Carlisle Barracks); Ms. Bridgitte Keller-Huschemenger, U.S. Information Service—Embassy of the United States of America; Ms. Joy B. Trulock, Valdosta State College; Ms. Janet B. Schwarz, Virginia Historical Society; Ms. Diane B. Jacob, Virginia Military Institute; John B. Straw, Virginia Polytechnic Institute and State University; Mr. Mark Scala, Ms. Ella Gaines Yates, Mr. Ted Polk, Mr. Donald L. Morecock, and Ms. Carolyn S. Parsons, Virginia State Library; Mr. John C. Frye, Washington County Free Library; Ms. Peggy Bledsoe, Washington County Historical Society; Ms. Dorothy Anne Reinhold, Waynesboro Public Library; and Ms. Sylvia B. Kennick, Williams College.

Maj. Gen. "Jeb" Stuart and Staff

PART ONE

Stuart
and
His Staff

History

We followed, almost at the top of our speed, thinking that at every fork of the road we would turn to the right and come out in front of the enemy; but to our surprise, at every fork, Stuart's indomitable feather was wont to bear to the left taking us directly behind the enemy's lines.[1]

—Sgt. B. J. Haden, 1st Virginia Cavalry

THE STORY OF the men who followed "Stuart's indomitable feather" began in May 1861 when newly commissioned James Ewell Brown Stuart reported to Col. Thomas J. Jackson at Harpers Ferry, Virginia. Jackson ignored Stuart's appointment as a lieutenant colonel of infantry and instead placed the youthful officer in charge of the cavalry forces of his command. Jackson's decision proved to be one he never had cause to regret. By late July, Stuart was a full colonel in command of the 1st Virginia Cavalry.

Regarding Stuart's assignment to the cavalry, Jackson can be credited with having had the ability to discern an individual's talent in order to place him in a position where he could render the greatest service. Stuart also had this ability: As he forged the cavalry companies assigned him into a regiment, he kept aware of men with unique talents, exceptional courage, and a desire to excel. Such men, Stuart knew, would be valuable should the war drag on longer than the few months some optimistically predicted.

In his position as commander of the 1st Virginia, Stuart had the opportunity to gather about him men who quickly demonstrated their usefulness. A Marylander named Luke Tiernan Brien came to volunteer his services. The Reverend Dabney Ball, fresh from his pulpit in Baltimore, found a niche as chaplain of the regiment. Peter Wilson Hairston traveled all the way from North Carolina to ride beside Stuart, his cousin and brother-in-law, as a voluntary aide. These and others showed their mettle at 1st Manassas. On that bloody field, Lt. William Willis Blackford's conduct attracted Stuart's attention, as did that of Lt. Richard Byrd Kennon and Sgt. Maj. Philip Henry Powers. "High praise" was accorded to Lt. Robert Franklin Beckham, whose talents as an artilleryman Stuart would call upon in the years ahead. One more future staff officer, Lt. John Pelham, also began to carve out his reputation at Manassas, but Stuart was not in a position to see his stubborn heroics, though perhaps he heard of them. In any event, Stuart would soon come to appreciate Pelham's gifts firsthand in the Stuart Horse Artillery.

On September 11, 1861, Stuart made a reconnaissance toward Lewinsville, Virginia. During the expedition, Rev. Ball and P. W. Hairston again "rendered valuable assistance" and displayed conspicuous daring. Another individual, who would later serve on the staff, received mention in Stuart's report. Cpl. William "Henry" Hagan was "entitled to special mention for good conduct and valuable service."[2] Stuart gradually added names to the list of men he had marked for future advancement.

Colonel Stuart, who had been highly complimented for his part in the first major battle of the war, received a reward for his services on September 24, 1861, when he was commissioned a brigadier general. Shortly thereafter, on October 2, Stuart issued General Orders No. 1, which announced his assumption of the command of the newly organized cavalry brigade and named the first members of his staff. These officers were Capt. Luke Tiernan Brien, assistant adjutant general and chief of staff; Capt. Roger Williams Steger, assistant quartermaster; and Capt. Dabney Ball, chief of subsistence. From this date until his fall at Yellow Tavern on May 11, 1864, forty-eight men would serve on Stuart's staff. Over two hundred more would be a part of his headquarters company at various times. Some would remain for months; others would be there only briefly. Stuart knew most of them personally, and almost all were hand-picked by him. His gift of insight rarely failed him, and he established the reputation of having one of the finest staffs in the Confederate Army.

In late September 1861, a future staff officer had briefly been part of cavalry headquarters. George Freaner had escaped from Hagerstown, Maryland, and made his way south to join Stuart's command as a volunteer aide. Also, until mid-October, Stuart continued to enjoy the services of P. W. Hairston. His talents were much appreciated, and Stuart offered him a commission on the staff. Hairston, however, preferred the freedom that came with retaining civilian status and, after turning down his cousin's offer, went back to North Carolina to attend to affairs on his family's plantation. Within a month of Hairston's departure, Captain Steger also left the staff for unknown reasons. Despite these losses, the staff grew in number, and by the middle of December it totaled five officers. In addition to Captains Ball and Brien, there were Lt. Chiswell Dabney, aide-de-camp; Lt. John Pelham, responsible for organizing the Stuart Horse Artillery, which he would then command; and Capt. William Eskridge Towles, aide-de-camp.

On December 20 the staff had its first opportunity to test itself against the enemy. Stuart received orders to accompany some of the army's wagons on a forage for hay in the vicinity of Dranesville, Virginia. Unfortunately for the new brigadier, five regiments of Pennsylvania infantry along with the 1st Pennsylvania Artillery and the 1st Pennsylvania Cavalry had been dispatched toward the same locale. When the two forces collided, Stuart found himself at a numerical disadvantage and encumbered by the wagon train he was assigned to protect. Nevertheless, he managed to extricate his command from the situation, and his staff officers responded as he had known they would. In his report he cited a few of the men who had helped him accomplish the feat. Capt. L. T. Brien and Lt. Chiswell Dabney had performed "valuable services on the field." Future staff member and scout Redmond Burke had served in Stuart's escort on this occasion and was, with the rest of the escort, accorded special thanks for "promptness and accuracy in conveying orders and instructions." Hagan garnered the greatest praise of all: "Corporal Henry Hagan, of First Virginia Cavalry, was of great service in showing the first Kentucky its position in line, and proved himself on this as on every other occasion worthy of a commission."[3]

The first half of 1862 brought many changes in personnel. The army was undergoing both internal and external upheaval. Names that were to become linked with Stuart's began to appear on orders and requisitions. By early May, fourteen men held positions on Stuart's burgeoning staff. There was to be one significant loss: Capt. L. T. Brien had been promoted to lieutenant colonel in the cavalry and would soon leave to assume his new position. In spite of this, Stuart would continue for a time to use Brien as his chief of staff and would mention him as such in his report of the action at Williamsburg. Brien had greatly impressed Stuart and would be missed.

New to Stuart's headquarters were Lt. Redmond Burke, voluntary aide-de-camp and scout; Lt. John Esten Cooke, ordnance officer; Talcott Eliason, medical director; Capt. William Downs Farley, scout; Lt. Henry Hagan, acting aide-de-camp; Lt. James Thomas Watt Hairston, acting assistant adjutant general; Capt. Samuel Harden Hairston, voluntary aide-de-camp; Rev. John Landstreet, voluntary aide; Maj. Philip Henry Powers, quartermaster; and Capt. Samuel Granville Staples, voluntary aide-de-camp. With these men and those already on his staff, Stuart launched into the 1862 summer campaign.

The landing of Maj. Gen. George B. McClellan's Union Army at Fort Monroe on the Virginia Peninsula prompted the Confederate fortification of the area around Williamsburg. Gen. Joseph E. Johnston eventually decided that the network of forts and entrenchments could not be defended and ordered a withdrawal up the peninsula toward Richmond. Stuart's rear guard duties brought on a clash with the enemy on May 4. In recounting the action, Stuart mentioned two officers by name.

My volunteer aide, Capt. S. G. Staples, who joined me but a day or two before, participated in the charge with the Hampton Legion Cavalry.

I will, however, mention the fearless daring and cool and determined courage always so conspicuous in Capt. W. D. Farley, attached as volunteer aide. He manages to get into every fight, and is always conspicuously gallant. He is a young man of rare modesty, merit, and worth, who can scarcely be replaced.[4]

On May 5 the advancing Federals again struck at the retiring Confederates and precipitated the Battle of Williamsburg. Stuart, with the cavalry and the newly organized Stuart Horse Artillery, was again involved. Pelham and the horse artillery were especially conspicuous, and in his report of the battle Stuart wrote, "I ordered it [the Stuart Horse Artillery] forward under the gallant Pelham. . . ." This was the first but not the last time Pelham was called gallant in an official report. It had not taken Stuart long to appreciate his gifted young artillerist. Stuart also called his commander's attention to a number of other officers and men of his staff and escort. He recorded the following, in part:

> The conduct of Lieutenant-Colonel Brien, First Virginia Cavalry, my chief of staff, is deserving special mention. His efficiency as a staff officer on the field was hardly excelled by his gallantry as a soldier.
>
> Maj. Dabney Ball, in action always transformed into the "bold, dashing huzzar," displayed all the admirable qualities which he has so often had ascribed to him on the field.
>
> Lieut. Chiswell Dabney, my aide-de-camp, was active and brave in the discharge of every duty.
>
> Lieut. Redmond Burke was ever under great personal danger, and led more than once the re-inforcements sent to Colonel Jenkins to their positions.
>
> Lieut. J. T. W. Hairston, C.S. Army, on duty with my brigade, rendered very essential and gallant service during the action.
>
> Captain Towles, to whose daring reference has already been made, is entitled to high commendation for the continued exhibition of a quality so desirable in cavalry service.
>
> Capt. W. D. Farley has always exhibited such

admirable coolness, undaunted courage, and intelligent comprehension of military matters that he would be of invaluable service as a commanding officer assigned to outpost service.

Rev. John Landstreet, chaplain First Virginia Cavalry, was as conspicuous for gallantry and usefulness on the field as he is distinguished for eloquence in the pulpit, and I am greatly indebted to him for the voluntary and important assistance rendered me during the day as well as on previous occasions.

Two gentlemen, who had joined me but a few days before as volunteer aides, Capts. Samuel Hardin [*sic*] Hairston and Samuel G. Staples, gave evidence, by their coolness, intelligence, and conspicuous gallantry, of future distinction in arms, and were of invaluable service to me.

It gives me pleasure to record my obligations to my escort . . . Corpl. Henry Hagan, First Virginia Cavalry, who was fully up to his reputation for brilliant and dashing courage previously earned. . . .[5]

Brigadier General Stuart was justifiably proud of the 1,289 men under his command. The Stuart Horse Artillery had proved worthy in its baptism of fire, its young commander laying the foundation for one of the most celebrated units of the war. The cavalry chieftain's staff and escort had earned the commendations their commander had heaped upon them in his reports. Their conduct set the precedent for those who were to come. Yet even with all of this success, a greater feat still lay ahead.

As May drew to a close, Gen. Joe Johnston concluded that he could retreat no farther. Indeed, for the Federal advance units, the spires of Richmond's churches stood out against the sky, and the pealing of their bells could be heard distinctly. Johnston had to fight, and he did so at Seven Pines. The sanguinary battle that developed gave no advantage to either side but cost the Southern army its commander. President Davis replaced the badly wounded Johnston with his military advisor, Robert E. Lee. Lee needed information about the enemy, and he called his young cavalry brigadier to his headquarters for a consultation. The result was the Chickahominy Raid, which Stuart carried out from June 12 through the 15.

This Ride Around McClellan, as it came to be known, established Stuart as a cavalry commander of considerable ability. The combination of daring and resourcefulness he displayed on the one-hundred-mile expedition behind the enemy's lines fired the South's spirit and set the

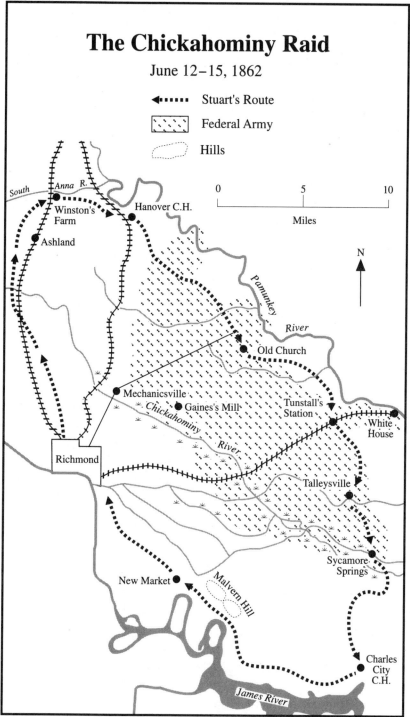

The Chickahominy Raid

June 12–15, 1862

◄······ Stuart's Route

Federal Army

Hills

South *Anna* R.

Winston's Farm

Hanover C.H.

Ashland

Pamunkey

0   5   10

Miles

River

N

Old Church

Mechanicsville

Chickahominy

Gaines's Mill

Tunstall's Station

White House

Richmond

River

Talleysville

Sycamore Springs

New Market

Malvern Hill

Charles City C.H.

James River

stage for Robert E. Lee's emergence as the "Savior of Richmond." When Stuart filed his report, he generously praised his staff, which now included two new members: Capt. Johann August Heinrich Heros von Borcke, an aide but soon to be assistant adjutant general; and Lt. Jones Rivers Christian, acting aide-de-camp. With these and the others Stuart shared the credit for his remarkable accomplishment.

> I am most of all indebted to . . . Second Lieut. Jones R. Christian and Private R. E. Frayser [a future staff officer], Third Virginia Cavalry, who were ever in the advance, and without whose thorough knowledge of the country and valuable assistance rendered I could have effected nothing.
>
> Asst. Surgeon J. B. Fontaine [another future staff officer], Fourth Virginia Cavalry (the enemy giving him little to do in his profession), was bold and indefatigable in reconnaissance, and was particularly active in his effort to complete the bridge.
>
> Capt. Heros von Borcke, a Prussian cavalry officer, who lately ran the blockade, assigned me by the honorable Secretary of War, joined in the charge of the First Squadron in gallant style, and subsequently, by his energy, skill, and activity, won the praise and admiration of all.
>
> To my staff present my thanks are especially due for the diligent performance of the duties assigned to them; they were as follows: First Lieut. John Esten Cooke, ordnance officer, my principal staff officer for the occasion; First Lieut. C. Dabney, aide-de-camp.
>
> Rev. Mr. Landstreet, Captains Farley, Towles, Fitzhugh [*sic*], and Mosby rendered conspicuous and gallant service during the whole expedition.
>
> My escort, under Corporal Hagan, are entitled individually to my thanks for their zeal and devotion to duty. . . .[6]

In an enclosure to his report, Stuart made recommendations for the promotion of certain officers he thought particularly deserving.

> 4. Assist. Surg. J. B. Fontaine to be surgeon of his regiment (Fourth Virginia Cavalry), now without one. Dr. Fontaine is a man of signal military merit and an adept in his profession.
>
> 5. M. Heros von Borcke, a Prussian cavalry officer,

has shown himself a thorough soldier and a splendid officer. I hope the Department will confer as high a commission as possible on this deserving man, who has cast his lot with us in the trying hour.

6. First Lieut. Redmond Burke to be captain, for the important service rendered by him on this occasion.

7. Capts. W. D. Farley and J. S. Mosby, without commission, have established a claim for position which a grateful country will not, I trust, disregard. Their distinguished services run far back toward the beginning of the war, and present a shining record of daring and usefulness.[7]

Despite Stuart's efforts on behalf of his staff and others, however, the military situation left little time for the Confederate War Department to concern itself with commendations and promotions.

General Lee, with the information brought him by his cavalry commander, set about planning the undoing of his adversary and the securing of Richmond. In the midst of the coming and going of troops in and around Richmond, three officers found their way to Stuart's camp and joined the staff just before the Seven Days Campaign opened. These were Capt. William Willis Blackford, engineer officer; Capt. Norman Richard FitzHugh, assistant adjutant general; and Capt. James Hardeman Stuart, signal officer.

For a cavalry officer of less initiative, the terrain over which most of this campaign was fought would have offered an excellent excuse for remaining where the bullets were not as thick. Stuart, however, was not one to lag in the rear and kept his troops active while the opposing infantry forces tore at each other from Mechanicsville to Malvern Hill. On July 14, 1862, while the tired cavalry regiments recovered their strength in camp near Hanover Court House, Stuart wrote his account of what had transpired during the days that decided the fate of the Confederate nation. As before, he was munificent in his praise for his men.

Capt. John Pelham, of the Horse Artillery, displayed such signal ability as an artillerist, such heroic example and devotion in danger, and indomitable energy under difficulties in the movement of his battery, that, reluctant as I am at the chance of losing such a valuable limb from the brigade, I feel bound to ask for his promotion, with the remark that in either cavalry or artillery no field grade is too high for his merit and capacity. The officers and men of that battery emulated the example of their captain, and did justice to the reputation already won.

Capt. William W. Blackford, of the Engineers, assigned to duty with me the day before the battles, was always in advance, obtaining valuable information of the enemy's strength, movements, and position, locating routes, and making hurried but accurate sketches. He is bold in reconnaissance, fearless in danger, and remarkably cool and correct in judgment. His services are invaluable to the advance guard of an army.

Capt. J. Hardeman Stuart, Signal Corps, was particularly active and fearless in the transmission of orders at Cold Harbor, and deserves my special thanks for his gallant conduct.

Capt. Norman R. Fitzhugh [sic], assistant adjutant-general, chief of staff, though but recently promoted from the ranks, gave evidence of those rare qualities, united with personal gallantry, which constitute a capable and efficient adjutant-general.

Capt. Heros von Borcke, assistant adjutant-general, was ever present, fearless and untiring in the zealous discharge of the duties assigned to him.

Maj. Samuel Hardin [sic] Hairston, quartermaster, and Maj. Dabney Ball, commissary of subsistence, were prevented by their duties of office from participating in the dangers of the conflict, but are entitled to my thanks for the thorough discharge of their duties.

The following officers attached to my staff deserve honorable mention in this report for their valuable services: Capt. Redmond Burke; Lieut. John Esten Cooke, ordnance officer; Lieut. J. T. W. Hairston, C.S. Army; Lieut. Jones R. Christian, Third Virginia Cavalry; Lieut. Chiswell Dabney, aide; Capts. W. D. Farley and W. E. Towles, volunteer aides, they having contributed their full share to whatever success was achieved by the brigade.

My escort did good service. Private Frank Stringfellow, Fourth Virginia Cavalry, was particularly conspicuous for gallantry and efficiency at Cold Harbor.[8]

By July 14, when Stuart wrote this report, he had lost the services of five officers: Jones Christian went back to his cavalry company; Philip Powers left because of ill health; John Landstreet resumed his full-time chaplain duties; Samuel Staples retired because of an accident; and William Towles rejoined his former comrades in the artillery. Even with these losses, the staff totaled fourteen men, all of whom had seen some of the action that transpired from May through early July. At the end of April, Stuart had had ten men attached to his staff; in a little more than two months, that number had increased to a high of seventeen in mid-June before dropping back to fourteen. The staff's growth was significant, even though some members had been attached for only a few weeks while campaigning in a familiar area, because this growth mirrored the growth of the cavalry in general and the added responsibility being placed on Stuart.

On July 25, 1862, Stuart was rewarded with a major generalcy for his part in Richmond's redemption. Several members of his staff profited by their association with one of the South's new heroes and received appropriate promotions in rank. Stuart's new commission entitled him to a larger staff, and during the first few days of August he added two men: Maj. William J. Johnson, chief of subsistence; and Lt. Richard Channing Price, aide-de-camp. But a loss somewhat offset these gains: After a disagreement with Stuart, Dabney Ball resigned his position as commissary officer on July 15. Thus at the opening of the 2nd Manassas Campaign in August 1862, the staff totaled fifteen.

Robert E. Lee, determined to eradicate the threat of Maj. Gen. John Pope to northern Virginia, formulated plans that gave an important role to Stuart and his cavalry. Fate and garbled orders intervened. On August 18 Stuart and his staff members N. R. FitzHugh, Heros von Borcke, C. Dabney, John Singleton Mosby (who was attached to the staff's couriers but acted as a scout), and Mosby's friend Lt. Samuel B. Gibson found themselves in the small hamlet of Verdiersville without the general's usually alert escort and at the mercy of an enemy patrol. Though failing to capture Stuart, the 1st Michigan Cavalry did succeed in taking FitzHugh. The adjutant, who had just received his major's star, had the comfort of seeing his chief and fellow officers escape but found himself in prison. He was the first of Stuart's staff to be captured in the war, and it was undoubtedly an honor he would have preferred to decline. Even worse, he had with him Lee's orders for the deployment of the army against Pope, who, forewarned, managed to evade the Confederates.

Stuart had suffered the loss of his hat and cape, and he vowed revenge. He raided Pope's headquarters at Catlett's Station and captured the Union commander's dress coat. He then joined Gen. "Stonewall" Jackson on one of his famous flank marches. Along with the "Savior of the Valley," who had something to prove himself after his own lackluster performance during the Seven Days Campaign, Stuart and his command descended upon the Federal supply base at Manassas Junction. The subsequent Battle of 2nd Manassas ended in the total discomfiture of Pope.

Stuart and his men deserved the credit accorded them by the high

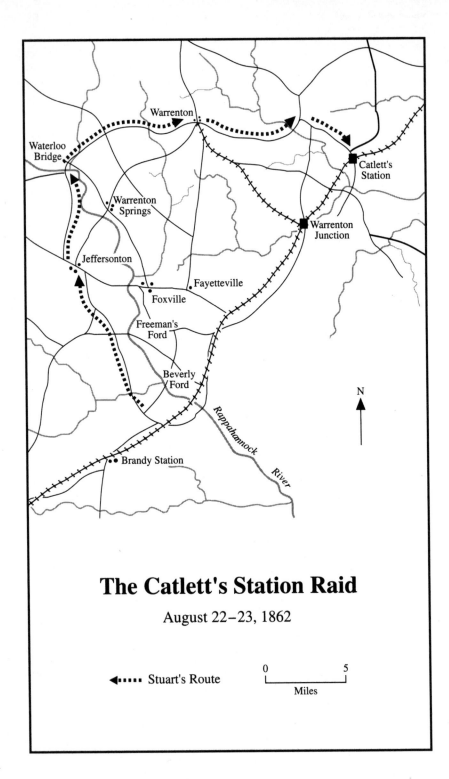

The Catlett's Station Raid

August 22–23, 1862

◀••••• Stuart's Route

0   5

Miles

command, but cavalry headquarters was stunned by the news that the cavalry chieftain's cousin Hardeman Stuart had fallen in the midst of the final infantry attack of the day. Though the armband of mourning was to be worn for thirty days, the business of war still had to be conducted. To replace his fallen cousin, Stuart called upon Capt. Richard Edgar Frayser, of Chickahominy Raid fame, to serve as signal officer. It was not until February 28, 1863, that Stuart wrote his report on the cavalry's role in the campaign. He stated, in part:

> During the day [August 30, 1862] I sent Capt. J. Hardeman Stuart, my signal officer, to capture the enemy's signal party on View Tree, an eminence overlooking Warrenton, and establish his own flag instead; the sequel shows with what success.
>
> At one time on the 30th I noticed our front lines near the Chinn's house giving way, and looking back saw the reserve line stationary. I sent word to the general commanding (whose name I did not learn) to move up, as he was much needed to support the attack. That order was carried by Capt. W. D. Farley, volunteer aide, under circumstances of great personal danger, in which his horse was shot.
>
> My division surgeon, Talcott Eliason, besides being an adept in his profession, exhibited on this, as on former occasions, the attributes of a cavalry commander.
>
> First Lieut. R. Channing Price was of invaluable assistance as aide-de-camp.
>
> Maj. Von Borcke, assistant adjutant-general, and Maj. J. T. W. Hairston, C.S. Army, and Lieut. Chiswell Dabney, aide-de-camp, rendered important service throughout the period embraced in this report.
>
> My division quartermaster, Maj. Samuel Hardin [sic] Hairston, in coming on to join me, was put in command of a detachment of cavalry at Salem by the commanding general, and sent on an important reconnaissance toward Warrenton, of which his report is appended.
>
> Capt. W. W. Blackford, Corps of Engineers, was quick and indefatigable in his efforts to detect the designs of the enemy and improve the positions within our reach.
>
> I have to mourn the loss of Capt. J. Hardeman Stuart, signal officer, the particulars of whose death are given below.

Capt. J. Hardeman Stuart, who was sent to capture the enemy's signal party, was deterred by the number of the guard, but the man who had his horse left without him, and he marched afoot with Longstreet's column to Groveton, in which memorable battle he shouldered a musket and fought as a private. He was killed at the storming of Groveton Heights among the foremost. No young man was so universally beloved, or will be more universally mourned; moreover a young man of fine attainments and bright promise.[9]

In addition to the men of his own staff, Stuart recognized a volunteer aide serving on the staff of Gen. Beverly Robertson. The cavalry chieftain evidently was impressed, for this man would join Stuart's staff in October.

General Jackson, having arrived early in the day, took direction of affairs, and the day was occupied mainly in rationing the command, but several serious demonstrations were made by the enemy during the day from the north side, and in connection I will mention the coolness and tact of Mr. Louis F. Terrill [*sic*], volunteer aide to General Robertson, who extemporized lanyards, and with detachments from the infantry as cannoneers turned the captured guns with marked effect upon the enemy.[10]

As September dawned, the cavalry crossed the Potomac River into Maryland. The Sharpsburg Campaign did not give too many of the staff members opportunities to distinguish themselves. Pelham won plaudits for his command of the artillery on Jackson's left flank, while von Borcke "displayed his usual skill, courage, and energy. His example was highly valuable to the troops." One of the new staff members, Lt. Walter Quarrier Hullihen, who had become an aide-de-camp on August 29, 1862, quickly attracted Stuart's attention, as he "was particularly distinguished on the field of Sharpsburg for his coolness and his valuable services as acting aide-de-camp." The staff's new signal officer, R. E. Frayser, "rendered important services to the commanding general from a mountain overlooking the enemy on the Antietam."[11] Only one officer was added to the staff in September. On the fourth, the young and daring Lt. Thomas Baynton Turner joined headquarters as an aide. Turner's affiliation with Stuart would be brief but filled with adventures.

The Confederate cavalry followed the rest of the army back to Virginia,

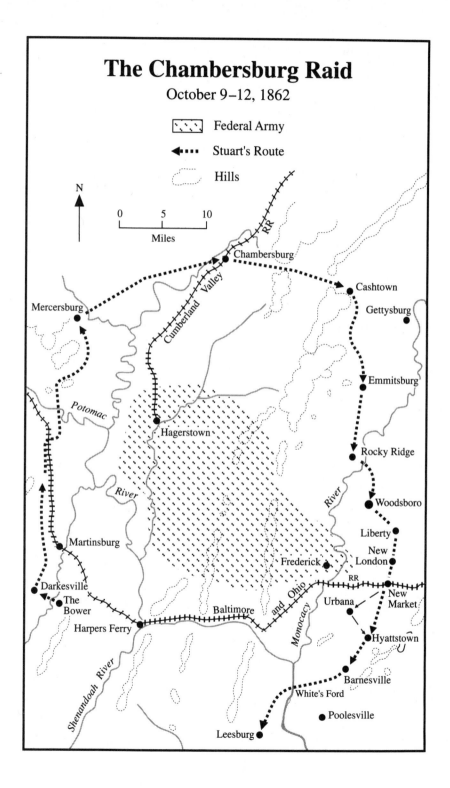

The Chambersburg Raid
October 9–12, 1862

Federal Army

Stuart's Route

Hills

N

0   5   10
Miles

Chambersburg

Cashtown

Gettysburg

Mercersburg

Cumberland Valley

RR

Emmitsburg

Potomac

Hagerstown

Rocky Ridge

River

Woodsboro

Liberty

Martinsburg

New London

Frederick

Darkesville

The Bower

Baltimore

and Ohio

RR

New Market

Urbana

Harpers Ferry

Monocacy

Hyattstown

Barnesville

Shenandoah River

White's Ford

Poolesville

Leesburg

where Lee granted a much-needed rest to his hard-fighting regiments. In early October Lee once again sent for Stuart to give him the orders that would launch a second Ride Around McClellan. The excursion took the gray cavalry all the way to Chambersburg, Pennsylvania, and proved to be an interesting one for Stuart's staff officers. Von Borcke may have been "untiring in the zealous discharge of the duties assigned to him," but his horses were not of the same mold. The huge Prussian was forced to remain behind for lack of a horse, a circumstance he abhorred but had brought upon himself by neglecting to care for his mounts properly. Those officers and men who did accompany Stuart experienced hard work and hard riding. During an exciting escape at White's Ford, Blackford and Price distinguished themselves for braving enemy fire to carry orders to the horse artillery. Pelham was in his glory as his guns kept the Federals at bay until the raiders were safe again on Virginia soil.

At least one officer so impressed Stuart on the raid that he was offered a staff position. Capt. Benjamin Stephen White, who had acted as a guide during the last portion of the raid, joined as part of the subsistence department. Stuart's account states, "I am especially indebted to Capt. B. S. White . . . whose skillful guidance was of immense service to me."[12] Stuart's practice of adding to his staff men who performed well under crisis situations continued to prove successful.

October also saw two other officers added to the staff. Maj. Lewis Frank Terrell, Beverly Robertson's former aide, accepted the post of inspector, and Capt. James Marshall Hanger assumed the position of assistant quartermaster. N. R. FitzHugh returned from captivity to resume his post as assistant adjutant general and immediately gained the praises of his commander during the cavalry's venture into Loudoun County between October 30 and November 6. Pelham and Blackford also received mention in Stuart's report of the operation. By the end of October, the staff totaled twenty officers.

For the rest of the year, the cavalry carried out its duties as the army's eyes and ears. Though the Battle of Fredericksburg did not offer the mounted arm occasion to add to its list of accomplishments, Pelham and the Stuart Horse Artillery gained immortality. The "gallant" one, with a section of Mathias Henry's Battery, held up the Federal advance against "Stonewall" Jackson for more than an hour. The feat became the topic of conversation for the rest of the winter. Pelham's talents as an artillerist were now desired by many officers, including Jackson and Longstreet, but Stuart would not part with him.

As the year drew to a close, time was found for additional raids, the most enterprising of which was Stuart's expedition to Dumfries, Virginia.

Christmas of 1862 would have been a happy time at the cavalry head-quarters except for the deaths of Redmond Burke, who was killed by Federal cavalry at Shepherdstown, and of little Flora Stuart, the general's young daughter. Lieutenant Hagan, who often gave Flora horseback rides when she visited her father, was especially crushed by her death, and the whole staff felt the loss of Burke, who would be difficult to replace.

January 1863 witnessed the departure of scout John S. Mosby. Although not actually a part of the staff, Mosby had continually distinguished himself and earned his independent command. With Stuart's blessing, he launched his career of harassing the Union Army within an area soon to be known as "Mosby's Confederacy." Not long after Mosby left, two new officers joined the ranks of the staff. Lt. Thomas Randolph Price, Jr., Channing's brother, became Blackford's engineer assistant; and Capt. James Louis Clark became an aide but spent his first few weeks in Richmond trying to recruit a horse artillery company.

The next four months brought about many changes among the men who "followed the plume." By June 1863, eight officers who had served Stuart for between five and seventeen months had either left or were incapacitated, while six others had joined the staff. Deteriorating health brought about the resignation of J. T. W. Hairston in early March. To replace him, Stuart secured a promotion for Channing Price, who had already assumed much of Hairston's work. March 17 saw the death of the "gallant" Pelham at the Battle of Kelly's Ford. The staff wore the black armbands of mourning, as they had done for Hardeman Stuart and Redmond Burke. These armbands would become almost a regular part of their uniforms during the next few months. On the last day of March, Samuel Hairston resigned.

Two officers joined the staff in March, though one would remain for only a few weeks. Capt. Harry Gilmor of the 12th Virginia Cavalry served as a voluntary aide-de-camp during the month. He was with Stuart at Kelly's Ford when Pelham fell, but he left soon afterward. Lt. Francis Smith Robertson was attached to the staff as another assistant to Engineer Officer Blackford.

In April Pelham's replacement arrived in the person of Maj. Robert Franklin Beckham, a most capable artillery officer, into whose hands now passed the Stuart Horse Artillery. Maj. Henry Brainerd McClellan of the 3rd Virginia Cavalry filled Norman R. FitzHugh's position as assistant adjutant general (FitzHugh having assumed Samuel H. Hairston's post as division quartermaster), and Capt. Andrew Reid Venable, who had so impressed Stuart during the Battle of Chancellorsville, joined the staff as assistant adjutant and inspector general, replacing Channing Price. One

final addition came late in the same month. Lt. Robert Henry Goldsborough assumed the post of aide-de-camp, which had been vacant since
Channing Price's elevation to major and assistant adjutant general.

The Chancellorsville Campaign in early May claimed three of the staff.
Channing Price was mortally wounded in the action on May 1. He might
have been saved if he had received prompt medical attention. Unfortunately,
none was available, and the talented and newly appointed assistant adjutant
general died of blood loss and shock. Lieutenant Hullihen fell with a
shoulder wound on May 2. He would later rejoin the staff and serve Stuart
for another six months. On the 4th, William Johnson was captured at
Shannon's Crossroads by Union cavalry. He had been carrying out his duties
far behind the lines but was in the wrong place at the wrong time.

Other changes also occurred as spring gave way to summer. Due to
an unfortunate set of circumstances, T. R. Price was relieved of his position
on the staff. Frank Terrell asked to be transferred. Both these men departed
cavalry headquarters in the early days of June 1863. Despite the losses,
the staff constituted twenty officers on the eve of the Battle of Brandy
Station, although not all were present for duty.

On June 1, Stuart issued the following order to his command.

Hdqrs. Cav. Div., Army of N. Va.,
General Orders,   June 1, 1863
No. 19.
I. The major-general commanding announces the
division staff as follows:
Maj. Heros von Borcke, assistant adjutant and inspector
general; Maj. H. B. McClellan, assistant adjutant-general;
Maj. A. R. Venable, assistant adjutant-general; Maj.
Norman R. Fitzhugh [*sic*], quartermaster; Maj. William
J. Johnson, commissary of subsistence; Capt. W. W.
Blackford, engineer department; Capt. John Esten
Cooke, chief of ordnance; First Lieut. Chiswell Dabney,
aide-de-camp; First Lieut. Robert H. Goldsborough,
aide-de-camp; Surg. Talcott Eliason, division surgeon;
Capt. W. D. Farley, volunteer aide; Capt. James L. Clark,
volunteer aide.
The following officers of the regular army are assigned
to duty with the cavalry division:
Capt. B. S. White, Provisional Army, C.S.; First Lieut.
R.B. Kennon, Provisional Army, C.S.; Cadet W. Q.
Hullihen, Provisional Army, C.S.

II. Lieut.Col. C. H. Tyler is relieved from duty as
assistant inspector-general of this division.

By command of Maj. Gen. J. E. B. Stuart:

H. B. McClellan,
Major, and Assistant Adjutant-General.[13]

Though the above appears to be a complete listing of Stuart's staff at this
time, the names of several officers then attached to cavalry headquarters are
not included: Maj. R. F. Beckham, chief of the Stuart Horse Artillery;
Capt. R. E. Frayser, signal officer; 1st Lieut. H. Hagan, Provisional
Army, C.S.; Capt. J. M. Hanger, assistant quartermaster; 1st Lieut. T. R.
Price, assistant engineer officer (about to leave the staff); 2nd Lieut. F. S.
Robertson, assistant engineer officer; Maj. L. F. Terrell, inspector (also
about to leave the staff). Just why these men were not included is something of a mystery, though in some cases reasons can be offered. Price's and
Terrell's omissions can be understood in light of their impending departures.
Hanger and Robertson may have been excluded because they were only
assistants. Hagan's "unofficial" staff position would have kept him from
being included with the staff, but he should have been listed with the
others "assigned to duty with the cavalry division." Beckham and Frayser
may have been omitted because the former was in the artillery and the latter
in the signal corps, but they should have been named as being attached to
the cavalry as was Blackford, though he was in the engineer corps.

Soon after the publication of the above order, the cavalry turned its
attention to pageantry. New uniforms and spit and polish were the order of
the day as the cavalry held its grand reviews (one had already taken place on
May 22) on the plains above Culpeper Court House near a small railroad
junction named Brandy Station. Once the grand display of the cavalry's
strength concluded, the mounted arm of Lee's mighty Army of Northern
Virginia was to initiate its commander-in-chief's orders for a second invasion of the North. At least, those were the plans. The Federals across the river
had other ideas, and on the morning of June 9 they put them into operation
and attacked Stuart on the very ground that so recently had been filled
with pageantry.

The largest cavalry engagement of the war ended with the withdrawal of the Union forces across the Rappahannock River. The Southern
cavalry lost about five hundred men, and Stuart's staff also suffered a
number of casualties. William Farley was mortally wounded, Benjamin
White was seriously wounded, and Robert Goldsborough was captured.

The situation had called for exceptional gallantry, and Stuart's staff
responded. Conspicuous in the day's action were von Borcke, McClellan,

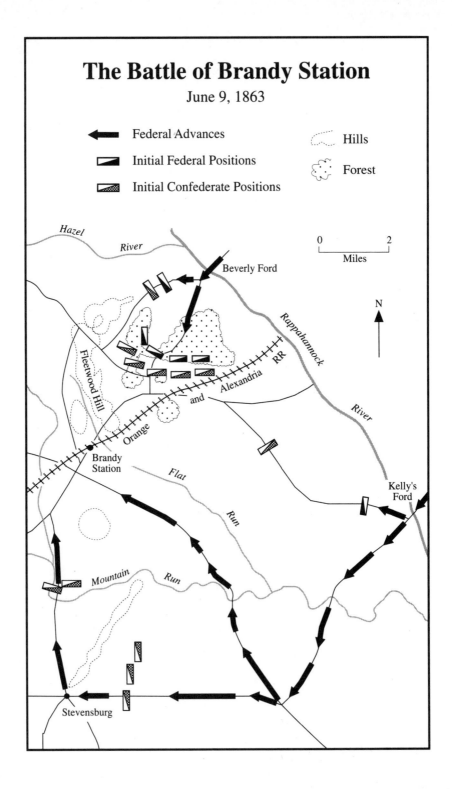

The Battle of Brandy Station
June 9, 1863

Federal Advances

Initial Federal Positions

Initial Confederate Positions

Hills

Forest

Hazel River

Beverly Ford

Rappahannock RR

River

N

0 — 2
Miles

Fleetwood Hill

Orange and Alexandria RR

Brandy Station

Flat Run

Kelly's Ford

Mountain Run

Stevensburg

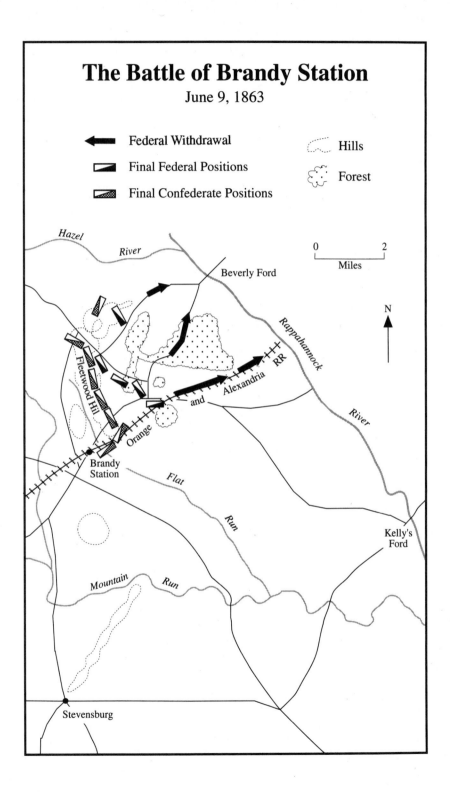

The Battle of Brandy Station
June 9, 1863

Federal Withdrawal

Final Federal Positions

Final Confederate Positions

Hills

Forest

Hazel

River

Beverly Ford

0   2
Miles

N

Rappahannock

RR

River

Fleetwood Hill

and Alexandria

Orange

Brandy
Station

Flat

Run

Kelly's
Ford

Mountain Run

Stevensburg

and Beckham. Others of the staff repeatedly braved enemy fire to carry
Stuart's orders or to help meet a blue regiment's charge. It is quite possible
that in no other action of the war was the staff exposed to as much danger
as in the battle around Fleetwood Hill. In his report Stuart recorded the
actions of his staff.

> Hearing from General Robertson. . . . I also sent Asst.
> Engineer F. S. Robertson to Brandy, to attend in person
> to the posting of a dismounted battalion of Hampton's
> brigade. . . .
>
> The conduct of the Horse Artillery, under that daring
> and efficient officer, Maj. R. F. Beckham, deserves the
> highest praise.
>
> Captain Benjamin S. White, of the regular army,
> serving on my staff, behaved with the most distinguished
> gallantry, and was wounded painfully in the neck.
>
> Col. M. C. Butler, Second South Carolina Cavalry,
> received a severe wound. . . . Capt. W. D. Farley, of South
> Carolina, a volunteer aide on my staff, was mortally
> wounded by the same shell. . . .
>
> My own staff, on this, as on all other occasions,
> acquitted themselves handsomely.
>
> Maj. Heros von Borcke, a gallant Prussian, who has
> fought bravely and served faithfully for one year, was
> everywhere, animating by his presence and prowess, and
> checking the wavering and the broken.
>
> Maj. H. B. McClellan, assistant adjutant-general,
> displayed the same zeal, gallantry, and efficiency which
> has on every battle-field, in the camp, or on the march,
> so distinguished him as to cause his selection to his
> present post.
>
> Surg. Talcott Eliason; Maj. Andrew R. Venable, assis-
> tant adjutant-general; Capt. W. W. Blackford, engineers;
> Capt. John Esten Cooke, chief of ordnance; Capt. J. L.
> Clarke [sic], volunteer aide; First Lieut. C. Dabney, aide-
> de-camp, and Maj. Norman R. Fitzhugh [sic], division
> quartermaster, all in their respective spheres acquitted
> themselves in a highly creditable manner. Surgeon Eliason,
> though without a superior in his profession, would, from
> his conduct on the field, excel as a colonel of cavalry.
>
> First Lieut. Robert H. Goldsborough, aide-de-camp,

while bearing an important message to Col. Wickham, was captured by the enemy.[14]

Also mentioned in the account was an officer, Lt. Richard Byrd Kennon, who would be an acting aide-de-camp for Stuart within a week of the battle.

> Capt. W. B. Wooldridge, Fourth Virginia Cavalry, Lieut. J. L. Jones, Second Virginia Cavalry, and Lieut. R. B. Kennon, Provisional Army, Confederate States, members of general court-martial, Fitz. Lee's brigade, lately adjourned, while en route to join their commands, met near Brandy a party of the enemy. Collecting a few stragglers, they attacked and routed the party, which was more than double their number, capturing a lieutenant, 6 privates, and a guidon.[15]

Following the battle, the summer campaign began in earnest. It was barely under way when two staff members left. Captain J. L. Clark was offered and accepted command of Harry Gilmor's old cavalry company in the 12th Virginia. He had been with Stuart a relatively short time. The other officer, however, Heros von Borcke, had ridden with Stuart for more than twelve months when on June 19, he was struck in the throat while riding by his chief's side near Middleburg. He would never do so again. The wound almost proved fatal. Only the Prussian's rugged constitution permitted him to survive.

For the remainder of the campaign, which eventually led to Gettysburg and then back to Virginia, the staff managed to escape with only a few bumps, bruises, and scratches. In Stuart's official accounting of the entire campaign, he was once more generous with his praise.

> I cannot here particularize the conduct of the many officers who deserve special mention, of less rank than brigadier-general, without extending my remarks more than would be proper. To my staff collectively, however, I feel at liberty to express thus officially my grateful appreciation of the zeal, fidelity, and ability with which they discharged their several duties, and labored to promote the success of the command.
>
> Maj. Heros von Borcke, assistant adjutant and in-spector general (that gallant officer from Prussia, who so early espoused our cause) was disabled in Fauquier, so as

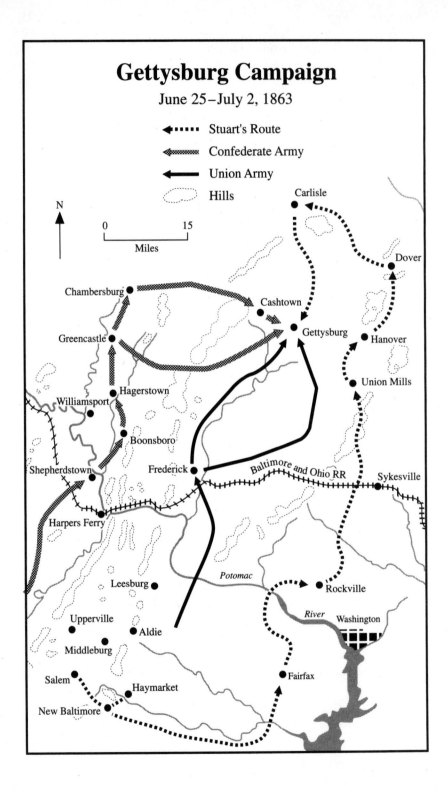

Gettysburg Campaign

June 25–July 2, 1863

◄▪▪▪▪▪ Stuart's Route

◄═══ Confederate Army

◄─── Union Army

Hills

N

0   15
Miles

Carlisle

Dover

Chambersburg

Cashtown

Gettysburg

Greencastle

Hanover

Hagerstown

Williamsport

Union Mills

Boonsboro

Frederick

Baltimore and Ohio RR

Sykesville

Shepherdstown

Harpers Ferry

Potomac

Leesburg

Rockville

River   Washington

Upperville

Aldie

Middleburg

Salem

Fairfax

Haymarket

New Baltimore

to deprive me of his valuable services on the expedition, but it is hoped that command will not long be deprived of his inspiring presence on the field.

Maj. Henry B. McClellan, my adjutant-general, was constantly at my side, and with his intelligence, ready pen, and quick comprehension, greatly facilitated the discharge of my duties.

The untiring energy, force of character and devotion to duty of Maj. A. R. Venable, my inspector-general, and Lieut. G. M. Ryals, C.S.A. Army, provost-marshal, deserve my special gratitude and praise.

The same qualities, united to a thorough knowledge of much of the country, are ascribable to Capt. B. S. White, C.S.A. Army, who, though still suffering from a severe wound received at Fleetwood, accompanied the command, and his services proclaim him an officer of merit and distinction.

Chief Surgeon Eliason, Captain Blackford, engineers; Captain Cooke, ordnance officer; Lieutenant Dabney, aide-de-camp; Asst. Engineer F. S. Robertson; and Cadet Hullihen, C.S. Army, and Lieut. H. Hagan, Virginia Provisional Army, all performed their duties with commendable zeal and credit.

Major Fitzhugh [*sic*], chief, and Capt. J. M. Hanger, assistant quartermaster, and Maj. W. J. Johnson, chief commissary, discharged their arduous duties in their usually highly creditable manner.

First Lieut. R. B. Kennon, Provisional Army Confederate States, temporarily attached, on two different occasions was entrusted with duties attended with great peril, which he performed in a highly successful and satisfactory manner—once in testing experimentally, at night, an unknown ford on the Potomac, and again in bearing a dispatch to the Commanding-General from Emmittsburg.[16]

From June 1863 to the new year, the cavalry of Lee's army fought a continually improving foe. As the South's resources dwindled, the North's grew. Stuart's staff officers continued to carry out their duties as their commander sought to provide Lee with the information he required.

During this period the staff underwent considerable change. Late in June Lt. Garland Mitchell Ryals had filled a new position on the staff, that of provost marshal. Lt. Henry Saxon Farley, brother of W. D. Farley, served as an aide from July 4 to September 3. Sometime in August, Lt. Col. Alexander Robinson Boteler accepted a position as voluntary aide-de-camp. Two new officers arrived at headquarters in September: Surgeon John Boursiquot Fontaine became assistant medical director of the cavalry, and Lt. Col. George St. Leger Grenfell was sent by Lee to be Stuart's assistant inspector general. In November Capt. Charles Grattan assumed the post of ordnance officer, and in December Maj. George Freaner filled the position of inspector in the adjutant general's department.

Though there were no further casualties from enemy bullets, some officers left the staff for various reasons. October brought the resignation of Talcott Eliason because of ill health, and in November Chiswell Dabney transferred to a cavalry unit. These two officers had been with Stuart longer than any others up to that time. They were the last of the 1861 staff members. To Blackford and Cooke now fell the title of "senior officers" of the staff. Also in November, R. B. Kennon and W. Q. Hullihen transferred to other positions within the cavalry. In December, St. Leger Grenfell left after a stay of only three months to rejoin Gen. Joseph Wheeler's cavalry in the western theater. At the age of fifty-four, he had been the oldest officer to serve on the staff.

Gen. Lee's abortive Bristoe Station Campaign in October had brought few results for the losses sustained. Stuart and the cavalry came in for their fair share of hard work. Although almost trapped at Auburn, Stuart escaped and hailed his men for their courage and ingenuity. The staff claimed a portion of the praise in their general's report.

> Maj. H. B. McClellan, assistant adjutant-general, was ever at my side night and day, and I am greatly indebted to him for the clearness with which orders and dispatches were transmitted.
>
> Maj. A. R. Venable, assistant adjutant and inspector general, deserves special mention for his soldierly bearing and conduct throughout, but particularly for his conduct in evading the enemy near Auburn, and reaching the commanding general with important dispatches on the night of the 13th.
>
> Maj. Heros von Borcke was, I regret to state, absent, disabled by his wounds received at Middleburg in June.
>
> Medical Director Fontaine and Captain Blackford (Engineers), and the rest of my staff, behaved with their usual efficiency.[17]

With the escape of the Union Army, the soldiers of both sides probably would have voted to call it quits for the remainder of the year, but the commander of the Army of the Potomac felt he could make one more effort to defeat Lee. Nevertheless, Maj. Gen. George G. Meade's Mine Run Campaign, which took place from November 26 to December 1, 1863, was no more successful than Lee's Bristoe Station Campaign had been. Once again a few staff officers received mention in Stuart's summary of the cavalry's activities.

> Capt. Charles Grattan, chief of ordnance of Cavalry Corps, had his horse killed at Parker's Store.
>
> My staff are entitled to my thanks for efficient and zealous assistance rendered throughout. The medical director, Surgeon Fontaine, was particularly efficient, all wounded as well as killed being removed safely from the field.[18]

Both armies at last settled down in their winter quarters for what was left of 1863. As of New Year's Day 1864, Stuart's staff numbered sixteen. The early months of 1864 brought more changes to cavalry headquarters personnel. January saw William Blackford's promotion and transfer to the newly formed 1st Regiment of Engineers. He deserved the appointment, but Stuart had to say good-bye to one who had served him for twenty-two months. Robert Beckham's tenure as chief of the Stuart Horse Artillery ended in February. He was the last of the staff to leave prior to Stuart's death.

Before the armies clashed again in the spring, Stuart added the final members to his staff. By February 1864, Dabney Ball had returned to headquarters, this time as chaplain for the Cavalry Corps. Lt. Theodore Stanford Garnett replaced Chiswell Dabney as aide-de-camp in March. In April the Stuart Horse Artillery command was given to Maj. Roger Preston Chew, who was handpicked by Stuart. He would hold this command until the war's end. When the Battle of the Wilderness erupted in early May 1864, Stuart's staff numbered seventeen: Ball, Boteler, Chew, Cooke, FitzHugh, Fontaine, Frayser, Freaner, Garnett, Grattan, Hagan, Hanger, Johnson, McClellan, Robertson, Ryals, and Venable.

On May 11, 1864, Maj. Gen. James Ewell Brown Stuart was mortally wounded at the Battle of Yellow Tavern. He died the next day.

Selection and Duties

I want an agreeable and efficient staff and <u>will</u> have the latter cost what it will in feeling.[1]

— Maj. Gen. J. E. B. Stuart

THE ENVIABLE RECORD accumulated by Stuart's staff during the various battles in which the cavalry arm of the Army of Northern Virginia participated accounts for only a small fraction of the story of these men and their general. Their bravery cannot be denied, and certainly one of the prerequisites for any staff officer had to be courage. But more than courage was needed to run a gigantic military enterprise, and if Stuart had made his selections based solely on this criterion, the effectiveness of the cavalry would have suffered. Stuart was quite aware of this. He wrote to his brother that selecting an aide was like picking a wife: It would be for better or for worse. Stuart was especially sensitive to the combination of talent and personality in the men he chose to ride by his side. He required men who could both do their jobs and get along with each other. Jealousy and clashing egos bred inefficiency, and inefficiency led to defeat—something that Stuart found abhorrent.

In his book *War Years with Jeb Stuart,* W. W. Blackford stated that Stuart's selection of staff and headquarters personnel was sometimes dependent on the general's sudden fancies for individuals who courted his good will.[2] (In all fairness, Blackford was quick to point out that if these men failed to carry out their duties efficiently they were soon dismissed.) But a careful examination of the men who served on the staff and at headquarters would seem to refute Blackford's view in most cases. Stuart does not appear to have appointed men to his staff in a haphazard fashion. He was not necessarily concerned with what the men could do but with what they could learn to do. An excellent example of this was the chief engineer's brother-in-law, Frank Robertson, whom Stuart chose to serve as an assistant engineer. Robertson knew nothing about the duties of the position, but

Stuart recognized the young man's talent, intelligence, and ability to learn rapidly. With no trepidation, he made him an assistant to Blackford. Robertson himself said within several weeks of his reporting for duty that he had become familiar with his work and no longer felt uneasy about what was required of him.

To further illustrate Stuart's ability to recognize talent, a glance at the staff members' prewar careers reveals that few were prepared for the jobs they were called to perform. Of those whose occupations are known, one was a writer, two were clergymen, two were doctors, three either came from the army or had been in attendance at the United States Military Academy at the war's commencement, six were farmers, seven were involved in business, eight were lawyers, and eleven came from the academic field (two teachers and nine students). Stuart placed some in positions for which they had training, but a significant number were asked to perform in areas in which they had had no experience. Two striking cases are J. E. Cooke, a writer who became ordnance officer, and Rev. Dabney Ball, who discharged the duties of commissary of subsistence.

Age did not figure too heavily when Stuart had to fill a staff position. Chiswell Dabney at seventeen was the youngest and Alexander R. Boteler at forty-eight the oldest of Stuart's appointees. (George St. Leger Grenfell was fifty-four, but he was appointed by R. E. Lee.) The average age of the staff was just under twenty-nine and a half, while its median age was twenty-seven. Stuart himself was twenty-eight years, seven months when he became a general. Twenty-one men, including Grenfell, were older than the general they served; eight of these were forty and older. Three officers (Dabney, Theodore Garnett, and Thomas Turner) were under twenty when they joined the staff.

Though Stuart chose his personnel for their particular attributes and abilities, it is not surprising that several were Stuart's relatives by either blood or marriage. The assigning of relatives to one's staff was a common practice of many officers in both armies. But for Stuart, at least, duty came first, and woe to any officer, kin or not, who failed in a critical hour. On the whole, Stuart's relatives served him and the cavalry well. He would not have kept them otherwise.

An individual who aspired to certain staff positions had to be willing to accept responsibilities that might affect his own family and fortune. An example of such a burden of responsibility is found in the records of Maj. Norman R. FitzHugh, one of Stuart's quartermasters. The war was big business, and Stuart's headquarters personnel were more often called upon to perform as executives than as soldiers.

Between August 1863 and June 1864, FitzHugh handled more than

$2,250,000 in quartermaster funds for the cavalry. His receipts for amounts totaling as much as $645,000 all bear the words "for which I am accountable to the Treasury of the Confederate States," followed by the major's bold signature.[3] Even taking into consideration the inflation of Confederate currency at that time, FitzHugh was conducting business on a huge scale.

When first assigned by Stuart to the post in March 1863, FitzHugh had to travel to Richmond to "fill his official bond." This meant he would personally assume any liabilities incurred through losses of funds or equipment, whether by accident or design, that could not be ascribed to the normal conduct of the war. Stuart also had to furnish the names of two other individuals, known as sureties, who would agree to cover any deficit beyond what FitzHugh could absorb.[4] Even with such circumstances, the number of candidates for staff positions was never lacking. In a letter to his wife, Flora, Stuart related that he had to reject applications for staff positions on almost a daily basis.[5]

Once an officer was assigned to one of the staff positions, he became responsible for outfitting himself in a manner that accorded with his rank and that would permit him to carry out his duties efficiently. Stuart made sure, on at least one occasion, that the newcomer had a complete listing of what was deemed necessary. Heros von Borcke's letter to newly appointed Aide-de-Camp R. Channing Price left little to Price's imagination and even less in his wallet.

29 of July 1862

Sir

Maj. Genl J E B Stuart directs me to send you a list of what articles you will require to have as an officer in the Staff

very respectfully
Heros von Borcke
AAG.

Equipment suitable for an Officer
of Cavallerie

A good Horse wich can be bot in Richmond or among the Rgts, the cost will be 400–500 Doll

A good Jenifer saddle and bridle, wich can be bot at the ordonance store for 62 Doll.

Arms will be sabre & Pistol, wich will cost from 80 to 100 Doll.

A Uniform trimed with yellow (Cav) or buff (Staff) either coat or jacket 80 to 100 Doll.

> Good Cavalry Boots with Spurs 50 Doll
> Grey or Black Hat 15 Doll.
> Saddle Blanket and other Blanket 20 Doll
> Oilcloth Coat 25–30 Doll
> Several little things not mentioned
>   (little Vallise, Comb, brushe etc etc)[6]

Von Borcke's difficulty with spelling did not cause Price as much trouble as did the acquiring of a horse. In his letters to his mother and sister, Price often bemoaned the fact that he desired a good horse but could not seem to obtain exactly what he wanted. At least one of his horses died unexpectedly, leaving Price without transport until he could have another animal brought to him. He considered for a time the purchasing of a little mare that had belonged to the deceased John Pelham. Price had occasion to ride the animal and found it quite satisfactory, but regrettably, there is no record verifying whether he obtained the animal. Von Borcke's problems with securing horses capable of supporting his huge frame are well documented, so Price was not the sole sufferer at headquarters when it came to having "a good Horse."

If Price took von Borcke's suggestions to heart, the young aide-de-camp would have found himself about $800 poorer. He soon discovered that the wear and tear of field service quickly took the shine off his new gear. He complained at times of his need for a new pair of pants or a new jacket. Contrary to popular belief among the troopers, staff officers did get dirty and wore out uniforms and accoutrements like everyone else. In addition to what Aide-de-Camp Price required in the way of a uniform and horse equipment, an officer assigned to a post such as engineer or adjutant might have had to supply himself with some of the equipment necessary to do his job. The Confederate Quartermaster Department was not always able to furnish the items required.

When spending any time in one location, the prudent staff officer made every effort to surround himself with as many homelike comforts as possible. Capt. John Esten Cooke, writing under the pseudonym of Tristan Joyeuse, provided a glimpse of his accommodations while lounging at "Camp No Camp."

The Inventory of goods and effects
of Tristan Joyeuse, Gent.

1 Table and Desk, the latter containing *Macaulay's History of England, Vol. V.*—Recreations of Christopher North—*Army Regulations—Consuelo, by George Sand—Bragelonne, by the great Dumas—The Monk's Revenge—*

and several official papers. A Bible and Prayer Book too, which Joyeuse still retains the habit, he is glad to say, of reading, night and morning. Flanking the literary contents —a bag of tobacco—a laurel pipe of curious design, the gift of Bumpo—an old ink bottle—a pistol, cartridges and sabre; the latter with a rusty scabbard.

2 Wooden chairs.

1 Mess chest, only half as convenient as the old cannon ammunition box, long used for a like purpose—with compartments, formerly for "spherical case," now serving to hold coffee, sugar, and much more.

4 Blankets, neatly folded, on a bed of straw, kept in its place by a log—one blanket having been brought to me lately from the North, and delivered in a Yankee camp, free of expense, the owner not even staying to take his receipt.

1 India rubber "Poncho," excellent for rainy days on horseback; also furnished gratis, on the same occasion, the agent of delivery having been suddenly called away. *My* Poncho, this is, fitting perfectly; but, doubtless, by mistake —marked with another's name.

1 Valise, black leather, formerly used on summer journeys to the mountains, now for a wardrobe. It lies at the head of my bed, and is always open by reason of ex- cessive cramming: containing as it does at present, the stowed-away spoils of Christmas in the shape of variegated shirts, cravats, ribbed socks, and all my most valuable effects.

1 Saddle, bridle and accoutrements, on a rack, at foot of bed, in the corner.

2 Overcoats, which have been through the wars, and will cheerfully be exchanged for one which has not.

1 Pile of wood, by fire, and

1000 other things "too tedious to mention," but convenient.

Such are the material surroundings, of your old friend Joyeuse, at this place of halt in his pilgrimage.[7]

Having accomplished his outfitting, although not immediately to the extent of Cooke, the officer's next undertaking was to become acquainted with his exact duties. Depending on the appointment, this "breaking-in" period could take days or weeks. Assistant Engineer Officer Frank Robertson was, at first, unsure just what was expected of him. The staff already had Blackford and Tom Price as engineers, but Robertson quickly was supplied with the task of coloring in one of Captain Blackford's maps. The nervous lieutenant spilled red ink on one area, but eventually got the hang of it. By mid-March 1863, after two weeks' work, he had both finished the map and gained considerable confidence in himself. Robertson had to not only adjust to his work, but also familiarize himself with Stuart's regimen and personal likes and dislikes, which may have taken some time as well. Once the officer acclimated himself to his new post, it became a matter of keeping everything at headquarters running as smoothly as possible—a task that was not always easily accomplished in the midst of campaigning.

When an officer finally joined Stuart's staff, he became part of the Headquarters of the Cavalry Corps of the Army of Northern Virginia. The sight that greeted his eyes as he first rode into camp must have been an inspiring one. An excellent description of one of Stuart's winter encampments, "The Wigwam," was written by "The" Garnett, one of Stuart's courier-clerks and later an aide-de-camp.

> The greater part of the month [November 1863] was consumed in building winter quarters. The camp was laid off with some degree of regularity, and old Hagan [Lt. Henry Hagan] took a special pride and delight in erecting the General's "Wigwam," as he called it. This was a large and commodious hospital tent, near the entrance of which Hagan had built a real *brick* chimney—none of your wooden affairs with barrel-tops—which was supplied throughout the whole winter with *cords* of the finest hickory wood. The inside was furnished with a plank floor, and a rough pineboard bedstead, on which the Generals blankets and buffalo robe was spread, making a resting place scarcely less comfortable than the feathery couches of luxury & ease.
>
> I have already given a brief description of this camp— "Wigwam"—as it was called by General Stuart, in memory perhaps of some of his camps in the far West, during the time when he was on the warpath against hostile Indians. I may as well, however, refresh the reader's memory with a fuller sketch as our sojourn here was probably of greater length than in any previous winter quarters, extending from about the 1st of Nov. 1863, to the 4th of May 1864. About one mile and a half northeast of Orange CH, in a

narrow valley thickly studded with pine and cedar trees, our tents were pitched; there was some regularity in the manner of laying off the encampment, a feature seldom found in any of the Corps, Division, or Brigade HdQrs of the Army of NoVa.

As you entered the valley from the direction of Orange CH, the road from which wound through the open, rolling fields belonging to the estate of Mr. Scott, you passed first, on the left, the camp and tents of Genl Stuart's escort of couriers, commanded by Lieut Hagan, a veteran who deserves honorable mention in these memoirs. Near this group of tents was the Forage-Sergt's quarters, easily distinguished by the two large stacks of hay and the piles of corn, with which Sergt. Buckner kept us so well supplied during the long and severe winter. Here too was the tent of Sergt. Ben Weller, the ante-bellem owner of the *Woolly-Horse;* he was also one of General Stuart's best and most reliable couriers; active, brave, keen-witted, and a good judge of horse-flesh; indeed, he supplied the General with one of the best horses that ever was brought to the Army—a powerful iron-grey, the horse, by the way, on which the Genl was mounted when he received his mortal wound near Yellow Tavern.

Following the road a hundred yards further on, the first tent on the left was Major McC's [Henry B. McClellan], our Adj.Genl, next to that and about 30 feet distant was Maj. [Andrew R.] Venable's, and then at about the same interval came the General's tent, a splendid specimen of canvass, beautifully pitched near an immense pine tree, having a brick chimney, a plank floor, a frame-door swing on hinges, in short, the most comfortable looking tent, inside and out, that I ever saw in any camp. Along in front of these three tents ran a saw-dust walk, terminating just beyond the Adj.Genl's tent at the door of a log-hut, which had been built for Maj. McC's clerks.

Behind this row of tents and about 20 yards further up the slope were three other tents pitched at the same intervals of distance from each other, and approached by saw-dust walks from the main walk. These tents were occupied by the remaining members of the staff: Capt. Charles Grattan, Ordnance officer, Capt. John Esten Cooke,

AAGenl, and Dr. Jno. B. Fontaine, Med Director, of the
Cavalry Corps. To the left and in front of Gen. Stuart's
tent, and almost in the bottom of the valley, was a solitary
tent-fly, raised about three feet from the ground, and
under which stood our mess table, a permanent structure,
made of pine boards and set off with rude benches—
chestnut-logs split in two and hewed down to some degree
of smoothness. A little further down the valley, during a
portion of the early winter stood the tent of Lieut.Col.
St. Leger Grenfel [*sic*], who occupied for a short time the
position of Inspector Genl of the Cavalry Corps.[8]

The site of the "Wigwam" winter camp may not have been as large as
some of Stuart's other encampments simply because many of the men
who would normally be attached to cavalry headquarters were home or
away on furlough during the lull in the war. Other camps, such as that
at "The Bower" or "Camp No Camp," could have been much larger.
Counting the staff, couriers, escort troops, clerks, wagon drivers, and
servants, Stuart's headquarters personnel might easily have numbered
around one hundred at any given time.

The staff itself was only a small, though vitally important, part of the
whole machine that kept Lee's cavalry working at peak efficiency. The total
number of officers serving on the staff fluctuated during the war. When
first formed in the fall of 1861, the staff numbered between five and ten
men. Not all of these individuals were actual members of the staff. Some
were volunteers, and others were only attached during certain expeditions
or engagements. By December of the same year, Stuart officially had five
staff officers at headquarters, but counting those who fell into the other two
categories, he actually had nine. From that point the staff grew in size.

W. W. Blackford wrote that the staff comprised the following: one
adjutant general, one signal officer, two assistant adjutant generals, one
quartermaster, two inspectors, one commissary officer, two aides-de-camp,
two engineer officers, one surgeon general, and one ordnance officer.[9]

Blackford, however, failed to include a number of other staff positions
that were known to have existed: commander of the Stuart Horse Artillery,
chief of couriers, chaplain, and provost marshal. Stuart also managed to have
scouts attached to his staff, and sometimes they were given the title of aide-
de-camp or voluntary aide-de-camp. Even civilian personnel had a tendency
to turn up riding with Stuart, as did Peter W. Hairston, another relative.

Of the staff diarists and chroniclers, R. Channing Price comes closest
to divulging a roster of staff members at a set time, but even he failed to

include some names of individuals known to be attached to the staff during his tenures as aide-de-camp and assistant adjutant general. All of this makes it difficult to state the exact size and composition of the staff during any given period, so the best that can be done is to make a well-calculated guess.

The actual work done by each staff officer requires some explanation. A brief description of the duties of each position follows.

Assistant adjutant general. Assistant adjutant generals were primarily responsible for all military correspondence between their general and the commanders of other units both superior and subordinate. They did not originate the correspondence but wrote or copied what their general dictated. On call day and night, an officer who aspired to this position had to be alert, accurate, and responsible. The outcome of a battle or a campaign might rest on his understanding of an order as dictated to him. Not surprisingly, good penmanship was not the least of the requirements.

Inspector. The title of inspector is an accurate description of the work this officer performed. His assignments usually involved examining troops and equipment and submitting a report to the general on what he found.

Engineer. The engineering officer undertook any job connected with the erecting of any structure that would serve a military purpose. He was the maker of maps, builder and destroyer of bridges, and designer of entrenchments, forts, and lines of defense. He might be called one day to draw a map of an area's roads and the next day to supervise the construction of a semipermanent encampment. Blackford wrote that during one engagement his job was to reconnoiter enemy positions and report any troop movements he observed. Without question, this officer was one of the most valuable on any general's staff.

Quartermaster. The quartermaster, in charge of distributing the equipment necessary to maintain the troops in the field, had one of the most difficult tasks of any staff officer. The accumulating and dispensing of clothing, tools, horse furniture, tents, and dozens of other items was a responsibility not to be taken lightly. Accurate record keeping and a miserly concern for getting the most out of every piece of equipment before replacing it could make the quartermaster's job a nightmare. A failure of this officer to perform his duties properly would greatly impair the efficiency of the soldiers who had to face the enemy day after day.

Signal officer. The tasks assigned to the signal officer centered on the sending and receiving of messages from stations that were in position to observe the enemy's movements or encampments. This officer might also be connected with the ever mysterious "Secret Service" that operated within the enemy's lines. The signal officer often found himself on some lonely perch high above the surrounding terrain trying to uncover and transmit information that would help his general make the right decisions. The signal officer's job was a dangerous one with little recognition.

Commissary officer or chief of subsistence. Commissary officer and chief of subsistence actually both refer to the same position (in fact, on an order dated June 25, 1862, Stuart refers to Maj. Dabney Ball as "commissary of subsistence"). This officer's main function was the acquiring and issuing of rations for the troops. This was a thankless position, considering the scarcity of supplies. The commissary officer made few friends issuing salted beef and pork along with hardtack and little else.

Ordnance officer. The ordnance officer, who was in charge of anything having to do with the weapons and ammunition used by the troops in the field, was essentially a type of quartermaster. The role most associated with him involves the artillery arm of the service, but he dealt with small arms as well. His duties were vital in that if he failed to supply the needed materiel, the men on the battleline could not do their job.

Surgeon general or medical director. No other officer on a general's staff had such a variety of duties as the surgeon general, who was the chief medical officer for thousands of men. He performed not only the functions of a doctor and surgeon, but also those of inspector, quartermaster, pharmacist, chief veterinarian, and, unbelievably, meteorologist. At one time the surgeon general of the cavalry (either Eliason or Fontaine, who was only twenty-three years old when he held this position) might have been responsible for as many as five thousand to ten thousand men and a like number of horses. Considering that the medical branches of both armies started virtually from scratch when war erupted, it is a wonder that they performed as efficiently as they did.

Aide-de-camp. Of all the positions on a general's staff, that of aide-de-camp is the most difficult to describe; an officer holding this title might be called upon to perform any of a variety of tasks. Channing Price recounted that he was called to do the job of adjutant general while still an aide-de-camp and that Chiswell Dabney was sent out to inspect the 10th Virginia Cavalry on one occasion, thus filling an inspector's role.

Commander of the Stuart Horse Artillery. The duties of the commander of the horse artillery need little explanation. Stuart created this position at the time of the organization of Pelham's Battery of Horse Artillery. With the addition of other batteries that fell under Pelham's command, it became difficult for the officer to be with any one battery on a constant basis, which may have been another reason for the continuance of the staff position.

Chief of couriers. This position was specially created by Stuart for Henry Hagan, who had served as a courier and escort trooper with Stuart early in the war. (Hagan's war record eradicates any doubt about his being worthy of a staff position, specially created or otherwise.) Duties centered on the organization of Stuart's couriers and, especially important, on the care of their horses.

Provost marshal. The provost marshal's duties focused primarily on four areas: enforcing orders dealing with military discipline, especially while campaigning; apprehending deserters; collecting and forwarding stragglers; and guarding prisoners of war. At least two men held this position on Stuart's staff, although in one case the post was temporary.

Chaplain. Whether the position of chaplain officially existed cannot be completely verified in the records, but on two forage requisitions, dated February 14 and March 16, 1864, Dabney Ball, formerly commissary officer on the staff, signed as "Dabney Ball Chaplain Cav. Corps." Ball had previously been chaplain of the 5th Virginia Cavalry, but that would not entitle him to sign as chaplain of the corps as a whole. A chaplain's chief concern would have been the spiritual welfare of the men in the cavalry. He might also coordinate his efforts with the chaplains of the various regiments.

How well the men of Stuart's staff performed the work described above can best be witnessed in the performance of the cavalry under Stuart, Hampton, and Fitz Lee. Even when the materiel of the South dwindled in the last two years of the war, the cavalry arm of the Army of Northern Virginia remained formidable. To verify this one need only read the accounts of such actions as Haw's Shop, Trevilian Station, and the numerous battles around Petersburg. True, there were defeats and even a few disasters in those last months of the Confederacy, but everything considered, the cavalry could be proud of its record, and those who had followed the plume could be proud of their contributions in achieving that record.

Stuart
and the Men

So I chatted round Stuart's staff of which he is the genuine soul, always full of life & humor. . . .[1]

— Jedediah Hotchkiss

It was dreadfully lonesome here all day and I wished very much that I was with the General as I have found that I am always happier when with him than anywhere else in this life we are now leading.[2]

— R. Channing Price

Hd Qrs Cavalry Corps
Sept. 21st, 1863.

Dear Lieutenant:

I deeply regret the continuance of your illness, for I had hoped by this time you would be able to join us. I know very well that you could not be kept from your post except by inexorable necessity. It needed no Surgeons certificate to satisfy me of it.

I am glad of the present opportunity of expressing to you my sense of the usefulness, the bravery, the devotion to duty and daring for which you were distinguished during your stay with me. I sent you through fiery ordeals at Chancellorsville and elsewhere from which I scarcely hoped to see you return, but rejoiced to see you escape. You will never forget those trials and I hope the kind Providence which so signally favored you will soon see you restored to the field and to your much attached comrades.

Present my kindest regards to your father's family and believe me

Your sincere friend,
J. E. B. Stuart
Major General.[3]

This letter rests in a quiet grave in Abingdon, Virginia, with the remains of Capt. Francis Smith Robertson, one-time assistant engineer officer on Stuart's staff. There is little difficulty in imagining the emotions of the then young lieutenant when he first read its words. The letter was treasured throughout the remainder of his long life.

In a broader context, the words Stuart penned to his invalid officer are representative of the feelings Stuart had for virtually all the men who rode with him. The letter conveys Stuart's innermost concerns for Robertson's health, both physical and mental, as well as his appreciation and admiration for the performance of a fellow officer and soldier in the most trying of circumstances. In his closing, Stuart reveals the secret of what bound his men to him: He was more than just their commander; he was truly their friend.

The letter also vividly points out that Stuart the soldier, regardless of his personal attachments to his staff, recognized that duty must transcend friendship. How the staff members reacted to this can be seen in the combat records and casualty lists. Where Stuart ordered them, they went. Stuart, of course, went with them, which was another reason for the mutual admiration and regard the general and his officers held for one another.

Stuart's sense of esprit de corps infected the entire headquarters company. His open, easygoing personality coupled with his willingness to be one of the boys bound men to him with a tenacious loyalty. In an article for the *Philadelphia Weekly Times,* John Esten Cooke recorded that Stuart's relationship with his staff was "more like a 'big boy' among a group of small ones, than a general enthroned among subordinates." Cooke admitted that Stuart's sense of humor was rough at times—"that of a cavalryman"—but if he thought he had offended anyone, he would take him aside and say, "Come, old fellow, get pleased. I never joke with any one unless I love them."[4]

Along with the camaraderie, Stuart became involved with many of his staff on a personal basis. He treasured their friendship and took pains to see to their welfare and their careers as soldiers and officers. When Stuart's cousin and aide-de-camp, Chiswell Dabney, became ill with typhoid fever in January 1862, he was forced to return home. Dabney was cared for by his sister Bettie. On January 29, Stuart wrote Bettie a letter in answer to one he had received concerning Chiswell's condition. He wrote, in part:

> Your petite note of 26th inst. was duly received and gave
> me great pleasure in all but one particular and that was the
> news of Chiswell's continued indisposition. However
> much I may miss him, still assure him that he loses nothing
> by being away, for we are having a very muddy and

disagreeable time, which he is fortunate to be obliged to miss, particularly in such society that his case is decidedly enviable. . . .

Take good care of Chiswell for me, tell him his commission was sent some days ago, to keep quiet and not give himself the slightest anxiety about his affairs here. His mare is doing well.

I think Chiswell will make a capital officer but he ought, in order to be the "bold, dashing huzzar" I would have him be, to take lessons from you in horsemanship. He doesn't sit erect in the saddle, but is rather given to doubling himself up as he rides along. A few hints and gentle admonitions <u>from you</u> he will appreciate.

Give much love to him and the hope for a speedy recovery.[5]

As he had in his letter to Robertson, Stuart once again took time to express his feelings for a friend and comrade in arms. His concern over Dabney's physical welfare was coupled with his interest in his lieutenant's becoming a good soldier. Stuart wanted Dabney to return not only healthy but a finer soldier as well. His appeal to a lady for help in making Dabney a better rider should not be surprising. Stuart was aware that a tender approach would often produce better results than all the swearing drill sergeants in the army.

The bond between Stuart and his staff deepened over the long months of war as they toiled and fought together. Illness and stress laid a number of the staff low for varying periods but claimed no lives. The enemy's cannon and muskets, however, claimed numerous victims, including Hardeman Stuart, Burke, Pelham, Price, and Farley. The war created deep scars, and Stuart carried his share, as did those who rode closest to him. Through it all, Stuart continued to be the spark that kept everything going. He and the staff still frolicked when the opportunity presented itself, but the memories of those no longer among them kept the joy from penetrating too deeply. At times the mere mention of a departed comrade's name brought tears to Stuart's eyes.

The closeness of Stuart to his staff was mirrored, more often than not, in the relationships between the staff officers themselves. The idea that the staff would run more efficiently if the individual officers were on friendly terms has already been mentioned, but working together on a military level does not presuppose that social interaction would occur. Officers who functioned smoothly as a team when performing their military duties might still be at odds personally when the work was finished. While the officers and men of Stuart's headquarters usually were on amiable terms, some problems did arise between Stuart and his staff and among the staff officers themselves. In any association or friendship, strife and jealousy do occur, but these do not destroy the relationship between true friends.

Blackford wrote of a falling-out with his tentmate, von Borcke, over a washbasin. After an exchange of words, both retreated into a cold silence. Such an occurrence illustrates how taut the nerves of both men were. Stuart was unaware of the difficulty between the two men, and neither Blackford nor von Borcke wanted him to hear of it. Maj. Norman FitzHugh had been present during the argument and was the only other person to know about the rift. When Stuart selected Blackford and von Borcke to accompany a patrol, FitzHugh felt he had to inform Stuart of what had happened.

Stuart immediately called von Borcke into his tent and asked for an explanation. After hearing one side of the story, he confronted Blackford with what von Borcke had said. In the end the two shook hands in front of their general and resumed their friendship as if nothing had occurred. Blackford recounted that his only reason for including the incident in his reminiscences was to illustrate how Stuart felt about the men of his staff and how much he disliked it when anything interrupted the good feeling between his officers.[6]

Another case of hard feelings between staff members can be seen in a letter written by Channing Price to his mother on April 5, 1863, in which he criticized von Borcke and Chiswell Dabney as being "ornamental officers" who never really did all that much work around camp. At the time the letter was written, Price was inundated with the work of two staff positions. He was an aide-de-camp but also was performing the job of adjutant since FitzHugh was being transferred to the quartermaster department. Price was under a great deal of pressure at the time he recorded his feelings. His impression of the work performed by von Borcke and Dabney may have been colored by the frustration he was experiencing over his own workload. In any event, Price's next letter returned to the usual camp gossip, and he wrote of both von Borcke and Dabney without any indication of a grudge or resentment.[7]

Stuart was not immune to similar feelings. His letters to his wife reveal periods when his patience with particular officers was wearing thin. Almost invariably, the reason for Stuart's displeasure or disappointment centered on the officer's performance of his duties rather than on his personality. If Stuart thought an officer was failing to meet the requirements of his position, he took steps to correct the situation. Sometimes all that was needed was encouragement or a furlough. In other instances a change of jobs rectified the problem. If all else failed, the officer was encouraged to resign, was reassigned, or was simply relieved. Chronic illness forced the resignation of a number of Stuart's staff, and in some cases the officers resigned at Stuart's request. A period of time usually was allowed for the officer to try to regain his health, as in the cases of Blackford, Dabney, Robertson, and others, but this was not always successful. Some hurt feelings may have resulted from Stuart's dedication to duty first. Nevertheless, he did not hesitate to replace officers who could not function according to his standards. Even his relatives were not exempt.

The personality clashes between Stuart and some of the cavalry officers have received considerable attention. On his staff, as well, Stuart had difficulty relating to a few individuals. Some of these relationships will be explored in the biographical section, but one needs to be mentioned here. John Esten Cooke was a relative of Stuart's and, in his writing after the war, demonstrated that he greatly admired the gallant cavalryman. Soon after Cooke joined the staff, however, he upset Flora by telling her that Stuart had shaved off his beard. The joke was not appreciated by Stuart. In at least two letters to Flora early in 1862, Stuart revealed that his attitude toward Cooke was one of tolerance rather than acceptance. Nevertheless, Cooke remained with the staff, though his duties as ordnance officer often took him away on business.

As the war continued, Stuart evidently began to alter his feelings toward Cooke to some degree. His reports of Cooke's service and performance during the various campaigns reveal that Stuart respected his cousin as a soldier. Cooke also accepted good-natured ribbing from Stuart after an incident when the lieutenant ducked a shell passing overhead and fell off his horse. The general and the others feared that he had been struck, and Stuart inquired if Cooke was all right. The somewhat embarrassed lieutenant replied that he was fine and that he had just dodged too far. That line became the joke of the camp for weeks as Stuart would occasionally call out, "Cooke, you dodged too far."

Stuart eventually transferred Cooke from the ordnance department to the post of assistant adjutant general, in which Cooke's talent as a writer was put to use in helping Stuart write out his battle reports. Stuart even presented one of his uniform coats to Cooke and told him to remove parts of the insignia until it represented a major's coat. The attempt to make Cooke a major failed when the War Department refused to confirm the appointment, but Cooke kept the coat as a memento. It hung on the wall of his home for years after the war and rests today in the Museum of the Confederacy in Richmond. By all appearances, Stuart had come to like Cooke. What had started out as a questionable association ended with Cooke serving on Stuart's staff for twenty-seven months—longer than any other officer.

One other aspect of Stuart's relationship with his staff and headquarters personnel needs to be explored. If, as has been intimated, Stuart's life was merely a posturing of some ideal of knighthood that Stuart had constructed for himself, then he managed to fool everyone who knew him. Stuart's staff officers lived, ate, fought, and some died with him as their commander. In their judgment, Stuart deserved their unswerving loyalty, and that judgment should be the measure of the man. True, there were three exceptions (Tom Price, George St. Leger Grenfell, and Lewis F. Terrell), but when the circumstances are known, nothing is found to diminish the appraisal of the remaining forty-five.

These staff officers were not all naive, impressionable young men. Their ages ranged from seventeen to fifty-four. They came to the staff from a variety of backgrounds. Many were very well educated; McClellan alone held four college degrees. Stuart could not possibly have deceived them as to his actual nature over such long periods of daily contact. Sooner or later he would have slipped, and then he would have lost their respect. That he did not is all the evidence required to refute allegations of a masking of his true self.

Much has been written about the "atmosphere" of Stuart's camps—the banjo playing of Sweeney; the singing and dancing of Stuart's servant, Bob; the wrestling matches; the romps with Nip and Tuck—but the frequency of occurrence of these events and the reasons for them seldom receive attention. Soldiers seek peace and quiet as well as revelry amid the noise of war. A titanic snowball battle among the divisions and brigades of John B. Hood, Richard H. Anderson, and Lafayette McLaws at Fredericksburg in the winter of 1862 is a classic example of the soldiers' need to play.[8] Stuart and his staff were no different in this respect. Even in the midst of his fun, however, Stuart was very much aware of his duty and knew when to call a halt to the merriment, as "The" Garnett recorded.

> Christmas [1863] came and found us all in low spirits at the prospect of a dull time. At night we would often get together our Amateur Glee-Club with old Sam Sweeney as leader of the band, Bob [Sweeney], his cousin, the lefthanded violinist, [Willie] Pegram with his flute, and occasionally Major Mc.Cl. [H.B. McClellan] with his fine guitar, and your humble servant with the triangle and all assembling in the General's tent, go through with a mixed program of songs, jokes, back-stepping and fun-making

generally until the general, tiring of our performances, would rise up on his buffalo-robe and say, "Well, Good evening to you all, gentlemen," and in five minutes thereafter the camp would be hushed in sleep.[9]

What Stuart's detractors, then and now, have failed to recognize at times are the long hours of duty, drudgery, and danger during a war that are spent not only on the battlefield but also in dirty campsites or in the mud-choked streets of villages and towns whose names occupy no significant place in history. In what free time the staff may have had, is it any wonder they sought solace in the soothing sounds of a banjo or in rough and tumble with a fellow soldier? Stuart was aware of the strain under which his men worked, and his willingness to furnish and even participate in such diversions suggests that the young general knew well his men and their needs.

Reviews and balls also entered into Stuart's plans for relieving the tediousness of camp routine. The most famous reviews Stuart held were the three at Brandy Station in late May and early June 1863. Their fame lies in the fact that they were the largest reviews ever staged by the cavalry and that the Battle of Brandy Station was fought the day after the last review, which was held on June 8. Historians strangely have forgotten, or perhaps ignored, the fact that it was Robert E. Lee, and not Stuart, who ordered that last review to be held. Lee had missed the one on June 5. Also forgotten are the dozens of reviews staged by other generals for exactly the same reasons Stuart held his. At all these grand displays, Stuart and his staff appeared in their finest uniforms, a sight that must have been something to behold.

The ball that has attracted the most attention from writers took place in early September 1862 in Urbana, Maryland. Von Borcke was put in charge of the decorations, to which he attended with enthusiasm. Numerous other balls and social gatherings were held, many of which are chronicled in von Borcke's memoirs. From Brien's and von Borcke's shadow plays to Stuart banging out a tune on a parlor piano in a friend's home, the staff knew how to turn their minds from the war, if only for a brief while. A condemnation of either Stuart or his men for doing so can only be attributed to a lack of understanding of human nature.

When the staff was broken up following Stuart's death, each officer took with him the prideful knowledge that he had served with the greatest cavalry chieftain of the time and, in many respects, of all time. In life Stuart had been the force that had held them together. In death his memory would do the same. Many lived within traveling distance of each other after the war. Confederate veteran reunions often brought them in contact with others who lived at greater distances. Sometimes it was difficult for the aging soldiers to recognize each other, as illustrated by this portion of a letter written by Chiswell Dabney to his wife on his visit to Richmond for the unveiling of Stuart's statue in 1907.

> Next day, Thursday, at the appointed hour, the carriage came round to carry me in the procession. I got in and drove to another house where a gentleman, old and grey, came out to the carriage—I asked him, "Who are you?" He replied, "Frank Robertson." I said, "I knew Frank Robertson like a brother 40 years ago, but I don't see him now." "Nevertheless," said he, "I am he—and who are you." I told him and we at once embraced.[10]

In the case of Walter Hullihen, there were some memories of the war he wished he could have forgotten. Stuart had had a nickname for him; for some reason the general had called him "Honey-Bun." At the time, Hullihen had had no difficulty with the sobriquet, but after the war he became an Episcopal minister and wanted to put the name behind him. His fellow staff officers would not hear of it. Charles Grattan, who lived in Staunton, where Hullihen resided, never ceased calling him "Honey-Bun," thereby causing the dignified servant of God much good-natured discomfiture. Grattan certainly enjoyed a laugh or two over the embarrassment he caused the poor priest, and as Hullihen flamed red, somewhere there undoubtedly was another burst of hearty laughter, and maybe a cry of "Cooke, you dodged too far!"

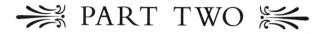

PART TWO

Stuart's
Staff
Officers

His [Stuart's] staff were greatly attached to him, for he sympathized in all their affairs as warmly as a brother, and was constantly doing them some "good turn." When with them off duty, he dropped every indication of rank, and was as much a boy as the youngest of them—playing marbles, quoits, or snowball, with perfect abandon and enjoyment. Most charming of all in the eyes of those gentlemen was the fact that he would not hesitate to decline invitations to entertainments on the plainly stated ground that "his staff were not included"—after which I need give myself no further trouble to explain why he was the most beloved of generals.

—John Esten Cooke[1]

THE BIOGRAPHIES OF Stuart's staff officers that make up this chapter will in many instances be the first recorded accounts of their lives. A handful of these men, W. W. Blackford, Heros von Borcke, H. B. McClellan, and John Esten Cooke, wrote accounts of their experiences while riding at Stuart's side but not necessarily of their lives before or after the war. Three of the staff, John Pelham, George St. Leger Grenfell, and Cooke, have had full biographies written about them. Theodore S. Garnett and others left scraps of memoirs. Peter W. Hairston, Philip H. Powers, R. Channing Price, Frank S. Robertson, and J. Hardeman Stuart wrote a substantial number of war letters. Of the majority, however, nothing has been written.

From October 2, 1861, to May 12, 1864, forty-eight men held one or more positions on Stuart's staff. The selection of the men to appear in this biographical section was based on their meeting at least one of two criteria: their records in the National Archives stated that they were assigned to Stuart, or Stuart mentioned them in his reports as being attached to his staff. Length of time on the staff, which ranges from one day to twenty-seven months, was not considered.

Comparison of the ensuing list with others that exist, notably that of Gen. Marcus J. Wright, will show that some names have been omitted while others have been added. Among the missing are ———— Bucks, Maj. Albert G. Dade, Norman, Maj. R. Norman, Lt. James E. Webb, and Maj. R. S. White. No conclusive evidence could be found to link Dade with Stuart's staff. Webb served as an assistant to Capt. Charles Grattan but was not officially a staff member. The remaining cases appear to be misnomers. Bucks is apparently a misspelling of Burke (Redmond). Both Norman and Maj. R. Norman seem to be a mistake involving a reversal of Norman R. FitzHugh's first name and middle initial. And R. S. White was most likely listed due to a misreading of B. S. White's first initial.

Several staff members were not included in Wright's list. Surprisingly, some of those omitted are well known: Roger P. Chew, Harry W. Gilmor, George St. Leger Grenfell, and John Pelham. Others, not as familiar, are James T. W. Hairston, Peter W. Hairston, Thomas R. Price, Roger W. Steger, Lewis F. Terrell, and Thomas B. Turner. Wright also spelled several of the staff officers' names incorrectly: J. S. Clarke for James L. Clark, Chriswell Dabney for Chiswell Dabney, Walter F. Hullehen for Walter Q. Hullihen, John Longstreet for John Landstreet, and S. G. Stables for Samuel G. Staples.

No claim is made that the roster in this chapter is complete, and names may need to be added or deleted in the future. A sincere attempt has been made to be as accurate as possible, however.

The positions of aide-de-camp and scout presented the greatest difficulty in determining an individual's staff membership. The shady area of aide-de-camp includes voluntary aide-de-camp, assistant aide-de-camp, and acting aide-de-camp. Several men fit into these categories, and Stuart named them as being members of his staff. Many men scouted for Stuart. Scouts W. D. Farley and Redmond Burke were also staff officers and have been included; John S. Mosby and Benjamin Franklin Stringfellow have not, because they held no official staff position, though they definitely were scouts for the general and members of his headquarters company.

The following staff biographies vary greatly in length and detail. While many of the staff survived the war, the stories of their lives often did not survive the ravages of time. As many sources as possible were investigated to establish correct names, dates, places, and other facts, but some of the men all but vanished. One, George St. Leger Grenfell, actually did, though he left a remarkable story behind. Despite these drawbacks, enough material was available to provide an outline of the lives of some of the men that have not heretofore been described.

Forty-eight men rode behind "Stuart's indomitable feather." What follows are their stories.

Maj. Dabney Ball

Chief of commissary and chaplain
October 2, 1861, to July 15, 1862, and December 1863 to May 12, 1864

Lt. William W. Blackford, adjutant of the 1st Virginia Cavalry, watched as a mounted figure emerged from the nearby woods and spurred his horse toward the waiting squadron of cavalrymen. As the rider drew closer, Blackford and the rest of the men sitting or lying near their horses sprang to their feet. The officer reined to a stop in front of Col. "Jeb" Stuart and with a crisp salute said, "Colonel Stuart, General Beauregard directs that you bring your command into action at once and that you attack where the firing is hottest."

The sounds of the bugle filled the air, and the column of men started off behind the colonel. Blackford's recollections of what happened next were vivid. The sounds of the struggle increased as they grew closer, and soon the battle came into view. The lieutenant was struck by the ever-shifting scene, as smoke obliterated first one area then another. Lines of men who were there one second disappeared in blinding flashes the next. Riding next to Stuart, Blackford made out a formation of scarlet and blue infantry. At first, doubt as to the identity of the regiment crossed both officers' minds, but a breeze unfurled the infantry's flag, and seconds later the cavalry was thundering down on the flank of the 5th New York Zouaves.

Surrounded by his charging comrades, Blackford somehow managed to keep aware of both the enemy and what was transpiring around him. Through the smoke and dust, he noticed a lone figure sitting calmly on his horse not ten paces from the enemy lines. Oblivious to their gunfire, this solitary cavalryman cocked and fired his pistol as if he were on the target range. Only after every chamber had been fired did the soldier turn his horse and ride off. Blackford recognized the bold trooper as the 1st Virginia's chaplain, the Reverend Dabney Ball, who that day not only left a lasting impression on Stuart's future engineer officer, but also established a reputation for courage and fearlessness.

Dabney Ball, who earned the sobriquet "The Fighting Parson" by his actions at 1st Manassas and on many other fields, was born in Fairfax County, Virginia, in May 1820. His parents, Dabney and Penelope Ball, were staunch members of the Methodist Church. Their strong beliefs were taught to their four sons, three of whom, including Dabney, would eventually become ministers. At fifteen, after attending local school, Dabney began to feel called to the ministry. By 1843 he was junior preacher on the Stafford Circuit.

From 1844 to 1861 Ball served churches in the following circuits or towns: Berkeley Circuit, Bedford Pennsylvania Circuit, Wardensville, Wrightsville, Westminster, Liberty, Hagerstown, Caroline Street Church (Baltimore), McKendree Church (Washington), Wesley Chapel (Washington), and Columbia Street Church (Baltimore). In 1845 while serving on the Bedford Circuit, Ball suffered what was thought to be a hemorrhage of the lungs—the first of many physical setbacks that would interrupt his career. He was compelled to quit his active duties for some months. His apparent complete recovery allowed him to continue his duties the next year on the Wardensville Circuit.[1] During this tenure, he met, courted, and married Mary D. Wisong of Darkesville, Virginia.

From February to May 1861, the confusion and turmoil caused by the approach of civil strife affected Ball. Early in the year he made several attempts to secure a chaplaincy in the United States Navy and repeatedly denounced secession and secessionists. A trip to Staunton, Virginia, for his church's conference in March did nothing but reaffirm his opinion that the states leaving the Union were totally in the wrong. While at the conference, Ball visited Alexander H. H. Stuart, former secretary of the interior under President Millard Fillmore, whose own strong Unionist feelings were not wasted on Ball.

The naval chaplaincy Ball desired failed to materialize, and to this disappointment was added grief over the loss of his small son, who died in April while on a visit to Ball's sister. He was buried in Mount Olivet Cemetery in Baltimore beside his sister and two other brothers. The death of four of his children within the span of about thirteen years must have been a heavy burden for Ball to bear. His own health continued to be a problem. Rheumatism, from which he had suffered for years, began to cause him much discomfort. Additionally, a throat condition prevented him from meeting his obligations as a preacher. His doctors advised a trip to a warmer climate, and with this in mind, he sought an appointment as a U.S. consul. He was especially interested in filling a position in either Foo Choo, China, or San Juan, Puerto Rico, but circumstances caused him to head in a different direction.

Ball's previously firm Union sentiments began to waver in the wake of the Baltimore Riots of April 19, 1861, which caused the deaths of four soldiers and twelve civilians plus the wounding of dozens more.[2] In a letter he wrote on April 21 to a friend in Washington, he outlined his fears and concerns. He stated, in part:

> The State [Maryland] evidently desires to remain in the Union, but at the same time is obviously determined not to be a party to the forcible subjugation of her Southern sisters. The peaceable passage of forces through her territory would be regarded as at least a tacit consent to Mr. Lincoln's policy as now developed. Even this would alienate the South effectually from her. The South is Maryland's chief market. She buys of the North, but sells to the South. Now, is it not very important to the government to keep Maryland in the Union? If so, ought she not to be permitted to maintain her neutrality at this critical junction?

> If Mr. Lincoln desires Maryland to stand under the Stars
> and Stripes, he has not a moment to lose in conciliating
> her people.
>   Again! It is alarming to see at this moment of extreme
> peril, his Proclamation, to blockade the Southern ports.
> For God's sake, for humanities sake, to spare the deluge of
> fraternal blood, if you have any influence, Mr. Samon, as
> I am sure you have, use it immediately, to induce him to
> modify his policy till Congress meets, and see if the
> providence of God will not offer some solution to the
> terrific problem which is before us.[3]

Ball's view of Maryland's situation was echoed by many other individuals, but Lincoln did not waver. Maryland would remain in the Union, and many industrious businessmen would still manage to "buy of the North and sell to the South" through all four years of conflict. For the majority of the state's populace, though, there came a time of decision. What Dabney Ball had experienced between February and May was enough to alter his position from committed Unionist to wavering Marylander. When the war finally erupted, Ball found it difficult to remain inactive and at last decided to align himself with the Confederacy. He left Baltimore and made his way south.

On July 1, 1861, Ball received an appointment as a chaplain from Virginia and joined the 1st Virginia Cavalry, commanded by Stuart. Following 1st Manassas, Ball continued to serve as the 1st Virginia's chaplain. One of the men who also served with Stuart at this time, Peter W. Hairston, mentioned Ball to his wife, Fanny, on at least three occasions. Hairston wrote that the regiment's "Fighting Parson" was ". . . quite a character—one of the bravest, coolest and most determined men I have known." In the same letter, Hairston also made reference to another clergyman, a Marylander, who had earned the title of "Foraging Parson." Due to a misreading of Hairston's letter, Ball has erroneously been labeled the "Foraging Parson" in a number of works focusing on Stuart.[4]

Along with his cool courage, Ball evidently had a sense of humor, as demonstrated in this story recorded by Hairston in a letter written to his wife on September 22, 1861.

> Our "fighting parson" Dabney Ball tells an amusing
> anecdote of himself. He was at Cape May one summer
> and was invited to preach. He accepted the invitation;
> but on repairing to the room designated he found a gay
> assemblage of persons—ladies and gentlemen in ball room

attire—the former with bouquets in their hands and engaged in lively conversation. He was invited up to the piano, took his seat behind it as a reading desk. Soon he had to call the congregation to order. He did not understand the matter until the next morning he saw in the newspaper, the joke of the service. Some <u>wag</u> had circulated the report there was to be a <u>ball</u> there that night. After the services were over his friends came up to him and tried to apologize but did not know how.[5]

When Stuart received his commission as brigadier general in late September 1861, he immediately set about appointing his brigade staff. Ball unquestionably had impressed him in a number of ways, for on October 2 the chaplain became a captain in the commissary department. After November 4 Ball was signing documents as a major, his new rank dating from October 2. The records would seem to indicate that Major Ball as chief of subsistence performed his duties with the same dedication and efficiency as had Rev. Ball the chaplain. Although often far behind the scene of action, the "Fighting Parson" managed to join in the fighting whenever there was an opportunity. Stuart's reports continued to mention Ball into the middle of 1862. Ball, however, was beginning to encounter more difficulty in gathering and shipping supplies to the troops under his care because of the Confederate government's lack of preparation. The chaos of the Peninsula Campaign apparently wreaked havoc with Ball's logistics. His inability to carry out Stuart's orders for supplies and the general's admonitions to surmount the problems in some manner led to frustration. Ball tendered his resignation to Secretary of War Randolph on July 15.

The incident that prompted Ball's resignation is explained in the following letter.

Atlee's Station
July 15, 1862

Dear General [Stuart],

I should have replied to your letter by the courier who brought it to me yesterday, but meeting him on the road as I was moving to this place, it was out of my power. I have the honour to report, in response to the inquiry it contained, that Col. Rosser's Reg't rec'd their rations yesterday, by his Commissary. Also that "arrangements" have been made to supply the three regiments east of Richmond that your orders specified, and also others

who are there. I am now at this place where I expect to
have supplies today for those in this vicinity.

I send herewith my resignation as commissary in the C.S.
Army which you will please do me the kindness to approve
and forward immediately to the government. Hoping you
may speedily fill the place with someone whose manner
of doing business will be less annoying to you, and who
will not be so "disconcerted and diverted" from the high
and responsible duty of feeding the men. I am with

> Great Respect—
> Your obt. svt.
> Dabney Ball
> Major & C.S.

P.S. I will continue to attend to duty for a few days as best
I may, if it is your wish I should, till the government has
time to act. D. B.[6]

Despite the apparent disagreement between Stuart and Ball over the
performance of the latter in getting supplies to the cavalry, both men still
admired and respected each other. On September 23, 1862, Stuart wrote a
letter recommending Ball for the position of major with the 11th Virginia
Cavalry. He obviously had high regard for Ball's leadership and fighting
ability. For whatever reason, the appointment was not made, and instead
Ball accepted the post of chaplain with the 5th Virginia Cavalry on
October 4, 1862. In January 1863, Stuart again tried unsuccessfully to
secure a majority in the 11th Cavalry for Ball. The "Fighting Parson"
remained with the 5th as chaplain until July 19, 1863, when he again
resigned, this time citing the inability to support his family on a chaplain's
salary.[7] Ball's family had been living in Baltimore before the war, and he
later arranged to move them from Baltimore to Salem, Virginia,[8] but the
costs of the move and the renting of a home in Salem made the family's
financial situation difficult.

In August 1863, in a further attempt to alleviate his family's problems,
Ball tried to obtain a commission as a major and adjutant general and an
assignment to Stuart's staff. Stuart had no objections to having Ball back
on his staff, as this letter indicates.

> Hd Qrs Cav Div A of N Va
> July 20, 1863

Major Dabney Ball, Chaplain 5th Va Cav
Major,

I regret exceedingly that the entire inadequacy of your salary for your support & that of your helpless & dependent family has made it necessary for you to resign from a post of so much usefulness. And I cannot consent for it to take place without making some effort to retain you in the service in another capacity. I hope you will see the Sec. of War therefore & represent to him that a Minister of the Gospel attached to my Division as Adjt. & Insp. Gen'l with the rank of Major, could with the military ability you have always displayed from the commencement of the war—and the experience derived in the Cavalry service, not only perform the duties of Inspector in the most satisfactory manner but besides devote much of your time to the dissemination of religious literature and influence, and the systematizing of religious services, with rules regulating chaplains of regts etc. etc. I do not know any one who could be more useful in such a capacity so desirable to the service, nor whose services & sacrifices are more deserving such consideration than yourself. I hope the Hon. Sec. of War will so decide.

Most Respectfully
& truly your obt svt,
J. E. B. Stuart
Major Gen'l
Comdg Cavalry[9]

The War Department did not grant the commission, however. Instead, Ball had to settle for a quasiofficial position as chaplain of the Cavalry Corps, a post he assumed sometime in December 1863 or January 1864.[10] Ball's military career after Stuart's death is unknown. Since his rank and position received no official confirmation, his "commission" would have lapsed when Stuart was killed. It is possible that Ball continued in his role under Hampton or Fitz Lee, but if so it was again in an unofficial capacity.

At the war's end, Ball returned to Baltimore and the Methodist Episcopal Church. He established the Bond Street Church and, from 1867 to 1869, was the presiding elder of the Roanoke District. During these years he suffered from rheumatism and erysipelas, which caused him great pain and discomfort. Nevertheless, as he had fearlessly faced his enemies on the battlefield, Ball bore his physical disabilities with like courage. At times he could scarcely stand while delivering his sermons but, refusing to sit, leaned heavily on the pulpit until he had finished. To his physical suffering was added mental anguish over the loss of at least two more children, but as one chronicler of his life wrote, "There was not a murmur, but always a certain steady marching forward to duty."[11]

While assigned to the Rockville Circuit in 1870–71, Ball's health eventually became such that he could ignore it no longer. He was forced to accept a transfer to the California Conference in the hope that his health would improve. By fall 1872 Ball remarkably was able to return to Baltimore, the climate of California having proved beneficial. He took charge of Central Church for two years before being appointed to Calvary Church in Baltimore. In 1875 he received appointment as presiding elder of the East Baltimore District. In May 1877 Ball's wife of thirty years died. Her death was a serious blow, and his grief surely helped undermine his physical condition. Slowly Ball's health gave way, until he became seriously ill with what was diagnosed as heart disease. He died at the home of William Coon in Baltimore at 9:30 A.M. on February 15, 1878. He was survived by two daughters and one son. Ball was laid to rest in Mount Olivet Cemetery. A biographer said of him:

> The temperament and character of Dabney Ball were conspicuously of the heroic type. We have never known a braver man. We have never known a man more inflexible in the maintenance of his purposes. In connection with these sterner features there appeared a sweetness of spirit, a deferential regard to the views and feelings of his friends, and the modesty of true manliness.[12]

Maj. Robert Franklin Beckham

Commander of the Stuart Horse Artillery
April 7, 1863, to February 16, 1864

> Hd Qts Cav Div Army of Nor Va
> Mar 26 1863
>
> General;
> I have the honor to request that Major R.F. Beckham Prov. Arty—be assigned to duty with my Division to take command of the Horse Artillery Batteries belonging to it, vice Pelham deceased.
> Major Beckham's services become available by the resignation of Major Genl G. W. Smith on whose staff he was serving as Ord officer.

I have known Major Beckham from the beginning of the war—he fought by my side at the first Manassas—and I am satisfied of his fitness for the place.

I respectfully recommend that he be assigned to duty as Lieutenant Colonel as his command is a very important one.

Most Respectfully
Your obt svt
J. E. B. Stuart
Major Genl

Gen. S. Cooper.
A&IG. Richmond Va.[1]

Eight days had passed since the death of Maj. John Pelham when Stuart penned this petition for the services of Robert Franklin Beckham to command his horse artillery. Stuart felt the loss of Pelham deeply. The young Alabamian had been more than the "gallant" Pelham to him; in fact, he had been almost a brother. But the war continued, and duty must supplant feelings. Stuart knew that Pelham's replacement would have to be an officer possessing special qualities. No evidence exists, however, that Stuart expected or wanted Beckham to fill Pelham's shoes. All Stuart desired was an officer who could fight his horse artillery the way it was supposed to be fought. In Beckham, Stuart found that officer.

Beckham was born May 6, 1837, in Culpeper, Virginia, the same town in which Pelham was to die. His father, John G. Beckham, moved the family to Warrenton sometime after Robert's birth. On July 1, 1854, at age seventeen, Beckham entered the United States Military Academy. His time at West Point was well spent. He proved to be a very good student, standing sixth in a class of twenty-two when he graduated in 1859.

After graduation, Beckham received a commission as a second lieutenant and an assignment to the Corps of Topographical Engineers. He was still attached to this branch of the service as a staff officer of George Meade stationed near Detroit, Michigan, when the war broke out. Over the next few months, he made a risky attempt to secure a commission in the Confederate Army while still holding his position in the Engineer Corps. In a letter written on March 6, 1861, by a fellow West Point graduate, Maj. Samuel H. Lockett of the Army of Alabama, to Confederate secretary of war L. P. Walker, Lockett tried to secure a commission for his friend.[2] The Confederate War Department plainly felt it had enough engineers, because on May 31 Beckham wrote a letter trying to obtain a commission in the regular Confederate Army. He had resigned from the U.S. Army on May 3, and at the time he wrote the letter he held a position in the Engineer Corps of the Provisional Army of Virginia. His friend Lockett was already in the regular army, and Beckham wanted to join him.

Once again Beckham was frustrated, for the War Department shelved his request, and the aspiring young officer had to be satisfied with his place in the Provisional Army of Virginia. He did not give up easily, however, as the following letter indicates.

Winchester Va
June 23, 1861

Hon Jeremiah Morton

Dear Sir, Learning that the Army is about to be re-organized & that the Provl Army is, in some <u>way</u> to be merged into the Con. S. Army, I have taken the liberty of writing to you to request that you would ask a place for me in the Southern Army. My reasons for writing are particularly these—that I fear that I may be called upon to serve in some corps with men who are of a <u>later date, above</u> me or that I may be appointed in some corps in which I do not wish to serve at all. In either case I should feel called upon to resign & then I would have to commence some new profession. At present I am holding a position in the Engineers of the Provl Army, having two or three men from Lexington ranking me—they being graduated <u>last</u> summer & holding the commission of Captain whilst I was honored with a Lieutenantcy. You will then understand that my object is not to obtain any exalted rank, but simply to get that place to which I conceive I am justly entitled— one on an <u>equal</u> footing with those who left the Military Academy with me <u>and above</u> those who came after me. If I can obtain the place of Captain in Engineers I shall be much gratified, but I would by no means be so presumptuous as to ask for it if in so doing I violate the law of Equity which I have mentioned above. I don't want to get above any one who has been above me before & I don't wish to be placed before any one who was before me. If I am not considered qualified for the Engineers, then I should like the Ordnance Corps and next to that the Dragoons. I do not wish to be put in the Infantry or Artillery. I wrote to Hon L. P. Walker some two or three weeks ago directing to Montgomery, but a few days after-

ward found that he was in Richmond & suppose he did
not get my letter. If you would do me the favor to ask a
position for me next to my friend & classmate Capt S. H.
Lockett of Ala. & let me know whether I may hope to
obtain the appointment I shall be under many obligations
to you. From present appearances we are likely to be at this
place for some time to come, as there seems to be no
enemy around here. For several days past I have been an
invalid under the tender care of Phil Williams Esq & his
lady. I am now however nearly well. Hoping to be excused
for this trespassing on your kindness I am very Respectfully
Yrs

R. F. Beckham[3]

Considering what he wrote, Beckham was not only unhappy about being
in the Provisional Army but also disturbed by the fact that he was outranked
by men from Lexington, an obvious reference to the Virginia Military Institute (VMI). Graduates of the United States Military Academy and VMI
would do battle over rank on many occasions during the next four years and
long after the war ended. Beckham's comments certainly were among the
opening salvos of a dispute that was never really settled. Perhaps the verbal
barb helped, though, because Beckham finally motivated the War Department to take action in his case. True to War Departments everywhere, it
placed the well-qualified engineer in the branch of service he desired least—
the artillery. In this instance, however, it would appear the men in Richmond
knew something Beckham did not.

One can imagine what Beckham must have felt when he read his new
orders for the first time. But then the deeply instilled discipline of his training
took over and he reported, with the rank of lieutenant, to his new command:
Groves's Culpeper Battery. This battery had enlisted on April 19, 1861, for
one year. It was not more than a month before Beckham found himself
on the field at 1st Manassas fighting with two of his guns under the eyes of
Stuart. The engineer-turned-artillerist conducted himself with courage and
efficiency. His behavior impressed Stuart and others, but his reward turned
out to be an assignment to the Reserve Artillery Corps. Then, on January 14,
1862, Beckham at last received the break he had been waiting for.[4]

Beckham's new orders sent him as a staff officer to Maj. Gen. Gustavus
W. Smith. Smith used his new staff member as an aide-de-camp but quickly
learned that Beckham held quite a reputation as an artillery officer. On
March 31, 1862, the Jeff Davis Artillery elected Smith's new aide captain
of their battery, even though he had made no effort to campaign for the

position. Although flattered, Beckham declined. Perhaps he recognized that opportunities for rapid advancement in that branch of the service were few and that he stood a better chance if he stayed with Smith. On August 16 he became a major, and Smith then assigned him to the post of ordnance officer.

Satisfied at last, Beckham performed his duties until Smith resigned in January 1863. For the next two months, Beckham had no command, though he held a commission as a major in the Provisional Artillery. Stuart's request for his services upon Pelham's death led Beckham into a phase of his career that may have been the most rewarding. He faced immense pressure at having to replace the greatly respected Pelham, but the fact that Stuart had requested him over many other officers must have made him feel more confident. Nevertheless, the horse artillery's new commander had misgivings about his new post, and on April 5, 1863, he expressed them in a letter from Richmond to his old commander-in-chief, G. W. Smith.

> My Dear General:
> I have received orders to leave here and report to General [Robert E.] Lee, and consequently will not have an opportunity of seeing you on your return to Richmond. I cannot begin to express the doubts by which I am troubled when now about to go into the field under an officer other than yourself. When with you I always felt sure of going very nearly in the right direction, but I now feel as if I must, for the future, rely almost altogether upon myself.[5]

On April 8, 1863, Beckham assumed command of the Stuart Horse Artillery. He had little time to familiarize himself with the officers and men of the batteries, for in less than three weeks the campaign season opened with the Battle of Chancellorsville. Part of the horse artillery, under Beckham, accompanied "Stonewall" Jackson on his famous flank march and charged with the 2nd Corps when it made its attack on the Army of the Potomac's 11th Corps. Beckham and Capt. James Breathed kept two guns firing down the Plank Road while managing to keep up with the headlong rush of Jackson's infantry. As the sun set and the battle died away, "Stonewall" rode up to Beckham and, shaking his hand, said, "Young man, I congratulate you."[6] It was Beckham's finest hour.

After Jackson's death, Lee's army underwent a reorganization. The cavalry and the horse artillery took the opportunity during the relatively quiet period to refit and prepare for the campaign ahead. A different kind of challenge now confronted Beckham. The South's reserve of horses was diminishing rapidly. Both the cavalry and the artillery struggled to secure horses in sufficient numbers. As commander of the horse artillery, Beckham was responsible for acquiring the proper number of horses for his guns. He somehow managed to obtain these plus extras to pull the guns Stuart had commandeered from those captured at Chancellorsville. Stuart, sincerely impressed by his artillery commander's achievement, again recommended him for promotion.

> Head Qts Cav Div A of N. Va
> May 21st 1863
>
> General S. Cooper
> Adjt Gen'l C.S.A.
> Richmond Va.
>
> General;
>
> I have the honor to request that Major Robt F. Beckham Com'd'g Horse Artillery be promoted to the rank of Lieut Colonel. He distinguished himself in command of a battery at First Manassas and has performed valuable service since. In the battle of the Wilderness May 2nd, he commanded the Artillery in advance & it is sufficient to say that he received <u>General Jackson's congratulations during the action</u>—. I hope his promotion will not be delayed. There are already 5 batteries attached to this Division soon to be increased to two more.
>
> Mo Respectfully
> J. E. B. Stuart
> Major Gen'l[7]

But the Confederate War Department would not grant the lieutenant colonelcy until the horse artillery battalion actually had the two new batteries. Beckham would have to wait for his two stars.

Over the next several months, the Stuart Horse Artillery passed through the Gettysburg and Mine Run Campaigns along with the rest of the army. The batteries' performances, especially during the withdrawal from Gettysburg, earned the battalion new laurels. Beckham fought when and where he could. He never had the entire battalion under his command at one time, as the batteries were assigned to the various cavalry brigades, which were scattered according to need. During October Beckham had two close calls. He, with Stuart and part of the cavalry, was surrounded at Auburn on the thirteenth and his horse was killed beneath him near Manassas Junction on the fifteenth.

On November 20 Beckham was again recommended for promotion, this time by Gen. William N. Pendleton,[8] whose plan would have put James Dearing in command of the horse artillery while Beckham went to E. Porter Alexander's 1st Corps Artillery. Nothing ever came of Pendleton's suggestions. On November 30 Beckham fought his guns near Antioch Church, after which the horse artillery was ordered into winter quarters. In December the battalion, except for Hart's Battery, began to erect its winter quarters near Charlottesville, but Beckham was not there; he was in Richmond under orders of Robert E. Lee as of December 24.

Just why Lee had Beckham in the Confederate capital is unknown, but the major did not remain there all the time. A letter written by Lt. Charles R. Phelps of Moorman's Battery on January 29, 1864, indicates that Beckham was in the horse artillery's camp on at least one occasion. Phelps wrote that his battery was to be inspected by "the Major," and Beckham was the only major in the horse artillery at this time. Also, in his other letters, Phelps always referred to Beckham as "Major B" or "the Major," so he probably was referring to Beckham in this instance.

Beckham seems to have divided his time between Richmond and the horse artillery camp outside of Charlottesville until February 16, when he was promoted to the temporary rank of colonel and issued orders to report to Lt. Gen. John B. Hood. Stuart said good-bye to his artillery chief in a telegram dated February 15, writing, "I never oppose the promotion of a deserving officer. I wish you all success."[9]

Although he was finally a colonel, the promotion took Beckham away from the Army of Northern Virginia and placed him in the Army of Tennessee. Hood at first gave Beckham command of all the artillery in the army, then placed him in charge of the artillery in Stephen D. Lee's corps. In this post, Beckham participated in Hood's ill-fated invasion of Tennessee. On November 29, 1864, Beckham brought his batteries into action near Columbia. During the action an unexploded enemy shell or solid shot struck a boulder behind Beckham, who was mounted and riding among his guns. A piece of the fragmented rock smashed into the back of his head. He was carried to "Hamilton Place" near Ashwood, Tennessee, where he died on December 5. He was buried on the tenth in St. John's Church Cemetery in Ashwood.

Capt. William Willis Blackford

Engineer Officer
June 24, 1862, to February 19, 1864

As a civil engineer, cavalry officer, engineer officer, author, professor, railroad construction engineer, sugar cane and oyster farmer, and a few other titles, William W. Blackford demonstrated a versatility of which few men can boast. That he performed well in all of them, exceptionally in some, illustrated the broad talents of one of Stuart's finest staff officers.

Blackford, the eldest son of William M. Blackford and Mary Berkley Minor, was born in Fredericksburg, Virginia, on March 23, 1831. He and his four brothers, Charles, Benjamin, Launcelot, anu Eugene, served with distinction in almost every branch of the Confederate Army. The complete story of this Southern family at war would make fascinating reading, since they witnessed it from so many different perspectives. Perhaps even more remarkable than their record of service is the fact that they all survived.

Blackford's early life differed little from that of other boys of his age and social standing until 1841, when President John Tyler appointed William's father chargé d'affaires to New Granada, now Colombia, South America. The Blackfords lived in Bogotá for two years, until the election of James Polk as president terminated his father's post. Upon returning home, William finished his schooling, selecting as his profession that of civil engineer. Blackford worked for three years as a laborer, earning enough money that at age twenty he could enter the University of Virginia. After two years he graduated and accepted a position as resident engineer for the Virginia and Tennessee Railroad.

During this period, on January 10, 1856, Blackford married Mary Trigg Robertson, daughter of Virginia's governor Wyndham Robertson and sister of Frank S. Robertson, who would become Blackford's assistant on Stuart's staff. Governor Robertson owned and operated a plaster mine at Buena Vista in Washington County, Virginia. Blackford gave up his position with the railroad to become a partner in the business.

In his own words, Blackford "was surrounded by every attraction of family affection and interest and, until the mighty war tempest arose, considered myself settled for life."[1] For Blackford the first signs of the tempest ahead came in the form of John Brown's raid on Harpers Ferry. The raid and the subsequent labeling of Brown as a martyr prompted Blackford to raise a cavalry company with William E. Jones, he of "grumbling" fame, as captain.[2] Blackford became first lieutenant. Among other members of the Washington Mounted Rifles was John Singleton Mosby. Blackford later recalled that there was nothing about Mosby at that time that would indicate his brilliant future as a partisan.

With the beginning of the war, the company marched to Richmond and, after spending a week or two at a camp of instruction, received orders to join the 1st Virginia Cavalry Regiment, then under the command of Lt. Col. "Jeb" Stuart. Another period of training ensued, followed by some action in the Shenandoah Valley. Shortly before the Battle of 1st Manassas, Stuart appointed Blackford adjutant for the regiment. Blackford's diet and lack of sleep caused him to become ill during the regiment's journey to Manassas. Being very disturbed lest Stuart think he was feigning illness on the eve of a battle, Blackford rested at a nearby home and, feeling refreshed the next morning, overtook the command before it reached Manassas. Blackford's performance in the battle was such that Stuart mentioned him in his report. Blackford described his experiences in a letter to his uncle.

> July 27, 1861
> Fairfax CH
> Head Q. 1st Reg. Va, Cav.
>
> Dear Uncle John
> The great battle has been fought & won and three of us have been active participants in it. Chas. is safe but I have not heard from Eugene. I got his friend Randolph McKim to go down to look him up yesterday. You can form but little idea of the [two words illegible] they sustained. We have supplied the whole army with almost every thing they needed. The roads are lined with abandoned wagons filled with property of every kind. I was in the charge made by Stuart's regiment, to which we are attached. Col. Stuart has made me Adjutant of the regiment, which position is a very imposing one and the comfort of my life is much greater. I was fortunate enough to make a draw of 80 prisoners with three men. I also captured a wagon and four horses. We are now here and our Colonel is in command of this brigade consisting of two regiments of infantry and one of cavalry and a company of artillery. We lost nine men killed sixteen wounded & nineteen horses in our charge. We charged in column by fours. I was two horses

length from the head when we struck the column of the
enemy who were the N.Y. Fire Zouaves. We slew them
at a great rate with our pistols. I doubled one fellow up
by a shot in the stomach as we dashed through which was
the only shot I got. I was not touched, nor my horse. I
had trouble in getting back over the dead horses. Chas I
saw after the battle and he was well. I must now close,
Love to Cousin [illegible] family. Your aff. Nephew

Wm. W. Blackford[3]

On October 3, 1861, Blackford received a commission as captain of his
company. Stuart's promotion to brigadier general on September 24 effectively ended Blackford's tenure as the 1st Virginia's adjutant. W. E. Jones had
also been promoted to colonel and was given command of the regiment, a
circumstance that Blackford soon had cause to regret. Jones had Blackford
arrested on charges of violating an order against having fires on the picket
line. After being under arrest for six weeks, a court-martial found the
captain innocent of the charges.

Blackford's absence from his company during his arrest cost him dearly.
When the army reorganized, he was not reelected as the company's captain.
Blackford returned to Richmond and found himself a captain again within
a very short time. That he had little trouble securing the new position can
be attributed, in part, to some of the friends he had made before the war,
as the following letter illustrates.

Junction, Hanover County
May 13th 1862

General G. W. Randolph
Secretary of War,
Sir

Mr. William W. Blackford is an applicant for a place in
the Corps of Engineers. He has been a Captain of Volunteers for a year and will present ample testimony of his
conduct & capacity as an officer from others.

It gives me great pleasure to say that he served years in
my Corps of Civil Engineers, and he displayed fine abilities
combined with a thorough education. In character also
he is every way worthy of your patronage.

I am, Sir, with great respect
Your ob. Servt
Chas. F. M. Garnett[4]

The impression Blackford had made on Garnett while he worked for him on the Virginia and Tennessee Railroad helped to reap the reward of a captain's commission in the Corps of Engineers dated May 26, 1862. After several assignments, including the building of a pontoon bridge across the James River, Blackford received orders to report to Stuart. He rejoined his old commander on June 24, 1862, the day before the opening of the Seven Days Battles.

Blackford's war service is excellently chronicled in his book *War Years with Jeb Stuart*. Besides his engineer duties, he drew many scouting assignments and even courier duty during battles. He missed only one major campaign, Chancellorsville, and that due to illness. Accidents nearly claimed him. According to von Borcke's memoirs, Blackford suffered what could have been a serious fall from a horse on October 26, 1862, during a fence-jumping competition.[5] The engineer made no mention of this in his reminiscences but did record a fall from a wagon on December 10, 1862, which inflicted a nasty head wound. In battle he was wounded only once, receiving a flesh wound in the leg on November 3, 1862. He had three horses shot beneath him, including Manassas and Comet. Both of these animals survived, as did Blackford's favorite, Magic, which passed through the war unscathed.

Throughout his book, Blackford mentions a special pair of field glasses that enabled him to see at greater distances than almost any other officer in the army. He was proud to note that because of the glasses he often ended up with the dangerous scouting missions.

The captain's most perilous moments, though, probably came during the Chambersburg Raid and had nothing to do with scouting. While crossing the Potomac back to Virginia at White's Ford, Stuart sent his engineer back to bring in the rear guard. At least three couriers had made the attempt and failed. Blackford attributed the greater portion of his success to Magic's strength and endurance. Having already ridden Magic nearly one hundred miles, the captain entrusted his fate to the horse. Stuart watched the engineer gallop away from the ford and, after many tension-filled minutes, return with the "lost" rear guard also at a gallop. No wonder the captain's memoirs contain numerous words of praise for what must have been a remarkable animal.[6]

By January 1864 Blackford had been a captain for longer than he cared to remember. Stuart had attempted to secure a higher commission for his fighting engineer, but Richmond always turned the recommendations down. But what Stuart could not do, necessity finally did. The raising of a regiment of engineers opened up positions of higher rank for a few deserving officers. Blackford's name had been included on a list for Secretary of War Seddon's consideration, and on February 19 Blackford received his commission as major. The thrill of the moment was somewhat lessened with the knowledge that he would have to say good-bye to Stuart and the cavalry. Nevertheless, he went, and by April 1 Blackford was a lieutenant colonel.

The 1st Regiment of Engineers spent virtually all of its existence in the lines protecting Petersburg. The greater portion of Blackford's time up until the fall of Richmond was spent directing countermining operations. He joined his regiment on the retreat to Appomattox, where he surrendered and was paroled along with the rest of Lee's army.

Soon after the war, he returned to railroading and became chief engineer for the Lynchburg and Danville Railroad, a position he occupied for two years. On May 22, 1866, Blackford's beloved Mary died from the effects of childbirth. His new daughter, born on May 1 and named after her mother, died on July 26, 1867. The Blackfords had had seven children in all: Elizabeth Robertson; Wyndam Robertson; Gay Robertson; Pelham; Lucy Landon (?–September 13, 1857); Landon Carter (August 26, 1859 –December 17, 1862); and Mary Robertson. With nothing tying him to Virginia any longer, he moved to Louisiana to try his hand at farming. He worked hard to build a sugar cane plantation, but it was destroyed in a flood in 1874.

In 1880 he accepted a position as professor of mechanics and drawing at Virginia Polytechnic Institute, where he also served as superintendent of buildings and grounds. A reorganization of the school in 1882 eliminated a number of faculty members including Blackford.[7] He turned again to railroading, working for the Baltimore and Ohio. He also directed the building of a railroad between Lynchburg, Virginia, and Durham, North Carolina. In 1890 Blackford retired to Lynnhaven Bay near Norfolk, Virginia, to take up oyster farming. He died there on April 30, 1905.[8] His remains were taken by the family to Abingdon, Virginia, and were laid to rest in Sinking Spring Cemetery.

Col. Alexander Robinson Boteler

Voluntary aide-de-camp
August 1863 to May 12, 1864

For the Confederate government, the early days of February 1862 were filled with an unanticipated anxiety that could not be attributed to anyone clad in Union blue. The difficulty had erupted from within and involved Gen. Thomas J. "Stonewall" Jackson, Gen. William W. Loring, Secretary of War Judah P. Benjamin, and President Jefferson Davis. A midwinter advance on the town of Romney, Virginia, had been the catalyst for an incident that almost cost the South one of its most celebrated generals.

Eleven of Loring's officers had signed a petition calling for the withdrawal of the Army of the Northwest, then under Jackson's command, to Winchester. Loring forwarded the mutinous document to Richmond via Gen. William B. Taliaferro, who placed it in the hands of the president. Davis decided that Jackson had made a mistake and had the secretary of war order Loring's command to concentrate at Winchester. Jackson complied but, disgusted and angered by what he rightly interpreted as interference on the part of Davis and Benjamin, also sent in his resignation.

Col. Alexander Robinson Boteler

Virginia's governor John Letcher became embroiled in the crisis when he received a letter from Jackson requesting an assignment to the Virginia Military Institute. Realizing that the Institute was no place for one of the South's rising stars, Letcher, with Secretary Benjamin's blessing, dispatched a letter to Jackson. The man who bore the crucial message and on whose shoulders fell the delicate job of persuading Jackson to reconsider his decision was Col. Alexander R. Boteler, Confederate congressman and close friend of Jackson's. He proved to be the right man for the job.

Before Boteler set out for Jackson's headquarters, he sent the ruffled general a plea to alter his position. Jackson's reply came swiftly. He was not going to change his mind unless he was assured that his decisions in the field would not be countermanded in Richmond. After Boteler's arrival at the general's headquarters in Winchester, his appeals to his friend's patriotism plus an avalanche of letters from all over the Confederacy finally convinced Jackson that he should remain in uniform. Loring was soon transferred, and Jackson went on to fashion a remarkable career. Boteler would serve the Confederacy in many capacities over the following three years, but none would be as vital as the service he performed that February in Winchester.

Born in Shepherdstown, Virginia (now West Virginia), on May 16, 1815, Alexander Robinson Boteler was the son of Henry Boteler and Priscilla Robinson. Henry had received a degree in medicine in Philadelphia and had settled in Shepherdstown, where he established his practice. His wife was the daughter of an affluent import merchant and ship owner from Baltimore. Her mother had been Angelica Peale, oldest daughter of artist Charles W. Peale. This may explain in part Alexander's talent in drawing, which he would use to great advantage during his long life.

Tragically, Boteler's mother died in 1820 when he was five, and his father sent him to Baltimore to live with his grandparents until he was eleven. During this time, he had all the advantages wealth could furnish.

Socially, he had many opportunities, even meeting Lafayette on his visit to Baltimore in 1825. In 1833 Boteler entered Princeton, graduating in 1835. While he was attending there, he met his future wife, Helen Macomb Stockton, through a mutual friend, A. S. Dandridge of "The Bower" (which would become the location of Stuart's headquarters in the fall of 1862). The young couple was married on April 26, 1836, but the happiness of their marriage was tempered by the death of Boteler's father the following summer.

They moved to "Fountain Rock," near Shepherdstown; here Boteler began a career in agriculture, which he pursued for the next twenty years. His farming experience plus his talent for public speaking eventually gained him a reputation as an authority on progressive agriculture. In 1850 he became president of the Jefferson County Agricultural Society, and during the following decade he had numerous opportunities to address some of the most important agricultural societies in Virginia, Ohio, and Maryland. His career seemed on the rise.

In 1852 disaster struck. Boteler's monetary support of a friend in the amount of $20,000 almost brought him financial ruin when the friend's business collapsed. Though he paid the debt, it cost him a large portion of his wife's inheritance and half of his "Fountain Rock" estate. For the rest of his life he struggled financially but died free of debt, his honesty and integrity intact.

While the year 1852 brought Boteler considerable hardship, it also saw the birth of his political career. A member of the Whig party, he became the delegate to the Whig convention in Richmond, where he received an appointment as a presidential elector. He cast his vote for Winfield Scott. In 1859 he won his first election and took a seat in the 36th Congress as a representative from Virginia. He held his seat until Virginia seceded, and then followed his state out of the Union. His political career did not end with his resignation from the U.S. House of Representatives; he was elected Jefferson County's delegate to the Virginia legislature in May 1861. Before he could enter into the duties of the office, however, he found himself a representative to the Confederate Congress from the 10th District.

Boteler's friendship with "Stonewall" Jackson brought him an appointment as voluntary aide-de-camp on May 30, 1862. He remained on Jackson's staff until that great leader's death in May 1863. During his tenure with Jackson, Boteler often acted as liaison between Richmond and Lee's volatile lieutenant. Perhaps Jackson had the incident of early February 1862 in mind when he called his friend to staff duty. Upon Jackson's death, Boteler returned to his position as a delegate in Richmond. On April 30, 1863, the Confederate Congress approved a resolution for the adoption of a coat of arms, better known as "The Great Seal of the Confederate States of America." Boteler played an important part in the designing of this and introduced the resolution for its acceptance in Congress.

In August 1863 Boteler became a voluntary aide-de-camp on the staff of "Jeb" Stuart. His letter of acceptance read, in part:

> Ballard House, August 15, 1863
>
> Hon. J. A. Seddon,
>   Secretary of War:
>   Sir: I accept the position of voluntary aide on Major-General Stuart's staff in the hope of rendering some little service by making myself practically acquainted with the causes of the present condition of the cavalry and in doing what I could to aid General Stuart in his zealous efforts to increase the strength and promote the efficiency of his command.[1]

By early February 1864, Stuart had come to respect Boteler to such an extent that he recommended him for the post of presiding judge in military court. The cavalry chieftain wrote to President Davis concerning the appointment.

> Feb. 6th 1864
>
> To His Excellency
> President Davis
> Mr. President—
>   Having already through the proper channels made a recommendation of Col. A. R. Boteler as a member (Presiding Judge) of a military court about to be authorized by Congress I beg to renew the same individually in his behalf as I am very anxious to secure his valuable services for that position. You are yourself so familiar with his ability that I need hardly refer to it, except to state that the Confederacy has no more zealous champion, or devoted patriot in or out of the field than Alex R. Boteler.
>
>   I have the honor to be
>   most Respectfully,
>   Your obt svt
>   JEB Stuart
>   Major Genl Comdg[2]

Some delay evidently occurred in the formation of the court, because Boteler did not receive his appointment until November 5, 1864. In the intervening period, Boteler continued to serve on Stuart's staff as a voluntary aide-de-camp until the general's death. No official record seems to exist of Boteler's status between May and November 1864. It is possible that he remained in Richmond as aide-de-camp to Gov. William "Extra Billy" Smith, a position he was known to have held during the war. The post would not have been new to him, as he had been aide to Smith's predecessor, Gov. John Letcher, in the same capacity.

While Boteler continued to serve his country, he suffered a personal loss that must have affected him deeply. On July 19, 1864, on the orders of Union general David Hunter, Boteler's home, "Fountain Rock," was burned to the ground. The colonel's wife, daughters, and three grandchildren, who were present when the Union soldiers came to execute Hunter's command, watched as their home was destroyed. They had been given no opportunity to save anything, but when one of Boteler's daughters entered the burning structure to play the piano one last time, a number of soldiers were touched by her resolve and assisted the family in rescuing a few possessions from the flames. The piano was among the first objects carried out of the house.

From November 1864 until Lee surrendered at Appomattox, Boteler continued as presiding judge on the military court. He evacuated Richmond with Lee's retreating forces and gave his parole with Lee's army on April 9, 1865. As with many other Southerners, there was little for Boteler to return to; nevertheless, he once again settled in the Shepherdstown area and began to work for the improvement of both himself and his community.

In 1871 he became one of the incorporators of Shepherd College and served on its board for many years. His political rights were restored to him on June 12, 1872, by a special bill that passed the Senate and the House of Representatives. The bill's passage allowed Boteler to become a commissioner for West Virginia to the Centennial Exposition in Philadelphia in 1876. He obviously was still held in high esteem by many in political circles. He also was appointed by President Chester Arthur as a member of the Tariff Commission in 1881, and he served as assistant attorney in the Department of Justice from 1882 to 1883 and as clerk of pardons in the Department of Justice from November 12, 1884, to September 12, 1889.

Boteler managed to find time for other endeavors as well. He was instrumental in establishing the telegraph in Shepherdstown and in having the Shenandoah Valley Railroad (later the Norfolk and Western) routed through the town. He authored various pamphlets and articles on the Civil War, including "Recollection of the John Brown Raid" for *Century Magazine*. He had already established himself as a writer of note with the publication of *My Ride to the Barbecue* in 1860. Although he had never had any formal art training, his talent at drawing played an important part in the publication of this book, as his illustrations were very popular. In 1887 the Military Historical Society of Boston purchased a collection of Boteler's paintings. Among the subjects of these works were portraits of R. E. Lee, James Longstreet, Jefferson Davis, and Wade Hampton.

Following his resignation from the Department of Justice in September 1889, Boteler lived in semiretirement until his death on May 8, 1892. He is buried in Elmwood Cemetery in Shepherdstown, where he is still remembered as one of the community's most revered citizens.

Capt. Luke Tiernan Brien

Assistant adjutant general and chief of staff
October 2, 1861, to April 23, 1862

On May 5, 1861, while encamped near Martinsburg, Virginia, Peter W. Hairston wrote to his wife, Fanny, that two "very nice gentlemen" from Maryland had "left their property & homes to fight our cause."[1] The circumstances that brought these men into the Confederate service were familiar ones. Maryland was torn between the Union and the Confederacy, and though she never left the Union, many of her sons fought for the South during the war.

One of these men was Luke Tiernan Brien, who had been born in Urbana, Maryland, on December 22, 1827. Brien was the son of Robert Coleman Brien and Ann Tiernan, the daughter of Luke Tiernan, who himself had a distinguished career of service to the state and for whom Brien was named. When Brien was seven, his family moved to Baltimore. There he received his education, graduating from Georgetown College in 1846. In 1847 he married Mary Virginia Nelson of Baltimore and settled on a farm at Mount Washington in Baltimore County. Brien remained on his farm until 1854, when he spent a year in Europe. Upon his return, he purchased a farm near Hagerstown. Possibly this was the "property & home" he left to join the Confederacy in May 1861.

Stuart first recognized Brien's services in his July 26, 1861, report of the Battle of 1st Manassas. At the time, Brien had no commission and was serving as a volunteer aide to Stuart along with P. W. Hairston and James F. Brown. All three displayed "meritorious conduct" and rendered "valuable assistance."

Whatever Brien did from his arrival in May until Stuart became brigadier general on September 24, 1861, it caught his commander's eye, and when General Stuart announced his staff on October 2, Brien received a commission as captain and an appointment as assistant adjutant general and chief of staff.

The lull that followed the clash at Manassas kept the newly organized cavalry brigade busy, but no mention of Brien is found in the records until Stuart's account of the Battle of Dranesville on December 20, when the adjutant is again commended for his "valuable services on the field." The new year dawned with the war once again reduced to minor skirmishing and capturing of pickets. Then, on April 23, 1862, Brien received a commission as lieutenant colonel of the 1st Virginia Regiment of Cavalry. The appointment came as a result of Brien's election by the men of the regiment. He had neither asked nor campaigned for the position, so his selection was quite a tribute to him. Also, the 1st was Stuart's old regiment, and he would not have agreed to Brien's appointment if he had not had great faith in him. The increase in rank and the added duties did not relieve Brien of his staff position, however. In Stuart's report of the fighting around Williamsburg, Brien was still referred to as "my chief of staff."

Brien's tenure as lieutenant colonel of the 1st Virginia continued until September 30, 1862, when he tendered his resignation. He cited no specific reason for doing so, though various accounts imply that his health had deteriorated to a point that forced him to retire at least temporarily from the service. Being a Marylander, Brien could not go to his home behind enemy lines. Peter W. Hairston, with whom he had become friends when the two served together as volunteer staff officers to Stuart, offered to let Brien stay on his plantation, "Cooleemee," in North Carolina, in exchange for his help as an overseer.

By March 1863, Brien had immersed himself in the problems on the Hairston plantation. He helped the Hairstons obtain a mill and additional land as a hedge against inflation. After Peter Hairston returned to the war following the Gettysburg Campaign, Brien assumed additional duties. He handled the problems attendant to the conscripting of slave labor by the government and even saw to the education of two of Peter's children, Sammy and Betty. The work Brien performed for the Hairstons further strengthened a friendship that would last beyond the end of the war until Hairston's death in 1886.

Brien eventually began to regain his health and sought to return to military service.[2] In April 1864, Gen. William H. F. Lee endeavored to have Brien commissioned as a major and appointed as his assistant adjutant general. Though the request was never acted on officially, Lee nevertheless made Brien his adjutant, a post Brien held until the war's end. David Cardwell of McGregor's Battery of the Stuart Horse Artillery gives a glimpse of Brien during the struggle around Five Forks.

> Our division kept its line and never wavered, though the infantry crowded them. They met the charges and after moved out under orders. It was an awful mixture. Gen. W. H. F. Lee took a flag and rode among them begging them to rally, but no, sir, they would not—they went their way.

Caught In A Charge

> We limbered up under order to do so, and moved out toward the right—down the road. As I attempted to follow with two other comrades, we were stopped by Col. Brien. I recall his splendid figure. He was in full dress Confederate uniform of his rank, and any one who has seen a full dress uniform of a Confederate colonel of cavalry, or of the staff, has seen something gorgeous. I have recently seen in the paper an account of the death of this splendid gentleman. He told us to pull down a fence in front of the second North Carolina cavalry "squadron front," and we did it. By so doing, we got (after we had mounted) terribly mixed up in a charge of that regiment. We were pressed back to the road and I was looking for a way out and I was looking hard, too.[3]

If Cardwell's recollection of Brien is correct, then perhaps the Marylander once again wore the stars of a lieutenant colonel on his collar.

Brien surrendered and was paroled at Appomattox with the rest of the army, after which he made his way back to Maryland. He went to New York later in 1865 to engage in the commission business but eventually drifted into railroad building. In 1874 he became assistant manager of the Illinois Central Railroad and moved to Chicago. During this period he accomplished one of the greatest engineering feats of the century by tearing up and relaying, at standard gauge, six hundred miles of track in a single day without stopping a single train. Over four thousand workmen were employed in the effort. A year before his death Brien stated, "I am prouder of that piece of work than of anything else I ever accomplished."[4]

In 1882 Brien returned to Urbana, Maryland, and purchased "Tyrone," a beautiful mansion that had been part of a military school prior to the war and sometime later had become the Shirley Female Institute. As a military academy it had been run by Virginia native John Robert Jones, who became a general in the Army of Northern Virginia. The academy was abandoned during the war, but one of its buildings housed Stuart's "Welcome to Maryland" ball on September 8, 1862.

On October 1, 1912, Brien moved to Frederick, Maryland, to spend the winter months there. He had been in failing health for a year with what was diagnosed as tuberculosis. Soon after the move he developed bronchitis, and complications quickly set in. On November 25, 1912, at 6:15 P.M., Brien died at age eighty-four. He is buried in St. Ignatius-Loyola Catholic Church Cemetery in Urbana, Maryland, with his wife, who had preceded him in death on November 21, 1907. He had at least six children—three sons, Robert C., William H., Lawrence W., and three daughters, Ada, Mary, and Annie—but none of them outlived him.

Capt. Redmond Burke

Aide-de-camp and scout
March 28, 1862, to November 25, 1862

An aura of mystery surrounds Redmond Burke today as it did when he fell victim to a Union ambush on November 25, 1862, in Shepherdstown, Virginia, now West Virginia. Labeled a guerrilla by his opponents, Burke served Stuart as a scout-aide-de-camp and was at one time part of the general's escort. If Burke did have a career as a guerrilla, it could not have been a long one, for his records show that he was most often found with Stuart and the regular cavalry forces.

So obscured are Burke's origins that it is impossible to give the date and location of his birth. Some writers have stated that he originally came from Texas (as even Stuart believed), but there is no evidence to support this. A descendant of Burke's holds to the opinion that his ancestor came from Ireland,[1] and this view finds support in a letter written by Peter W. Hairston, who rode with Burke early in the war. Hairston called Burke an Irishman and recorded that they had fought together in a rear guard action near Bunker Hill.[2] He mentioned the experience because he believed Burke had been captured and deeply regretted his loss. The scout managed to elude his pursuers and later rejoined Stuart's headquarters company. It is likely that Hairston had learned of Burke's origin from the scout himself. This fact, plus the findings of Burke's descendant, virtually confirms that Burke was born on the Emerald Isle and immigrated to America.

At the outbreak of the war, a number of the men of Shepherdstown formed a cavalry company, which would become Company "F" of the 1st Virginia Cavalry under Stuart. Burke, however, does not seem to have joined this company. His records indicate that he became a member of Company "B," 1st Virginia Cavalry on July 2, 1861.[3] The earliest reference linking him to Stuart's headquarters appears in Hairston's letter, which was dated September 26, 1861. Officially, Burke received no mention until Stuart's report of his fight near Dranesville on December 20.[4] In the report Burke is noted as having been in Stuart's escort.

Although he was part of the cavalry chief's headquarters, Burke did not join Stuart's inner circle until sometime in February 1862. Up to this time, Burke had no rank except that of private. Stuart requested that Burke be commissioned a lieutenant. In his letter, Stuart referred to his scout as Mr. Redmond Burke, which may indicate that he was no longer a member of the 1st Virginia. The letter was written on March 19, 1862, and must have brought immediate action, for in a report dated March 28, Stuart mentioned Burke as being a lieutenant. The commission did not become official until April 3, however, when Lieutenant Burke received his orders to report to Stuart for duty with the cavalry.

The fighting near Williamsburg on May 5, 1862, brought additional recognition to Burke. By this time, he was a voluntary aide-de-camp on the general's staff. On the Chickahominy Raid, he again displayed the kind of courage and stamina Stuart looked for in his staff personnel. He played an important role in building a bridge across the Chickahominy River at the end of the raid. The one-hundred-mile ride had been hard on many of the gray troopers, but Burke still had enough strength to carry out Stuart's instructions for the bridge's construction. His actions prompted Stuart to request a captaincy for Burke. This would be the last promotion he received.

With the repulse of McClellan from the outskirts of Richmond during the Seven Days Battles, the scene of action shifted north of the Confederate capital. August 20 saw Stuart's forces engaged near Brandy Station on what would become familiar ground to the cavalry of both armies. The Union regiments could not yet cope with the Rebel horse and were slowly, and in some places rapidly, forced back. In the midst of one melee, Heros von Borcke noticed a fresh Yankee squadron charging the Confederate flank. Gathering about eighty men, including Burke, "Von" launched them toward the oncoming blue wave. Seeing the charging Confederates, the Union squadron realized they no longer held the element of surprise, so they slackened their pace. As von Borcke's improvised command drew within forty yards of their line, the Yanks fired a ragged volley and broke for safer ground. Their scattered fire had little effect on the charging graybacks, but one missile found its mark: Burke was struck in the leg. Von Borcke halted his own pursuit of the enemy to tend to his comrade.[5]

The wound was Burke's second within a couple of weeks. At some time during a cavalry expedition near Fredericksburg in early August, he had been severely wounded in the wrist. The thought of fighting the Yankees with only one good arm clearly had not caused Burke any concern. His temerity earned him another scar and a few weeks' rest. By October, duty drew him back to Stuart, who wrote in a letter to Flora that Burke was again with him and doing splendid service.[6]

The captain's wounds had not completely healed before he returned to cavalry headquarters. Handicapped as he must have been by them, Burke nevertheless began to harass the Union forces north of the Potomac with his scouting-raiding forays into their lines. As a "guerrilla" fighter, Burke cannot be compared to John S. Mosby, Harry Gilmor, John "Hanse" McNeill, or Elijah "Lige" White. He raided no trains, abducted no generals, and destroyed few supplies. His priority was the gathering of information that would be of use to his chief. His "raids," if they can be labeled as such, could not have been sufficient to warrant the title of "guerrilla." In spite of this fact, the Yanks unmistakably felt that Burke had become more than a mere nuisance. They wanted him dead or alive, preferably the former.

The night of November 24 found Burke and a few of his fellow scouts, including his three sons, Edward, John Redmond, and William (better known as "Jug"), in familiar territory around Shepherdstown. They had succeeded in their information gathering and were returning to Shepherdstown for the night. In the morning they would return to Stuart. But the presence of the "guerrilla" band unfortunately had been communicated to the Union commander on the other side of the Potomac. Union sympathizers had volunteered to act as guides for a company of the 2nd Massachusetts Infantry. Plans were laid to cross the river and surprise the rebels.

The company with its civilian guides soon found themselves near Shepherdstown. One of the guides slipped quietly into town and located the home at which Burke would be staying. Minutes later the trap was set.

Burke's party, believing that a river separated them from their enemy, approached the home without any precautions. What happened next remains a controversy to this day. Local legend states that Burke dismounted in the yard and handed the reins of his horse (a gift from Stuart valued at $1000) to his son "Jug." He then walked toward the house. Before he reached the door, one of the Union's civilian guides stepped forward and, placing his pistol almost against Burke's chest, fired two shots. The captain died instantly. He had not been given a chance to surrender and, therefore, so the story goes, was murdered in cold blood. The rest of the party was captured except for "Jug," who mounted his father's horse and escaped.[7]

The Union version of the incident differs entirely, as would be expected. In the official report, Burke's death wound came as a result of his attempting to flee when he had been called on to surrender. According to the report, Burke was shot with an Enfield rifle in the back, the bullet passing through his heart. Recently, one Shepherdstown resident disputed the claim that Burke was fleeing, stating that his great-grandmother had seen Burke's body the following morning and that there were powder burns on his uniform, indicating that he had been shot at very close range. The true circumstances surrounding Burke's death will probably never be known.[8]

The captain in charge of the ambush found numerous papers on Burke's person. One of them was his captain's commission. Many of the others dealt with the Union forces on the other side of the Potomac. He also carried letters and some orders signed by Stuart that outlined Burke's mission. Burke's body was left behind in Shepherdstown when the Yankees made their escape. He was interred in the town's Elmwood Cemetery. His grave marker sheds little light on his life. It reads

Capt. Redman Burke
Jeff. Co. WVa.

The good citizens apparently did not know the captain too well, as they failed to spell his name correctly on his tombstone. Stuart, had he lived, would have taken care of the mistake. In a letter to Lily Lee of Shepherdstown, he promised to set up a marker over Burke's grave. He deeply lamented Burke's loss and had valued him as both a soldier and a friend. Stuart regrettably did not live to keep his vow, but in his General Orders No. 14, he expressed his feelings for Burke and shared his grief with the cavalry.

> Hd Qrs Cav Div
> December 3rd 1862
>
> General Orders
> No. 14
>   The Major General of Cavalry announces with the deepest regret the death of Capt. Redmond Burke whose valuable services and heroic conduct on our border are historic.

He was killed by a lurking foe in a night attack on his little band on the 25th ult'o at Shepherdstown where he had for some time been stationed on detached service.

He possessed a heart intrepid, a spirit invincible, a patriotism too lofty to admit of a selfish thought, and a conscience that scorned to do a mean thing.

A devoted champion of the South, his grey hairs have descended in honor to the grave leaving a shining example of patriotism and heroic devotion to those who survive.

By command of

Maj. Genl. J. E. B. Stuart

Heros von Borcke

A.A. Genl.[9]

Maj. Roger Preston Chew

Commander of the Stuart Horse Artillery
April 1864 to May 12, 1864

> Young men, now that you have your company, what are you going to do with it?[1]

These words were spoken by Gen. Thomas J. Jackson during an interview with the officers of the newly formed "Ashby" Battery of horse artillery. Organized on November 11, 1861, the battery consisted of thirty-six officers and men and three guns. It was the first battery of horse artillery formed in the Confederate Army. The officers standing before "Stonewall" that day were eighteen-year-old 2nd Lt. James Walton Thomson, seventeen-year-old 1st Lt. Milton Rouse, and the captain of the battery, nineteen-year-old Roger Preston Chew. All were graduates of the Virginia Military Institute, and all had been Jackson's students. Within a few weeks they had answered his question.[2]

The military career of Roger Preston Chew deserves a full biography, something not within the scope of this work. Indeed, he was not only a worthy successor to Pelham and Beckham but, according to some historians, more than equal to both in talent and courage. The record of the Ashby Battery speaks for itself, and few would dispute the claim that Chew was one of the finest artillery officers in the Army of Northern Virginia. Stuart recognized in Chew the abilities that Ashby had seen and was quick to recommend him for the position of commander of the Stuart Horse Artillery when Beckham was promoted and transferred. The battalion never had another.

Chew was born in Loudoun County, Virginia, on April 9, 1843,[3] the son of Roger and Sarah West (née Aldridge) Chew. Around 1848 the family moved to Charles Town, Virginia, now West Virginia, which would be Chew's home for the remainder of his life. Completing his early education at the Charles Town Academy, he enrolled at the Virginia Military Institute on July 30, 1859, and but for the war would have graduated in 1862. Because of the conflict, his class was declared graduated in July 1861. The VMI cadets performed many needed services during the early months of the war. In mid-April 1861 Professor T. J. Jackson and members of the color guard, including Chew, journeyed to Richmond via Staunton to drill recruits on the fairgrounds near the capital. Others in the party included Milton Rouse and Henry K. Burgwyn, who would be killed leading the 26th North Carolina at Gettysburg.[4]

The initial excitement over playing drill sergeant to civilian soldiers soon wore thin, and so when orders came transferring about a dozen of the cadets to Jackson's new command at Harpers Ferry, Chew considered himself fortunate to be among the number selected. The cadets' jubilation centered on the fact that several of them would be very close to their homes, and they expected numerous opportunities to spend time with their loved ones and friends. Jackson had other ideas. He refused to issue passes, believing that the cadets should set a good example to the raw recruits he commanded. Chew and Rouse, deciding Jackson had been unfair, went home anyway. When they returned to Harpers Ferry the following Monday, they paid for their indiscretion. On May 1 Jackson sent them packing back to VMI. The incident was the low point of Chew's career.[5]

After brooding for a time, Chew ultimately joined with other cadets in a second journey to Richmond, hoping for an assignment. When this failed to materialize, they traveled west and became part of a battery that had been in Gen. Robert S. Garnett's disastrous Rich Mountain Campaign. The battery's officers had become separated from the men and guns, and the cadets were put in charge until the officers returned on September 5. Chew enjoyed his association with the artillery and made up his mind to form a battery with Rouse and several of the other cadets. Their idea received Col. Turner Ashby's enthusiastic support, but they were told that Gen. Joseph E. Johnston would have to grant them permission to organize, since he was commander of the Valley Army. Johnston demurred, however, stating that he could not authorize the battery since he would soon be relieved of his command in the Shenandoah. He told the cadets that the new commander would be "Stonewall" Jackson and that they would need to get his permission. Though they feared he would recall their disobedience at Harpers Ferry, Chew and the others laid their case before Jackson, who, after giving it considerable thought, assented.[6]

From the formation of the battery, Chew was its heart and soul. His leadership molded the officers and men into an outstanding fighting organization capable of remarkable feats. On May 24, 1862, near Middletown, during Union general Nathaniel P. Banks's retreat toward Winchester, Ashby ordered Chew to charge the enemy with his artillery. In the excitement of the moment, Chew, by his own admission, did not stop to consider what Ashby had asked him to do; he ordered the guns limbered and charged the retreating Federals. The combination of Ashby and Chew had come up with an innovation in artillery tactics.[7] The young captain would not take the credit for it, but without his ready and willing response, it never would have been accomplished.

Ashby's death near Harrisonburg, Virginia, on June 6, 1862, caused Chew much grief. Because he had been fighting in a secondary theater of the war, Chew did not receive any recognition apart from Ashby. Though his battery always seemed to be in the heart of the action, little notice was taken of him outside the Shenandoah Valley. Meanwhile, Pelham was garnering deserved accolades fighting with the main army in the east. All this changed in August 1862, when Chew's Battery joined Stuart for the Catlett Station Raid just before the Battle of 2nd Manassas. The battery also performed excellent service at Crampton's Gap during the Sharpsburg Campaign, after which it returned to the Valley.

On June 4, 1863, Chew's Battery joined Stuart's cavalry at Brandy Station. The horse artillery of the Army of Northern Virginia was coming together to form a battalion under its new commander, Maj. R. F. Beckham, who had succeeded Pelham in April. While not a stranger to Lee's army, Chew, having performed most of his service in the Valley, probably felt that he had to prove himself in the eyes of his new commanders. He did not have to wait long for the opportunity. On June 9, as Stuart's cavalry and artillery lay in their encampment on the field around Brandy Station, they were attacked by Union cavalry. Chew and his battery found themselves in the thick of the fight. One of their guns, a Blakely, burned out at its breech after firing 160 rounds.[8] Gunner George M. Neese of Chew's Battery wrote to his old commander on October 22, 1900, and included the following anecdote about the battle.

> Since I saw you last, I heard of a circumstance that occurred at the big battle of Brandy Station complimentary

to the efficiency of your Battery on that memorable field. I got my information from a member of the 12th Va Cavalry who was captured that day and personally heard the remarks. In the evening after the fight was over General Pleasonton's Chief of Artillery reported at headquarters and asked the captives of the 12th Va, "What battery was that on that hill today, he told him Captain Chew's of Stuart's Horse Artillery." Then the chief turned to General Pleasonton and remarked, "I was all through the Mexican war and in this one from its commencement up to the present time, and I never saw a battery fire so accurately and effectively as that one did on that hill today."[9]

From Brandy Station until the army returned to Virginia after the Battle of Gettysburg, Chew and his battery demonstrated that they were one of the premier batteries in the army. By the time the horse artillery went into winter quarters near Charlottesville in December 1863, Chew had established himself as an officer of superior ability. Promotion had eluded him, however. His time in the Shenandoah Valley away from the main army had probably cost him more than one promotion.

Then an opportunity arose for Chew's talents to come into play once more. Union general George A. Custer conducted a raid toward Charlottesville, Virginia, near the end of February 1864. All that stood in his way were four batteries of the Stuart Horse Artillery commanded by its senior captain, Marcellus N. Moorman, in the absence of Major Beckham. Custer's forces numbered fifteen hundred men, while the horse artillery could barely muster two hundred. The battle should have been a slaughter. The Confederates should have been destroyed, as well as their guns and entire camp. They were not. Moorman, James Breathed, and Chew put up such a show of opposition that Custer, believing he might be facing a force considerably larger than his own, retreated. This helped secure the command of the horse artillery for Chew.

Not long after the Battle of Rio Hill, as the engagement with Custer has been called, Beckham was promoted and transferred out of the horse artillery. Captain Moorman also received promotion to major and left the battalion. Stuart made Chew the temporary commander and had it in mind to make the appointment a permanent one. Col. William N. Pendleton, though, had other ideas. He nominated James Dearing for the post with the rank of lieutenant colonel. Dearing was at the time a colonel in command of a regiment of cavalry, and he did not wish to accept the position if it meant a decrease in rank. He therefore refused to report. Stuart, after waiting several days for Dearing, wrote Gen. R. E. Lee requesting that Chew remain as commander. Lee agreed and Pendleton acquiesced. Chew became only a major, however. He would have to wait another year, until February 18, 1865, for his promotion to lieutenant colonel. By that time the number of batteries in the battalion had doubled to ten.

The final year of the war witnessed the slow decline of the Southern cavalry as horses and equipment became scarce. Through it all Chew somehow kept the horse artillery going. Guns were lost but not the fighting spirit. In the end Chew escaped Grant's stranglehold on Lee's army at Appomattox. He made one final effort to join Gen. Joe Johnston in North Carolina. On the way he buried twelve pieces of artillery in order to keep them from the enemy. The journey was for naught, however, because Johnston's army also had to capitulate. Chew gave his parole and began the long trek home to Charles Town. The Stuart Horse Artillery had fought its final battle.

The reputation Chew earned for himself during the war can best be illustrated through the words of the men who had commanded him in battle and had seen his courage and skill demonstrated on dozens of fields.

> Washington, March 13th, 1888
>
> My Dear Kenna:
> . . . I always regarded him [Chew] as the best commander of the Horse Artillery, though that gallant body of men had been under the command at different times of very able and efficient officers. . . .
>
> > Yours very truly
> > Wade Hampton

> 1747 F Street, Washington, D.C., March 7th, 1904
> Mr. Thornton T. Perry,
> > Charles Town, West Va.,
> Dear Sir:
> Replying to yours of the 18th ult., asking what my estimate was of Col. R. P. Chew as a soldier, I beg to say when I first met Chew in the Army of Northern Virginia he was a captain of a Battery of Horse Artillery and from that time to the end he was a conspicuous figure in that dashing branch of the service. I was with him on many trying occasions and he was one of the coolest men in battle I was ever associated with. He was then a very young

man, boyish in appearance, but no veteran in any army ever stood the shock of battle with more courage and composure than Chew.

Young and handsome, a superb horseman, always cool and self-possessed, he was the beau ideal of a Battery commander, and later as the commander of a Battalion of Horse Artillery. He was a most companionable, agreeable comrade in camp and as dashing a dare-devil in battle as ever drew a sword. I can scarcely find words to express my admiration and regard for Col. Chew as a soldier and man. Our relations have always been of the most pleasant character, and I am gratified that you give me this opportunity to pay this inadequate tribute to his character. What a splendid lot of young fellows of the Horse Artillery in that incomparable army—Pelham, Chew, Breathed, Hart, McGregor and others.

I can pay Chew no higher compliment than to say he was easily the peer of the best of them.

Very truly yours,
M. C. Butler

Charlottesville, Va., March 16, 1904

Mr. Thornton T. Perry,
Charles Town, West Va.,
Dear Sir:

Answering yours of the 27th inst., I will say that Colonel R. Preston Chew commanded the Horse Artillery of the Cavalry Corps of the Army of Northern Virginia after the death of the "Immortal" Pelham, and there was not an officer in the army of his rank, who stood higher in the estimation of our higher officers, in point of courage, military ability and enterprise than he, and there was no one of greater popularity and influence among our generals, or one who commanded greater respect or inspired greater confidence among the fighting men than Chew, and I regard him as one of the very best artillery officers I ever knew, and indeed, one of the very best officers of his rank in the Confederate Army.

Very truly yours,
Thomas Rosser[10]

Upon returning to Charles Town, Chew entered into farming, working the land as his father had done. On August 15, 1871, he married Louisa Fontaine Washington, daughter of John A. Washington, who had served on Gen. R. E. Lee's staff. The couple had three children, Christine, Roger, and Margaret, but no descendants are living today.

In the years following 1871, Chew became involved in various business enterprises including insurance and real estate. In 1882 his stature in the community led to his election to the state legislature. He won reelection in 1884, 1886, and 1888, when he also became chairman of the finance committee. He became an active member of the Confederate Veterans and on June 19, 1912, delivered the dedication address at the unveiling of Sir Moses Ezekiel's statue of Jackson at VMI. His interest in the war led him to begin gathering material in preparation for a history of the Stuart Horse Artillery. The project regrettably never advanced beyond this initial stage. On March 16, 1921, Chew died in Charles Town. He was buried in Zion Episcopal Churchyard just a few blocks from his home.

2nd Lt. Jones Rivers Christian[1]

Assistant aide-de-camp
June 12, 1862, to July 1862

Jones R. Christian never actually held an official position on Stuart's staff. His association with Stuart grew out of the general's need for information concerning the country in the vicinity of Christian's home. In order to have him close by when the need arose, Stuart had him temporarily attached to his headquarters as an acting aide-de-camp. The valuable role Christian played in the Chickahominy Raid and the Seven Days Campaign can be found in Stuart's reports in the Official Records.[2] Christian was not the only individual employed by Stuart in this manner. Stuart's desire to know every foot of the terrain over which he had to lead his cavalry prompted him to use natives of the areas as guides. Several became permanent members of the staff.

Born in New Kent County east of Richmond, Christian called "Sycamore Springs," his father's estate, home for much of his life before the war. He was one of five children, all boys. His father, also named Jones Rivers Christian, had married his cousin, Caroline Christian. Christian's early life is vague but seems to have been connected with his father's plantation. He never married.

Christian enlisted in the New Kent Light Dragoons (also known as the New Kent Cavalry) on June 28, 1861, as a private. His company was designated as Company "K" but later became Company "F" of the 3rd

Virginia Cavalry. On April 25, 1862, he was elected second lieutenant of the company.[3] The exact date of his attachment to Stuart's staff is uncertain, but his service with Stuart during June 1862 is a matter of record. In July, soon after the close of the Seven Days Campaign, he left the staff and rejoined his company.

On October 24, 1862, Christian received a promotion to first lieutenant, which was followed on November 11 by a promotion to captain. He continued to serve with his company until the Wilderness Campaign. On May 8, 1864, he was captured and imprisoned at Fort Delaware. His description at the time of his capture was as follows: height five feet, eleven inches; dark complexion; dark eyes; dark hair.[4] Christian became one of the "Immortal 600" held under fire on Morris Island in Charleston Harbor. He was later transferred to Hilton Head, South Carolina. His release came on June 16, 1865.

All that is known about Christian's postwar career is that he worked as a clerk in the Richmond post office. On March 1, 1893, he entered the R. E. Lee Camp Soldiers' Home in Richmond, suffering from neuralgia. He died there on May 20, 1895, and was buried in Hollywood Cemetery.

Capt. James Louis Clark

Aide-de-camp
January 1863 to June 17, 1863

Born in 1841, James L. Clark was, in today's terminology, an "army brat." His father, Maj. Michael M. Clark, a Virginian, served in the U.S. Army for thirty-five years. Clark did not choose to follow in his father's footsteps, however, and pursued a law career. Educated in Washington City, Clark attended the Rugby Academy before beginning his studies for the bar. As with so many of the young men of his day, the war altered his carefully laid plans for the future. A Baltimore resident at the war's start, Clark had to decide whether to offer his services to the United States or to leave everything behind and join the Confederacy. Strong though the memory of his father's years in the U.S. Army must have been, Clark allied himself with the South, attaching himself to the 1st Maryland Infantry in September 1861.

Clark almost immediately managed to secure a captaincy and an appointment as quartermaster for his regiment. The commission, however, dated November 20, 1861, was contingent on his being able to file bond (obtain financial backers), which he was unable to do. At this point the first of many inconsistencies in Clark's records appears. Though he had failed to meet the major requirement for retaining his commission, he continued to perform the duties of quartermaster until June 13, 1862, when he resigned. Since he had been dropped from his infantry company's muster roll on February 24, 1862, because he had become regimental quartermaster, his resignation gave him the freedom to do what he pleased.

Unfortunately, what Clark chose to do was visit his home in Baltimore. This led to his capture on July 21, 1862. He gave as his unit the 1st Maryland, to which he technically no longer belonged. Luckily, the Federals were in no position to know just what their prisoner's military status was, so Clark spent only a short time behind bars. He was exchanged on August 11, 1862, and quickly made his way back to his old regiment. Somehow he obtained the post of acting assistant quartermaster and along with it the rank of captain. But Clark must have realized that his situation, tenuous at best, could not last very long. Not wishing to return to the ranks, he applied for a lieutenancy in the regular Confederate Army on September 29, 1862. Though he received the endorsement of Gen. Joseph E. Johnston, the Confederate War Department took no action.

Refusing to give up, Clark reapplied on December 1, 1862. Again, he had the support of an influential individual, who wrote the following endorsement.

> The above applicant has served with me in the field and I take pleasure in recommending him as a meritorious, gallant and [word illegible] gentleman and well qualified for the position sought.
>
> R. S. Ewell
> Maj. Gen.[1]

The War Department again, however, took no action. But Clark's luck soon changed, for on January 24, 1863, he was signing documents as a captain in the Stuart Horse Artillery. Once again, the records do not show precisely how he acquired his commission. Stuart probably had something to do with the assignment, which bears a close similarity to J. E. Cooke's brief attempt to raise a horse artillery company before joining the staff as ordnance officer.

Unlike Cooke, Clark's association with the horse artillery may have lasted for the entire time he served with Stuart. One of the Marylander's jackets preserved in the Museum of the Confederacy bears the rank insignia of a captain (three horizontal gold bars on the collar) and the red trim of the artillery. As he had done with Cooke, Stuart may have attached Clark to his staff after obtaining a commission for him in the horse artillery. No evidence exists that Clark ever formed a company of horse artillery or ever fought as an officer with the famous battalion. Still, he claimed to have been Pelham's tentmate, which is possible, although it is not substantiated by any other source.

Had he chosen to write his memoirs as did von Borcke, Clark may have garnered equal fame as a storyteller. The claims he made in just one letter are enough to start any Confederate cavalry historian digging for references to support or refute Clark's statements.[2] Not only did Clark claim to be Pelham's tentmate, but he also recalled that on the morning of Pelham's departure for Culpeper Court House (and death at Kelly's Ford) he had loaned the dashing artillerist his "handsome plush lap robe with a yellow tiger on one side and black on the other that I had brought from Baltimore" to use as a poncho. According to Clark's version of Pelham's death, which he received from no less a source than Harry Gilmor, the robe was found by Gilmor on the very spot where Pelham was struck by the shell fragment that killed him. Clark also stated that Gilmor kept a piece of Pelham's skull as a souvenir of the "Gallant One."

In the same letter, Clark also claimed to have collected Will Farley's leg from the battlefield of Brandy Station and to have placed it in the ambulance beside the mortally wounded scout. If Clark did indeed do so, this was very possibly one of his last acts as a member of Stuart's staff. On June 17, 1863, Clark was appointed captain of Company "F," 12th Virginia Cavalry, Harry Gilmor's old company. The appointment came as a result of Gilmor's recommendation and a petition signed by the members of the company requesting Clark as their captain. Stuart endorsed the unorthodox procedure, stating that the men of the company had waived all their rights in signing the petition and that he had no objections to Clark's replacing Gilmor.

The new captain passed through the Gettysburg Campaign with his new command but then suffered two setbacks. From October 18, 1863, to February 2, 1864, he was hospitalized (first in Culpeper then in Richmond) with "scoties."[3] Soon after he reported for duty, he was arrested for unspecified charges. Clark eventually returned to lead his company during the Wilderness Campaign. His horse was killed beneath him at Todd's Tavern on May 6, 1864, and he lost another to enemy fire at Ashland on June 6.

In July Clark and his company became part of the 2nd Maryland Cavalry and as such were attached to Gilmor's command. Clark rode with Gilmor through much of Gen. Jubal Early's Shenandoah Valley Campaign. Clark's war career virtually ended on August 7, 1864, when he was captured by Union general William W. Averell's cavalry during its attack on the Confederate cavalry brigades of Bradley T. Johnson and John McCausland at Moorefield.

Incarcerated first at Camp Chase, where he was described as being twenty-three years old, five feet nine inches tall, with a light complexion, blue eyes, and light hair, Clark was transferred to Point Lookout on February 12, 1865. He was exchanged shortly after his transfer and traveled to Petersburg, arriving just before the Federal breakthrough at Five Forks. According to one source, he was ordered to escort one of Gen. R. E. Lee's daughters back to her mother's home in Richmond. While he was there, news of the retreat flashed through the capital. Clark immediately rejoined the army and accompanied it to Appomattox, where he surrendered.

Though on his parole Clark gave his destination as Baltimore, he did not remain in the city. Little has been recorded of his life after the war, though it is known that he became a lawyer and lived for some time in Columbine, Routt County, Colorado. In his old age he returned to Baltimore and applied for admittance into the Maryland Line Old Soldiers' Home in Pikesville, Maryland, on September 4, 1910. The committee that reviewed his application endorsed it on September 6, even though Clark had died on the day he filed his application, at age 69. Clark is buried in Loudon Park Cemetery on Confederate Hill near the spot where Harry Gilmor rests.

Capt. John Esten Cooke

Voluntary aide, ordnance officer, and assistant
adjutant general
March 25, 1862, to May 12, 1864

John Esten Cooke was a writer. He worked very hard at being a soldier, but he wrote all through the war, using his pen more frequently than his sword. When he finally laid aside his uniform for good, he reminisced of the war and the one man who had been his hero, "Jeb" Stuart. As one who never quite fit the mold of a soldier, Cooke managed to capture the essence of one who did: His portraits of Stuart are alive with the vitality of the man they describe. It is doubtful that Cooke could have written about the great cavalry chieftain as well as he did, if he had not been a soldier himself.

Born at "Ambler's Hill" in Winchester, Virginia, on November 3, 1830, Cooke traced his lineage back to Hereford County, England. His father was John Rogers Cooke, a lawyer who had helped write Virginia's new constitution in 1829. His mother was Maria Pendleton of Berkeley County. The couple had thirteen children, but only five lived beyond adolescence. John Esten was the second of their children to bear that name, the first having died in infancy.[1]

Cooke's early years differed little from other Virginia boys of his time. Many hours were spent roaming "Glengary," the Pendleton estate that had become the family's home. More often than not, his companion was his brother Henry Pendleton Cooke. Henry was slightly older than "John Ety," as his mother called him, and the two were almost inseparable. Cooke greatly admired another of his brothers, Philip Pendleton Cooke, who, fourteen years his senior, attended Princeton and became an author of some merit before his death in 1850.

In 1838 "Glengary" was destroyed by fire, forcing the family to move to Charles Town, Virginia. Cooke had his first exposure to schooling in Charles Town, and his reaction to education after having spent his time wandering freely in the country can be imagined. He had scarcely begun to adjust to Charles Town when the family again moved, this time to Richmond. March 1840 saw the Cooke clan established in a house just below the Capitol Square. Cooke reacted to his new surroundings with enthusiasm. School and books became important to him, and by age sixteen he began to study law under his father's tutelage. Cooke hoped to enter the University of Virginia in 1847, but financial difficulties prevented this. The family's monetary woes continued, and after the fall of 1849 passed without his having sufficient funds to enroll, he gave up the idea of studying law and turned instead to writing.

Cooke experienced two tragic losses in 1850, as first Philip and then his mother died. Their deaths plunged him into a gloomy state from which he had great difficulty emerging. He continued to write, however, and after having had several manuscripts published between 1848 and 1853 (*Avalon* in 1848 had been his first), he saw his first book, *Leather Stocking and Silk,* come off the presses in 1854. Other books followed. *Henry St. John, Gentleman,* published in 1859, was the last before the outbreak of the war.

In 1851, with a number of years of private study behind him, Cooke formed a partnership with his father and tried to establish a law practice of his own. But Cooke could not keep his mind where it had to be to make the partnership work. His writing interfered to the extent that he resolved to cease writing altogether. But his desire to write was too strong, and once he began to receive money for his pieces, it was only a matter of time before the law practice suffered permanent damage. His father's death in 1858 sealed the fate of his future at the bar. No more would Cooke practice law.

Cooke became immersed in the conflict between North and South at an early stage. He had joined the Richmond Howitzers sometime in the late 1850s, for reasons that remain unclear, and when the elite company was dispatched to Harpers Ferry at the time of John Brown's Raid, Cooke accompanied it. The outbreak of open hostilities saw the company raised to battalion strength. Cooke became a sergeant and as such fought at 1st Manassas, serving his gun so enthusiastically that, according to George Cary Eggleston, he was hatless, coatless, and covered with the grime of battle.[2]

Cooke remained a member of the Howitzers until January 31, 1862, when he was discharged with the rank of sergeant. The next few months of his military service are sketchy. Records indicate that on March 25 and again on April 15 Cooke acted as Stuart's voluntary aide. Then on May 19, 1862, Cooke was commissioned a lieutenant and ordered to report to Stuart. His assignment was to recruit a company for the horse artillery in Richmond. Stuart definitely was interested in the horse artillery at this time, but Cooke's venture met with little success. Strangely, by this time Pelham's Battery had been in existence for some months and had earned accolades during the fighting around Williamsburg. Perhaps Stuart envisioned another battery or at least an increase of Pelham's. Whatever prompted Cooke's orders to recruit another horse artillery company, the situation on the peninsula, and possibly a lack of volunteers, changed Stuart's mind. Cooke was recalled and appointed ordnance officer on the staff.

This period marked Cooke's most significant active service. Though he would come under fire in the future, his ordnance duties more often than not kept him behind the lines, where he saw little except the wounded and enemy prisoners. His performance during the Chickahominy Raid and the Seven Days Battles earned him Stuart's praise and a promotion, which came on August 8, 1862. It was to be his last despite the efforts of Stuart and Robert E. Lee to have him commissioned a major in 1863. Cooke never understood why he failed to achieve a majority. In a biography of Cooke, John O. Beaty speculates that his writing during the war irritated and offended certain officials in Richmond and that those officials were, unfortunately for Cooke, in a position to keep him a captain for the duration. Cooke had written articles criticizing the administration's policies, so Beaty's hypothesis has merit. Cooke had to be satisfied with his captain's bars, though he always felt he should have been given a higher rank.[3]

The Battle of Brandy Station gave Cooke a rare chance to combat the enemy. Stuart, in his report of the action, congratulated Cooke along with the rest of the staff.[4] Just how much Cooke got involved in the fighting that day is not known, but the entire staff was exposed to more dangers than at almost any other engagement up to that time. There is no reason to doubt that Cooke saw his share of the fighting as he carried out his duties.

Following the Gettysburg Campaign, Stuart found himself somewhat behind in filing his reports and decided to use Cooke's gift for writing. On October 27, 1863, the chief of ordnance became an adjutant on the staff, and Stuart put him to work on the reports. Their relationship, from Stuart's perspective, had not been a close one, but time and Cooke's hard work with little complaining won over his commander. If Stuart did not like Cooke as well as he did some of the other officers on the staff, Cooke never knew it, and Stuart never attempted to remove Cooke from his staff.

With Stuart's death, Cooke received an assignment as adjutant to the staff of Gen. William N. Pendleton. These final months of the war held no golden memories for Cooke. He seemed to have lost a great deal of his enthusiasm after Stuart's death and to have accepted in his heart and mind that the war could not be won. His general and many of his comrades were gone. He did not cease to do his duty, but he became depressed and performed more out of force of habit than patriotic zeal. He kept the depth of his sorrow hidden. When the end came at Appomattox, it is said he buried his silver spurs on the field. With them he buried the warrior he had tried to be.

In the years after the war, Cooke wove his experiences into a variety of books and stories. His idol, Stuart, the Last Knight of the Confederacy, rode again in *The Wearing of the Gray* and other books. Farley, Pelham, and Ashby all lived anew through Cooke's writing. He now became the chronicler of their exploits. He championed their deeds. He struggled to see that they would not be forgotten. Though the quality of his works varies, no one would deny that Cooke made a major contribution to Confederate literature. Lamentably, he could have done more. As Beaty wrote, "It seems almost a loss to the world that the young captain of artillery, an already famous novelist, should have written his biographies without regard to style or sufficient data, and above all should have vitiated notes of the utmost value by blending with them an outworn strain of fiction. What an opportunity he lost! How famous he might have become as the only writer of note who served from first Manassas to Appomattox and set down with accuracy and brilliancy the little as well as the large aspects of the great struggle! Such a work—alas unwritten!—would have been a classic for the twentieth century."[5]

Most of Beaty's criticism centers on Cooke's major biographical efforts. His work on Jackson, written in 1863, was rushed into print and contains numerous errors. *Surry of Eagle's Nest* fits into Beaty's description of a mixture of real and fictional characters. In all justice to Cooke, however, he does present very clear and accurate pictures of his subjects in some shorter biographical works. Cooke's tribute to Pelham and descriptions of Stuart are among the most quoted passages in Civil War literature, but his struggle between realism and romanticism in this period of his life was definitely won by the romantic side of his nature. It could not have been otherwise. Many of his heroes were dead, taken by the war. He remembered them as sacrifices on the altar of independence. To him, the failure of the Confederacy meant they died for nothing. Cooke could not accept that, so he wrote of them as of the knights of old. They could dwell victoriously in a fictional world.

Life in the real world went on for Cooke. On September 18, 1867, he married Mary Francis Page of Clarke County, Virginia. The newlyweds at first lived with the bride's parents at "Saratoga," then moved to "The Briars," which would be Cooke's home for the rest of his life. The couple had three children, Susan Randolph (b. July 11, 1868), Edmund Pendleton (b. May 23, 1870), and Robert Powell Page (b. October 12, 1874). The last son would grow up to become a doctor who, during the Spanish-American War, worked under Walter Reed as a human guinea pig to help disprove the theory of "foamites" as the cause of yellow fever. He died in 1952.[6]

Supporting a family by writing alone proved impossible. Cooke tried his hand at farming, but fate and fluctuating prices kept him from being completely successful. He managed to maintain a precarious financial stability, however. To the worry over his monetary situation was added grief over Mary's death on January 15, 1878. The family soon split so that the children could receive what Cooke felt was proper care. Susan was entrusted to Mary's sister, Mrs. William Carter, while the boys remained at "The Briars," though they made extended visits to their aunt.

Cooke's final years saw him continue his writing, but as an author, he was not growing. His works retained the same style as those he had written before the war. His last book, *The Maurice Mystery,* was written in 1885. He had contributed much to American literature in his time but admitted that he was not able to change: "I was born too soon, and am now too old to learn my trade anew."[7] In the summer of 1886 his health began to fail. He contracted typhoid fever but refused to give in to the illness until he fainted in his chair. Put to bed, he died the next day, September 27, 1886. He is buried in the Old Chapel Cemetery in Clarke County, Virginia.

On February 11, 1865, Cooke had penned what may well be called his philosophy of life. Seldom quoted, it provides a fitting epitaph for the warrior-writer.

> Just read Leigh Hunt's Life. He was honest kind, accomplished, but wanted muscle.
> His old age like many others was clouded.

How to make manhood and age happy? Here it is.

Avoid *passion,* that is, not feeling (have as much as possible) but wearing, tearing *passion.* Be calm, steady, moderate. Make the most of simple pleasures, and small enjoyments. First and foremost cultivate hygiene. Half of the ills of life spring from want of exercise, irregularity in eating or drinking—late hours etc. *Be regular*—be calm: be a philosopher. If anybody says "The Yankees are charging us!!!" with all the horrours in his voice: ask "Where did you say they were?" Get in the saddle but keep cool.

Don't be flustered. Don't hate or envy. They are dark sins—they are also *unhealthy.* Nothing is more wholesome than kindness. Be kind to all, and of modest Simplicity—not humble, not proud: courteous: the considerate gentleman. The French say you can't be too humble before God, or too defiant with men. It is only true—the latter—in the sense of defying their foolish opinions of you, to dishearten you. Be Just and fear not.

Excess, irregularity, hurry, flustration—are the hugest follies. Be regular, calm, cool,—they will soon become habits. I wish what poor Pelham said of me was true—that he named his horse after me because all his spurring in battle couldn't *hurry him.*

Be kind; be pure. love all—don't bite anybody but rascals on occasion, and then use all the teeth.

Be cool, calm, considerate. Eat regularly, sleep regularly, drink moderately or never—smoke temperately: read, talk, write, ride—fill up your day: read your Bible, and fall asleep—by *ten.* Rise early & da capo.

Make God the first and last.[8]

1st Lt. Chiswell Dabney

Aide-de-camp
January 14, 1862, to November 19, 1863

In the dark morning hours of August 18, 1862, a small party of men rode quietly into the tiny village of Verdiersville. One of the riders was Maj. Gen. "Jeb" Stuart, commander of R. E. Lee's cavalry. Those accompanying him were Maj. Heros von Borcke, Maj. Norman R. FitzHugh, Lt. Chiswell

Dabney, scout John S. Mosby, and Lt. Samuel B.
Gibson. Wearily, all but one of the men turned their
horses into the yard of the first house they encountered. Major FitzHugh continued on down
the road in search of Gen. Fitz Lee's column of
cavalry, with whom the group was to rendezvous.

Back in the yard, Stuart and the others tried
to rest during what hours of darkness remained.
Lieutenant Dabney removed his belt and laid it aside,
along with his pistol and saber. He spent a few
moments inquiring as to why von Borcke insisted
on making himself so uncomfortable by keeping

1st Lt.
Chiswell Dabney

his weapons buckled about his waist. At last, with each man settled in his
place, all became quiet. It did not remain that way for very long.

With the coming of dawn, the party heard the sounds of an approaching
cavalry column. Gibson, the first to react to the advancing horsemen, roused
Mosby, who in turn awakened Stuart. The cavalry chieftain dispatched
Mosby and Gibson toward the column, which was believed to be the tardy
Fitz Lee. Seconds later the two riders, pistol balls flying about them, galloped
back to the house. A warning was unnecessary; the shots had already alerted
Stuart, von Borcke, and Dabney to the danger. Everyone scattered. Stuart,
who had been standing at the gate of the yard, ran for his horse. Von Borcke,
Mosby, and Gibson made their escape down the road. Stuart and Dabney,
knowing they could not reach the gate ahead of the Federal cavalry, jumped
their horses over the fence and rode rapidly away.

Safe at last, the men regrouped to take stock of their situation. Major
FitzHugh had been captured, but he proved to be the only casualty.
Dabney—without his belt, pistol, saber, and gauntlets[1] —sat on his horse
before von Borcke. The Prussian recounted that the young lieutenant "made
a sorry appearance." With a touch of maliciousness, von Borcke inquired as
to whether Dabney was quite "comfortable" now.[2] Undoubtedly embarrassed, Dabney made no recorded reply. A lesson had been learned, however.
There is no account of Dabney losing his arms and equipment anytime
afterward.

Chiswell Dabney was born at his father's plantation, "Vaucluse," in
Campbell County, Virginia, on July 25, 1844. His family, which had come
to Virginia in 1660, descended from the Huguenot D'Aubigné family. His
father was the Reverend John Blair Dabney and his mother the former Elizabeth Towles. He received part of his education at New London Academy, a
nearby school. He had enrolled in the University of Virginia in the autumn

of 1861, but like many of his classmates, he could not concentrate on his studies and thought only of the war.

Dabney left the university to enlist in the Confederate Army. He became a courier and was assigned to Stuart's headquarters. His performance in December 1861, especially at Dranesville, earned him a promotion to lieutenant and an appointment as one of Stuart's aides-de-camp on January 14, 1862. At the age of seventeen, he had the distinction of being the youngest to serve on the staff. But he was furloughed home because of typhoid fever and was not present at cavalry headquarters when his lieutenant's commission arrived. Sometime in February or March 1862 he returned to duty with Stuart and served through all the major campaigns of the army. He became a captain in the Adjutant General's Department on November 19, 1863, and was transferred from Stuart's staff to Gen. James B. Gordon's brigade as inspector.[3] During the fighting around Gaines' Mill, Salem Church, and Haw's Shop on June 2, 1864, Dabney was wounded in the right arm. Following his recovery, he became brigade inspector for Gen. Rufus Barringer on July 3, 1864, a position he held until the end of the war.

After the war, Dabney wrote an account of his participation in the Battle of Brandy Station. He recalled how, at the first sound of firing from the pickets stationed at Beverley's Ford, Stuart and his staff mounted their horses and rode toward the camps of Generals W. E. Jones and W. H. F. Lee near St. James Church. Upon reaching the camps, Stuart and his staff joined the charge of the 6th Virginia Cavalry. Dabney remembered riding boot to boot with von Borcke as each pursued a Union cavalryman. After firing every round in his pistol, Dabney finally trapped his quarry when the Yank's horse failed to jump a water-filled ditch at the base of a hill. Dabney tells what happened next:

> The man disengaged himself [from his horse, which had fallen back into the water] and crawled up on the other bank and began handling his carbine, when I leveled my pistol at him and played a bluff game, ordering him to drop his gun or I would blow his head off. Fortunately he did not know my pistol was empty. I made him wade over. The bullets were flying pretty thick and he said, "Don't keep me here or I will be shot by my own men," so I sent him running to the rear where he was picked up by the provost guard.[4]

After stabilizing the situation at St. James Church, Stuart's attention was drawn to Fleetwood Hill. Dabney rode with his general and the rest of the staff toward the new area of crisis.

> We had nothing there at that time but one gun in charge of Lt. [John Wright "Tuck"] Carter, of [Capt. Roger Preston] Chew's Battery, who had gone back to replenish his ammunition chests and had only a few rounds, but this gallant officer was not dismayed, but planting his gun on Fleetwood Hill he opened fire at once and checked Gregg's advance. General Jones was nearly two miles away, but as soon as he heard the firing he dispatched the 12th Regiment to the danger point. The gallant Col. [Ashur Waterman] Harman was in command, but before he reached Fleetwood Hill, Stuart and his staff were there, who seeing the danger ordered me to gallop to General [Wade] Hampton and order him to bring his brigade up at once. . . . I was just returning to General Stuart from the front when I was caught in the midst of White's [Lt. Col. Elijah Viers White of the 35th Battalion of Virginia Cavalry] retreating men and was carried along with them as was von Borcke whom I met about that time. . . .[5]

Dabney carried at least one additional message for Stuart that day, riding to Col. J. Lucius Davis with orders from Stuart to hold Buford in check. By the time he returned, the battle was essentially over. His reminiscences of Brandy Station also include a recounting of the unusual manner by which the Confederates captured a Union flag.

> On the top of Fleetwood Hill was an ice house. The top was gone and so hardly pressed were the enemy at this point by Hampton that the Color Bearer of one of Gregg's regiments went headlong into the hole as he fled and was killed as well as his horse by the fall. The colors became one of the trophies of the fight.[6]

Despite the above account, Dabney appears to have written little about the war in his later life. He kept in touch with some of his fellow staff members and other veterans, but for the most part his life was consumed by a new mission, that of the ministry. Immediately after the war, Dabney tried his hand at farming. He did not consider making it a lifetime endeavor, however. He was simply trying to survive in a time of severe hardship. He eventually began to study law under the tutelage of his father and by 1870 had established an office in Chatham, Virginia.

In 1874 Dabney married Lucy Fontaine, daughter of Col. Edmund Fontaine and sister of Maj. John B. Fontaine, Stuart's medical director. The couple lived at Chatham and became members of the Emmanuel Church. Their increasing involvement with this church was to change Dabney's life, especially after the arrival of Rev. Clevius Orlando Pruden in July 1884. Rev. Pruden displayed a missionary zeal, which soon inspired many in his congregation. New churches were founded throughout his parish, which encompassed some seven hundred square miles.

Rev. Pruden recognized that it was impossible to cover the entire area single-handedly, so he began to rely on his lay people to stand in for him while he traveled the circuit of his churches. One of the men he came to rely on was Chiswell Dabney, and the more he relied on Dabney, the closer Dabney became to the church. From 1886 to 1896 Dabney continued as a lay reader, and at last he decided to take up his father's profession and become a full-time minister. Since he could not attend a seminary while supporting his family, he studied under Rev. Pruden and Bishop Randolph. During this same period, Dabney wrote a booklet entitled *The Episcopal Church: A Manual for Enquirers,* which was published in 1895.

Dabney was ordained a deacon in July 1896. On May 31, 1900, Bishop Randolph ordained him a priest at Emmanuel Church where Dabney had been serving as assistant rector since becoming a deacon. He had also become involved in the diocese's church schools, helping Rev. Pruden obtain funds to rebuild the Chatham Episcopal Institute when it burned in 1906. The two men saw their hard work rewarded with the erecting of Pruden Hall in 1907 and Dabney Hall in 1910.

Rev. Pruden resigned his rectorship of Bannister Parish in 1917, and the parish was divided in 1918. Part of it retained the name Bannister, while the rest was named Pruden Parish. Dabney became the rector of Pruden Parish and continued the work of his mentor, who died in 1921. A new community house, named the Dabney House, and a parochial school were built in Peytonsburg in 1922. At this time Dabney was seventy-eight. The winter of 1922–23 saw him continue to perform his daily duties, but the strain was beginning to weaken his health. After a brief illness, Dabney died on April 28, 1923, and was buried in Chatham Cemetery, Chatham, Virginia. Upon Dabney's death, the following was written by the editor of the *Pittsylvania County Paper.*

> Few men live as long as he lived in the same community,
> among the same people and their offspring, taking interest

in all things public, in all issues, political and otherwise, frank and outspoken in his opinions, and uncompromising in his stand for the right, hewing strictly to the line, walking steadfastly in the path pointed out to him by his own opinion, fighting for his principles, asking no quarter and giving none, and then come down to the end of such a life with the love of all who knew him and the respect accorded to but a few.

Mr. Dabney was the friend of man, and there can be no higher thing said of anyone. It was his desire to serve and few have ever turned to him and failed to find the deepest sympathy and warmest encouragement.[7]

Surgeon Talcott Eliason

Medical director
January 1862 to October 1863

"My dear fellow, your wound is mortal, and I can't expect you to live till the morning. . . ."[1] The cavalry's chief surgeon, Dr. Talcott Eliason, spoke these few words in a voice choked with emotion. His patient, Heros von Borcke, lay in the doctor's home in Upperville, where he had been taken after being struck in the throat by a ball while riding at Stuart's side. (The Prussian remained in the doctor's home until Union cavalry threatened, when he was whisked away by Gen. James Longstreet's personal ambulance.)[2]

Von Borcke had scant reason to doubt his good friend's prognosis. He had seen Eliason tend wounds and break such news to others under his care. The doctor had seldom erred.

But as Eliason's blind daughter wept at von Borcke's bedside, the Prussian summoned all the strength of his huge frame and determined that in this instance Eliason would be wrong. Von Borcke's subsequent recovery could certainly be attributed more to his own stamina than to anything Eliason or any other surgeon of that time could have done for him. No record exists of Eliason's reaction to having had his diagnosis overturned, but being wrong in this case surely did not bother him in the least.

Stuart's first chief surgeon of the cavalry was born in 1826 in Beaufort, North Carolina.[3] His father, William Alexander Eliason, had graduated first in his class at West Point in 1821. In March 1839 William Eliason died while stationed at Fortress Monroe. Talcott and his brother, Landon C. Eliason, eventually moved with their mother, the former Mary Landon Carter, to Alexandria, Virginia, which Talcott gave as his residence while attending Jefferson Medical College in Philadelphia, Pennsylvania. He graduated from the school in 1847, having written his thesis on coxalgia (also known as coxitis), an inflammatory disease of the hip joint.[4]

Shortly after his graduation, Eliason established himself in Upperville, Virginia, where he began his practice. On October 5, 1848, Eliason married Sarah (Sallie) W. Chunn in Emmanuel Episcopal Church in Middleburg, Virginia.[5] The couple's first child, Mary S., was born on June 30, 1853, and a second daughter, Mary McIntyre, on May 14, 1855. According to von Borcke's memoirs, one of Eliason's daughters (ten years old when von Borcke knew her) was blind, a circumstance that must have weighed heavily on Eliason and his wife.[6] Twin boys were born to the Eliasons on March 19, 1858, but neither the twins nor their mother survived, and Eliason was plunged into mourning. By 1860 Eliason was living in a rented home in Upperville with his mother and his surviving children.

Eliason began his service with the Confederacy as assistant surgeon under Dr. T. H. Williams at Manassas Junction on August 29, 1861. He does not seem to have been affiliated with a particular regiment or command until September 2, 1861, when he was appointed assistant surgeon from Virginia with orders to report to Gen. P. G. T. Beauregard. From this time until his assignment to Stuart, Eliason appears to have been attached to the 1st Virginia Cavalry under W. E. Jones, who attained command of the 1st after Stuart's promotion to brigadier general on September 24, 1861. Lee mentioned the doctor in a report concerning a scout in the vicinity of Falls Church on November 18, 1861, giving Eliason's rank as assistant surgeon (captain). Lee stated that Eliason was "as conspicuous with his pistol making wounds as he was afterward with other instruments healing them."[7] This tendency of Eliason's to be a trooper also caught Stuart's eye later in the war and ultimately led to a recommendation that the surgeon would make a good field officer.

On January 23, 1862, Eliason signed a report of casualties as medical director of Stuart's brigade, which would seem to indicate that he had become part of Stuart's staff. He was probably attached to the staff late in 1861, but this is the first date that can be officially confirmed.[8] By April 17, 1862, he had received his commission as surgeon, equivalent to the rank of major, along with orders to report to Gen. J. E. Johnston. This must have been just a formality. Johnston was commander of the army at that time, and he undoubtedly assigned Eliason to Stuart as soon as the doctor reported to him.

When Johnston fell wounded at Fair Oaks and Robert E. Lee took command, Stuart's cavalry entered into its golden age. Eliason accompanied Stuart on many expeditions, having a horse killed under him early in the Dumfries Raid. The year 1863 proved to be a pivotal one for Eliason. He was announced as chief surgeon of the cavalry on June 1; he actually had held this post for months, but the reorganization of the army and the addition of more cavalry to Stuart's command necessitated an official pronouncement. Eliason's health almost immediately began to fail, though he was still at his post on June 17, for it was he who cared for the wounded von Borcke.

Eliason rode with the cavalry through the Gettysburg Campaign, but it was his last. On July 18, 1863, Stuart wrote Flora that John Fontaine was acting medical director because Eliason had become sick.[9] Fontaine actually had been assisting Eliason for weeks and had slowly been assuming the chief surgeon's duties as Eliason became more and more indisposed. The doctor's illness at that time remained unidentified, but it continued to plague him. In October Stuart finally replaced him permanently with Fontaine. Stuart wrote to Flora on October 3, 1863, that he had made the change and that although he liked Fontaine more, he thought that Eliason was the better surgeon.[10]

After Eliason's removal, his health deteriorated to the point that he entered Richmond's General Hospital #4 on November 19, 1863, with what was diagnosed as morbi cutis, a form of skin disease.[11] Two weeks later he returned to duty. There is reason to believe that he was serving in some medical capacity in or around Richmond. On January 27, 1864, he received orders to report to surgeon W. A. Carrington, medical director at Richmond, for reassignment. Eliason evidently remained in Richmond until July 7, when he was transferred to Charleston, South Carolina. On July 9, 1864, he tendered his resignation, which was accepted on July 15.

Eliason's participation in the war, if any, from the date of his resignation to Robert E. Lee's surrender at Appomattox is unknown. His name appears in the list of the "Medical Faculty of Fauquier county," which published a fee schedule on December 23, 1865.[12] Since the group had met to vote on the schedule on October 23, Eliason was probably back practicing medicine in Upperville soon after the end of the war. Later, the 1870 census recorded him as living alone in his house in Upperville. He was forty-five.

In the early 1870s Eliason moved to Hancock, Maryland, where he again practiced medicine. For a time he and his mother lived as boarders with the family of Mrs. J. Delaplane, but eventually he owned property in the town. His mother died on January 25, 1886, and soon after her death Eliason married Lena Theresa Hansroth. The couple had five children, three boys and two girls. The children were John Landon (September 16, 1890–July 18,

1916); Carl Grammer (1892–June 6, 1921); Fannie (?–May 12, 1951); Talcott, Jr.; and Nancy Carter.

Death came unexpectedly to the old cavalry surgeon on October 22, 1896, at his home in Hancock. The previous day he had been in Cumberland, Maryland, testifying in a will case. Asked to state his age, he replied, "Seventy years, and as hearty as a buck."[13] Returning home, Eliason appeared in excellent health when he retired for the night. He awakened at about 11:00 P.M. feeling ill. Not able to sleep, he sat down in a chair and in a short time expired. His funeral was held in St. Thomas Episcopal Church in Hancock, and he was buried in the family plot in the Presbyterian Cemetery.

Lt. Henry Saxon Farley

Aide-de-camp
July 4, 1863, to September 30, 1863

Early morning darkness still enshrouded Charleston Harbor. It was scarcely four hours into the new day, April 12, 1861. Surrounded by sand dunes, Capt. George S. James stared into the darkness from his post at Fort Johnson on James Island. He commanded two Confederate batteries of ten mortars, a great responsibility since they were poised to fire on Fort Sumter, then held by U.S. forces. A Mexican War veteran, James understood quite clearly that if Sumter refused to surrender, there would be war. He also understood that because of his position, the duty of firing the first shot would fall to him and his batteries. Calm and resolute, he waited.

Standing among the artillerymen, Dr. W. H. Prioleau, the post surgeon, felt the air fill with tension as Capt. Stephen D. Lee, aide to Gen. P. G. T. Beauregard, approached Captain James. After speaking to Lee, James ordered his men to their posts. When all had reached their stations, James turned to a young lieutenant who stood, lanyard in hand, near the mortar he commanded. At a word from the captain, the lieutenant jerked the lanyard and sent a shell screaming into the night sky. By Dr. Prioleau's watch it was approximately 4:30 A.M. War between the Union and the Confederacy had begun.[1]

The youthful lieutenant who found himself thus participating in one of history's pivotal moments was Henry Saxon Farley, younger brother of William Downs Farley. He was born on February 11, 1840, in what was then Laurensville, South Carolina. His father, William R. Farley, originally from Charlotte County, Virginia, had moved to South Carolina when about twenty-one years old to practice law and had married Phoebe M. Downs of Laurensville on April 7, 1831.

The Farleys had a proud heritage that could be traced back to Viking king Joar Vidfadine, who ruled in A.D. 600. Almost five hundred years later, William de Falaise, who fought under William the Conqueror in 1066, began the Farley line that eventually came to America.[2] Though they had no knowledge of their distinguished progenitors, both Henry and William, along with younger brother Hugh Legare, demonstrated the same determination, resourcefulness, and courage that had brought their ancestors first to England and then to America.

Little is known of Farley's early life in Laurensville. He received some of his initial military training at the Citadel in Charleston, South Carolina. On July 1, 1858, he entered West Point, where he remained until November 19, 1860, when he resigned and left the academy. The growing tension between North and South weighed heavily on the twenty-year-old. Though South Carolina had yet to secede, Farley felt led to return to his native state and offer his services. The choice that confronted Farley at this time was the same that faced all Southern cadets in early 1861; Farley, however, was the first to decide to commit himself wholeheartedly to the South.[3]

Upon his return to South Carolina, Farley received a commission as a second lieutenant of infantry in the Confederate Army on March 16, 1861. He simultaneously held a commission as second lieutenant in the 1st South Carolina Artillery. His acceptance of a position with the latter unit brought him to Charleston, where he found himself attached to one of the batteries facing Fort Sumter. His own words regarding the historic occasion were recorded in a letter to Dr. Robert Lebby sometime in 1893.

> The circumstances attending the firing of the first gun at Sumter are quite fresh in my memory. Captain James stood on my right, with watch in hand, and at the designated moment gave me the order to fire. I pulled the lanyard, having already carefully inserted a friction tube, and discharged a thirteen-inch mortar shell, which was the right of battery. In one of the issues of a Charleston evening paper, which appeared shortly after the reduction of Fort Sumter, you will find it stated that Lieutenant Farley fired the first gun, and Lieutenant Gibbes the second.[4]

Following his historic role in the firing on the fort, Farley remained in the artillery, receiving a promotion to captain. He commanded three batteries around Charleston. Sometime in 1862, he set aside the war temporarily and married Mary C. Hamilton. The couple had at least two children, a son, Brooke, and a daughter, May.

On May 30, 1863, he resigned his commission in the artillery, stating that he desired duty elsewhere under his commission as second lieutenant of infantry, which he still held. Apparently Farley did not wait until his resignation was accepted, on June 22, to attach himself to the Army of Northern Virginia. At least one source states that he was on temporary duty with Stuart on June 23. It was not until July 4, however, that he received orders to report to R. E. Lee for assignment. Lee sent him to Stuart, where he remained until September 30, when he was relieved of duty with the Army of Northern Virginia. Col. P. M. B. Young noted that Farley commanded some scouting parties during his tenure with the cavalry and that he also served with Gen. Wade Hampton in some capacity. Considering all the evidence, Farley's time with Stuart must have been relatively short.[5]

Though it appeared that Farley's tour of duty with the Army of Northern Virginia was at an end, on November 6, he was appointed a major (temporary rank) and ordered to report to Gen. P. M. B. Young for duty with the cavalry. Farley remained with the cavalry and at some time was given command of those men who found themselves without a mount and with little prospect of obtaining one. Just when Farley made this transition from mounted cavalry to foot dragoons cannot be determined, but it was certainly before September 1864. Beginning late that month, Farley demonstrated his fitness for command and his fighting tenacity.

As Grant attempted to tighten his stranglehold on Petersburg by pushing ever westward to stretch the Confederate lines, Gen. Wade Hampton, Stuart's eventual successor, became increasingly handicapped by his cavalry's lack of horses. By the end of September 1864, fully 35 percent of his force was without a mount.[6] Charged with the task of containing the Federal cavalry raids against the railroads supplying Petersburg, Hampton used his mounted men as a mobile strike and counterstrike force. His foot dragoons under Farley were less mobile but could garrison strong points along Hampton's lengthy front. In this capacity Farley fought through the various Federal offensives and attained a reputation as a fine officer with a combative nature.[7] An inspection report dated December 31, 1864, shows that as of this date he was still in command of the dismounted cavalrymen near Hicks Ford.[8]

Farley's military career after December 1864 is obscure. He appears to have ended the war as a major, but his assignment at that time is unknown, though he probably remained with the cavalry's dismounted contingent.

Summarizing Henry Farley's war service is difficult because the records are so fragmentary. His desire for a different assignment in May 1863, even at the sacrifice of his rank, denotes his willingness to serve in any capacity. But except for his command of the foot dragoons, which could give only limited service, he does not seem to have had the opportunities that fell to William and Hugh. Most of the assignments he received during the early part of the war kept him away from the main theaters. When he did have the opportunity, he showed his mettle as a fighter. His life subsequent to the war would exhibit his variety of talents, but he was not able to showcase them to any degree through a more active role during the conflict. Nevertheless, he carried out his assignments with the same devotion to duty as did his more famous brothers.

When at least peace returned, Farley managed to acquire some training in law and established a practice in New York. Soon, however, he returned to the military life he had grown to love, working as an instructor in a number of military academies. He spent some time at the Mount Pleasant Military Academy in Sing Sing (now Ossining), New York. The academy's monthly newspaper, *The Mount Pleasant Reveille,* for January 1873 lists Farley as "Drill Master and Instructor in Mathematics, Horsemanship, and Gymnastics."

By January 1874, Farley had moved on. He taught at an academy in Chicago for some time before journeying to California, where he became involved in gold mining. He then returned to the East and settled in Columbia, South Carolina, becoming the editor of a newspaper. Known as an excellent speaker, Farley entered upon a career as a lecturer on the Chautauqua circuit. His addresses, mostly of a political nature, attracted considerable attention in the northern and western parts of the country. In his later years, when he returned to California on vacation, he briefly became involved with the embryonic motion picture industry. His distinguished appearance and dignified bearing brought him to the attention of a number of producers. One managed to persuade Farley to appear as a judge in a movie starring Constance Talmadge. He also had roles in a few other films, but did not wish to make acting a permanent part of his life, so he eventually left California and settled in Flushing, New York, where he lived with his daughter. Farley spent his last years among his family. He died on June 3, 1927, and was buried in Flushing Cemetery, the last of Stuart's staff to pass away.

Capt. William Downs Farley

Scout and voluntary aide-de-camp
May 1862 to June 9, 1863

Hd Qrs Cav. Brigade
June 5th 1862
To Hon. Geo W. Randolph
Sec of War
General:
I am influenced by a desire to promote
the efficiency of my Brigade, by asking you
to commission W. D. Farley as Major of Sharp Shooters in this
Brigade. The enemy fight their cavalry much on foot in wooded
regions, hence it becomes necessary to have our cavalry thor-
oughly versed in fighting on foot. Mr. Farley is the man for it.
His name is in this army synonymous with intrepidity, bravery,
good judgment, and intelligence.

Most Respectfully,
General
I remain your obt sert
J. E. B. Stuart
BrigGen of Cavalry [1]

This letter clearly illustrates two important facts: Stuart had come to appreciate the talents of William Downs Farley very quickly (Farley had served
with Stuart for only about a month when the letter was written), and the
cavalry chieftain had realized quite early in the war the need for fighting his
cavalry dismounted in certain terrains and situations. Secretary of War
Randolph regrettably failed to act on Stuart's request. Farley never got his
commission, and Stuart never had an officially recognized unit of sharpshooters under his command. He did, however, have Farley.

William Downs Farley was born in Laurensville, South Carolina, on
December 19, 1835. William, brother of Henry Saxon and Hugh Legare,
was the third child of William R. Farley and Phoebe M. Downs. As a youth
Farley displayed a passion for reading poetry, and later in life he was fond of
writing verse. The gentle side of his nature was counterbalanced by his
athletic talents, which he strove to develop to their fullest.[2]

He studied at the University of Virginia, and while in attendance there
he journeyed with a number of other students to the Natural Bridge near

Lexington. A practice of visitors to the site in those days was to attempt to climb as high as possible and carve their initials into the soft rock. Farley's physical training enabled him to climb higher than any of his classmates. The story goes that he could have gone higher still but would not do so because he did not wish to carve his initials above those of George Washington, who had accomplished the feat many years earlier.[3]

Before graduating, Farley took another trip, which was to bring him great benefits during his wartime service. At seventeen, along with an older friend, he made a walking tour of northern Virginia and, as a result, gained significant knowledge concerning the terrain and location of paths and roads; he would later be able to use this knowledge as a scout under Stuart.

After obtaining his degree, Farley returned home to assist his ailing father with the family business. His interest in the political affairs of South Carolina and the nation had to be curtailed during his father's illness, but after William R. Farley died on June 24, 1860, his son became more active. His commitment to the states' rights movement led him to advocate secession with enthusiasm, and he helped build support for it at home.

Following South Carolina's secession and the formation of the Confederate States of America, Farley made frequent visits to Charleston, hoping to be present if an attack was made on the city. But much to his chagrin, during one of his short absences, the bombardment of Fort Sumter took place. The family was represented by his brother Henry, however. The rapidly occurring series of events that ensued took Virginia out of the Union and brought Farley to the defense of the state he loved second only to South Carolina. One account states that he was the first South Carolinian to come to the aid of Virginia.[4]

Farley enlisted in Col. Maxcy Gregg's 1st Carolina Regiment of Infantry. After the six months' regiment's time had expired, Farley became an independent operator, though he did attach himself to Brig. Gen. Milledge L. Bonham as an aide-de-camp with the rank of private. Prior to 1st Manassas, he secured valuable information about the enemy for Generals Bonham and P. G. T. Beauregard, and then fought valiantly in that engagement despite a raging fever brought on by the measles.

His daring began to attract the attention of his superiors as the army entered into a period of stalemate after Manassas. Upton's Hill became the scene of one of his grand exploits when, accompanied by only three other men, he took and held the position in the presence of a superior enemy force. Perhaps it was Farley's successes that led him to attack the head of a Union cavalry column (Col. George D. Bayard in command of the 1st Pennsylvania) with, again, just three men. The audacity of the attack almost gave Farley a remarkable little victory, but he and all his companions were either captured or killed, and the bold scout found himself incarcerated in Old Capitol Prison in Washington for a short time.

The relationship between Stuart and Farley began in the early days of May 1862, after the latter had been released from prison. Stuart, aware of the South Carolinian's reputation, coveted his services and managed to snatch him from other officers who had similar ideas. The scout and the general had much in common, and both respected each other's abilities. With Stuart, Farley was able to use his talents to their fullest. Stuart, knowing that Farley could be counted on in any circumstance, gave his newest staff member carte blanche as an operative. There is no record that either of the men was ever disappointed in the relationship.

The scene of action had shifted to Williamsburg on the peninsula, and Farley, living up to his previous standards of intrepidity, threw himself into the battle that erupted around that town. In a letter to his mother, he described some of what had transpired.

> New Kent C.H.
>
> May 9th, 1862. 5 o'clock A.M.
>
> My dear Mother:
>
> Knowing how anxious you would feel about Hugh and me when you heard about the Battle of Williamsburg, I write this the first opportunity. We are both un-injured—
>
> Hugh's Brigade was not engaged. I made two very narrow escapes the day before the battle: lost my own horse, lay concealed in the bushes for half an hour, then joined in a fight against the enemy's Cavalry with our Cavalry; captured another horse,—splendid fellow; was again cut off by the enemy, was chased for a mile and had my horse wounded in two places; had to take to the woods for second time, on foot I worked my way by eleven or twelve o'clock at night to our friends.
>
> Monday morning, having no horse, I told General Stuart I would go into the fight with the Infantry, capture another horse and then act as his aide again.
>
> Went into the 19th Miss, Regt.—then on picket in front of the enemy killed four men before the battle commenced; one of them the Capt. of the 47th N.Y. Have his sword, a fine one. Soon afterwards the whole Regt. advanced, made a charge, the Col. was killed (Col. Motte) we kept advancing and falling back, fighting

all the time, and steadily driving the enemy before us. This part of the Battlefield is universally considered the hottest. Two of the flag bearers of the 19th Miss. were shot down in succession, I caught up the colors myself and bore them for some time, until one of the Officers of the Regt. requested me to give them to a member of the Regt. I did so, he was immediately shot down; another took it, and I <u>think</u> he was wounded.

There was considerable confusion in this part of the field on account of the death and absence of Field Officers; and I actually took command of the 19th Miss., the 9th Ala., and some shattered companies from other Regts. Leaping upon the stumps and logs, I discovered that the enemy's battery was silenced by our cannon from the Forts. Shouting to the men to come on and take it, we did so. Running forward some distance in front, and our own Forts not knowing (on account of the smoke) that we were friends who had taken the enemy's battery, continued firing upon us, and I was struck by a piece of our own shells in the breast, and knocked down, but not much hurt. I leaped up and caught one of the Yankee Officer's fine horses which was left with the battery, and rode full speed to our Forts and stopped them from firing upon us; then went to Gen'ls Johnston, Longstreet, and Stuart—who I found together, and communicated the first joyful intelligence that we had whipped the enemy and taken their battery. The enemy afterwards received reinforcements and continued the fight until night.

It was considered necessary by our Genl's. to continue a backward movement, chiefly on account of nothing to eat for our army; so we had to leave that night, and left almost all of our wounded at Williamsburg. We sent some fifteen of our Doctors under a flag of truce to attend to them.

We had a considerable fight with the enemy (day before yesterday 7th) who had landed from their gun boats to our right and drove them back, killing and capturing some two or three hundred of them.

I have written this in great haste, on my saddle. I have slept and ate little for several days, but am perfectly well and can stand anything. Hugh is looking finely.

I had, in the hottest of the fight all day, only one ball to
touch even my clothing; that was done while carrying the
flag; the blow from the shell hurt me a little that night
but I do not feel it now.

God bless you all and keep the detestable Yankees from
your home.

Pray for the Success of our Confederacy.

Your Aff. Son,

W. D. Farley[5]

Farley was to carry the sword he mentioned in the letter until his death, but
the story of the weapon did not end at Brandy Station. Passed down through
the family, the saber came into the possession of Annie B. Farley, the only
granddaughter of Farley's mother. Annie married Ellison D. Smith on
October 31, 1906. E. D. Smith became the senior United States senator
from South Carolina, and in November 1923, Mrs. Smith and the sword
were both present at the United Daughters of the Confederacy's annual
meeting in Washington, D.C. Also in attendance was a General Wales from
New York, a descendant of the man from whom Farley had taken the sword.
He was there because Mrs. Smith was returning the sword to its owner's
family. Her speech was an inspirational one, recounting Captain Farley's
capture of the sword and its journey through the years within the Farley
family. She closed with these words:

> I do not know the history of your sword before it came
> into our keeping but I can well believe that it has a proud
> and noble record.
>
> I do [not] know all the high adventure, all the daring
> exploits—all the gallant fights—that your sword took part
> in, while it was in the possession of my uncle, but I do
> know this—that he added great glory to its record and
> kept its honor bright—and I proudly return it to you—
> stainless.[6]

Undoubtedly Mrs. Smith spoke with a great deal of pride in the accomplishments of her uncle and possibly with a small amount of Southern bias as well.
She had every right to both feelings, however, for Farley continually demonstrated that he was more than worthy of the accolades he received from comrades and civilians alike. His character was described as pure and beyond
reproach. The only strong spirits that ever passed his lips were taken at 1st
Manassas when he was sick with fever but still in the fight. His love of literature plus an extensive library in his father's home caused one chronicler

to state that "few men of his age possessed a finer fund of literary knowledge."[7] Consequently he was a man whose life and deeds demanded respect, even from his enemies.

Farley was described as being "of medium height, elegantly formed, graceful, well knit, and from habitual exercise on the gymnasium, possessing a remarkable degree of strength and activity. His hair was dark brown; his eyebrows and lashes were so dark, and so shaded the dark grey eyes beneath, as to give them the appearance of blackness."[8] This then was the man Stuart welcomed into his headquarters family in those early days of May 1862. By the time the battles and skirmishes around Williamsburg were over, Stuart had every reason to congratulate himself on his choice, and Farley had just begun to prove his usefulness.

The long withdrawal up the peninsula before McClellan's army culminated in the Battle of Seven Pines, which, because of Gen. Joseph E. Johnston's wounding, led to Robert E. Lee's appointment to the command of the army. During that engagement Farley somehow managed to capture a Federal uniform from the headquarters of Gen. Silas Casey. This appropriation of enemy equipment became Farley's trademark. He never accepted pay, uniforms, weapons, or horses from the Confederate government. Everything he needed to make war he obtained from his foe, and he never ventured out on a mission without being fully equipped.

Soon after Lee had assumed command, he sent Stuart to scout the enemy's right flank, a mission that the intrepid cavalry commander turned into his first Ride Around McClellan. Farley's performance in the expedition was such that he received a sword from the governor of Virginia. From this point on, Farley became a thorn in the side of the Union forces. He acquired what is believed to have been an English Whitworth rifle, which he used to kill Federal officers and blow up enemy artillery limbers and caissons with explosive bullets.

Farley served in all but one of the army's campaigns through 1862 and into 1863, missing only that of Chancellorsville, when he took a much-deserved furlough home to South Carolina. When Farley returned to the army, he found it preparing for the upcoming summer campaign. The cavalry gathered in strength around Culpeper Court House, and Stuart took the opportunity to hold reviews of his newly enlarged command.

Just prior to the Battle of Brandy Station, which would claim Farley's life, the daring scout encountered the only enemy that ever routed him. Stuart and some of his staff had come upon a yard with a tree full of ripened cherries. At their general's behest, several of the staff, including Farley, dismounted and climbed the tree to secure some of the tempting fruit. Throwing some cherries down to Stuart and the remainder of the staff, the men in the tree settled on a comfortable branch to enjoy their treat. Without warning, an old lady suddenly appeared from around the corner of the house carrying a long pole, which she began to wield with considerable dexterity against those men still in the tree. Farley was knocked from his perch to the ground. The woman continued to ply her weapon with a vengeance on Farley, causing Stuart, who caught his breath between bursts of laughter, to shout, "Biggs blow the retreat!" A badly bruised Farley, along with Stuart and the rest, withdrew rapidly, leaving the old woman to savor her triumph.[9]

Early on the morning of June 9, 1863, Stuart's camp on Fleetwood Hill was awakened by the sounds of pistol and carbine fire coming from the direction of the Rappahannock fords. Lt. Frank S. Robertson, the assistant engineer officer, remembered Farley throwing his hat into the air and shouting, "Hurrah, we're going to have a fight!"[10] Stuart sent his staff off in numerous directions to rally the cavalry regiments to the defense of the fields around Brandy Station. He dispatched Farley with orders to Col. Matthew C. Butler of the 2nd South Carolina Cavalry. As the two officers sat side by side on their horses, an enemy shell tore through both men. The projectile removed Butler's foot and severed Farley's leg at the knee. The wound was mortal. Farley requested that his leg be brought to him, after which he was carried from the field on a trough. A short time later he died from loss of blood and shock. An account of his death was given later by Captain Blocker, an eyewitness.

> As soon as I heard that Col. [Matthew C.] Butler, [of the 2nd South Carolina Cavalry] was wounded, I went immediately to him and reached him just as they were putting him in the horse trough . . . and assisted in getting him to a private house. After being there a short time, Col. Butler told me he wanted me to go to Culpeper to telegraph to Governor Pickens for him. When I left him he told me to look after Capt. Farley. I soon overtook the ambulance with Capt. Farley. He asked about Col. Butler and asked where I was going. I asked him if I could do anything for him. He then asked me to go to a Dr. Jones and see if I could get him in there. Dr. Jones told me certainly to bring him there. After sending Col. Butler's dispatch, I went back and met the ambulance, and Capt. Farley was carried to Dr. Jones's. I assisted in carrying him in the house, where we found a mattress on the parlor floor for him. As we laid him down I attempted to draw my arm from under his head. He said: "Hold on Blocker; let your arm stay under my head." He then closed his eyes for a few seconds, then opened them and looked around the room and said in a

very clear, distinct, and demanding tone, "To your post, men! to your post!" and those were the last words he ever spoke. He died in a few moments.[11]

The campaign that followed left little time for Stuart to convey his condolences to Farley's mother, but eventually he wrote the following letter expressing his feelings for his friend and comrade.

Hd. Qrs. Cav. Div.
A. of N. Va., Aug.10, 1863.

My dear Madam:

Permit me even at this late day to throw a garland over the grave of your dear boy the beloved and the brave Capt. W. D. Farley who did me the honor to serve so long, so faithfully, though without emolument or commission, as a member of my staff.

The events embracing the battle of Fleetwood and the Pennsylvania campaign crowded upon each other with such absorbing interest that I never could command time and composure of mind sufficient to enable me to write to you as I desired. And even now I write confronted with that same army of the Potomac and my guns planted on the heights of Fleetwood, not knowing but what before this is completed those guns will be hurling death and defiance at our foes.

But I cannot longer postpone a tribute due to one of Carolina's noblest sons, universally admired and beloved. It is needless to tell his mother what were his noble traits of character; but I thought it might be gratifying to her broken spirit to know from me how much her son was appreciated and how sorely his loss is felt. His bravery amounted to heroism of the highest order, and there are letters on file in the War Department attesting his merit, which I felt it my duty, unsolicited by him, to write.

In my official report of the battle of Fleetwood I used the following language concerning your son:

"Capt. W. D. Farley, of South Carolina, a voluntary aide on my staff, was mortally wounded by the same shell that wounded Col. M. C. Butler, and displayed even in death the same loftiness of bearing and fortitude which have characterized him through life. He had served without emolument, long, faithfully and always with distinction.

No nobler champion has fallen. May his spirit abide
with us."

His high qualities as a patriot and a soldier were height-
ened by his modesty and gentleness of demeanor and the
purity of his private character.

Be assured, my dear madam, you have my tears of sympathy in this sad bereavement, and in this I am sure I am
joined by his comrades who were devoted to him while
living and cherish dearly his memory now that he is no
more.

With the sincere prayer that He who tempers the wind
to the shorn lamb, will administer to you that consolation
which is the offspring of a Christian faith.

I am sincerely
Yours and your son's friend,
J. E. B. Stuart.[12]

Not long before the Battle of Brandy Station, Farley had spoken to some of
his friends in Culpeper that if he fell in battle he was to be wrapped in his new
coat of Confederate gray and sent home to his mother. For whatever reasons,
however, this did not happen. Captain Farley—though according to what
Stuart wrote, Farley never really held an actual commission as captain but
was more than deserving of one—was buried in Fairview Cemetery in
Culpeper. His tombstone's inscription reads:

> *A South Carolina Volunteer*
> *Capt. Wm. Downs Farley*
> *of Gen. Stuart's Staff*
> *Born Dec. 19, 1835*
> *Fell in defense of his*
> *country in cavalry en-*
> *gagement at Culpeper, Va.*
> *June 9, 1863*

Maj. Norman Richard FitzHugh

Adjutant and quartermaster
June 24, 1862, to May 12, 1864

The cell door clanged shut and a much dejected but greatly relieved Maj.
Norman R. FitzHugh made himself as comfortable as possible in his new

"home." He had just been incarcerated in Old Capitol Prison in Washington, D.C., after being captured at Verdiersville on August 18, 1862, by the 1st Michigan Cavalry. Important papers he had been carrying related to Gen. R. E. Lee's new offensive were now spread before the eyes of the Union high command. On these two points, FitzHugh had little to bolster his morale. On the other hand, he could feel some relief that he and the plans were all the Michiganders had rounded up that day; if things had gone a bit differently, he might be sharing the prison with Gen. Stuart, who had barely escaped.

FitzHugh's time in prison might have passed more slowly than it did had not a charming female prisoner occupied the next cell. She was the young, spirited Belle Boyd, arrested as a Confederate spy in late July 1862. She, along with his cellmate, Major Morse of Gen. Richard S. Ewell's staff, were able to make the best of a bad situation.[1] Fortunately their incarceration was brief. On August 29 Boyd and FitzHugh stepped into a carriage that whisked them to a ship, the *Juniata,* at anchor on the Potomac River. They set sail the next day. The major had been especially detailed to accompany Boyd. They were among the first contingent of prisoners to be exchanged under a new agreement worked out by the Federal and Confederate governments.

The jubilant party's arrival in Richmond attracted the attention of the Richmond *Daily Dispatch,* which duly recorded the event. FitzHugh bid adieu to his celebrated traveling companion and made plans to rejoin Stuart and the cavalry. His first experience as a prisoner of war had not been too unpleasant. But FitzHugh, though lucky when it came to dodging enemy bullets and shells, was not quite so fortunate in avoiding capture. He would have the opportunity to partake of Yankee "hospitality" again.

Norman R. FitzHugh, the son of Norman R. and Mary Ann Fitz-Hugh (née Vowell), was born December 8, 1831. His father died in September 1835, leaving a wife and four children. The loss of her husband and the strain of trying to raise a family by herself may have contributed to her own death in 1840. The four young children were raised either in a boarding school or by a member of the Vowell family.[2] In any event, Fitz-Hugh's early life could not have been too stable.

Of the years between 1840 and 1862, only bits and pieces are known. Blackford alluded to the fact that FitzHugh often entertained the staff around the campfire with tales of his life among the Indians out West.[3] Unlike St. Leger Grenfell's stories, which were more fiction than fact, FitzHugh's appear to contain a reasonable amount of substance. He most assuredly was in Utah in 1859, as he married Mary Foot Lynde at Camp Floyd on June 26 of that year. Another source stated that FitzHugh had been captured by the Sioux and had been adopted by a chief.[4] This presumably occurred before his marriage.

FitzHugh returned to Virginia, where he inevitably became pulled into the conflict between North and South. He did not enlist until April 1, 1862, however, which could indicate either that he had just arrived from the West or that he had tried to remain out of the war as long as possible. He joined Company "E" (the Mercer Cavalry of Spotsylvania County) of the 9th Virginia Cavalry. FitzHugh's talents must have been recognized prior to his enlistment, since he was immediately appointed a corporal. Then, less than three months after his enlistment, Stuart asked for his commission as assistant adjutant general.

> Hd Qrs Cavalry Brigade
> June 21, 1862
>
> General:
>   I have the honor to nominate for appointment as asst adjt General to my brigade—
>
> Norman R. FitzHugh
>
> and to request that his commission issue at the earliest practicable moment. The post was made vacant by the promotion of L. Tiernan Brien to Lt. Col. 1st Va Cavalry.
>   I have the honor to be very
>
> Respectfully
> Your obt svt
> J. E. B. Stuart
> Brig Gen'l
> Co'd'g
>
> General:
>   S. Cooper
>   Adjt & Insp. General
>   Richmond, Va.[5]

From the beginning of his association with Stuart's staff, FitzHugh was one of its hardest working officers and best-liked men. His relationship with his chief also developed quickly into a close bond of friendship, so close that on July 27, 1862, Stuart stood as godfather to FitzHugh's son, Norman R. FitzHugh, Jr. The service was held at cavalry headquarters at Hanover Court House.[6] Less than a month later, FitzHugh was a major and had received accolades in Stuart's report for his role as adjutant and chief of staff during the Peninsula Campaign.

Whatever euphoria the newly commissioned major may have experienced, he soon was jolted back to reality by his capture at Verdiersville. Unlike some other officers, though, FitzHugh had a relatively brief prison stay. He was officially exchanged for Maj. James D. Potter of the 38th New York Volunteer Infantry on September 21, 1862, though he had returned to Richmond on September 2.[7] In early October, soon after his official exchange, FitzHugh made his way north to rendezvous with Stuart and staff, then headquartered at "The Bower" about eight miles southeast of Martinsburg. Everyone was happy to have him back, Channing Price stating that "everything moves smoothly when he is about."[8]

As the Army of Northern Virginia positioned itself near Fredericksburg, W. W. Blackford took the time to compose a poem and dedicate it to FitzHugh.

Lines written on a bale of smoking
tobacco presented to my Comrade, Mess-mate,
and Friend, Major Norman R. FitzHugh,
of Stuart's Staff, before the battle of Fredericksburg

When first Sir Walter Raleigh drew
A whiff, with Indian Chieftains round,
The gallant Knight but little knew
The wondrous weed that he had found

Let swag'ring Comrades snuff and chew
But this battle 'eve will you and I
E'en puff in peaceful pipes Fitz Hugh
This golden bale of "cut and dry"

And while the smoke to heaven ascends
Our frosty moon-bright prayer shall be
For him whose soul tomorrow sends
A sacrifice to Victory

Head Quarters, Cavalry Corps
Army of Northern Virginia
Near Fredericksburg
December 12th, 1862[9]

In early March 1863, Stuart, concerned about Federal cavalry incursions, used FitzHugh's 640-acre farm as his center of operations for several days.

Known as "Forrest Hall," the farm was located just south of United States Ford on the Rappahannock River above Fredericksburg, in Spotsylvania County. Just when FitzHugh purchased the farm and how long he lived there before the war (if at all) are unknown. From March 30 through the first few days of April, FitzHugh was absent from cavalry headquarters while he took care of necessary army business in Richmond and then moved his family out of harm's way to Albemarle County, Virginia.[10] After the war, upon his release from prison camp, he gave his home as Albemarle County and not Spotsylvania County.[11]

The resignation of Maj. Samuel H. Hairston in March 1863 left the staff without a quartermaster. Stuart transferred FitzHugh to the quartermaster post and made Channing Price his adjutant. The general had originally intended to move Maj. W. J. Johnson from the commissary department to quartermaster and put FitzHugh in his place,[12] but he finally chose to replace Hairston with FitzHugh and leave Johnson as commissary. Again, FitzHugh did not disappoint his commander, quickly learning the quartermaster's job of supplying the men. No record exists of FitzHugh's reaction to the change in position, other than his energetic hard work.

The winter of 1862–63 brought a strange episode in FitzHugh's military life. From February 20 to April 20, 1863, the brigade of Gen. Carnot Posey and part of the brigade of Gen. William Mahone encamped on FitzHugh's farm at U.S. Ford. In order to keep warm, the men burned a considerable amount of wood (estimated at fifty acres or 1250 cords plus 350 panels of worm fence). FitzHugh filed claim against the Confederate government for damages and after almost a year collected $2,675. If the claim was paid in Confederate currency, FitzHugh was all the poorer for it. The rest of his fencing and his home eventually were burned as well, the fencing by the Yankees and the house "accidentally" while the Northerners had possession of it.[13]

After Stuart's death, FitzHugh was assigned to the staff of Gen. Wade Hampton as quartermaster of the cavalry. He continued in this post until December 1, 1864, when he was captured at Stony Creek south of Petersburg by the Union's 2nd Cavalry Division. He spent the remainder of the war in Fort Delaware. He was released on June 4, 1865, at which time he was described as being six feet tall with blue eyes, light hair, and a ruddy complexion.[14]

FitzHugh's life immediately after the war is almost as mysterious as it was before the conflict. With his home burned, he apparently made little or no effort to return and start anew. With his wife and at least one child, he packed up and headed west. In 1871 he was in Minnesota, where his son Isaac was born.[15] By 1876 he had moved again, this time to Picolata, St. Johns County, Florida. The 1880 census shows that his family consisted of his wife; two sons, Norman, Jr., and Isaac; and Mary, a daughter born in either Virginia or Washington, D.C.[16] Also living with him were his wife's parents and brother. They were all engaged in orange growing. FitzHugh also served as justice of the peace and notary public.[17]

In 1910 FitzHugh was seventy-nine years old. He and Mary had had six children, three of whom were still living. Their widowed daughter, Mary, lived with them. Back in 1907 and again in 1909, FitzHugh had applied for a pension from the state of Florida. At the time of his application in 1909, the examining physician had described him as being "very feeble & infirm from great exposure and age."[18] FitzHugh died on May 13, 1915. He was buried in Evergreen Cemetery in Jacksonville, Florida.

Surgeon John Boursiquot Fontaine

Medical director
October 20, 1863, to May 12, 1864

Around noon on October 1, 1864, Gen. Wade Hampton, riding at the head of a column consisting of the 9th and 13th Virginia Cavalries, made his way from his position near the Harman Road southwest of Petersburg toward the Vaughan Road. The cavalry chieftain's ultimate goal was to confront Union forces in the area of the Vaughan Road. Riding with Hampton was John B. Fontaine. That morning, Fontaine had left Camp Early accompanied by Capt. Charles Grattan and Maj. George Freaner, also officers on Hampton's staff, in search of the general. They had found him just about an hour before Hampton made his decision to make the reconnaissance in force.

The Confederate column did not reach its destination until 3:00 that afternoon. A relatively slow advance had been necessary in order to avoid a possible ambush, and the horrible condition of the roads, turned into quagmires by recent storms, also retarded movement. Nevertheless, Hampton found that their approach had gone unnoticed by the Union troops west of Arthur's Swamp, the side closest to the advancing Confederates. The general quickly made preparations for a surprise attack. But one brigade unfortunately went astray, causing the Confederate attack to be launched piecemeal and without the aid of a flanking column. Instead of crushing or capturing the two Yankee regiments west of the swamp, all the cavalry succeeded in doing was driving the enemy across the boggy ground to join their main body east of the swamp.

Having failed in the initial attempt, the Southern commander made
do with some shelling by Capt. James F. Hart's and Capt. Edward Graham's
batteries of horse artillery while determining his next step. A heated dis-
cussion arose over the best approach to take. Gen. John Dunovant and his
superior, Gen. Matthew C. Butler, could not agree on the best method
of attack. Butler favored a flanking maneuver, while Dunovant wanted to
launch a frontal attack straight down the road. Dunovant eventually had
his way, and soon his South Carolina brigade thundered down the slope
toward the enemy. What transpired next is best told by an eyewitness.
Maj. George Freaner recorded the events in a letter to Mrs. Fontaine just
five days after the battle.[1]

> It was about four o'clock when the battle was joined and
> it began furiously. In about ten minutes a courier dashed up
> to Gen. Hampton and informed him that Gen. Dunovant,
> Comdg a So. Carolina brigade, was mortally wounded.
> As soon as the announcement was made Dr. Fontaine
> put spurs to his horse, and calling to his courier Patterson
> to follow, dashed at the gallop in the direction of Gen. D.
> He passed one of our batteries which was in full play and
> being replied to by the guns of the enemy. When about
> twenty paces in front of the battery, a shell from the
> enemy's guns exploded about thirty paces in his immediate
> front, a piece of which—a very small fragment, struck him
> upon the chin and glancing downward entered the left side
> of the throat near the socket. He did not fall, but dropped
> the reins of the bridle on his horse's neck, leaned backward
> and remained so until lifted from his horse by Patterson
> and laid on the ground. All this occurred as soon almost as
> I have written it and was announced to the General a very
> few moments after the doctor left us. Capt. Grattan and
> myself were about to start to his rescue when we were
> informed that he was approaching on a litter. As the litter
> bearers approached he rose up and was spoken to tenderly
> by all but was unable to speak and reply. Dr Gilliam Chf
> Surgeon WHF Lee's Div Capt. Grattan and myself started
> with the litter bearers to convey him to the nearest house,
> which was about two hundred yards in the rear of the road
> upon which we met him. As we approached the house he
> rose on the litter, and gesticulating with his arm gave us
> to understand that he wished to be carried further to the

rear. One of us galloped on and found a house about a quarter of a mile distant to which we carried him. It proved to be a dwelling of a widow lady of apparently moderate circumstances, named Mrs. Tucker. Here he expressed his willingness by a nod of the head to be taken from the litter and have his wound examined. A hasty pallet was made on the floor and he was placed upon it. Dr Gilliam took position by his side and watched the developments of his case with a tenderness and sympathy that was truly affecting. It was soon ascertained that the Doctor was suffering from internal hemorrhage and that his case was hopeless. He managed to speak to Dr Gilliam twice in a low and almost inaudible voice—once saying that he knew he was bound to die—and again "what will become of my poor wife" or words to that effect.

[three words illegible] him on the pallet we endeavored to administer some stimulants, but he had lost the power of swallowing and gestured it away. He breathed heavily and with great labor—once or twice he pointed to his breast indicating that the seat of his suffering was there. About 6 o'clock P.M. he had a profuse hemorrhage under which he fainted and to all appearances his suffering spirit had flown, but after a few minutes of lethargic stupor, he rallied, became strong and intelligent of persons and things around him. No relief could be afforded him. It made our duty so much the more painful and melancholy that we could not aid him, or assuage his suffering.

About ½ past seven o'clock after intense and restless suffering he became suddenly quiet and in a few moments passed calmly away. His body was immediately placed in an ambulance and in charge of Captain Grattan and myself, was carried to Dr Guild's Quarters, where it was neatly dressed and started for Richmond.[2]

Fontaine was only twenty-four years old when he suffered the fate of so many of his fellow soldiers and friends. On numerous occasions he had stood by helplessly and watched them die, unable to save them or ease their sufferings. In the end, his friends had been equally powerless to alleviate the anguish of his final moments. As a doctor he knew that his wound was mortal, and the soldier in him faced that truth with a calm courage. In his few short years he had risen rapidly and had demonstrated his remarkable abilities as a surgeon and soldier under the most trying of circumstances. At the age of twenty-three he had become the cavalry corps medical director under Stuart, caring for more than six thousand men as well as their horses. His death could be directly attributed to his intense devotion to duty and his desire to fulfill his Hippocratic oath.

Born at the Fontaine home near Beaver Dam Station on April 1, 1840, John Boursiquot Fontaine was one of the eleven children of Edmund Fontaine, Sr., and his wife, the former Louisa Shackelford. Fontaine's training for a career in medicine began on April 1, 1858, when he enrolled in the Richmond Association of Medical Instruction. His "instruction" consisted of working as an apprentice to a physician. By doing so, he fulfilled one of the requirements for entering medical school.

On October 5, 1858, Fontaine entered the Medical College of Virginia at Richmond. He completed his course in March 1859 and journeyed to New York City, where he enrolled at New York University for the summer. Returning to Richmond, he began his next course of instruction on December 28, 1859. He successfully concluded his education on March 8, 1860. From the time of his graduation until the outbreak of the war, it is believed that Fontaine practiced in Ashland, Virginia.

Fontaine offered his services to the Confederacy and received an assignment as assistant surgeon to the 5th Virginia Regiment of Volunteers on May 21, 1861. This order was almost immediately countermanded, and on May 29 he reported to Major Harrison's cavalry command at Manassas. The month of June saw Fontaine attached to Lt. Col. Walter H. Jenifer's cavalry stationed at Sangster's Crossroads. On July 1, after what must have been a helter-skelter first two months of service, Fontaine was transferred to Gen. P. G. T. Beauregard's forces at Manassas.

At the 1st Battle of Manassas, Fontaine confronted the horrors of war on a scale few men of the period had imagined. The dead and wounded of both armies littered the countryside. Late in the day, as the battle drew to its close, the Hanover Light Dragoons were launched in pursuit of the retreating enemy. Fontaine was the medical officer on duty when the first casualty of the Dragoons' gallant charge arrived for medical attention. The young surgeon must have stared in disbelief as his older brother, Edmund, Jr., was laid before him. A quick, careful examination told John all he needed to know. The wound was mortal, and he could not save his brother's life.

Fontaine continued his affiliation with the Hanover Light Dragoons after the company became part of the 4th Virginia Cavalry on September 4, 1861. Assigned to the regiment and promoted to surgeon (equal to a major's rank) on February 14, 1862, the young physician began to attract the attention of his senior officers. By November 1862 he had become surgeon to Gen. Fitz Lee's entire brigade, which included the 4th Virginia. His new position brought him to the attention of Stuart, who witnessed the doctor's courage at the Battle of Kelly's Ford on March 17, 1863, where Fontaine's horse was severely wounded beneath him. It was a close call, as Fontaine's claim for reimbursement indicates.

> Head - Quarters Lee's Cavalry Brigade
> April 18th 1863

> I hereby certify that my horse appraised at $175.00 in April 1862 was so wounded and disabled in the fight near Kelly's Ford on the 17th March 1863 by a shot from the enemy that he had to be abandoned and killed immediately to relieve suffering, his left fore-leg being broken just below the shoulder joint so that he could not get up after being shot down.
>
> J. B. Fontaine, Senr Surg.
> Lee's Cav. Brigade.[3]

Fitz Lee's promotion to major general brought Fontaine additional responsibilities, as he became the new division's medical director. Though he had a number of doctors working under him, he continued to perform the functions of surgeon, veterinarian, and dentist just as he had done when he had been the 4th Virginia's surgeon, but he now had the added burden of paperwork and divisional reports as well.

Despite all his obligations, Fontaine still managed to find time to court the lovely Elizabeth Winston Price of "Dundee" near Richmond. Sometime in January 1863 the young couple was married. Stuart and von Borcke arrived for the wedding after a thundering forty-five-mile ride. The event proved to be a bright interlude for the three men in an otherwise dismal winter of lonely camp life. Fontaine had a few weeks away from the war but was back again by March 2.[4]

In the aftermath of the Gettysburg Campaign, Stuart's medical director, Talcott Eliason, began to suffer from an illness that frequently made him incapable of remaining on duty at cavalry headquarters. At those times, Stuart called on Fontaine to assume Eliason's post. By October 9 Fontaine was in fact the cavalry corps medical director, and on December 17 Stuart finally moved to make the position permanent.

Headqrs. Cav Corps ANV
Dec 17, 1863

Gen. S. Cooper,
    A. & I. Gen. Confederate States
General,

I have the honor to request that Surgeon J.B. Fontaine,
4th Va. Cav., be assigned to duty at these headquarters as
Medical Director of the Cavalry Corps.

Although not the senior Surgeon of the Corps, he was
senior in Gen. Fitz Lee's Brigade—afterward, Chief Surgeon of his Division—and has now been for nearly three
months acting as Chief Surgeon of the Cav. Corps. I can
recommend him as an officer of high character and attainments, and bear my testimony to the fact that his official
duties in this laborious and responsible position, have been
discharged with zeal, intelligence and efficiency.

His appointment would I am sure prove an excellent
one, and highly beneficial to the service.

I am, General
Most Respy Your Ob sevt
J. E. B. Stuart
Maj Genl.[5]

Fontaine continued as Stuart's medical director until the general's death. It
was Fontaine who first examined Stuart's wound while the general lay in an
ambulance. The surgeon knew the wound was mortal, but he nevertheless
called in other doctors after Stuart was in bed at the home of Dr. Charles
Brewer, Stuart's brother-in-law. Fontaine's diagnosis was confirmed, and the
surgeon made his patient as comfortable as possible and waited for the end.

Little is recorded of Fontaine's service from May 12 until August 11,
1864, on which date he received orders to report to Gen. Wade Hampton
for assignment. Until his death on October 1, he held the post of chief
medical director of the cavalry corps. He was buried in the family plot on
the plantation near Beaver Dam Station.

Capt. Richard Edgar Frayser

Signal officer
August 31, 1862, to May 12, 1864

In selecting men for his staff, Stuart was greatly influenced by an individual's
performance under difficult circumstances. Several officers were added to

the staff solely because Stuart had seen them in action and had observed their talents. One of this number was Richard E. Frayser, who had enlisted in the New Kent Light Dragoons on June 28, 1861.[1] The Dragoons later became Company "F" of the 3rd Virginia Cavalry. Nothing in Frayser's records with the 3rd Virginia indicates that he was any-thing special as a cavalry trooper; his life prior to the war is equally unimpressive. When an opportunity presented itself, however, Frayser showed that he had the kinds of abilities Stuart always looked for. In less than three months from his first contact with the cavalry's commander-in-chief, Frayser was on Stuart's staff.

Capt. Richard Edgar Frayser

Son of Rev. Richard Frayser, a Methodist minister, Richard E. Frayser (he does not appear to have been named after his father) was born in Octo-ber 1830 in New Kent County, Virginia. He was orphaned at an early age and went to work in a country store to help pay for his keep. After several years he ventured out on his own and journeyed to Richmond, where he took a post office job. Frayser resigned in 1854 and returned to New Kent County to establish his own mercantile business. His earlier experience coupled with hard work brought him a modicum of success. In 1861 the war intervened and Frayser joined his local company.

The initial months of Frayser's military service were filled with the normal soldier's routine of duties. On December 6, 1861, he was marked absent on the company muster roll with a sick furlough; he remained so through part of January 1862. His break came in June, when Gen. George B. McClellan's Union Army, which had successfully driven up the James River Peninsula, stood before Richmond. The Confederate Army's new commander, Robert E. Lee, issued orders to Stuart for a reconnaissance of the Federal Army's right flank. Stuart's scouting expedition was to turn into the famous Chickahominy Raid, as he circled the Union forces in three days.

Part of the Confederate cavalry's route lay through New Kent County. Stuart called on two men who knew the countryside intimately: Lt. Jones R. Christian and Pvt. Richard E. Frayser. According to his own account of the adventure, Frayser first became involved when Stuart ordered him to go in advance of the column somewhere between Old Church and Tunstall's Station. This may have occurred near Smith's Store, which lay near the Hanover–New Kent county line. Approaching Tunstall's, Frayser tried a ruse to keep the Federals occupying the station long enough to be surrounded and captured. But the Union officer in charge did not believe that the cavalry in his front was the 8th Illinois as Frayser had told him, and he and his men rapidly escaped down the road to the White House.[2]

Frayser continued to act as guide until the cavalry was safely across the Chickahominy. Stuart ordered a halt near the home of Col. J. M. Wilcox in Charles City County to allow his weary troopers a much-needed rest. The general, Frayser, and a courier paused only briefly and then started out for Richmond about thirty miles away. Somewhere close to the capital, Stuart instructed Frayser to ride to Virginia governor John Letcher with the news of the mission's success. Upon his arrival at the executive mansion, Frayser was informed that the governor was asleep and that he should return later in the morning. Frayser insisted on an interview, telling the servant who barred his way that he had come from General Stuart. Entrance was gained immediately. So pleased was Governor Letcher that he presented Frayser with a requisition order allowing him to select any sword he wished from the state arsenal. It was a true cavalryman's reward.[3]

Having played no small part in the final outcome of Stuart's foray, Frayser returned to his regiment proud in the knowledge that in his general's official report he had received recognition for his role. His feelings of elation were tempered quickly, however. On July 6, near a place called Fallsville, Frayser was captured.[4] His incarceration lasted until August 5, when he was exchanged at Aiken's Landing, Virginia. He rejoined his company just in time for the 2nd Manassas Campaign.

The fighting that raged over the already bloodied fields in the vicinity of Manassas Junction claimed thousands more soldiers, both blue and gray. One of them was Stuart's signal officer, J. Hardeman Stuart, who fell in the day's final assault. On August 31, 1862, the general wrote to the Secretary of War recommending Frayser as the replacement. Considering Stuart's alacrity in responding to the vacancy on his staff, he probably had never had anyone but Frayser in mind for the position, nor did he await Richmond's reply to his request. Private Frayser became Captain Frayser overnight, and he immediately assumed the duties of his new post.

Considerable surprise over Frayser's appointment existed, however, among the personnel of the signal corps who had served under Hardeman Stuart. In a letter to his uncle dated September 3, 1862, Edward Stuart, Hardeman's younger brother and a fellow member of the signal corps, stated his belief that Frayser's accession to the position was based solely on his association with General Stuart during the Ride Around McClellan. He further asserted Frayser's total ignorance of the system of signals used by the corps. Edward felt that the new signal officer was a kindhearted man but completely unsuited to replace his brother, who had gained his experience by hard service over many months.[5]

Despite his lack of experience, Frayser performed well in his initial campaign as signal officer. Stuart's report of his command's actions during the Sharpsburg Campaign commends Frayser for his "important services to the commanding general from a mountain overlooking the enemy on the Antietam."[6] The new captain obviously found ways of circumventing his deficiencies.

Frayser's service with the signal corps sometimes took him away from Stuart and the cavalry to which he was officially attached. On June 5, 1863, Gen. R. E. Lee wrote to Gen. A. P. Hill, commander of the 3rd Corps of the Army of Northern Virginia, that "Capt. [R. E.] Frayser, signal officer, is at Port Royal and has been instructed to report to you."[7] At this time the cavalry was gathered in the vicinity of Brandy Station, preparing for Lee's summer campaign. Frayser's records are unclear as to how long he remained at Port Royal, but one document dated December 17, 1863, mentioned him as being captain of Stuart's signal corps stationed at Port Royal. By January 11, 1864, he was in Richmond under the authority of Gen. R. S. Ewell.[8]

On May 12, 1864, Frayser's service with Stuart came to an end in two ways. Sometime during the confused fighting around Spotsylvania, Frayser was captured by the Federals for a second time. His commander had been mortally wounded the day before and died that evening. Stuart did not live long enough to learn that he had lost another of his staff, and the signal officer probably did not find out for several days about his commander's death.

A great trial lay ahead for Frayser. After being incarcerated at Fort Delaware for three months, Frayser, along with a large number of his fellow inmates, celebrated upon learning in mid-August that they were to be taken south for exchange. The Confederates embarked on the steamer "Crescent City" on August 20, but they soon began to doubt their captors' words. The promised exchange did not take place; instead, the ragged prisoners were unloaded eighteen days later at Morris Island in Charleston Harbor, South Carolina. Here, six hundred Confederate officers endured six weeks of a most unusual imprisonment. They had been placed on Morris Island in order to prevent the Confederate batteries in and around Charleston from firing on Union artillery positions. Frayser and the rest endured bad medical treatment, poor rations, and the fear of being shelled by their own compatriots. Miraculously they all survived, only to face additional imprisonment in either Fort Pulaski, Georgia, or Hilton Head, South Carolina.[9]

After this, many of the remaining "Immortal 600," as they came to be called, were sent back to Fort Delaware. Frayser was not among them. His deteriorating physical condition led to his exchange in February 1865 at Charleston under a cartel that allowed for the exchange of sick and disabled. He recovered to some extent, returned to duty with the Army of

Northern Virginia, and was among the tattered remnants that surrendered at Appomattox.

Soon after the Confederacy's collapse, Frayser settled in a devastated Richmond. He became mailing clerk on the *Dispatch* and held this position for many years. Remaining in the newspaper business, he later became business manager for the *Whig* and held a similar post on the *Commonwealth*. In 1883 Frayser established the *Richmond Mercantile and Manufacturing Journal,* which he managed for several years. He became interested in politics, holding the office of superintendent of public printing for a number of years and running for the House of Delegates in 1893. He also gained a law degree and established a small law practice.

Frayser's wife, Mary Armstead Williamson, died May 10, 1891. In January 1899 Frayser suffered an attack of grippe from which he never really recovered, and his health began to deteriorate rapidly. Another attack, this time of typhoid-malaria, struck him in July. Though he improved enough to return to his own apartment in Richmond, by late October he was confined to the Retreat for the Sick, where, after much suffering, he succumbed on December 22, 1899, at 4:30 A.M. to a combination of illnesses, Bright's disease being the most serious. He was sixty-nine years old. He was buried in Hollywood Cemetery the following day.

Maj. George Freaner

Assistant adjutant and inspector general
December 7, 1863, to May 12, 1864

Richmond 2nd Nov 1861

Col W. H. S. Taylor
2nd Auditors Office
Dear Sir

I am desirous of obtaining a position in your office. I am a native of the state of Maryland and a lawyer by profession of some years standing. I was also a member of her recently dispersed legislature. In consequences of my persistent advocacy of the rights of the South in our unfortunate national quarrel I was compelled to abandon my home and effects and am unprepared to meet the contingencies of a life of exile. I was also one of a committee appointed by the last southern rights convention to submit an address to the people of Md.

If it be permitted me I will further remark that I was a democratic member of the Electoral College of 1856 from the state of California and as such cast one Electoral vote for Buchanan and Breckinridge. If any Maryland references now accessible is necessary to sustain this application I will engage to furnish it.

Hoping that it may meet with the favor of the Department I am

Respectfully yours
George Freaner[1]

With this letter, Stuart's future inspector general conveyed the turmoil and anxiety that plagued the people of Maryland at the opening of the war. His term "exile" clearly defines the position in which many Marylanders found themselves. Like Dabney Ball and L. T. Brien, Freaner had to make a choice between remaining with his state in the Union or siding with the South. Freaner's political beliefs made this choice clear.

The remainder of the letter briefly outlines the prewar career of one of Stuart's most talented and distinguished staff officers. That his name did not become eternally linked with Stuart's, as did von Borcke's, McClellan's, and Blackford's, can only be ascribed to his short duration of service with the cavalry chieftain.

Born in Hagerstown, Maryland, on January 20, 1831, to Henry Freaner and the former Sarah Chambers, Freaner demonstrated quite early a gift for public speaking. So noticeable was his talent that after he graduated from Hagerstown Academy, his father decided he should receive a classical education and enrolled him at Dickinson College in Carlisle, Pennsylvania.[2] Freaner entered the school in 1848 but left in 1851 before receiving his degree. His reason is revealed in an excerpt from a letter to fellow classmate, Christian Philip Ziegler Humrich, a Carlisle resident.

Hagerstown Aug 1851

Dear Christ,

Mully [illegible] has just come to town and informed me that he is going to Carlisle and I snatch these few moments to inform you that I am well. I am at the law and very well satisfied so much so that I fear I will not have the pleasure of returning to college. . . .[3]

The "law" to which Freaner referred was located in the offices of Alexander Neill, Sr., where he read for some time. He was admitted to the bar of

Washington County in 1853. He then moved to California, settling in Oakland, where he established a law practice. His business did not flourish, and he accepted the position of editor for *The Times and Transcript*. His success in this venture brought him the editorship of a paper in Yreka, which was located in Siskiyou County in northern California.

Through the paper, Freaner became the champion of the "Law and Order" advocates who opposed the Vigilance Committee. In the 1856 presidential campaign, he headed the delegation from Siskiyou County to the state convention, where his oratory impressed all in attendance. By acclamation he was chosen as one of the two electors-at-large, and eventually he was selected to carry the vote to Washington. His career in California seemed assured, but upon his return to the East in 1857, he decided to open up a law practice in his native county. He also became editor and part proprietor of the *Hagerstown Mail*. In 1859 Freaner, running on the Democratic ticket, won election to Maryland's House of Representatives, where he immediately made an impact as the chairman of a special committee investigating alleged frauds in the Baltimore elections.

The triumph was short-lived. Unknown to Freaner and those who supported him for election, the time he had spent in California put him in violation of a state regulation that did not permit the holding of a state office by an individual who did not have residency in the state for at least the past three consecutive years. He quickly resigned his seat, much to the regret of his colleagues, and returned to Hagerstown, where he resumed his law practice until the outbreak of the war.

Either Col. W. H. S. Taylor never answered Freaner's letter concerning a position with the auditor's office or there were no such positions available, for Freaner never entered into service in that department. According to the records, he joined the 1st Virginia Cavalry in the fall of 1861 and received an appointment as first lieutenant and adjutant from Virginia on October 4, 1862, to date from August 8.[4] Prior to his commission he had acted as the regiment's adjutant under another Marylander, L. T. Brien. Freaner had met Stuart as early as September 1861, when he fled Maryland to fight for the Confederacy, but now his service under Brien brought him closer to cavalry headquarters and Stuart. Brien resigned his colonelcy in October 1862, the same month as Freaner's appointment, and for a time Freaner served as assistant adjutant to the brigade to which the 1st Virginia was attached.

A letter Freaner wrote to Stuart on January 28, 1863, shows that in addition to his adjutant's duties, he functioned as a judge advocate on a military court. After his return to the 1st Virginia, he resumed his duties as assistant adjutant general to Fitz Lee. Stuart's admiration for Freaner led to the following letter, which stated in part:

Hdq. Cav Div ANV
July 31st 1863

General:

I have the honor to recommend the following officers as Brigade Inspectors for my command viz:

George Freaner (now adj. 1st Va Cav) now of Fitz Lee Br.

Jono M. Lee (already appt)—W. H. F. Lee's Br.

Henry Bolling (Maryland) Fitz Lee's Br.

Joseph V. Nash (now adj 13th VA Cav) W. H. F. Lee's Br.

R. B. Kennon (1st Lt) PACS.

Walter Q. Hullihen (now Cadet CSA) PACS.

Chiswell Dabney (now 1st Lt ADC) PACS.

I desire to have the first name (George Freaner) appointed additional Division Inspector with the rank of Major as he is an officer of decided ability and merits and as my command is so extensive as to require another Inspector.

These selections have been made with a view to the peculiar ability and fitness of those recommended.[5]

The government responded so slowly to Stuart's request that it was not until November 20, 1863, that Freaner received his commission as major and orders to report to R. E. Lee for assignment to the cavalry corps. Freaner's association with Stuart mirrored R. B. Kennon's. Both officers entered into their duties at a time when little was transpiring, and therefore they did not have the opportunity to exhibit their talents during active campaigning. On May 14, 1864, during the reorganization of the cavalry following Stuart's death, Freaner was temporarily assigned to Fitz Lee's division, where he performed the role of assistant adjutant general. Then on August 11, he received orders that sent him to the staff of Gen. Wade Hampton. He remained with Hampton as both assistant adjutant general and assistant inspector general until January 19, 1865, when he again was temporarily attached to Fitz Lee's cavalry command.

Freaner's final posting was on March 27, 1865, as assistant adjutant general to Hampton. Hampton was in North Carolina while Freaner was in Virginia, however, and it would appear that the major never joined Johnston's army. According to the records, Freaner was paroled in Winchester, Virginia, on April 24, 1865. In all likelihood, when Lee surrendered at Appomattox, Freaner recognized the end of the conflict and was making his way home when he gave his parole in Winchester. His papers stated that he was thirty-four years old and five feet, eight inches tall, with a light complexion, dark hair, and blue eyes. Also recorded was the fact that his last duty was as inspector to Fitz Lee's cavalry division and that he had been stationed at Nine Mile Road.

Freaner returned to Hagerstown, where, his old law firm having been dissolved, he entered into partnership in 1866 with Andrew K. Syester, who later became attorney general of Maryland. In 1867 Freaner was appointed auditor of the courts for Washington County, a post he held until his death. On January 19, 1871, he married Mrs. Sallie A. Murray, daughter of George and Mary E. Fechtig, of Hagerstown. In 1874 he was elected to the Maryland House of Delegates on the Democratic ticket and quickly established an enviable record. On June 15, 1877, Freaner, along with Henry Kyd Douglas, welcomed Gen. Fitz Lee to Hagerstown for the ceremonies dedicating a part of Rose Hill Cemetery as a final resting place for Confederate dead exhumed from battlefields in the area. Freaner, treasurer of the cemetery association, delivered a historical sketch of the cemetery during the program.[6]

Freaner's death on November 10, 1878, was unexpected. Though he was not well, his condition had not been diagnosed as life threatening. He was buried in Rose Hill Cemetery, Hagerstown, Maryland. One of his pallbearers was Henry Kyd Douglas. Freaner left a wife and two daughters.

1st Lt. Theodore Stanford Garnett, Jr.

Clerk, courier, and aide-de-camp
January 27, 1864, to May 12, 1864

On May 30, 1907, before a crowd of thousands, an elderly, dignified gentleman arose to present a testimonial speech at the unveiling of an equestrian statue of General Stuart in Richmond, Virginia. "The," as Theodore Stanford Garnett, Jr., was known among his comrades on the staff, did not disappoint those in attendance, nor could he have.[1] His topic was dear to them all: the life of their beloved cavalry commander. The program committee had chosen well, for Garnett had ridden beside Stuart for a year and had been present with the general during the final scenes at Yellow Tavern and at Dr. Charles Brewer's home in Richmond. He had stood in hushed silence as the general's remains were lowered to their final resting place in Hollywood Cemetery. To his dying day, Garnett spoke with great difficulty about Stuart; the emotions he felt were always fresh, even after many years. Those feelings undoubtedly affected him on this day as he rendered his tribute.

Garnett was born on October 28, 1844, in Richmond, Virginia. He was named after his father, a civil engineer, and his mother was Florentina Isidora Moreno of Pensacola, Florida. Before Garnett was ten, the family moved to Hanover County, Virginia. During the summer of his tenth year, he had the experience of working with a bricklayer. (Subsequently, Garnett always felt that every boy should be exposed to a form of manual labor as he grew up.) That same year he entered Episcopal High School near Alexandria, Virginia. He was still enrolled there at the outbreak of the war.

Hurrying back to Hanover, the fifteen-year-old Garnett enlisted in a light artillery battery that became known as the Hanover Artillery. But when he arrived at Richmond with the battery, the enrolling officer refused to accept him, stating that he was too young. Even an interview with President Davis's military advisor, Gen. R. E. Lee, who knew the Garnett family, failed to get the youth and two equally young companions into the army. Instead Garnett ended up as a clerk in the Navy Department, a post that did not exactly coincide with how he had envisioned his role. For more than eighteen months he toiled in this capacity. But it turned out to be the skills he developed during this period that eventually led to a post with Stuart.

Garnett's "fast and flowing hand" made him the leading candidate to fill General Stuart's request for an individual to assume the position of clerk on his staff. Garnett joined Company "F," 9th Virginia Cavalry on May 15, 1863, and found himself immediately assigned to duty at Stuart's headquarters. He may actually have managed to join Stuart earlier: By one account he was present with Stuart at Chancellorsville. Lt. Frank S. Robertson remembered that he and Garnett slept between two graves on the night of May 3.[2] It is possible that Garnett joined Stuart earlier than the records indicate and was serving with cavalry headquarters while waiting for the paperwork to catch up with him.

Stuart may have wanted a clerk, but he soon discovered he had received much more. Garnett's eighteen months of relative inactivity in Richmond had made the young cavalryman eager to make up for what he felt was lost time. While he did indeed write with a beautiful hand, Garnett quickly demonstrated that he knew how to handle a saber and pistol as well. Soon he was one of Stuart's most trusted couriers, a post that gave Garnett all the action and adventure he could have desired.

Some of that adventure occurred during the Gettysburg Campaign. Robertson and Garnett, tentmates when the cavalry was in camp, experienced what ultimately happened to nearly all cavalrymen: the breakdown of their horses. The two went horse hunting near Carlisle, Pennsylvania, without benefit of escort. It was just the sort of expedition that had laid low many a *beau sabreur*. But the two emerged unscathed and with two new horses. Neither had any misgivings about their deed, which the farmers of the region would have labeled horse stealing. They had left their own horses in exchange, and in Robertson's case the Yankee farmer got the better of the deal.[3]

If a cavalryman did not find adventure, it sometimes found him. A close call could occur at any moment, usually when he least expected it. Garnett had many such encounters during his service with Stuart. He recorded an incident that occurred in late November 1863.

> On Sunday morning, November 29th, bright and early, Gen'l Stuart rode with his staff and escort over to the extreme right of our lines, then well established along the west side of the valley through which Mine Run flows, and after sending orders to Gen'l Hampton to bring his division down the Catharpin Road, set out in that direction himself. I well remember the impatience with which he waited to learn that the command was on the way to join him, and how he sent courier after courier to hurry them up. The road was in bad order, muddy and slippery, and the horses traveled with difficulty. What on earth was up? Where were we going? No man but Stuart knew.
>
> After marching probably 6 or 8 miles, we left the Catharpin Road and struck off through some farms and woodland in the direction of the old railroad which was once intended to run from Fredericksburg to Orange Court House or Gordonsville. As we approached the line of the railroad, traveling a swampy difficult road through a thick body of woods, the sharp report of a pistol just in front rang out on the morning air followed by the crack of a carbine and the whistle of a ball over our heads, causing us to straighten up in our saddles and unbuckle our holsters, for every man felt that we were in the presence of the enemy. In a few seconds, [M. B.] Chewning, the scout . . . , came galloping back and informed the General that he had fired at a picket standing on the railroad bank, who had returned his salute and then retreated.
>
> Gen'l Stuart reproved him sharply for firing his pistol and rebuked him for not taking the man off his post

without making such a row. But Chewning replied that he didn't feel exactly authorized to be so rude, in view of the fact that there were three or four other Yankees with the first named gentleman, for he saw them all ride back together. Here we were then, nothing but the staff and escort of couriers, some 20 men in all, close upon the enemy's outposts. No time must be wasted or the whole effect of the surprise would be lost. What we were to do must be done quickly. So without a minutes hesitation, Gen'l Stuart turned to his staff and couriers and told us to *Charge.*

"Here we go boys! The General's leading us. There's no getting out of this matter,"—and away we went! Reaching the railroad embankment, we found it clear, but in the field beyond we could see the backs of the retreating pickets. Over we go, and raising a savage yell, our little column dashed gallantly across the field. Thunder and Mars! What is that I see standing in the Plank Road at Parker's Store? *Cavalry,* by the Powers! Yankee Cavalry,—in some confusion, it is true, but still enough to eat us all up at one mouthful!

Bang! Bang!—the smoke rises all around them, and Whiz! Thud! there goes Archie's (my messmate's) horse down on his nose, and his rider playing leap-frog over his head. Zip!—a ball hits the pommel of my saddle, and I rein my horse in, somewhat doubtful of the success of this little affair.

Some half a dozen of us halt about 75 yards from the Plank Road, and blaze away into the thick crowd of men and horses standing there, bringing down only two or three, that I could see, hardly enough to pay for our powder and ball. Whereas it seemed to me almost impossible to shoot into such a crowd without hitting something, and yet I ask any unprejudiced person or persons if it isn't a very difficult matter to hit the side of a barn if you are in momentary apprehension that the aforesaid barn is going to return the compliment.

[Nelson W.] Toler has gotten off a little to one side, on their flank, and is putting in some good shots. Channing Smith is firing right straight ahead and attracting their attention almost exclusively, for which I thank him with my whole heart, though I do feel really alarmed for him, and hope he won't be hit. George Woodbridge is busy too. I join Toler in the bushes on the left and after firing the only remaining load in my pistol, begin to think of leaving.

Just then they break, and we advance to the road. In the bushes beyond is the camp of two regiments of Pennsylvania Cavalry, deserted and now in the hands of a *half dozen* of Stuart's *couriers*. Is it possible, I thought to myself, as I rode up to untie a splendid horse from the tree where his owner had left him, is it possible that those fellows are going to give up their camp without any more fighting than this?

Before I could reach the horse, however, my question was fully answered. The clatter of horses' feet on the other side of the camp was heard, and in another second I saw them returning to the charge. I had scarcely time to turn my horse into the road and give him the spur, before they were back in the camp, and but for the intervention of a few friendly bushes, I would have been a prisoner.

We retreated across the field back to the railroad bank; the time occupied in this little scrimmage could not have been more than 5 minutes in reality. It seemed to me, however, at least a half hour.[4]

The impression Garnett made upon Stuart in this and similar encounters with the enemy rapidly brought reward. A recommendation for a lieutenancy in the cavalry in February 1864 was followed by Garnett's commission as a first lieutenant and aide-de-camp on March 11, 1864. Stuart informed Garnett of his recommendation for promotion in typical Stuart fashion.

I had retired for the night, or in soldier's phrase, "turned in" to my bunk in Maj. McClellan's tent and was peacefully dreaming, when I felt a heavy hand on my shoulder and turning over recognized Major Venable, who had waked me, saying "get up, General Stuart wants to see you in his tent." It didn't take me more than a minute to complete my toilet, which consisted of pulling on a heavy pair of cavalry boots and slipping on my jacket, and rubbing my drowsy eyes, I groped my way to the General's tent. Knocking at the door I was told to "Come in," and entered finding the General stretched out on his couch

with Venable sitting near him. I wondered what was coming, and thought some trick or joke was about to be played
on me by my laughter-loving chief; for I had fancied I
could detect a suppressed smile on Maj. Venable's countenance. Pointing to his open desk, on which the General's
private letter book was lying, with pens, ink, and paper, he
very quietly said, "Sit down there, Garnett, and copy that
letter for me." I did as I was told, and taking up a pen, not
even yet fully awake, commenced to write, as follows:

> "HdQrs Cavalry Corps
> Army of No'n Va
> January 27, 1864

Gen. S. Cooper, A&I Genl.
    Richmond.
      General,
       I have the honor to recommend Private Theodore
S. Garnett, Jr., of Co. "F" 9th Va Cav, for appointment
as 1st Lieut. and Aide-de-Camp, to be assigned to duty on
my Staff, vice Lieut. Chiswell Dabney promoted."

Before finishing that sentence, I rose from my seat,
blushing like a girl, and stammered out my thanks to
General Stuart, grasping his strong hand in both of mine
and pledging him my life-long gratitude and service. He
burst into the heartiest laughter and seemed to enjoy
hugely my utter surprise and confusion. Major Venable,
joining in with his powerful lungs, and thus making it
"worse confounded." I finished the letter to Gen. Cooper
and after a short conversation with the Genl went back to
my blankets, but not to sleep, for my heart was thumping
away and every pulse throbbing with pleasure and pride,
at this the first mark of that great soldier's esteem for me,
a pleasure and pride which I can never again experience,
and for which I would not exchange now any memory
of my life.

The next morning, the 28th of January, I was invited to
breakfast with General Stuart, and received the congratu-
lations of my brethren of the Staff.[5]

Shortly thereafter, the cavalry began to prepare for the spring campaign
season. Since his aide-de-camp duties would not have been too different

from what he had been doing previously, Garnett probably settled into his new position without the adjustment problems some new staff officers experienced. Sadly, he did not have long to enjoy his new post.

The Battle of Yellow Tavern brought Stuart his mortal wound. Garnett was one of the staff who assisted in transporting the general to Richmond. He left Stuart's ambulance at Mechanicsville to ride ahead and see that a bed was prepared at Dr. Brewer's home. He also carried a message to Gen. Braxton Bragg informing that officer of the fighting around Yellow Tavern and the wounding of Stuart. Garnett was stunned by Bragg's unemotional reaction to the news. Bragg appeared indifferent and "expressed no sympathy, either by word or in manner, and he indicated no interest in me or my message."[6]

Having completed his mission to Bragg, Garnett returned to Dr. Brewer's. Here, according to his own account, he felt Stuart's pulse until the general was aroused by a commotion in the street. Stuart sent Garnett to investigate. The lieutenant quickly discovered that yet another price had been extracted for the defense of Richmond. Gen. James B. Gordon, one of Stuart's brigadiers, had been mortally wounded near Meadow Bridge and was on his final journey through the city. He would die on May 18.

When Garnett returned to Stuart, he did not tell him of Gordon's wounding. The general spoke with a few others who had gathered at the house and saw to the distribution of his few personal belongings and his horses. At approximately 7:38 P.M. on May 12, 1864, Stuart died. Garnett took the loss of his chief very hard, but the war continued, and he still had duties to perform. One of those was attending Stuart's funeral, after which Garnett discovered that his commission had elapsed with his general's death. Shortly thereafter, on June 1, 1864, he was recommissioned at his old rank and posted as aide to Gen. W. H. F. Lee. On March 15, 1865, after having served in this capacity for almost nine months, Garnett received a commission as captain and was assigned as assistant adjutant general to Gen. William P. Roberts. He held this position until the army's surrender at Appomattox.[7]

The war had interrupted Garnett's education, which became his primary concern once he overcame his shock at the Confederacy's fall. He entered the University of Virginia in the fall of 1865 and graduated with a law degree in 1866. Initially settling in Warrenton, Virginia, Garnett taught classes in a private school until he could establish himself as a lawyer. The competition proved intense, and not being able to accumulate sufficient clientele, he left Warrenton in 1869 and moved first to Norfolk and then to nearby Suffolk. Garnett was elected to a county judgeship in 1870. He voluntarily resigned in 1873 to return to Norfolk. There he formed a law partnership with William H. White, which was to last until Garnett's death.

Active in the Confederate veteran organizations, Garnett became commander of the 1st Brigade of the Virginia Division in 1900. He succeeded to the command of the division in 1906, and by 1912 he was promoted to command the Department of Virginia, with the rank of lieutenant general. His speech at the unveiling of Stuart's statue was expanded into a monograph and published in 1907. It remains as an excellent source of information on Stuart.

In the later years of his life, he received many honors. His years were cut short by an occurrence that today would be considered most rare. Garnett was having trouble with one of his teeth and visited a dentist during the latter days of February 1915. It was necessary to extract a tooth, and blood poisoning developed.[8] He died at his home at 11:00 A.M. on April 27, 1915, at the age of seventy-one. He had been married twice, first to Emily Eyre Baker of Norfolk, and then to Mrs. Louise Bowdoin of Northampton County, Virginia. His second wife survived him, along with a daughter and a son. He was buried in Elmwood Cemetery in Norfolk. His tombstone reads:

Sacred to the Memory of
Theodore Stanford Garnett
Born October 28 1844
Died April 27 1915

What doth the Lord require of thee
but to do justly, to love mercy, and
to walk humbly with thy God?
Micah-VI-8

A separate marker contains these words:

Confederate
States of
America
T. S. Garnett
Aide Gen. J. E. B. Stuart

Capt. Harry W. Gilmor

Voluntary aide-de-camp
March 1863

Harry Gilmor's career with Stuart was one of the shortest of any staff officer. He had just been exchanged after having spent five months in Fort McHenry as a prisoner of war and in actuality was killing time while waiting for a new opportunity to present itself.[1] Gilmor, an independent operator in the mold of "Hanse" and Jesse McNeill and John Mosby, could boast of various successes that illustrated his value as a partisan. His stay with Stuart was only temporary until he could obtain the authority to raise a new company and return to what he did best.

Born in Baltimore, Maryland, on January 24, 1838, Gilmor was a descendant of Robert Gilmor, who emigrated from Scotland to settle in Oxford, Maryland, in 1769.[2] Robert's son William became a banker in Baltimore and was the father of Harry and his brother, Robert III, who served for several years as an attaché at the American Embassy in Paris. Harry was given a private education at the family estate, "Glen Ellen," where he also dabbled in farming. His adventuresome spirit led him west, where his attempts at homesteading failed. He returned to Maryland, joined the state militia, and became involved in the argument over secession.

When Federal troops occupied Baltimore, Gilmor fell under suspicion of being a spy. His arrest followed, and he spent approximately two weeks in prison in August 1861. He instantly headed for Virginia, where on August 31 he enlisted in Turner Ashby's cavalry, becoming a private in Company "G," 7th Virginia Cavalry. Within a few weeks, his usefulness and intrepidity had earned him a promotion to sergeant major courtesy of Ashby himself.[3]

Gilmor proceeded to prove that what he had accomplished thus far had not been a flash in the pan. His exploits and bravery brought him a captain's commission on March 27, 1862. He raised a company of Marylanders for service in the 12th Virginia Cavalry. Designated Company "F," Gilmor's command operated almost entirely independently of the 12th. Unfortunately, little is known of the men who served in the company. Either Gilmor kept few records or they were lost.

After "Stonewall" Jackson's victory at McDowell, the Valley Army advanced to Winchester and beyond. Jackson sent Gilmor to keep an eye on Gen. John C. Frémont, who was on the other side of the Shenandoah

Mountains. When Frémont moved in an attempt to close off Jackson's line of retreat up the Valley, it was Gilmor who brought "Stonewall" the news of the Union advance, enabling the Confederate commander to withdraw and eventually whip Frémont at the Battle of Port Republic.[4]

Skill and dash coupled with good fortune helped Gilmor forge a reputation as a bold partisan chieftain. Then, just when he had everything going his way, he committed a blunder of immense proportions. During the Army of Northern Virginia's invasion of Maryland in September 1862, Gilmor broke away from the main column to visit some friends who lived seven miles from Baltimore. Not surprisingly, he was captured. He was imprisoned until February 1863,[5] after which time he became attached to Stuart's staff as a volunteer aide.

The intrepid captain's tenure on the staff might have passed virtually unnoticed except for the part he played at the Battle of Kelly's Ford on March 17, 1863. Just how he came to be with Stuart is unknown, but he was with the general at Culpeper, where Stuart was testifying in a court-martial. When the Federals attacked on the seventeenth, Stuart, Gilmor, and Maj. John Pelham left Culpeper and rode together toward the sounds of battle. Gilmor and Pelham stayed together or at least met again during the fight, but they became separated from Stuart. According to Gilmor, the two were sitting on their horses near the 2nd Virginia Cavalry, which came under fire from a Federal battery. Pelham was struck by a shell fragment and fell from his horse, which galloped off. Noticing the artillery major's still form on the ground, Gilmor dismounted and with some assistance draped Pelham over his own horse and hurried away. Gilmor turned Pelham over to two cavalrymen, ordering them to place the wounded officer in an ambulance and transport him to Culpeper. He then returned to the battlefield to inform Stuart of what had happened to Pelham.

Gilmor's adventure did not end with his reporting to Stuart. Later he overtook the two cavalrymen, who, thinking Pelham was already dead, had proceeded at a leisurely pace toward Culpeper. Discovering that the major was still alive, an enraged Gilmor commandeered an ambulance and had Pelham taken to the Shackelford home, where he subsequently died. There have been numerous versions of Pelham's death, but Gilmor was one of the few eyewitnesses. Though problems with his account do exist, it cannot be denied that he was present and that it was his horse that brought Pelham off the field. His stay with Stuart may have been brief, but Gilmor always seemed to manage to get in the middle of things. The Battle of Kelly's Ford and the death of the gallant Pelham were no exceptions.[6]

Gilmor's sojourn with Stuart ended soon after Kelly's Ford. Traveling to the Confederacy's capital, Captain Gilmor became Major Gilmor on

May 27, 1863, and obtained permission to raise a battalion of cavalry, which would become known as the 2nd Maryland Cavalry.[7] By June, his credentials secured, Gilmor rode north to join the columns of Gen. Richard S. Ewell's newly constituted 2nd Corps as they wound their way through the Shenandoah Valley en route for Maryland and Pennsylvania. When in mid-July Lee's army crossed the Potomac back into Virginia, Gilmor went back to his role as partisan, riding among the hills and valleys that made up the no-man's-land between the two great armies.

In January 1864 Gen. Jubal Early attempted to alleviate the paucity of food in the Confederate Army by conducting a raid into West Virginia. While the incursion did not succeed as Lee had hoped it would, Gilmor did collect significant quantities of food and military supplies. Late in the month Early was ordered to make a second foraging expedition, and again Gilmor and his command went along for the ride. Once more luck was with the dashing partisan. Gilmor was fired on during a skirmish with the enemy, but his life was saved by a deck of cards. They were all penetrated by a musket ball save one—the ace of spades. The close call did little to discourage the major from further escapades.[8]

Stuart gave Gilmor his next assignment: the cutting of the B&O Railroad in order to keep Union troop reinforcements from reaching the Army of the Potomac. Selecting a site about eight miles from Martinsburg, the partisan chieftain halted one train and might have done more damage had he not been interrupted by another containing Federal infantry, which caused the Confederates to retreat hastily. The raid almost brought Gilmor's career in the army to an end. As an officer, Gilmor was responsible for the conduct of his men. The accusation that they robbed defenseless passengers and threatened to kill them put Gilmor in an awkward position. The outraged Yankee citizenry, backed by the Northern press, pressured the Confederate high command into bringing charges against Gilmor. He was tried before a court-martial convened in Staunton. The accused denied knowing of the robberies, and the court, made up of officers from the 7th Virginia Cavalry, acquitted Gilmor after one week.[9]

The invasion of the Valley by forces under the command of Union general Franz Sigel gave Gilmor an opportunity to get back in the saddle. Gilmor and his men helped make life miserable for Sigel's cavalry, and Sigel was defeated at the Battle of New Market on May 15. In actuality, Gilmor should have been elsewhere. On May 5 he had received an order stating that he and his band of Partisan Rangers were to be mustered into the Confederate service as cavalry. Gilmor was to report with his men to Camp Maryland at Staunton, Virginia, and present himself to Maj. Gen.

Arnold Elzey, who was to command the Maryland Line. Ignoring the order, Gilmor chose to remain with Breckinridge and face Sigel. That nothing came of his insubordination can probably be attributed to the fact that the Maryland Line did not become a reality at that time.[10]

During Gen. Jubal Early's advance on Washington, D.C., in June–July 1864, Gilmor rode ahead of the Confederate infantry. He disrupted communications and raided near Baltimore with the idea of destroying the Gunpowder Bridge on the Philadelphia, Wilmington, and Baltimore Railroad. He accomplished his mission and succeeded in rejoining the Confederate forces at Poolesville after a narrow escape. He had fallen asleep in the saddle and had become separated from his men. He then was challenged by a Federal sentry but managed to convince the man he was a Unionist, after which he slipped quietly into the night to find his column.[11]

Gilmor participated in Gen. John McCausland's retaliation raid on Chambersburg, Pennsylvania, in late July. In command of the advance guard, two Maryland battalions of about two hundred men all told, he successfully attacked a Union force near Clear Spring, Maryland, on July 29. In Chambersburg, a chivalrous Gilmor spared the home of Federal colonel William H. Boyd, telling the colonel's wife that since her husband was a gallant soldier who only made war on armed men and not on helpless civilians, he would do likewise. This was the same Boyd who had forced Mosby, the Confederacy's "Gray Ghost," to seek refuge on a tree limb in his nightshirt.[12] If he knew of the incident, Gilmor chose not to avenge the embarrassment. The equally chivalrous Mosby would have passed up the opportunity as well, not being in favor of making war against women.

Returning to Virginia, Gilmor became attached to the cavalry of Maj. Gen. Lunsford Lomax. On September 3, while commanding his own battalion and the 18th Virginia Cavalry, Gilmor was wounded in the shoulder during an engagement with Federal cavalry around Darkesville. He spent what he called one of the happiest times of his life recuperating at the Winchester home of a widowed friend, Mrs. O'Bannon. On the nineteenth, his idyllic reverie ended in the midst of the Battle of Winchester. Forced to flee, Gilmor had to find first his clothes and then a means of escape. One of Mrs. O'Bannon's nieces solved the first problem by bringing him his pants, but the partially clad partisan had no horse on which to make his getaway. One of Gilmor's men saw him standing on the porch and, dismounting, assisted his commander into the saddle. Gilmor galloped off down the road and disappeared among the fugitives of Early's army.[13]

Not until October did Gilmor return to duty. During the winter he spent some time in South Carolina, returning to find that he had been appointed by Early to the command of all the Rangers in the area encompassing the commands of Jesse McNeill and Blake Woodsen. Arriving at Moorefield, Gilmor waited for fair weather to resume operations. His task would not be easy, as neither McNeill nor Woodsen was inclined to cooperate. Then on February 4, 1865, the Federals entered the town and captured Gilmor. Under special orders from Phil Sheridan, Maj. Harry Young caught the partisan chieftain with his guard down, and Gilmor was imprisoned for the remainder of the war.[14]

He was not freed until July 24, 1865, at which time he returned to Maryland and took up residence in Baltimore. He married Mentoria Strong, and the couple had three children, Alice, Harry, and Elsie. Gilmor held various positions in postwar Baltimore. In 1871 he was a clerk and in 1873 the state weigher. He was elected police commissioner in 1874 and served until 1879, after which he entered into the insurance business.

The onset of the disease that would eventually take his life occurred in 1881. Sharp pains below his left eye forced him to seek medical attention from his sister's husband, Dr. G. Halsted Boyland. Gilmor received treatment for what was diagnosed as neuralgia and improved somewhat. In September 1882, however, the pain increased and soon was accompanied by paralysis. Gilmor died on March 4, 1883. An autopsy performed at his own prior request revealed a tumor that had grown toward the back of his head.[15] The pressure on the spinal column had caused the paralysis. Gilmor was buried in Loudon Park Cemetery. An impressive obelisk marks his final resting place. Its four sides are engraved as follows, beginning with the front and proceeding around the monument counterclockwise.

In
Memory of
Harry Gilmor
Lt. Col. 2nd Maryland Cavalry
Army of Northern Virginia
C.S.A.
GILMOR

Mentoria N. Strong
Beloved Wife of
Harry Gilmor
Born
February 6, 1845
Died
December 13, 1879
"Death is swallowed up in
Victory."

OUR GALLANT HARRY

Dauntless in Battle
Splendid in Success
Constant in Defeat

This dashing Cavalry Chief
Outrode the Storm of War
And in the Noontide of Life
Entered the Valley of Death
Where he was Conqueror

Life's Battle ended he sleeps well
Beside the wife
Who on Earth as in Heaven
Heralding the better life
Was a helpmate worthy of a hero

HARRY GILMOR
Born
January 24, 1838
Died
March 4, 1883

Distinguished in Eighteen
Hundred and seventy-seven as
POLICE COMMISSIONER
In the service of his native
State and City

Lt. Robert Henry Goldsborough

Aide-de-camp
May 16, 1863, to June 9, 1863

Some men are lucky in war. They somehow manage to emerge unscathed from the midst of the hottest fire, and they pass through the most severe trials and hardships seemingly unaffected. Others, like Robert H. Goldsborough, are not so fortunate. His courage was never doubted, his ability never questioned. Young, handsome, talented, Goldsborough could have epitomized the Southern cavalier at his finest—until his luck went from good to bad to catastrophic in less than two years.

Born near Easton, Maryland, on January 15, 1841, Goldsborough came from a distinguished family. His father, a farmer, was William Goldsborough of "Myrtle Grove," and his mother was Mary Tilghman Goldsborough, daughter of Gov. Charles Goldsborough of Maryland. As with a large number of Stuart's staff, there is a lack of information about his early life.[1] According to his military files, his initial involvement in the war did not occur until late in 1862, when he joined Capt. William H. Chapman's Company of Virginia Light Artillery eight days before it was cut to pieces at Sharpsburg. Special Orders No. 209 of October 4, 1862, disbanded Chapman's Company and assigned the men and horses to Capt. William J. Pegram's Battery.[2] Goldsborough chose not to remain in the artillery and instead traveled to Richmond, where on October 29, 1862, he enlisted in what became Company "B" of the 39th Battalion of Virginia Cavalry.[3] This company was also known as Capt. William F. Randolph's company, and its men were especially organized to serve as scouts, guides, and couriers. Before the company's incorporation into the 39th Battalion on March 9, 1863, it served as escort or bodyguard to Gen. Richard S. Ewell.[4]

Goldsborough was discharged from Randolph's company on May 2, 1863, to serve with Stuart. He was officially appointed to Stuart's staff on May 16, but the process to bring him to cavalry headquarters actually had begun much earlier when Stuart wrote to Gen. Samuel Cooper, adjutant and inspector general of the Confederate Army.[5]

> Hd. Qrs. Cav. Div. A of N Va
> April 6th 1863
>
> General:
>
> I have the honor to request that Robert H. Goldsborough of Randolph's Cavalry be commissioned as 1st Lt. and A.D.C. on my staff vice R. Channing Price promoted Major A.A.G.
>
> I beg leave to state that I make this recommendation with the full conviction of his merit and ability and desire his commission to bear the date April 1st 1863.
>
> Most Respectfully,
> Your obt svt
> J. E. B. Stuart
> Major Gen'l
> Comdg
>
> Gen S. Cooper
> A & I Gen'l C.S.A.
> Richmond, Va.[6]

Channing Price, whom Goldsborough would be replacing, was not unaware of Stuart's nominee for his old post. In a letter to his mother on March 30, Price mentioned Goldsborough as Stuart's choice for the aide-de-camp position he had recently vacated.

> He [Stuart] has offered the position of aide-de-camp to a young man named Goldsborough from Maryland, a private in a Cavalry Company serving as Gen. Early's [*sic*] escort: he [Stuart] has not heard from him, as the Company has gone back into the interior to recruit the horses. Goldsborough is the son of a great friend of the General's in Maryland & is I think a fine young man, from what I have seen of him. He will no doubt accept the offer, as it is a place not to be scorned,—A.D.C. to the Chief of Cavalry.[7]

Indeed, Goldsborough did not scorn Stuart's offer. Lamentably, though, his affiliation with the staff was to be brief. The appointment was the zenith of his military career. Fortune soon turned its back on the young Marylander: His first engagement in his new post was to be his last. The Battle of Brandy Station began Goldsborough's run of bad luck, which would end at Sayler's Creek.

When the battle erupted in the early morning hours of June 9, 1863, everyone at cavalry headquarters scrambled to prepare for the fighting ahead. Stuart dispatched riders in all directions to find out just what he was facing. In a very short time he knew he was to be challenged that day as he had never been before. Among those officers sent on missions to various parts of the field was Goldsborough. It is known that Lt. Frank Robertson carried several orders that day from one end of the field to the other, and chances are that Goldsborough was kept quite busy as well.

Ultimately Stuart became concerned about his right flank. Though he had directed Brig. Gen. Beverly H. Robertson to secure Kelly's Ford, he remained troubled about a possible threat from that quarter. He decided to take further precautions and sent Goldsborough with an order to Col. William C. Wickham of the 4th Virginia.[8] The youthful aide galloped off, knowing the graveness of the situation that confronted the Confederate cavalry and remembering that every second counted. In Blackford's account of what transpired, Goldsborough rode headlong into a Yankee column and was captured. The engineer attributed the lieutenant's capture to his inexperience, lack of caution, and the fact that dust may have covered the dark blue Union cavalry uniforms, leading Goldsborough to believe the soldiers were Confederates.[9]

All of the reasons Blackford gave for Goldsborough's capture make sense in light of the Marylander's career up to Brandy Station. The swirling fighting that raged from St. James Church to Stevensburg was in all probability beyond anything he had experienced in the 39th Virginia. Though as an escort trooper and courier for General Ewell, Goldsborough may have carried orders prior to Brandy, the conditions would have been greatly different. Carrying dispatches for Ewell could not have been overly dangerous, since the general was incapacitated with an amputated leg from late August 1862 to May 23, 1863, during which time Goldsborough was serving with the 39th. Most certainly Goldsborough's inexperience, coupled with the excitement of being in such a battle, led to his error of riding into the Federal column. The good luck he had in gaining the appointment quickly changed to terrible misfortune.

For the next twenty months, Goldsborough was shunted from prison to prison. At first he was incarcerated in Old Capitol Prison, the same facility in which Major FitzHugh had been held. On August 8 he was transferred to Johnson's Island, where he remained until February 20, 1865. Then he was moved to Point Lookout, which proved to be his final stop.[10] Soon after his arrival, he was exchanged, probably because his physical condition had deteriorated.

While Goldsborough remained in prison, Stuart, the cavalry, and the rest of the army passed through the Gettysburg Campaign. During the lull following the invasion of the North, Stuart attempted to secure his aide's release. On August 5, 1863, Stuart proposed an exchange of aides-de-camp—Goldsborough for one of Brig. Gen. John Buford's aides, who had been captured during the campaign.[11] Nothing came of the proposal, however.

When he finally was exchanged in March 1865, Goldsborough found that his lieutenant's commission, which he had enjoyed for about a month, had elapsed due to Stuart's death. After he regained his health, he accepted a new position as aide-de-camp to Maj. Gen. G. W. Custis Lee. Goldsborough assumed his new duties at the beginning of April 1865 and quickly became part of the mass retreat from Petersburg and Richmond. Moving west with Custis Lee's force of Richmond clerks, mechanics, and other government personnel, Goldsborough entered the bottomlands surrounding Sayler's Creek on April 6. He rode among the remnant of "Stonewall" Jackson's proud 2nd Corps, to which Custis Lee's force had been attached, now commanded by Gen. Richard S. Ewell.

When a gap appeared in the Confederate column, the pursuing Union Army seized the moment and struck. The ensuing Battle of Sayler's Creek ended with the surrender of Ewell and most of his corps. During the 2nd

Corps's desperate attempt to free themselves from the trap, Goldsborough was struck by a shell fragment and mortally wounded. He died shortly thereafter. He had returned to the army just in time to perish in its final campaign, and as might be expected, he was the last member of Stuart's staff to be killed in the war. His family recovered his body, and he rests in the family cemetery at "Ashby" in Talbot County, Maryland.

Capt. Charles Grattan

Ordnance officer
October 27, 1863, to May 12, 1864

The Grattan family of Rockingham County, Virginia, was like many other Southern families who sacrificed so much for the Confederacy during its brief period of existence. Four sons of Maj. Robert Grattan and his wife Martha Divers Grattan (née Minor) joined the Army of Northern Virginia. Two, Robert Ridgeway Grattan, a lieutenant in the cavalry, and Peter Minor Grattan, also in the cavalry, perished during the conflict. Robert succumbed to typhoid fever on December 27, 1862, and Peter died of wounds received at the Battle of Yellow Tavern. Peter is buried at Beaver Dam Station on the plantation owned by Edmund Fontaine, father of Stuart's medical director, John B. Fontaine. A third son, George Gilmer Grattan, suffered the loss of a leg, the result of a wound he received at 2nd Cold Harbor.[1] The eldest son, Charles, somehow managed to emerge from the war unscathed, though he often had faced the enemy in battle and once had had his horse killed beneath him.

Charles Grattan was born at "Ridgeway," his mother's former home in Albemarle County, Virginia, on December 8, 1833.[2] He was reared at the Grattan family's home, "Contentment," near Mount Crawford in Rockingham County, Virginia. Grattan was of Scottish lineage. His ancestors had immigrated to Ireland to escape "Bloody Mary," and one of them, John Grattan, later came to America and settled in Pennsylvania.[3] The Grattans eventually moved to the Valley of Virginia, where Charles's father was born, studied law, and turned farmer when he inherited the family estate. Charles also decided to pursue a law career and entered the University of Virginia in 1853. His education was interrupted from time to time for reasons that are not entirely clear, though the death of his father in 1855 probably caused him to miss that year. In 1859 he was elected to the state legislature from Rockingham County. He was reelected for a second term in 1861 but was attending law lectures at the University of Virginia when the war began.

At that time, Grattan received word from Maj. John A. Harman, later to be "Stonewall" Jackson's quartermaster, that a plan was being formulated to march down the Shenandoah Valley and seize Harpers Ferry. In a short memoir he wrote in 1896, Grattan reveals some of his feelings and activities, including how he managed to get involved with the expedition.

> Major Harman was Genl. Harper's [Maj. Gen. Kenton Harper commanded the Virginia militia that would attempt to capture Harpers Ferry] Q.M. and thought he was Quarter Master General of the State of Va. and I who was his assistant thought the same, we did not think there was any other army in the world
>
> On our way down [the Valley], Major Harman informed me that he was to occupy the position of Q.M. on the General's Staff and asked me to assist him. I being willing to do anything to aid the cause, readily consented, thinking in my extremely fresh condition, that the only duty of a Q.M. was to find a place to camp and sleep the troops. I did not apprehend much trouble, or that my attention would be very seriously directed from the prominent object, that of killing Yankees. I was mistaken in this as in many other notions I entertained about war and things pertaining thereto.
>
> We did not have a single copy of Army regulations in our office and if an officer had come to me with a regulation I should have thought he was putting on airs and wanted taking down.
>
> One thing the Major had though, that was indomitable energy, and push, with a very good share of good sense, and this energy he infused into all the boys in his office. He bought everything he could lay his hands on and turned it over to the needy commands daily arriving, depending upon his office force to keep him straight, we trying by a sort of military double entry to do so. How lamentably we failed, I suppose only the collapse of the cause prevented being seen and known. The Major did not confine himself to Q.M. supplies, but bought and issued commissaries as well, made and fitted up caissons and did anything that no one else did and that meant pretty much all. In fact

we did not know where the line was that divided the different fields and had no guide but our own crude ideas of the varied wants of the troops daily coming in with nothing.

It goes without saying that we were worked day and night, but that did not matter so long as we were permitted to hope, we would soon be allowed to try our hand on the Yankees as we called them and every one of the asst. Q.M. clerks like old settlers in the Indian days, worked day and night with his musket within reach and on one or two occasions we were summoned to arms by false summons of the approach of an enemy. I think it was the universal dread that the war would close before we had a chance to drive the Yankees from the sacred soil.[4]

Grattan continued in this capacity until word came from Richmond in the spring of 1861 that a new commander would soon arrive. Col. Thomas J. "Stonewall" Jackson supplanted Harper and, in observing what had transpired during the latter's tenure, came to the conclusion that Major Harman had accomplished much as quartermaster. While the generals of militia and their staffs packed for home or their next assignment, Jackson approached Harman and asked him to stay on as his quartermaster. Harman, in turn, inquired of Grattan whether he would be willing to continue as assistant quartermaster. Grattan assented but had some misgivings. In his reminiscences he explained what he did to clear them from his conscience.

By this time it had begun to dawn upon me that in a sure enough war a Q.M. was rather a non combatant and as I had seen no fight as yet and was spoiling for one I said as much to the Major [Harman], telling him I did not object to the work, though it had been very hard up to that time, but that unless I could have the opportunity afforded me of cutting off some Yankee heads, that all would go for nothing. He proposed we should interview the Col. The absurdity of the thing makes me smile after the lapse of 35 years, I, who had never smelled powder other than in a bird gun, demanding from the future Stonewall, who had distinguished himself in Mexico, the privilege of cutting off heads as the price of my work in the Q.M. department. Nevertheless we went. . . .

After requesting us to take seats, Maj. Harman in a few words stated the case. The Col. gave us a calm and earnest survey as though to see if we were in earnest in our absurdity and then lapsing into one of his kindly smiles, he said in his sharp, quick, nervous style, "The first duty of a Q.M. is to look after his train, but I suppose an opportunity may be afforded." This was all that was to be expected and the interview, the first of many with this great and good soldier closed.[5]

Grattan, in continuing as Harman's assistant, was able to witness the manner in which Jackson transformed his new command into a fighting force. Jackson's methods were seldom greeted with enthusiasm, but as the drilling continued, the militiamen became soldiers and their officers learned their duties or suffered the consequences. Grattan recalled that ". . . cocked hats, long sashes, jingling spurs, rattling sabres, glittering epaulettes and whole companies of aides, couriers, and etc. like the Arab had quietly folded their tents and slipped away. . . ."[6] The change had been necessary, and Jackson's iron will made it happen. That iron will was accompanied by a personality some viewed as grim and others as downright foreboding. The newly organized staff did not as yet understand their sober leader, and having to dine with him was an experience dreaded by all. Grattan finally had had enough of silent meals and determined to alter the situation by testing Jackson's humor.

The Col. and his staff, including his blood thirsty Q.M. and his assistant, messed together. We took our meals in one of the government buildings on the hill, vacated by the late commandant or one of his subordinates. We of the Q.M. department were kept employed from daylight until late at night . . . but we did not grumble, we imagined we were performing a patriotic duty and our names would linger on the tongues of after ages. The only moments of relaxation we enjoyed were those we spent at meal time, but here we were met by the grave, solemn countenance of our Commanding Colonel: all were afraid of him . . . and we ate as silent as mutes, ever and anon casting a stealthy eye upon the Col. to see if he ate like other men, or bolted raw meat and gnawed bloody bones. What was to be done? The Surgeon, the Adjutant, the Aid and all the others sat like oysters, they ate but spoke not. Who was to bell the cat? I the youngest . . . declared my intention of getting off a joke at this *festal board*. My messmates held up their hands in holy horror and advised me against any such rashness: told me my doom would be the guard house at the least, and declared they would under no circumstances be considered participants in such reckless folly.

How be it my mind was made up, blessed is he whose situation is so poor it can't be worse . . . and so one day at dinner during the awful silence, unbroken but by the subdued rattle of the knives and crockery, I got off as a feeler a very diluted and mild joke. Not one of all that crowd of guzzlers even looked up or noticed I had said a word, but cut a glance at Col. Jackson out of the corners of their eyes to see what he would do. I suppose it was sometime since the Col. had had a joke poked at him, for he evidently did not seem to know exactly what to do, had a half startled appearance, then subsided into a smile, then all those long faced Jeremiahs laughed, the ice was broken, we were saved from dyspepsia and learned to esteem the genial qualities of our great Commander as we admired his wonderful genius.[7]

Grattan had successfully survived the "fearful" Jackson and continued in his position as assistant quartermaster, though his rank had been reduced to quartermaster sergeant as a result of the change in command. He had enlisted as a private in Company "I" of the 1st Virginia Cavalry on May 1, 1861, but, because of his service in the quartermaster's department, never rode with the regiment.[8] In December 1861 he gave up his post and went to Richmond to take his seat in the legislature. At the close of the session, he took the ordnance examination, finished third, received a first lieutenant's commission, and was assigned to Col. Henry C. Cabell's battalion of artillery on March 5, 1863. About a month later, Grattan tried to secure a transfer and a captain's commission with the following letter:

Ordnance Office Cabell's Arty Battn
Hdqrs McLaws Division
Hamiltons Crossing
April 9th 1863

Hon'ble A. T. Caperton
Dear Sir
I stood the examination for Ordnance held in Rich-

mond—passed third as Captain. Am now assigned to Cabell's Arty Btn as Acting 1st Lt. As I understand, the Chief of Ordnance of the 2nd Corps (Jackson's) has applied to have me commissioned as Captain and assigned to him. Genl Jackson has approved this & I doubt not Col. B. G. Baldwin Ch of Ord of A.N. Va. Now I wish you would see Mr. Seddon about this as also, to ask Col Baldwin if the [word illegible] to do the same & have the matter accomplished. I passed third—the two above me Allen & Little have been commissioned some time as Capts. Nobody will be hurt, & all parties be pleased by this movement.

Respectfully Your Obt Sert,

Charles Grattan

Acty 1st Lt & Ord Off Cabell's Arty Battn

Col J. Gorgas Ch Ord C.S.A.[9]

The officer who had petitioned for Grattan's promotion and transfer to Jackson's Corps was Maj. W. Allan. He had wanted Grattan as his assistant and had received "Stonewall's" blessing. Both Allan's and Grattan's requests fell on deaf ears, however. Col. Josiah Gorgas, the Confederacy's chief of ordnance, refused to grant the transfer or the commission. Major Allan would try again in June, but nothing came of this either. Still holding his lieutenant's rank, Grattan participated in a number of battles, and his actions at Chancellorsville brought a commendation from Cabell in his report of the battle. He wrote, "I desire to call attention to the gallant conduct and energy and efficiency of Lieutenant Grattan, my ordnance officer."[10] The lieutenant also received mention in the report of Maj. S. P. Hamilton: "Lieutenant Grattan, ordnance officer, performed his very arduous duties with the greatest zeal and efficiency, and is worthy of especial praise."[11]

On June 9, 1863, Grattan, still a lieutenant, received orders transferring him to the 2nd Corps artillery, where he continued to serve through the Battle of Gettysburg. After the army returned to Virginia, Grattan remained with the 2nd Corps until October 6, 1863, when he was at last promoted to captain. His promotion removed him from the 2nd Corps, and he reported to Col. Josiah Gorgas, head of the ordnance department.

On October 27, 1863, Grattan became ordnance officer with Stuart's cavalry corps. Just how or why the cavalry's commander-in-chief chose Grattan as a replacement for John Esten Cooke, who had moved into the assistant adjutant's post, remains a bit of a mystery. Perhaps Grattan was just in the right place at the right time.

Grattan did not have to wait long for action. On November 26, 1863, the Confederate and Union cavalries began a series of maneuvers that were precipitated by the latter's crossing of the Rapidan River in the vicinity of Germanna Ford. Numerous skirmishes erupted, and at Parker's Store on November 29 Grattan had his horse killed beneath him. The incident turned out to be one of the captain's closest brushes during the war. Soon after the Mine Run Campaign ended, the cavalry went into winter quarters. For the most part, Grattan's active campaigning with Stuart was over.

Somehow, among all his duties, positions, and transfers, Grattan had found the time to court and win the heart of Elizabeth Crawford Finley, who lived on her father's plantation near Piedmont. The two made plans to be married, but first Grattan had to obtain a furlough. In late December 1863 Captain Grattan applied to Stuart for a pass and a furlough from his duties. The request was granted with the following endorsement written in Stuart's hand.

Hd Qrs Cav. Corps

27 Dec. 1863

Approved and respectfully forwarded as Capt. G's business is very urgent & cannot be transacted by proxy.

J. E. B. Stuart

Major Genl[12]

The sentiment and humor of that endorsement was not lost upon Grattan, who kept the document as a remembrance of his gallant leader. The wedding took place on January 6, 1864. Grattan may have wished to name a son in honor of Stuart, but he was not given the opportunity. The young couple would have seven children—lovely girls all: Mary (1864-?), Virginia (1867-1951), Sarah (1867-1899), Martha (1869-?), Louisa (1871-1877), Elizabeth (1876-1958), and Minnie (1878-1970).

For the young captain, the quiet moments with his new bride must have passed all too swiftly. Soon, with spring's return, the war called. Riding with Stuart in early March 1864, Grattan had another close call during a brief encounter with Gen. George A. Custer's raiders, who were withdrawing from the Battle of Rio Hill outside of Charlottesville, Virginia. Stuart, with less than a brigade, tried to stop the Union cavalry's retreat, only to be pushed aside by superior numbers. During the short fight, Grattan's horse was wounded. The circumstances surrounding the incident were recorded by "The" Garnett, who had been sent by Stuart to order a small body of men to withdraw from an exposed position.

The Yanks were now getting ready to dash upon us, and in another moment they commenced a charge. After a parting salute, our little squad, having made the best stand they could, wheeled and ran. There was but one opening in the rail fence which surrounded the field, by which we could escape, and I shall never forget the uncomfortable sound of those Yankee carbine balls as they whistled over our backs when we crowded through the gap. To my amazement they failed to hit a man or a horse, and I turned around after getting through the fence to observe a dozen Yankees within 20 paces, yelling "Surrender" at the top of their voices. This same party galloped their horses along the fence until they came within easy pistol shot of Gen. Stuart and Capt. Grattan, to whom they gave chase. The General seeing that they could not get at him over the fence, cantered along down the lane rather too leisurely, turning every now and then to his ordnance officer and saying, "Shoot that fellow, Grattan! Shoot him!" pointing to a Yankee who was plugging away at them both. But instead of Grattan shooting him, the Yankee shot Grattan's horse, inflicting a severe wound in his hind-quarters and laming him for the rest of the day.[13]

Custer managed to escape, and Stuart led his staff back to winter quarters near Orange Court House. With only minor interruptions, they remained there until the opening of the Wilderness Campaign, which led to Stuart's mortal wounding at Yellow Tavern. Grattan's reaction to Stuart's death is unknown, but he undoubtedly mourned with the rest of the staff and the army. He then became part of Wade Hampton's staff, serving in the same capacity as he had with Stuart. In a letter Grattan wrote to his sister, Mary, on July 19, 1864, while stationed near the North Carolina border about twenty miles below Petersburg, he described his situation and outlined his duties.

I am very singularly situated & have been since Genl. Stuart's death, reporting to Col. Baldwin [Lt. Col. Briscoe G. Baldwin, chief of ordnance on Gen. R. E. Lee's staff] & no one else. I pick up my traps & go where I please within the command & all that ties me to any locality more than another is being near to the Qr. Mr. & Commissary so as to draw rations for man & beast & to be in some central point so that I do not give any portion of the command too much riding to get at me. I go on the "grand round" every four or five days from Stoney Creek to Petersburg & generally but for the hot weather & dust have a good time on them as I select good places to stop at. Tomorrow I am going on one of these to Petersburg & shall go with Major [William J.] Johnson [formerly chief of subsistence on Stuart's staff] the Commissary who stops with his [word illegible] & gets the best to eat. So you see I have an eye for the inner man though in the midst of the Arabian desert.[14]

When Hampton went to the Carolinas, Grattan received orders attaching him to Fitz Lee's cavalry. On February 24, 1865, he was assigned as ordnance officer of the Valley District and proceeded to Staunton, where he attempted to gather artillery to replace that lost in Gen. Jubal Early's Valley Campaign. He was returning to the army under orders he had received on March 27, 1865, when he learned of Lee's surrender. Grattan was paroled in June.

Upon his return to civilian life, Grattan entered into farming in Augusta County, Virginia. In 1871 he moved his family to Staunton and resumed his law practice. He served at some time as superintendent of schools in Augusta County and as commissioner of immigration for Virginia. In 1888 he was elected to a judgeship in Augusta County and in 1894 was reelected for a six-year term. He stepped down at the end of his term and spent the remaining years of his life at "Cherry Hill Farm," his home on the west side of Staunton. He died at 11:30 A.M. on June 20, 1902, at the age of sixty-eight, of heart disease and kidney failure.[15] He was buried in Thornrose Cemetery in Staunton. One of his pallbearers was Maj. J. Marshall Hanger, once quartermaster of Stuart's cavalry.

Lt. Col. George St. Leger Ommanney Grenfell[1]

Assistant inspector general
September 14, 1863, to December 26, 1863

In his lengthy biography of Lt. Col. George St. Leger Grenfell, author Stephen Z. Starr successfully dissipated the fog that surrounded the life of one of the Confederacy's most legendary figures. Starr, while retaining his objectivity, nevertheless described a man whom the reader came to pity, not for his lack of ability as a soldier but rather for what he might have been. Grenfell's life was by no means dull, but it possessed few moments of real accomplishment. Failure stalked him from one venture to the next.

Grenfell was born in London on May 30, 1808.[2] It is apparent from his date of birth that he was the oldest by about seven years of any of Stuart's staff, the next being A. R. Boteler. His parents, George Bevil Granville Grenfell and Caroline Granville, who were cousins, had him christened George St. Leger Ommanney Grenfell. Even at the start of his life fate conspired against him: St. Paul's baptismal register misspelled his name as "Greenfell." The Grenfells were fairly well off financially and possessed a name of some note. Grenfell did not manage to add to the family's wealth, but he did supply additional color to its history.

Education for the future adventurer began with schooling in Penzance and ended with college in Holland. A trip throughout Europe followed, after which Grenfell settled in Paris. Here he became involved in the French Revolution of 1830, fighting against the Bourbons. In 1833 he married Hortense Louise Wyatt. They had three children: Caroline Hortense, Marie Emilie Jeanne, and Blanche Isabel. The couple separated in 1855. During the early years of his marriage, he worked for his father in one of the family's banking firms, which had a branch in Paris. Grenfell proved a dismal failure at finance. His father, ruined by having to make good his son's ill-conceived speculations, disowned him. Grenfell was tried *in absentia,* convicted, and sentenced to six years' imprisonment by a French court. By 1840 he had fled France to avoid prison and returned to England.

For the next twenty years, Grenfell carved the life of adventure that would be the source of the stories with which he enthralled John Hunt Morgan's men during the Civil War and anyone else who would give him an ear. Not surprisingly, most were blatant untruths, while others were merely exaggerations of considerable proportions. Several aspects of his stories were true, however. He did travel to many lands. Gibraltar, Morocco, Turkey, and Argentina were all his home at one time or another. Grenfell's "work" in these exotic locales included a position at the British consulate in Tangiers and a job as a gun runner. In 1855 he served as a British officer in a Turkish cavalry regiment that never saw any action in the Crimea because its horses could not be put ashore. His association with this unit furnished the setting for the stories dealing with his "participation" in the Crimean War. It also provided the military training he would put to good use while with the Confederate cavalry.

In the six years just prior to the Civil War, Grenfell appears to have lived a quieter life. Although he later claimed to have taken part in the Sepoy Mutiny in India and to have fought in Giuseppe Garibaldi's South American Legion, corroborating evidence is lacking. Grenfell's penchant for embellishing his past casts serious doubt on either claim. One verifiable fact does emerge from this period: Grenfell was in Argentina sometime before his coming to North America. In all probability he dabbled in some manner of husbandry, the details of which are unknown.

Why Grenfell joined the Confederacy remains a mystery. Perhaps his venture into farming had failed or, more likely, his wanderlust had gotten the better of him again. Whatever his motive, he left South America, returned to England, then journeyed to France, where he met John Slidell of "Trent Affair" fame before sailing for the United States. In April 1862 he arrived in Charleston, South Carolina, aboard the blockade-runner *Nelly*. Slidell had supplied Grenfell with a letter of introduction to Robert E. Lee, who was seemingly impressed by the Britisher's military record and training. Lee decided to send him to the Western theater, where Grenfell began his association with John Hunt Morgan.

Grenfell and Morgan took an immediate liking to each other. Joining the 2nd Kentucky Cavalry, Grenfell became the regiment's adjutant. During his time with Morgan, Grenfell gained the respect of many of the men he rode with. Basil Duke became an unabashed admirer of the Englishman who wore a red forage cap in the midst of battle. Duke and others were awed by Grenfell's fearlessness in battle and astounded at some of his quirks, such as bathing in every stream the regiment crossed. Though he bragged and regaled the Kentuckians with wild stories of his "experiences," Grenfell did make numerous friends. He may not have been overly popular with the rank and file due to the strict code of discipline he endeavored to enforce as regimental adjutant, but he surely captured the men's fancy and esteem. At the same time, the relationship between Morgan and the Britisher, which had been so strong, underwent a significant change.

John Hunt Morgan's marriage to Martha Ready opened up a rift between Grenfell and the intrepid raider. Grenfell had voiced his opposition to the marriage and could not very well remain in Morgan's command. There may have been other factors as well. In December 1862 Grenfell left the 2nd Kentucky and for a time served with Gen. Braxton Bragg as a volunteer aide. Bragg mentioned Grenfell's performance at the Battle of Murfreesboro in his report, stating, "G. Saint Leger Grenfell, of England . . . served me most efficiently."[3]

Impressed with Grenfell, Bragg appointed the Britisher inspector of cavalry and sent him to Maj. Gen. Joseph Wheeler. The appointment, when finally approved in Richmond, brought with it a lieutenant colonel's commission. His courage and military acumen had gained him an important and responsible position, but Grenfell promptly ruined everything: An alleged theft of horses, equipment, and money from an individual whom Grenfell accused of being a deserter landed the newly commissioned officer in jail. Bragg posted bail, and Grenfell left Tennessee in June 1863. He apparently suffered no military disgrace, for his request for another assignment was granted. He reported for duty with Stuart's cavalry corps as assistant inspector general on September 14, 1863.

With the exception of Pelham, Grenfell was the only officer ever assigned to a position on Stuart's staff without Stuart's requesting the appointment himself. A good reason must have existed for Grenfell's installation as inspector, since Stuart already had two such officers, George Freaner and A. R. Venable. Gen. R. E. Lee unquestionably felt that his cavalry and especially the horse artillery would benefit by having Grenfell as inspector. The commanding general had not been overly happy with the condition of the horse artillery, and the cavalry was beginning to experience the shortage of horses and small arms that would hamper it in the coming campaigns.

Stuart had been doing his utmost to keep his troopers and his artillery in the field. Nevertheless, he was beginning to encounter difficulties that neither he nor Lee would be able to surmount. Indeed, the entire Army of Northern Virginia had begun to feel the shortages of essential materiel. Stuart could only hope to conserve what he already had, and in a war of attrition conservation becomes increasingly impossible. Perhaps this idea of conservation was what Lee had had in mind when he sent Grenfell to Stuart, but if he had hoped that Grenfell would in some way alter what was happening, he was greatly mistaken.

Stuart's own reaction to Grenfell's appointment is unrecorded, but to say that Grenfell received a cold reception at Stuart's headquarters would be an understatement. H. B. McClellan made his feelings about the Britisher quite clear in his book *I Rode with Jeb Stuart,* and W. W. Blackford devoted but eleven words to Grenfell in his memoirs. Stuart's engineer had little to say or, more likely, decided to say little, but McClellan virtually accused the Englishman of cowardice and painted a thoroughly negative and greatly unfair picture of Grenfell. The Englishman may have been many things, but a coward was not one of them. Considering McClellan's statement, Grenfell could not have felt very welcome in Stuart's camp. Although no evidence exists that Stuart treated Grenfell badly, the Britisher could only have deemed the actions of the staff as unfriendly. He also came to believe that Stuart disliked him as well.

Grenfell's response can well be imagined. He could be obstinate and vindictive. One of his actions surely did not win over any of his compatriots. In November the cavalry encamped around Brandy Station. John Minor Botts, an ardent Unionist, owned a farm in the vicinity. Grenfell stayed in Botts's home for two weeks while Stuart and the staff camped elsewhere. Such behavior may have been an outgrowth of Grenfell's feelings of alienation at Stuart's headquarters, but it could not help but widen the schism between Grenfell and the rest of the staff.

An interesting view of Grenfell at this time can be found in the *War Sketches* of Theodore S. Garnett, Jr., who was then serving as a courier clerk on Stuart's staff.

> A little further down the valley, during a portion of the early winter, stood the tent of Lieut. Col. St. Leger Grenfell, who occupied for a short time the position of Inspector Genl of the Cav. Corps. This officer had come to Gen. Stuart from the Western Army, and was assigned to this duty by the War Dept. at Richmond. He was a curious compound of soldierly qualities and personal idiosyncrasies; at times, he would talk with officers & couriers in a sort of general harangue, relating some of the most wonderful anecdotes that were ever heard, and again, he would avoid all society confining himself closely to his tent, in company with his big yellow Bull-dog, and appearing only at meals, or at work on his two magnificent horses with curry comb and brush, allowing no other groom to touch their velvet coats. He disappeared from our midst about X-mas, 1863, and I heard of him no more. . . .[4]

Garnett heard "no more" of Grenfell because by December the state of affairs had degenerated to such an extent that Grenfell could not have been able to exercise his authority had he so desired. He claimed that Stuart conspired to get rid of him, but the only documentation supporting the Englishman's accusation comes from letters he wrote and not from official sources.[5] Whatever occurred, Grenfell was relieved of his duties with Stuart's cavalry on December 26, 1863, and was again assigned to Wheeler's command. Rather than report to Wheeler, Grenfell resigned his commission in an effort to join Morgan, who was trying to raise another command, as a private soldier, but this failed to materialize. Grenfell left the Confederacy for the North on May 12, 1864, the same day Stuart died.

While Grenfell had been riding with Morgan, he met a young, adventurous soldier named Thomas Henry Hines. Now, while in Richmond following his stay with Stuart, Grenfell heard of a conspiracy formulated by Hines to free prisoners of war in Chicago and establish a "Northwest Confederacy" with the help of Copperheads. The colonel's previous association with Hines opened the way for his participation in the scheme. Upon his arrival in the North, one of Grenfell's first acts was to meet with U.S. secretary of war Edwin M. Stanton to establish the fact that he had put the Confederacy behind him and was once again just another British citizen touring North America. The always suspicious Stanton was not fooled for an instant and did not appreciate being lied to, something Grenfell did with relish.[6]

The plot proved to be a disaster due to faulty planning on the Confederates' part and a lack of backbone on the Copperheads' part. On November 7, 1864, scores of men supposedly connected with the plot were arrested. Among them was Grenfell—by one account the first of the conspirators to be captured.[7] Seven men were eventually tried and convicted by a military court, but Grenfell was the only defendant to receive a death sentence, later reduced to life imprisonment. Incarcerated first in Columbus, Ohio, Grenfell was finally transferred to the Dry Tortugas, where the Lincoln assassination conspirators were also imprisoned. He survived a yellow fever epidemic, during which he displayed all the qualities of a hero.

Grenfell finally realized that those who had been trying to secure his freedom would not be able to succeed (all the other defendants were free by this time), and he decided to attempt an escape. On the night of March 6, 1868, Grenfell and two other prisoners, with the help of a guard, secured a boat and set sail for Cuba. The boat and all aboard disappeared without a trace.

Lt. William Henry Hagan

Chief of couriers and aide-de-camp
May 1862 to May 12, 1864[1]

Better known by his middle name than his first, Henry Hagan has become one of the most maligned members of Stuart's staff simply because the majority of historians have accepted George Cary Eggleston's demeaning appraisal of Hagan in his 1875 book, *A Rebel's Recollections*. Eggleston's description of Hagan is completely unflattering, to say the least.

> Almost at the beginning of the war he [Stuart] managed to surround himself with a number of persons whose principal qualification for membership of his military household was their ability to make fun. . . . He had another queer character about him, whose chief recommendation was his grotesque fierceness of appearance. This was Corporal

Hagan, a very giant in frame, with an abnormal tendency to develop hair. His face was heavily bearded almost to his eyes, and his voice was as hoarse as distant thunder, which indeed it closely resembled. Stuart, seeing him in the ranks, fell in love with his peculiarities of person at once, and had him detailed for duty at head-quarters, where he made him a corporal, and gave him charge of the stables. Hagan, whose greatness was bodily only, was much elated by the attention shown him, and his person seemed to swell and his voice continued to grow deeper than ever under the influence of the newly acquired dignity of chevrons. All this was amusing, of course, and Stuart's delight was un-bounded. The man remained with him till the time of his death, though not always as a corporal. In a mad freak of fun one day, the chief recommended his corporal for promotion, to see, he said, if the giant was capable of further swelling, and so the corporal became a lieutenant upon the staff.[2]

If Eggleston wrote the above passage to add color and humor to his book, he succeeded at the expense of both Stuart and Hagan. Stuart may have enjoyed a good joke and a hearty laugh, but to state that he added individuals to his staff based solely on their "ability to make fun" or their "grotesque fierceness of appearance" seems to stretch the truth a bit too far. The concern Stuart demonstrated over acquiring quality staff personnel would seemingly refute Eggleston's allegation. Further evidence that Eggleston was exaggerating can be found through a careful examination of Hagan's life and war record.

Born April 6, 1821, in Braddock Heights, Maryland, Hagan moved with his family to Shepherdstown, Virginia, now West Virginia, when he was still quite young. By 1847 he had married Hester Ann Lemen and had settled in Cumberland, Maryland. They returned to Shepherdstown sometime later. At the commencement of the war, Shepherdstown raised a company of cavalry, which became Company "F" of the 1st Virginia Cavalry. Hagan joined this company on April 18, 1861.[3]

Hagan served with his regiment for three months, and on July 24, 1861, he was attached as a corporal to Stuart's headquarters. The date of his promotion is unknown, but it appears to have occurred before he joined Stuart. Hagan's record over the next few months should not be ignored by those who would judge his value to Stuart. The corporal's courage was attested to by Stuart himself. Hagan, given the post of commander of Stuart's escort, frequently earned his commander's praise over his conduct in the face of the enemy. The position of commander of Stuart's escort would not be given to just anyone, nor would it be placed in the hands of a person who had been added to headquarters just in order to have a good laugh. The post required a responsible, intelligent individual whom Stuart could count on in emergencies. Hagan apparently had those qualifications.

Early April 1862 saw Hagan still attached to cavalry headquarters, but his name also appeared on the rolls of the 1st Virginia. Then on April 18, Stuart wrote the following letter:

> HdQrs Cav Brig
> Richmond April 18, 1862
> I beg leave to call your attention to the peculiar claims of Corporal Henry Hagan of the 1st VA Cavalry who has won a commission on the march & the battlefield if ever man did. His services are indispensable to me, while his valuable services as recognized in every report I ever made entitle him to such a mark of confidence. He would adorn the position of Lieutenant and I hope it will meet with your pleasure to give him the appointment.
>
> The Generals who have witnessed his conduct would cheerfully endorse this.
>
> Most Respectfully
> Your obt svt
> J. E. B. Stuart Brig Genl[4]

The high recommendation given to Hagan by Stuart in this letter brought him a lieutenant's commission. He continued to serve at Stuart's headquarters in various positions, most notably as chief of couriers. He also undoubtedly maintained a place in the general's escort, where he had performed exceptionally well. Hagan had his closest brush with death on October 12, 1863, when his horse was killed beneath him. The circumstances surrounding this event are unknown, but Stuart approved and signed a voucher so that Hagan could be reimbursed for his loss.

After Stuart's death, Hagan joined the staff of Gen. Wade Hampton and served as an aide-de-camp until the end of the war. He was paroled in North Carolina on April 26, 1865.

Hagan returned to Shepherdstown, where he became known as "Major" Hagan. The title must have been honorary, since there is no record of his having been promoted to that rank. He eventually became president of the Potomac Cement Mills and held the position for a number of years. The town's local newspaper commented:

> We are glad to learn that Major Henry Hagan, who has
> command of the Potomac Cement Mills, is running them
> to their fullest capacity, and making an excellent quality
> of cement, all of which is shipped to Washington, where
> there is a great demand for it.[5] The Major "puts things
> through very lively."[6]

In the late 1870s, when his health began to fail, Hagan left the company
and became proprietor of the Entler Hotel in Shepherdstown.[7] In April
1882 he gave up the hotel and opened a small boardinghouse. He and his
wife continued to live as a respected couple in Shepherdstown for many
years. No records exist of their ever having children, but if they did, none
survived them. Hagan died on June 18, 1895. He was buried in Elmwood
Cemetery in Shepherdstown. His tombstone reads:

> *William H. Hagan*
> *Died*
> *June 18, 1895*
> *Aged*
> *74 yrs. 2 m. 12 d.*
> *Them that sleep in Jesus will God bring with Him*

The evidence would seem to suggest that Hagan was more than just a
hairy giant. His achievements while a member of Stuart's headquarters
family should not be overlooked when judging the man. Including his
time of service as corporal and commander of the general's escort, Hagan
followed the plume of Stuart longer than did any other individual among
the hundreds who were associated with Stuart's headquarters. This fact
plus his excellent military record should confirm his value to the general
and earn for him the respect due a gallant soldier.

Maj. James Thomas Watt Hairston

Assistant aide-de-camp and assistant adjutant general
September 11, 1861; January 16, 1862, to March 1, 1863

J. T. W. Hairston's career in the Confederate army might have been entirely
different had it not been for the rheumatism that plagued him intermittently
throughout the first two years of the war. The malady would first force
him to leave his position with his cousin Stuart and then to resign from
the army altogether.

Watt Hairston, as he was often called, was born on January 26, 1835, the seventh son of Harden and Sallie Stovall Hairston (née Staples), at the family's home, "Old Fort," in Lowndes County, Mississippi.[1] He was a younger brother of Samuel Harden Hairston and cousin of Peter W. Hairston. The Hairston clan, descendants of Scottish immigrant Peter Hairston, owned more than thirty-five thousand acres of land in Mississippi, Tennessee, North Carolina, and Virginia before 1865.[2] Five generations had carved out large farms and plantations from the wilderness in the rural South.

Maj. James Thomas Watt Hairston

Watt Hairston inherited from his family a love for the land, but his education was not centered on agriculture. He attended the W. L. Bingham School in Hillsboro, North Carolina, and then enrolled at the Virginia Military Institute in 1854. Graduating in 1858, Hairston decided to return to his family's holdings in Mississippi and raise cotton. The pull of the land was strong.

In the years just before the war, Hairston and many other young men from Lowndes, Noxubee, and Oktibbeha counties in Mississippi organized a company of infantry they christened the "Prairie Guards." Hairston became captain of the company, which later would become Company "E," 11th Mississippi Infantry. Soon after Mississippi seceded, the company was called into service, along with several others, for the purpose of securing the navy yard at Pensacola, Florida. With the help of other troops from Alabama and Florida, the "Prairie Guards" fulfilled their mission, only to be disbanded at its completion. Hairston traveled to Montgomery, Alabama, and by mid-March had succeeded in obtaining a lieutenant's commission in the infantry. Meanwhile, recognizing that war loomed in the near future, the "Prairie Guards" reorganized and again elected Hairston their captain.[3]

On April 27, 1861, the company received orders to march for Corinth, Mississippi. Arriving on April 30, the "Prairie Guards" officially became part of the 11th Mississippi Infantry, and with that regiment they were mustered into the Confederate service on May 13 at Lynchburg, Virginia. The regiment was sent on to Harper's Ferry, where it arrived on May 19. Sometime during this period, Hairston first began to suffer from the rheumatism that would gradually undermine his health and end his military service. When Gen. Joseph E. Johnston withdrew his forces from Harper's Ferry to Winchester, Hairston was ill to the point of almost being disabled. The threat of a Union advance early in July brought Hairston from his sickbed. Rejoining his regiment, he waited in vain for the enemy to strike, but all had been rumor. His patriotic devotion to duty brought on a complete collapse of his health and forced him to request thirty days' leave, which was granted effective July 11.

Recovering slowly, Hairston decided that his condition would not allow him to remain with the infantry, and he resigned his commission in September 1861. On September 11 Hairston had his first taste of service with Stuart. An enemy reconnaissance column occupied the small village of Lewinsville between the two armies. Stuart felt obliged to give them a Virginia welcome and with that intention led a small mixed force of cavalry, infantry, and artillery toward the village. Hairston volunteered to accompany Stuart as an aide.[4] The Federals had not expected serious opposition and suffered a sound defeat. Hairston emerged without a scratch and might have made an effort to stay with Stuart had he completely recovered his health.

Hairston, though he had resigned one commission, had retained the lieutenancy he had secured in Montgomery. In October he reported to Gen. J. H. Winder in Richmond. His fragile health would not enable him to accept too strenuous an assignment, but he did want to serve. Winder found a niche that Hairston could fill and appointed the lieutenant commandant of Libby Prison, a position Hairston held from October 21, 1861, to January 16, 1862.[5] At the time he was in charge of the prison, the conditions were not as bad as they would become later in the war, when overcrowding and a lack of provisions became serious problems for the captured soldiers.

While Hairston gradually recovered his health, Stuart actively campaigned to have him assigned to his staff when the lieutenant was once again ready for field service. On January 16 Hairston was relieved of his duties as Libby Prison's commandant and given a one-month furlough to complete his recovery and prepare for his next assignment. At the end of his furlough, he was ordered to report to Gen. J. E. Johnston for duty with Stuart. One small problem still had to be eliminated. Stuart, having requested Hairston for his staff, now wrote to headquarters to have Hairston transferred from the infantry to the cavalry.

> Hd Qrs Cavalry Brigade
> Centreville Jan. 23, 1862
>
> General:
>   Lt JTW Hairston CSA who has been ordered to report for duty to me at the expiration of his leave belongs to the infantry and is desirous of a transfer to the cavalry. If compatible to do so I hope you will gratify his wishes, for I feel assured from long acquaintance that he is well fitted

for that branch of service and will be an ornament to it.
                                              Most Respectfully
                                                      General
                                                  Your Obt svt
                                                   JEB Stuart
                                                   Brig genl
                                                   Comdg[6]

The transfer was not immediately forthcoming, however. The delay was what probably led Stuart to attach Hairston to his staff with the nonpermanent title of voluntary aide-de-camp. This soon became acting assistant adjutant general. As late as July 14, 1862, Hairston was still only a lieutenant attached to the staff.[7] At last, on August 8, his majority and appointment in the adjutant general's department arrived. His commission was to date from July 25, 1862.[8] The abrupt change occurred when Stuart was promoted to major general on July 25, 1862, and Hairston benefited from the general's good fortune. He continued to serve as Stuart's adjutant and on at least one occasion—the Chambersburg Raid—acted as provost marshal.[9]

With the coming of the winter of 1862-63, Hairston had another onset of rheumatism. He was repeatedly unable to fulfill his duties, and others, including young Channing Price, had to be pressed into service. Stuart made every effort to keep Hairston on his staff but finally had to ask him to resign for the good of the service. In compliance with his commander's request, Hairston wrote the following letter.

                                        Camp at Hd Qrs Cav Div
                                                March 1, 1863
General
    I have the honor hereby to tender my resignation as Major A.A.G. upon your staff.
    I have been suffering from Rheumatism all winter and am frequently unable to attend to my duties, and would most respectfully ask that my resignation be accepted as the post is important and requires one more able to perform its duties.

                                              I am General
                                            Most Respectfully
                                             Yr. Obt. Sevt.
                                            J. T. W. Hairston
                                            Major AAG[10]

Stuart's medical director, Talcott Eliason, confirmed Hairston's condition, and the request was granted. Even though Hairston was related to Stuart, he understood that when he could no longer perform his duties, it was time to leave and allow another to assume his post. Soon after his resignation, Hairston returned to Mississippi. He never reentered the military. In a letter he wrote to his alma mater in January 1867, he states how much he was affected by his illness.

> Crawfordville Miss
> January 28th 1867
>
> Gen'l F. H. Smith
> Respected Sir
> In reading over a list of graduates of the Institute killed during the late disastrous war saw my name mentioned. It must have been intended for my cousin Lieut J. A. Hairston.
> I was retired from the army early in the year 1863 from ill health and did not reenter. (Nor have I entirely recovered as yet) When retired was Major & A.A.G. on Major Gen'l JEB Stuart's Staff—Cavalry Division A.N.Va.
>
> Respectfully etc.
> J.T.W. Hairston
>
> PS. Lt. H[airston]. was killed
> Williamsburg 5th May 1862[11]

At the time he wrote the above letter, Hairston was having problems with the Freedman's Bureau, which was trying to confiscate his Mississippi holdings as abandoned land. He fought stubbornly and succeeded in retaining some, if not all, of his property. In 1873 he married his cousin Bettie Perkins Hairston, daughter of Marshall and Ann Hairston of "Beaver Creek" plantation in Henry County, Virginia. The couple had two sons: Marshall, who died in infancy, and Watt, who died in 1916 at age forty.[12] There are no living descendants.

Hairston spent the remainder of his life as a farmer, planting tobacco in Virginia and cotton in Mississippi. He died at his home near Columbus, Mississippi, on January 19, 1908, at age seventy-two. His remains were brought back to Virginia, and he was buried in the family cemetery at "Beaver Creek" near Martinsville.

Peter Wilson Hairston

Civilian volunteer aide-de-camp
May 1861 to October 1861

Head. Qrs Cavalry Brigade
Camp Beverly Oct 12th 1861
This is to certify that Peter W. Hairston of North Carolina, has for the past
five months been associated with me as
volunteer Aide, during that time he has
borne the hardships and privations of out-
door campaign with the most commendable zeal
and cheerfulness. His duties with the 1st Cavalry have
time and again brought him in the presence of the enemy,
and he has never failed to show determined courage—
intelligent apprehension of orders, and conspicuous daring.
As an aide his services have been invaluable.

On the battlefield of Manassas, he was constantly
exposed to a destructive fire, but bore himself handsomely
throughout, having twice crossed the battlefield bearing
dispatches from me to our Generals. In several less important engagements with the enemy both in the valley of the
Shenandoah and Potomac, he has received for his gallant
and efficient conduct my high commendation.

He has been long enough a close observer of cavalry
drill and outpost service to make him particularly efficient
in that duty, and I hope the country will continue to have
his services, but in a much higher grade than that heretofore filled. Given under my hand at the Head quarters
Cavalry Brigade, Army of the Potomac Confederate States
of America the day and year above written.

J. E. B. Stuart
Brig. Gen'l[1]

With the above testimonial in his pocket, Peter W. Hairston bid good-bye
to Brig. Gen. "Jeb" Stuart, his cousin and brother-in-law, and returned to
his beautiful plantation, "Cooleemee," in North Carolina. At the beginning
of the war, Hairston had rushed to Stuart's side, bringing with him a
splendid horse, George, as a gift.[2] During the intervening months, Hairston
had earned the plaudits of Stuart and others, but he had also retained his

civilian status, passing up an opportunity to join officially both the army and Stuart's newly formed staff as aide-de-camp.[3] He was one of the few private citizens to function in a staff position, though his period of service after Stuart became a general lasted only about three weeks.

Peter W. Hairston shared the same ancestry as his cousins J. T. W. (Watt) and Samuel H. Hairston. Peter's father, Samuel, was the brother of Samuel and Watt's father, Harden. Peter was born at "Oak Hill" in Pittsylvania County, Virginia, on November 25, 1819. His mother was Agnes Wilson Hairston, the only daughter of Peter and Ruth Hairston Wilson. Young Peter received some of his education at "Oak Hill"; then, at age twelve, he was enrolled in the W. L. Bingham School, the same school Watt Hairston would attend. He later received a master's degree from the University of North Carolina. From 1837 to 1839 he studied law at the University of Virginia, but illness sent him home in December 1839 and he never returned.

For the next several years, Hairston immersed himself in the business of running a plantation. He also became increasingly concerned, as did the rest of the family, over the health of his brother George. He journeyed with George to Philadelphia to seek medical help. There, a doctor suggested that a trip to Europe might be beneficial. Soon afterward, a decision was made to send George, accompanied by Peter, to southern Italy in the hope that George's health would be restored in a warmer clime. They left New York on October 7, 1843, and returned in February or March of the following year.

Once Hairston returned to "Cooleemee," he tackled in earnest the job of running his plantation. Though he was kept very busy, he managed to court "Jeb" Stuart's sister, Columbia, and on November 7, 1849, they were married. They were very happy, and the new bride fit in quite well at "Cooleemee." The couple had four children, but Columbia died in August 1857 after giving birth to the fourth child, which lived only long enough to be baptized. None of the other children lived into their twenties. Archibald died when he was a year old, Samuel at seventeen, and Elizabeth at thirteen.

At the end of a year of mourning, Hairston became reacquainted with Fanny McCoy Caldwell, and on June 22, 1859, they were married. They honeymooned in Europe, returning to "Cooleemee" in March 1860. The political climate was quickly beginning to deteriorate by August, when their first child, Agnes, was born. Hairston went to war on April 29, 1861. He journeyed north and joined his brother-in-law "Jeb" Stuart in Richmond as a volunteer aide. The two were soon off to Harpers Ferry.

The letters Hairston wrote to his "Dear Fanny" during the next several months are filled with material relating to the war, politics, sickness, weather, rumors, generals, and numerous other topics. In many instances they contain some of the earliest references to many of Stuart's future staff members. Among those Hairston "introduced" to his young wife back home were the Reverend Dabney Ball, whom Hairston greatly admired as both a minister and a soldier; Luke Tiernan Brien, a Marylander who became Hairston's lifelong friend; George Freaner, another Maryland refugee; Peter's cousins, James Thomas Watt and Samuel Harden Hairston; Redmond Burke, one of Stuart's daring scouts; and even the charming informant, Antonia Ford.[4] Hairston saw the waste of war and more than once commented in his writings that he felt some of the generals needed to be prodded. He esteemed Stuart, was speculative about President Davis, thought Lee was an excellent engineer but a poor general, and placed great confidence in Joe Johnston.

As the months passed, Hairston became more and more concerned about "Cooleemee." Fanny increasingly pressured him to return. He approached Stuart about leaving but received an appeal to his and Fanny's patriotism and a plea to remain. Hairston, however, had made up his mind, and Stuart could not order him to stay. Instead, the newly commissioned brigadier wrote the highly complimentary document quoted earlier. Hairston went home but was back in Richmond in July 1862. His actual position with the army at this time is not known. He remained until at least the early days of August, when he again went home to "Cooleemee." He found that he was indeed needed and soon realized that running a plantation in wartime was a challenge worthy of the most astute businessman. He received some help from Luke Tiernan Brien, but inflation and the uncertainty bred by the war tested both him and the Marylander.[5]

When Hairston felt it was necessary for him once again to enter the conflict, he did not rejoin Stuart's staff but instead secured a position as a volunteer aide with Maj. Gen. Jubal Early, who was also a relative. Though Hairston had had a few narrow escapes while he rode with Stuart, they did not compare with the one he had early in November 1863. His description of the incident was recorded in the diary he kept at the time. The narration begins in midsentence because preceding pages have been lost.

> . . . glasses I had on to look and I was in the act of handing them to him, when my horse was killed by a shell passing through him, having entered his right flank and coming out at his tail cutting it off entirely. It passed thro' my saddle blanket and coat tail and yet did not injure me. I can not be too thankful for my almost miraculous escape.[6]

Hairston continued as Early's aide for the remainder of the general's career. When Sheridan managed to wrest control of the Valley away from Early, Lee had no choice but to take the command of the 2nd Corps away from Jackson's successor. Hairston set out for "Cooleemee," arriving sometime after Lee's surrender at Appomattox.

The economic situation at "Cooleemee" and the other plantations owned by Hairston after the war was such that he decided to try his fortune in Baltimore. Arriving in September 1865, he soon was made to feel at home by Brien, who had left "Cooleemee" in the spring of 1864 to rejoin the army. On September 26 Hairston announced in a letter to Fanny that he had gone into partnership with Col. James R. Herbert, a former commander of Maryland troops in the Confederate Army.[7] As commission merchants, the two entrepreneurs prospered. Hairston brought his family to Baltimore but still maintained his hold on his land. It was fortunate that he did.

Colonel Herbert died in August 1884, and Hairston discovered that his partner had borrowed money from their business for personal use. Herbert's estate could not make up the loss, so Hairston had to assume responsibility. To his credit, every last cent was paid. Tragedy had also struck the family through the years following the war. Both of his children by Columbia Stuart had died, Elizabeth in 1865 as a result of a fall and Samuel in 1867 of typhoid fever. Hairston's brother, George, had died in 1866, his grandmother in 1867, and his father in 1875. His burdens increasing, Hairston's own health began to weaken. The strain over Colonel Herbert's financial indiscretions took a heavy toll. While sitting at his desk one February day in 1886, Hairston suffered a massive stroke and died before medical help arrived. He was buried in the family cemetery at "Berry Hill" in Pittsylvania County, Virginia.

Maj. Samuel Harden Hairston

Volunteer aide-de-camp and quartermaster
May 5, 1862, to March 31, 1863

On April 27, 1870, members of the legislature, lawyers, judges, police officials, reporters, and visitors crowded the state capitol building in Richmond, Virginia. The occasion was the rendering of a decision in a case contesting the constitutionality of what was known as the "enabling act." Great interest in the case had been spawned, since it involved the office of the mayor of Richmond. Just after 11:00 A.M., as the final preparations were being made to begin the business of the day in the court of appeals, a piece of ceiling panel beneath the gallery of the courtroom fell to the floor. Almost immediately a girder supporting the gallery broke, and the gallery, along with the people in it, came crashing down to the floor of the court of appeals.

The impact and the additional weight were too much for the floor to bear, and it too gave way, sending debris and people down on the heads of those in the house of delegates' chamber below the court of appeals. Dozens of people were killed and many others hurt. Among the dead was Maj. Samuel Harden Hairston. He had survived bullets, shells, sickness, and the violence of the battlefield during the long years of war only to die horribly in the collapse of a floor in his state's capitol building. He was forty-eight years old.

Samuel Hairston, born at "Old Fort" in Patrick County, Virginia, in April 1822, was the third child of Harden and Sallie Staples Hairston[1] and the brother of James Thomas Watt Hairston. His early life was similar to that of his younger brother's, but his later education differed. Samuel attended William and Mary from 1845 to 1847. At twenty-three years of age, he was one of the older students at the college. He studied law, junior moral, and philosophy his first year, and law, senior political, and chemistry his second year.[2] Whether he practiced law for any length of time remains unknown, but he was nominated county judge for Henry County, Virginia, before the war. Hairston married his cousin Alcey Hairston, daughter of Samuel and Agnes Wilson Hairston of "Oak Hill" in Pittsylvania County, Virginia. The couple's first child, Harden, was born in April 1857. They had two other children, Ruth and Sarah.[3]

Hairston's role at the beginning of the war mirrored his brother's in some respects. On April 26, 1861, he enlisted in his brother's company, Company "E" of the 11th Mississippi Infantry. He soon attained the rank of fourth sergeant. Abruptly, just as had James, Samuel began to suffer from chronic rheumatism. Try as he might, he could not perform his duties and was discharged from the regiment at Camp Fisher on October 3, 1861. At this time he was described as being six feet, two inches tall with dark hair, blue eyes, and a fair complexion. He gave his occupation as farmer. One discrepancy emerges from Hairston's records with the 11th Mississippi. Upon his enlistment he gave his age as thirty; he was actually one year shy of being forty.

Hairston, not wanting to be kept out of the war, sought an alternative to service with the infantry. His records do not reveal just exactly when he attached himself to cavalry headquarters, but on May 5, 1862, Stuart reported that Samuel Hairston had been acting as his voluntary aide for a number of days. His rank was given as captain. Stuart soon made a move to attach Hairston to his staff in a more permanent way.

Hd Qrs Cavalry Brigade
June 11th 1862

Col A. C. Myers
  Qr Mr General CSA
Col:

I have the honor to request that if after reconsideration
of the subject with an eye to the best public service, you
still decline to allow Capt. Geo. Johnston to accept the
position of Qr Mr of my Brigade, that you will nominate
as soon as practicable <u>Sam Harden Hairston</u> to that position
as soon as possible in order that he may enter into bond
and assume the duties at a very early day.

Most Respectfully
Col your obt svt
JEB Stuart
Brig Genl
Comdg Cavalry [4]

The position of quartermaster had become vacant, or rather Stuart knew it
would become vacant, with the resignation of Maj. Philip H. Powers,
formerly of the 1st Virginia Cavalry. Stuart evidently had made a request on
behalf of Captain Johnston but, because of some difficulty with his confirmation, felt that Hairston might be more acceptable to the authorities in
Richmond. He proved correct when Hairston's commission as major and
quartermaster came through on August 30, 1862. By then, Hairston had
been serving in the position since June 17, the date of his appointment.

All seemed to be well, and according to Stuart's reports Hairston
performed his duties efficiently. But then, abruptly, on January 14, 1863,
Hairston submitted the following:

Off. QMaster Dept Cav. Div.
14 Jan 1863

Genl

I have the Honor respectfully to tender my resignation
as Major and Qmaster of the Cavalry Division, and request
that it may take effect immediately.

I have the Honor to be
very
Respectfully
Genl S. Cooper   your obt svt
Adjt & Inst Gen   Sam Harden Hairston
C.S.A.   Maj & QM Cav Div.[5]

Unfortunately, Hairston did not reveal his reason for resigning. Since his resignation has a date preceding his brother's resignation by about six weeks, he could not have been motivated by Stuart's asking Watt to resign because of poor health. Additionally, Samuel appears to have remained with Stuart for some time after January 14. He requested and received a thirty-day leave on May 2. On May 31 his resignation was accepted, and he left the staff permanently.

Hairston's career subsequent to his service with Stuart is unclear. After the war he returned to Henry County to raise tobacco and, by one account, prospered until his untimely death in Richmond. He is believed to have been buried in the family's cemetery near Martinsville, Virginia.

Capt. James Marshall Hanger

Assistant quartermaster
October 31, 1862, to May 12, 1864

The military career of James Marshall Hanger typifies that of thousands of men who worked industriously behind the scenes in order that the troops on the front lines might have the food, arms, clothing, and equipment necessary to meet the enemy in battle. Gallantry they may have had in abundance, but seldom did an opportunity arise for them to demonstrate it. Forever in the rear echelons, Hanger and the others who endured the hardships of active campaigning without the glory nevertheless contributed toward whatever victories the army achieved. The satisfaction of knowing that they had performed their duties to the best of their abilities was sometimes the only reward they received. Yet such reward must have been sufficient, for they remained at their posts, took the abuse of generals and privates alike, and continually searched for ways to provide for the army amid the crumbling economy of the Confederacy.

Marshall Hanger, as he preferred to be called, was born to Peter Hanger III and Martha Elizabeth Hanger (née Crawford) near Waynesboro in Augusta County, Virginia, on November 12, 1833. He could trace his Virginia roots back to 1750, when his great-grandfather, Peter Hanger, settled in Augusta.[1] Hanger received his early education in Augusta County, then the University of Virginia, where he studied law. After graduating, he returned to Augusta and settled in Staunton, forming the firm of Baylor and Hanger. He maintained this association until the outbreak of the war, at which time he enlisted in the cavalry.

By May 1862 Hanger's name appeared on the rolls of the 1st Virginia's Company "E." In July and August he was detailed as a private to the brigade quartermaster. Up until autumn, his experiences differed little from that of thousands of other cavalrymen. Then on October 4, 1862, Hanger received a promotion to captain and an assignment as assistant quartermaster to the 17th Virginia Battalion,[2] but almost as soon as these orders were issued they were canceled, leaving Hanger in limbo. Why this occurred is not known, but Hanger's situation brightened again when on October 31 he was appointed captain and assistant quartermaster from Virginia with orders to report to Stuart. Initially his superior officer was Maj. Samuel H. Hairston, but after May 16, 1863, he would serve under Maj. Norman R. FitzHugh.

Although it appears that Hanger seldom saw much action, he did manage on at least one occasion to venture close to the enemy, as evidenced by the following document:

> This day personally appeared before me John W. Catron and made oath that on or about the 12th day of March 1864, one horse the property of the Confederate States in the possession of Captain J. M. Hanger died from wounds received in action and that the said J. M. Hanger, AQM is in nowise blamable.
>
> Given under my hand and seal this 13th day of March 1864.
>
> > N. R. FitzHugh
> > Major & QM[3]

This skirmish, in which Hanger's horse was killed, went unrecorded, lost among the thousands of other small actions whose casualties added together would probably surpass those of some of the major battles of the war. Neither Hanger nor any of his associates who chronicled the war thought to immortalize the brief fight with a word or two. Still, it must have been a narrow escape, one Hanger may have looked back on later in life as his "moment of glory."

Soon after Stuart's death, Hanger was upset to discover that his commission as captain had never been confirmed. He had to write to Richmond to apply for reinstatement. His letter dated July 23, 1864, contained the signatures of Maj. Gens. Wade Hampton and Fitz Lee; Brig. Gens. Matthew C. Butler, Lunsford Lomax, and Williams C. Wickham; and Majs.

George Freaner and Norman R. FitzHugh. His statement of the facts and the endorsements ostensibly brought results, and Hanger was reinstated as captain and assistant quartermaster on August 10, 1864, to date from July 29, 1864. Somewhere in the confusion he had lost twenty-one months of seniority as captain, but nothing indicates that he complained. August 11 brought him orders to report to Hampton and assume again the duties of assistant quartermaster of the cavalry corps.[4]

Hanger probably would have remained FitzHugh's subordinate had not that officer been captured by the enemy's cavalry at Stoney Creek. Hampton then acted to replace FitzHugh with Hanger. On December 15, 1864, he wrote to Richmond and said, in part:

> [Captain Hanger] . . . proved valuable and energetic officer. Major N. R. FitzHugh, Chief of QM of this Corps, was captured by the enemy on the 1st instant. During his absence I have assigned Capt. Hanger to duty as Act Chief QM. I have the honor to request that raise be given him commensurate with his duties and as a servant of long and faithful services.[5]

Hampton's efforts on Hanger's behalf failed to gain a favorable response from the higher authorities, however. Though Hanger was now responsible for the duties once performed by FitzHugh, he did not receive the rank.

During the Confederacy's final months, Hanger was transferred twice. On January 19, 1865, he was assigned temporarily to W. H. F. Lee's Division, but on January 25 the orders were altered to Fitz Lee's Corps in the Valley. On March 9, 1865, Richmond finally granted Hanger his majority to date from February 15, 1865. They had waited almost too long to recognize his dedicated service. Hanger accompanied Lee's retreating army to Appomattox, where Lee surrendered on April 9.

The ex-quartermaster returned to Staunton, Virginia, and resumed his law practice. He remained a bachelor for the rest of his life and lived in various hotels, not wishing to purchase a house of his own. In 1869 he was elected to Virginia's House of Delegates and for the next fourteen years served in that capacity. From 1871 to 1877 he was speaker of the house, gaining the respect of many of his fellow representatives. In the 1882 elections, his allegiance to the "debt payers" as opposed to the "readjusters" cost him his seat, and he retired from political life.[6]

Hanger again returned to Staunton, where, for the next ten years, he continued in law. He also found time to serve on the board of visitors of the Virginia Military Institute from January 1, 1889, to December 31,

1891. In 1893 Hanger was called by President Cleveland to be consul to Bermuda, where he lived until 1897. His final years were spent in his beloved Staunton. According to one source, he remained active to within a few weeks of his death. He entered the King's Daughters Hospital around August 20, 1912, with what was diagnosed as intestinal paralysis followed by gangrene. He died just past 11:00 A.M. on August 26, 1912. Major Hanger is buried in Thornrose Cemetery in Staunton.

2nd Lt. Walter Quarrier Hullihen

Aide-de-camp
August 29, 1862, to November 19, 1863

In the quiet confines of the Trinity Episcopal Church grounds in Staunton, Virginia, stands a small obelisk that marks the grave of Walter Quarrier Hullihen. Fittingly, Hullihen rests near the church he served as rector for forty-six years. Amid such peaceful surroundings, visualizing Hullihen as the soldier who was twice wounded during the war becomes difficult. The image of the warrior fades still more when his portrait, that of a dignified, elderly man of God, is seen hanging on the dark, wood-paneled wall inside the church. Beneath his tranquil exterior, however, beat the heart of a fighter who tenaciously faced his opponents.

Born on June 14, 1841, in Wheeling, Virginia, now West Virginia, Walter Quarrier Hullihen was the fourth son of Dr. S. Peter and Elizabeth Fundenberg Hullihen. His early education is not known, but he felt drawn to the ministry, which makes his decision to enter the Virginia Military Institute somewhat difficult to understand. He enrolled on August 16, 1858, and quickly discovered that the school did not suit his needs. (He had desired to take Latin and Greek, while the school taught mathematics and French.) A letter written by his mother explained to the institute the problem her son had encountered.

Wheeling Sept 3rd 1858

John T. L. Preston Esq.
My Dear Sir,
Your letter of the 30th inst. was received this morning. I have given my son Walter permission to leave the Institute which he finds after a short trial to be as I have always

thought entirely inconsistent with his taste, temperament and purpose in life.

You mention in your letter having enclosed a bill. It must have been forgotten as the letter did not contain one. I will attend to the payment of my son's bill as soon as you send it. With many thanks for your kindness, I remain

Gratefully and respectfully

E. Hullihen[1]

His mother had known full well that VMI would not fulfill her son's requirements, but the seventeen-year-old Hullihen must have been quite obstinate. With her husband dead, Hullihen's mother may have decided to let Walter have his own way in order to learn from his mistake.

Shortly after this, Hullihen entered the University of Virginia. He was not destined to finish his education, however, as the problems between the North and South began to escalate toward open conflict. Hullihen adhered to the Union until Virginia seceded. As he stated, "When Virginia went out, I went out too."[2] He became involved with the "Southern Guards," a unit organized by students at the university. Marching with the company as a substitute for his roommate, who had to remain behind to study, Hullihen took part in the occupation of Harpers Ferry in April 1861.

This short taste of the soldier's life led to Hullihen's decision to leave the university. He journeyed to Yorktown, where he enlisted in the second company of Richmond Howitzers on May 27, 1861. At the time of his enlistment he was described as being twenty-one years of age, standing five feet, ten inches tall, with a dark complexion, gray eyes, and brown hair. On June 10 Hullihen participated with the Howitzers in the Battle of Big Bethel and remained with the unit until after the Battle of Seven Pines.

Then on July 24, 1862, Hullihen received an appointment as a cadet from Virginia in the Confederate States Army. Orders assigning Hullihen, with the temporary rank of second lieutenant, to Captain Moody's Madison Artillery from Louisiana were issued on August 1. The young lieutenant's affiliation with the battery lasted only a short time. By August 28 he was relieved of duty with the artillery, and on the following day he reported to Gen. R. E. Lee for duty with Stuart.[3] Stuart promptly made him one of his aides and put Hullihen to work. An early mission, strictly voluntary, was an unsuccessful foray behind enemy lines in mid-December to rescue Gen. R. E. Lee's daughter, Mary. Stuart's Dumfries Raid followed, though what part Hullihen played is unrecorded.

The opening of the spring campaign in late April 1863 quickly brought the Army of Northern Virginia and the Army of the Potomac together in the tangle of the Wilderness. The Battle of Chancellorsville proved to be "Stonewall" Jackson's last battle. It was almost Hullihen's as well. Once, when pressed to tell of the incident, he related the following:

> General Stuart had sent me with a message to General Jackson, and told me which road to take to rejoin the staff. After delivering the message, I started back to find the staff, and came upon a battery of artillery which had just taken part in an action with the Federals. It was unlimbered right in the road. I asked the officer in command, a big, surly fellow, if he had seen Stuart's staff. He answered "No," in a discourteous way, and I rode on down the road, as I had been told by the General that it was the one to follow. It was night. Suddenly I was challenged:
> "Halt! Who is there?"
> "An officer of Stuart's staff," I replied.
> I was told to advance, and being fatigued and not on the alert, I didn't notice that I had ridden into a Federal picket, at first. But suddenly, I realized that I was in the enemy's lines. The squad that was awaiting me was not 15 yards off. I dug my spurs into my horse. He responded instantly, and as I wheeled him, the whole picket started to fire. It sounded like the whole Yankee army to me. A bullet hit me in the right shoulder, and the range was so short and the force so strong that it nearly knocked me out of my saddle. I was crouching forward, or it would have hit me in the neck or head, I expect.
> I rode back into the artillery battery that had failed to warn me that the Federals were ahead. They were in pandemonium, thinking the enemy was on them. I rode on, and a short distance away found the staff, and had my wound dressed.[4]

Hullihen's nurse at Stuart's bivouac was Heros von Borcke, who did the best he could to make his patient comfortable. But Hullihen required serious medical treatment.[5] He was sent to Richmond, where he spent several months recovering at the home of Dr. Charles Minnegerode, rector of St. Paul's Church. The care he received in the good doctor's home restored Hullihen's health, and there apparently were no ill effects from the wound. Meanwhile, the army had been to Pennsylvania and back. Stuart, when he finally found the time, made an effort to secure a promotion for his courageous aide. In a letter he wrote on September 15, 1863, Stuart requested that Hullihen be appointed a captain in the Provisional Army of the Confederacy and a brevet second lieutenant in the regular army. He also desired that Hullihen be assigned as an inspector to one of the cavalry brigades.[6]

Stuart's application brought Hullihen his captaincy on November 19, 1863, and his lieutenancy on December 12. The latter appointment came through a board of examiners that consisted of Stuart, Gen. Fitz Lee, and Gen. Lunsford Lomax. The description of Hullihen accompanying the report stated, "Moral character good, physical constitution strong & healthy. His intellectual attainments and military acquirements, and scientific knowledge were such as to justify his promotion—while his services in the field were represented to have been of a character illustrating coolness, and bravery united to a conscientious devotion to duty."[7]

A cadet no longer, Hullihen reported to Gen. R. E. Lee, who assigned him as assistant adjutant general to Lomax's cavalry brigade. Hullihen reported for duty on December 7, 1863. He served with Lomax until October 9, 1864, when he was severely wounded at the Battle of Tom's Brook in the Shenandoah Valley. The exact circumstances of his wounding are unclear, but his records indicate that he was struck in the right leg. His horse, a small bay with white hind feet and a white patch on its nose, was killed. More than likely the horse, valued at $3,500, had been struck by the same missile that wounded its rider.[8]

The wound proved difficult to heal. Hullihen's records show that he applied for and received at least two leave extensions. The healing process caused a contraction of the tendon in his leg, which gave him considerable discomfort. His last leave extension request, dated February 21, 1865, was for thirty days. Sometime during or immediately after his recovery period he again reported for duty and was assigned to Gen. William H. F. Payne's cavalry brigade.[9] His active service with his new commander had to have been brief, but it was not without adventure. On November 21, 1916, Hullihen, in a letter to William Gordon McCabe, recounted an incident that occurred on April 6, 1865, at High Bridge during the retreat to Appomattox Court House.

> Staunton, Nov. 21st/16
>
> Dear McCabe:
>
> I am sending you the enclosed "address" which you and Armistead Gordon expressed a wish to read—he was so much pleased with it, that he said it ought to be published in pamphlet form.

You will see when you read the description of Major Breathed's fight with the two captains that I was not relating something about which a soldier could feel at all proud of doing—but it is a good thing to tell, sometimes, the plain truth about one's self, if it will furnish a good background for showing the splendid bravery of a fellow soldier.

I read the address in manuscript to Genl. Rosser who said that he remembered well the incident of our looking on at Breathed fighting the two Captains.

Toward the end of the lecture I mentioned an incident—the capture of a flag by an officer and a private—the fact that it was the very last flag (as I think) captured by anyone belonging to the Army of Northern Virginia lends added interest to it.

I could not of course mention my own name in connection with it, but I may tell you some time all about it if you should care to hear it for it was my good fortune (as a soldier) to be the officer alluded to. For when Rosser in a loud and ringing voice called out "Charge 'em" my eye fell upon the flag—guidon—as the enemy fled in disorder and I said to myself now is your chance to capture a flag and I was successful with the incidental assistance of a private, for after a chase, I managed to catch up with and halted the flag bearer, but he was on the opposite side of a fence and as both my hands were fully occupied, the right hand covering with pointed pistol the man three feet away and the left holding the reins of my horse, I could not reach out and take the flag staff which was extended toward me— at that moment, however, a Confederate private rode up on the far side of the fence and the incident became closed and I rode off immediately leaving the private with the flagbearer. I had to use some very threatening language to the flagbearer, but have been deeply thankful ever since that I did not shoot him.

I remain,
Yours sincerely,
Walter Q. Hullihen[10]

The use of "some very threatening language" may have shocked his future parishioners had they been close enough to hear, but Hullihen's rejoicing over not having shot the man reveals much about his character. The war had not corrupted him, nor had it altered his basic goal in life, for following his surrender at Appomattox three days after his capturing of the flag, he resumed his pursuit of a ministry career. His progress was slightly delayed when, after returning to his mother's home in Wheeling, Hullihen was forced to hide for a few months with relatives in Pittsburgh. His flight from enemies unknown may have been prompted by fantasy rather than fact, but many other former Confederates were taking no chances either. Not surprisingly, Federal authorities were after larger game than captains of the adjutant general's department, and Hullihen's exile ended shortly after it had begun.

In the fall of 1865 Hullihen entered the Virginia Theological Seminary at Alexandria, where his professors crammed three years of work into two so that he was able to graduate in 1867. He was ordained immediately thereafter and spent the year of his deaconate in the Fincastle and Buchannon parishes of Botetourt County. After he became a priest, he spent two years in charge of St. Andrew's Church in Louisville, Kentucky. On March 21, 1870, Hullihen married Amelia H. Campbell of Wheeling. The couple would eventually have five children: Elizabeth, Meta, Jennie, Louise, and Walter, Jr.[11]

Hullihen functioned as rector at the Church of the Messiah in Baltimore for about two years before coming to Trinity Church in Staunton in April 1872. For the next forty-six years, until his retirement in June 1918, Hullihen played an active role in all that transpired at Trinity. Though some of his actions at times made him the center of controversy, he weathered all storms, and his sincerity won him the respect of many.

Even after Hullihen's retirement, he continued working in the church. His successor, Rev. John J. Gravatt, was with the American Army in Europe, and Hullihen carried out the many duties required of a rector though officially he no longer held the position. Hampden-Sidney College conferred upon him the degree of doctor of divinity in June 1922.

One of Hullihen's most treasured moments may have been the dedication of the Soldiers' Monument in Thornrose Cemetery in Staunton, Virginia, on September 25, 1888. His long and fervent prayer on that occasion included Robert E. Lee's oft-quoted "duty is the sublimest word in human language" and a reference to "Stonewall" Jackson's "Let us cross over the river and rest under the shade of the trees."[12]

Later, Hullihen wrote to Jefferson Davis and included a copy of his prayer. The ex-President of the Confederacy responded with the following letter.

Beauvoir Missi
20th June 1889

The Revd
Walter Q. Hullihen,
Dear Sir,

Please accept my thanks for your kind remembrance of me and for the beautiful and patriotic prayer of which you enclosed me a copy. I hope the words will sink deep into the hearts of all the rising generations & that the time may never come when the heroic efforts of our veterans will cease to be honored by the People of the South. Surely it is not needful in common effort for the common good, to question the virtue of our heroes or the justice of our cause.

Fraternally yours,
Jefferson Davis[13]

On May 30, 1907, Hullihen was called upon to present the prayer at the unveiling of the equestrian statue of Stuart in Richmond. He offered an eloquent if rather long prayer (much to the chagrin of Frank Robertson and Chiswell Dabney, who had hinted to Hullihen that on such occasions the prayer should be brief).[14] Joining Hullihen on the speaker's platform that day were Andrew R. Venable, who presided over the ceremonies, and Theodore S. Garnett, who delivered the dedication address. The occasion would be one of the last times that so many of the staff gathered.

The devoted man of God greeted the year 1923 with the same dedication of soul and spirit that had driven him in years past. But the pace had become too great, and Hullihen's doctors warned him that his heart could no longer stand the strain. Heeding their advice, he allowed himself to rest but refused to become totally inactive. Until two weeks before his death, he faithfully attended church services and made visitations to parishioners. On April 8, 1923, Hullihen died at his home in Staunton. The Stonewall Jackson Camp, Confederate Veterans, of which he was a member, and the J. E. B. Stuart chapter of the United Daughters of the Confederacy attended his funeral. His gravestone reads:

Walter Q.
Hullihen
A Soldier of the
Confederacy

for 46 years Rector
of Trinity Church
Born in Wheeling, Va.
June 14, 1841
Died in Staunton, Va.
April 8, 1923

Maj. William J. Johnson

Chief of subsistence
August 1, 1862, to May 12, 1864

The name Shannon's Crossroads (Shannon's Hill) is not one that immediately comes to mind when discussing the history of the war. For Maj. William J. Johnson, though, the two country roads that intersected about ten miles south of Louisa Court House would always have special meaning. There for a few minutes on the morning of May 4, 1863, he came face-to-face with the war that subsistence officers rarely encountered. For Johnson the war was fought with requisition forms, wagons, stubborn mules, irritable wagoners, and tons of supplies, not with pistol and sabre. Vital as his work was, for most of the war Johnson was a rear echelon officer who seldom saw armed Yankees, much less fired on them.

Whether he took advantage of his opportunity to get off a few rounds that morning is not known. Most certainly the Yanks managed to scatter a few carbine balls in his direction before capturing Johnson, who spent the next three weeks sampling Union rations in Old Capitol Prison before being exchanged and returning to his "war" of supplies, requisitions, and cantankerous mules.

A virtually unknown staff officer, William J. Johnson does not rate even a single word in any of the standard works on Stuart. His name does not appear in von Borcke's memoirs, McClellan's account of Stuart's campaigns, or the letters of Channing Price and Frank Robertson. The only mention of his association with the staff occurs in Blackford's *War Years with Jeb Stuart,* and then not in the text but in the incomplete list of Stuart's staff officers in the book's appendixes. And there the usually reliable Blackford erred by recording Johnson's middle initial as "S" instead of "J."[1] One other reference to him occurs in a letter written by Charles Grattan to his sister on July 19, 1864.[2] Beyond these two citations, Johnson's only claim to having followed the plume is his war record, which fortunately confirms his place on the staff.

Born on February 3, 1828, in Louisa County, Virginia, William J. Johnson, according to one account, did not venture far from his native county until his involvement in the war. He enlisted as a private in Company "C," 1st Virginia Cavalry, in Lexington, Virginia, on April 18, 1861. By May 12 Johnson was quartermaster sergeant. Appointed from Virginia on October 8, 1861, as captain and assistant commissary of subsistence for the 1st Virginia Cavalry, Johnson secured and forwarded his official bond on November 30, 1861. This procedure was similar to that which Dabney Ball, Norman R. FitzHugh, and the other quartermaster and commissary officers had to undergo before assuming their duties.

Johnson remained with the 1st Virginia until Dabney Ball resigned his position as the cavalry's commissary officer on July 15, 1862. Stuart wasted little time in having Johnson assigned to his staff. Commissioned major on August 1, to date from July 17, Johnson took over for Ball almost immediately. His work would not have varied much from that which he had done with the 1st Virginia.

The Federal major general George Stoneman launched his raid behind the Army of Northern Virginia on April 30, 1863. As a military expedition, it met with limited success and has generally been condemned for robbing the Union Army of the Potomac of the majority of its cavalry during the ensuing Chancellorsville Campaign. About the same time, Major Johnson was performing his duties supplying Stuart's cavalry with its daily rations. He was unaware of Stoneman's foray but soon learned of it firsthand.

Capt. James E. Harrison of the 5th U.S. Cavalry, with the eighty men of his command, received orders the night of May 3 to secure the Confederate outpost at Shannon's Crossroads, which was at that time about six miles in the rear of Stoneman's column. He successfully completed his mission, though a brief clash with a portion of Gen. Wade Hampton's brigade occurred in the vicinity of the crossroads. Somehow in the skirmishing that took place Johnson was captured. Stoneman credits a Lieutenant Tupper of the 6th U.S. Cavalry with taking Johnson during the brief fighting in and around the crossroads.[3] Three other Confederates were also taken prisoner.[4]

Following his brief stay in prison, Johnson continued as Stuart's chief of subsistence. After Yellow Tavern, he was transferred to Hampton's staff and later served with Gen. Fitzhugh Lee. On March 27, 1865, Johnson was assigned once again to Hampton and reported to that officer in Raleigh, North Carolina. As part of Gen. Joseph E. Johnston's army, Johnson was paroled on April 26, 1865.[5]

Though his military career pales when compared with that of others on the staff, Johnson evidently excelled as a commissary officer. His record does not contain a single blemish. With the exceptions of the time he spent as a prisoner and a twenty-day leave of absence, Johnson remained on duty from October 1861 until the surrender.

Johnson settled in Richmond after the war and put into practice what he had learned during four years of conflict. Entering into a partnership with a man named Hunt, he formed a wholesale grocery business. The firm of Johnson & Hunt did well enough, but upon the death of his partner some years later, Johnson founded W. J. Johnson & Co., which, under his astute business leadership, soon became one of the leading wholesale grocery houses in the South. His wealth and obvious business sense soon took him into new fields of endeavor. In 1882 Johnson was elected president of the Citizens' Bank in Richmond. At various times he was also vice-president of the United Banking, Building, and Loan Company, vice-president of the Burton Electric Company, and director of Merchants' National Bank.

In his private life, Johnson had both happiness and sorrow. He was married twice, first to Mrs. Helen Lane (née Clark) of Richmond and after her death to Mrs. Sarah Friend (née Tifley) of King George County. By his first wife he had two children: a son, Cameron, at one time a Presbyterian missionary to Japan; and a daughter, Virginia, who was unmarried at the time of his death. There were no children from the second marriage.

Johnson's health began to fail in the winter of 1894–95. His problem was diagnosed as heart trouble. In April 1895 he journeyed to Boston to consult a close friend who was a physician. The trip proved too much of a strain, and Johnson was forced to enter a hospital in Washington. He remained there until August 10, when, having improved slightly, he made the trip back to Richmond. His condition began to worsen, and he was bedridden from September 1 until his death on October 4, 1895. Richard E. Frayser, Andrew R. Venable, and Francis H. Deane, all of Stuart's staff or headquarters company, were pallbearers at Johnson's funeral. He is buried in Hollywood Cemetery in Richmond.

Lt. Richard Byrd Kennon

Assistant adjutant general
April 26, 1863, to November 19, 1863

Richard Byrd Kennon rests today in a little, out-of-the-way cemetery just south of the Virginia–North Carolina state line. In a sense his presence in such a place reflects his association with Stuart's staff. Though he was a capable officer, Kennon's time of service with Stuart was brief and, except for the Gettysburg Campaign, extended over a period of relative inactivity, so only the most dedicated of Stuart scholars recognize his name.

Born in Norfolk, Virginia, on November 10, 1835, Kennon appears to have been the only child of Dr. George Tarry and Ann (née Bousle) Kennon. He was the grandson of Gen. Richard Kennon, whose distinguished service with Virginia's 5th Infantry Regiment during the Revolution gained him such renown that President Thomas Jefferson appointed him governor of Louisiana.[1]

Kennon chose to pursue his father's profession and began to train for a medical career, but the war interrupted his studies. It also may have affected his personal life. With the war on the horizon, some couples decided to postpone their nuptials until the conflict was over. Kennon and his future bride were not deterred, however, and were married on June 21, 1860. His new wife was Louisiana Barraud Cocke, daughter of Phillip St. George Cocke, who later became a Confederate general. The couple was married at the bride's home, "Belmeade," along the James River in Powhatan County, Virginia. It was to "Belmeade" that General Cocke returned in shattered health after eight months in the field. He died on December 26, 1861.[2]

Kennon did not profit militarily from his marriage to General Cocke's daughter; Cocke had declined to use his influence even to assist his own sons in securing commissions. On May 8, 1861, prior to his wedding, Kennon had enlisted in Company "I" of the 4th Virginia Cavalry. This company had been organized in Richmond before the war with the fanciful title "Governor's Mounted Guard." Kennon became a first lieutenant in the company and on July 21 was present at Manassas, where the company was stationed on the extreme right of the Confederate line at Union Mills and was thus out of the action. Kennon, though, had been detailed as a courier for Col. "Jeb" Stuart and saw much of the fighting on the left flank. At one point, while on a reconnaissance, he felt a minié ball strike the sheath of his saber and glance away. Kennon carried that saber and sheath for the remainder of the war. The indentation left by the ball was a constant reminder of how close his first battle had been to becoming his last.[3]

Following his resignation from the 4th Virginia on September 21, 1861, Kennon was appointed first lieutenant and adjutant in the Confederate States Army from Virginia on December 31, 1861, to date from November 25.[4] He was ordered to report to the 8th Virginia Cavalry Regiment. His service with the 8th evidently demonstrated his competence, for on April 26, 1863, he received an assignment to Stuart's staff as assistant adjutant general.

When Stuart and a portion of the cavalry started on their ride around the Union Army in an attempt to rendezvous with Lt. Gen. Richard S. Ewell's Corps in Pennsylvania, Kennon went along as part of the cavalry chieftain's staff. On the night of June 27, Stuart reached the Potomac River in the vicinity of Rowser's Ford. Part of the cavalry under Wade Hampton had already succeeded in crossing the river, but Stuart felt justifiable concern over whether his artillery could duplicate Hampton's feat. He called for a volunteer to test another spot in the river to see if it would better accommodate the horse artillery. Kennon was the first to step forward. Kennon later described the event to his daughter Clara as follows:

> Gen. Stuart called for a volunteer to cross the Potomac in the vicinity of Rowser's ford in hope of finding it better. I was riding a thoroughbred horse named "Big Indian." I volunteered to try. The Potomac was about a mile wide, the water deep and the current strong. I made the plunge in early night. The horse swam magnificently. When tired I would get off on a boulder, holding the bridle to let him rest. I reached the Maryland side. The night was calm, but no moon. Some rest for the horse was indispensable. However, as soon as the breathing of "Big Indian" came back to normal I sprung to the saddle and we took the plunge to return. Reaching the Virginia side, a man emerged from the heavy growth of trees and bushes. I did not recognize him until the horse had its front feet on the bank. The man placed his hand on the bridle. When I dismounted, the arm of Gen. Stuart encircled me. (I had recognized him when he placed his hand on the bridle.) He said, "God be praised. I never expected to see you again."
>
> I saluted and said, "Where did you come from General?"
> "I have been here all the time. Can we make it?"
> I told him of the current and other disadvantages which all in all offered no advantage over Rowser's ford.[5]

After Stuart expressed his concern for Kennon's horse, he informed his aide that he had decided on Rowser's Ford. Kennon was left in the care of his servant, Sterling, to get what rest and food he could and was ordered to catch up later. The next morning, taking his servant's horse in place of Big Indian, whose exertions had ruined it for further riding during the campaign, Kennon crossed the Potomac yet a third time and caught up with Stuart at Rockville.[6]

The general had promised Kennon a majority when he had emerged from the dark waters of the Potomac on his nearly dead horse. According to Kennon, he received his promotion certificate from Stuart's own hands at Rockville.[7] The promotion does not appear to have been confirmed, and Kennon never reached the rank of major. He served throughout the remainder of the campaign and on August 24, 1863, became inspector for one of the cavalry brigades. Following a thirty-day sick leave during October, Kennon was appointed captain in the adjutant general's department on November 19 and assigned as brigade inspector to Gen. Thomas L. Rosser.[8] He held this post until the end of the war. Although one account states that when he surrendered at Appomattox he was assistant adjutant general to Gen. James Dearing, this cannot be substantiated.

Louisiana Cocke Kennon had inherited a significant amount of land in Brunswick County, Virginia, through her mother's family, the Bowdoins. The land included two plantations, "Meherrin" and "Pea Hill." After the war, Kennon and his family moved to "Pea Hill," where they spent the remainder of their lives. Between 1863 and 1878, ten children were born: Phillip St. George (1863); Annie Bousle (1865); Courtney Byrd (1867); William Henry (1869); twins Louisiana Barraud and Rosalie Bradfute (1871); twins George and Rebecca (1873); Sally Bowdoin (1875); and Clara (1878). Three of the children did not survive to adulthood: Philip died in 1867, and George and Rebecca died in 1874.[9] Despite this large family, there are no descendants of Captain Kennon's living today. The last of the immediate family, Louisiana, died in 1965.

Kennon's career after the war centered around "Pea Hill" plantation, though he did become very involved with the county in education, politics, and public health. Kennon died at "Pea Hill" on December 14, 1892, at age fifty-eight. He is buried in the Kennon family plot at St. Luke's Episcopal Church Cemetery in Northampton County, North Carolina.

Rev. John Landstreet

Volunteer aide-de-camp
May 5, 1862, to June 15, 1862[1]

Stuart had a deep and abiding concern for things spiritual, so his keeping a man of the cloth close to his headquarters in some capacity throughout most of his wartime service should not come as a surprise. Stuart's first affiliation with organized religion had come in 1848, when as a new student at Emory and Henry, he had joined the Methodist Church. Then, early in 1859, he was confirmed in the Episcopal Church, to which his mother and wife belonged. The war did not weaken Stuart's faith but rather, as with many others, deepened it.

Stuart's first encounter with the Reverend John Landstreet came when the forty-three-year-old Methodist Episcopal minister enlisted as a private in the 1st Virginia Cavalry early in 1861. From that time Landstreet became a familiar figure around cavalry headquarters. Though his place with Stuart received official recognition only during the Peninsula Campaign and the Chickahominy Raid, he remained close to the cavalry's commander after McClellan was hurled back to Harrison's Landing.[2] Their friendship, based on their common faith, flourished during Landstreet's tenure as the 1st Virginia's chaplain and continued until Stuart's death.

Born to John and Anne Verlinda Orme Landstreet in Baltimore on April 23, 1818, John Landstreet received his early education at Baltimore High School. His father, a merchant, may have wished that his son would stay involved in the family business, but Landstreet was converted at a camp meeting while still a young man and was committed to the church from that time on. He attended Dickinson Seminary, the forerunner of Lycoming College in Williamsport, Pennsylvania. After graduation he began to prepare for the ministry under the tutelage of Bishop Waugh of the Methodist Episcopal Church and received his license to preach on September 24, 1847. Like Dabney Ball, who was of the same denomination, Landstreet served many churches before the war. Until March 1848 he ministered on the Bladensburg Circuit in Maryland, after which, between 1848 and 1861, he pastored the following towns or circuits: Bladensburg (a second time) and Georgetown, Maryland; Shippensburg, Pennsylvania; Fairfax, Leesburg, Lexington, the Loudoun Circuit, Stafford, Warrenton, and Woodville, Virginia; and Martinsburg, Virginia, now West Virginia.[3] In 1852, while stationed at Georgetown, he married Mary F. Swink of Fairfax County, Virginia. The union would produce seven children.

The war ended Landstreet's peaceful lifestyle. The middle-aged minister was forced to choose sides. Though a Marylander by birth, much of his life had been spent serving churches in Virginia, and his wife was a Virginian. He decided to align himself with the Confederacy.

During the Methodist Episcopal Church's annual conference, held March 5–14, 1862, Landstreet withdrew from the Church's Baltimore Conference; he had been a member since 1847.[4] This action was only his first step. Sometime before the Battle of 1st Manassas, he enlisted in the 1st Virginia Cavalry. He was not at this time the regiment's chaplain but fought alongside his future "parishioners" as a private. He was slightly wounded by a saber cut at 1st Manassas but continued as a trooper with the 1st Virginia until February or March 1862. The regiment's lack of spiritual leadership led Landstreet to assume the role of chaplain unofficially. His work did not go unnoticed, and sometime in late March or early April, the officers of the regiment asked that he become the unit's chaplain.

On April 8, 1862, Landstreet wrote from Culpeper Court House to the Hon. Alexander R. Boteler regarding his request. He stated, in part:

> Like many others I am a refugee from home. The Officers of the 1st Reg't Va. Cavalry invite me to become their chaplain, and in that capacity I have been acting for several weeks. A few days ago they sent to the Secretary of War a formal application for my appointment endorsed by Gen'l J. E. B. Stuart. Last evening the Gen'l suggested that I write to you in reference to it. . . .

The letter had the desired effect, and Landstreet received the confirmation of his appointment as the 1st Virginia's chaplain on April 17.[5]

Not long after assuming his new position, Landstreet was called by Stuart to be a volunteer aide on his staff. The exact dates of Landstreet's service in this capacity are difficult to determine. In his report of the fighting around Williamsburg on May 5 (see pages 5–6), Stuart acknowledged Landstreet's contributions to the successes attained. He also mentioned that it had not been the first time that Landstreet had been of service to him. Just what Stuart meant by this remains unclear, but it does establish that the chaplain had been attached to Stuart in some role before Williamsburg.

The records are also ambiguous concerning the length of Landstreet's time on the staff. His official status apparently ended after the first Ride Around McClellan, though he maintained some connection with Stuart and the staff, as he is mentioned in letters written by the general and other staff members. He was regarded with great respect by all, and he made abundantly clear his own feelings toward Stuart in a letter he wrote to his wife from "Camp Brien" on August 12, 1862.

> My Darling Wife,
>
> Hoping fondly and reasonably from events now transpiring that I may drop in suddenly upon you some of these days or nights, my every inclination leads me to prepare a letter in the event an opportunity presents of communication with you prior to that time.
>
> I enclose at the same time the Official report of the famous Chickahominy scout—called here Bro. Stuart's Round on Chickahominy Circuit—also another notice the nature of which you will understand at a glance.
>
> Since my last (on foolscap paper) which I fondly hope has reached you ere this, I have been on another of equal

success & exposure. Like the former it was mainly a daylight adventure but for risk, gallantry, and result such a
one as our gallant Leader alone could prosecute.[6]

Success and luck continued to ride with the zealous chaplain. He accompanied the cavalry into the 2nd Manassas Campaign and witnessed the
triumph of Lee, Stuart, and Jackson over Pope. But the situation abruptly
darkened when Landstreet was captured. Sgt. B. J. Haden of Company
"E," 1st Virginia Cavalry described Landstreet's capture as follows:

On passing a road which led in the direction of Falls
Church, he [Stuart] directed a picket of three men to be
placed on that road, for fear some of the enemy might
come from that direction, and get behind us. My company being in front, I had to make the detail Sergeant.
E. G. Fishburne, W. D. McClausland, and Henry Canady
were accordingly sent with orders to let no one pass. We
then moved down the road until the distance between us
and the retreating column was only a few hundred yards,
when a battery of Stuart's horse artillery, which always
accompanied us, opened on them, causing a considerable
stampede with their wagon train and artillery. We then
turned to the left in the direction of Flint Hill. Colonel
Drake, of our regiment, and the chaplain, Parson Landstreet, rode out a short distance from the column to a
house to get something to eat, when they were fired on
and pursued by the enemy. The firing was so heavy that
the Parson stopped and was captured. The Colonel, who
was a wicked man, turned, hollering as he ran, "G——
d—— it parson, why don't you run." The Colonel made
good his escape, but the Parson, thinking a good stand
better than a bad run, obeyed the command to halt.[7]

While a prisoner, Landstreet managed to meet with Pope and several other
generals. His relationship with Stuart became known, and Pope asked the
parson to transmit a message to his chieftain. It turned out to be an offer
for an exchange of "prisoners": Pope's coat for Stuart's hat.[8] Landstreet
also conveyed the fact that the Federal officers with whom he had conversed
"spoke kindly" of Stuart, something the cavalry commander must have
enjoyed hearing.

The good parson's incarceration proved to be rather brief. The opportunity to deliver Pope's offer and the other information he had accumulated came rather unexpectedly. On September 2, the day after Landstreet's capture, Stuart, while driving the Union cavalry before him, liberated the chaplain at Fairfax Court House. The reunion must have been lively considering all that Landstreet had to say. Though he had been treated quite royally while a prisoner, he certainly was glad to be back with Stuart and the 1st Virginia once again.

Along with his service to Stuart, Landstreet continued to perform the duties that fell to him as chaplain of the 1st Virginia. A fellow soldier wrote of Landstreet after the chaplain's death, stating:

> The history of Stuart's Cavalry during the entire war was replete with many incidents, in which our favorite chaplain was a most conspicuous character; ever ready to lend a helping hand, to administer comfort to the sick and wounded, and to offer consolation to the dying soldier on the field of battle. He never neglected an opportunity to hold divine service in the regiment whenever an opportunity presented itself, and that in an able, zealous, and impressive manner. His services among the wounded and dying soldiers, sons of his old friends and relatives, were of the most affecting character. He would march and fight with our regiment all day, and spend the night administering comfort and consolation in the hospital, or bear the sad tidings of death to the home of afflicted parents.[9]

As the above quote illustrates, not all of Landstreet's duties were pleasant. One of his more sorrowful tasks was related by Col. William A. Morgan of the 1st Virginia Cavalry.

> I remember a circumstance that tested his [Landstreet's] nerve and the duty of his responsible office: One of our army corps was encamped around Orange Court House; our cavalry was also in that neighborhood, the parson, (as we all familiarly called him) and myself had received an invitation from Gen. Stuart to dine with him on that day at his headquarters. On our way out, while passing through the Court House, we overtook a file of soldiers following immediately behind a cart in which two men

were seated. We had passed by without noticing the circumstances, but turning and stopping my horse to take another look at the party, saw at once that it was a death detail. A few yards on one side I noticed a firm post but recently planted, which told me in my army experience that the man then sitting on his coffin in that cart was to be "shot to death by musketry."

I at once called the parson's attention to the fact that the lieutenant in charge of the file of men was about to execute that man, and as he had no spiritual advisor, would he go at once to him and pray with him. After taking in the situation he asked me to accompany him to the spot, where he was then being bound to the post, one of them binding a bandage over his eyes and placing a handkerchief in his hand to be dropped on the ground when he was ready to die. I begged from going with him, saying to him that I could not witness the shooting of one of our men, but insisted upon his going at once.

Handing me his bridle rein, he quickly dismounted and approached the poor man just in time, as the file of men were in a position to fire. There upon the fresh earth, thrown out to plant that fatal post, he dropped upon his knees, uncovered his head and with one hand resting upon the breast of the soldier and the other raised to heaven, he made one of the most feeling, earnest and eloquent petitions to the throne of mercy and grace in behalf of this poor man. I can never forget that scene. The prayer finished, the parson arose and stepping quickly to one side, the condemned man dropped the signal promptly, the word "fire" was immediately given, and a report followed.[10]

In January 1863 Landstreet's ministrations to his fellow cavalrymen ended abruptly when, for the second time, he was captured by the enemy. The records indicate that he was imprisoned on January 31, 1863. On this occasion Stuart could not save him from a stay in Old Capitol Prison. Still, he was not without friends. A number of them plus his brother, William, commander of the 11th Maryland (U.S.) Infantry, went to his aid and secured his release. He immediately crossed into the Confederate lines and, finding his regiment, reported for duty.[11]

Landstreet passed through all the campaigns of the army with the 1st Virginia until October 1864, when the regiment's roll of the twentieth stated that he had been absent sick since the eighteenth. On January 30, 1865, he admitted himself to the Charlottesville General Hospital with carbuncles. He submitted his resignation on February 2, 1865; his physical condition may have been a major factor.

There are indications that he considered accepting another post, but either he never did or his records were not updated. The evidence suggests that he never held another position. He was discharged from the hospital on April 17, 1865, and gave his parole at Fairfax Court House on April 22. At that time he was described as being forty-seven years old and five feet, nine and a half inches tall, with dark hair, brown eyes, and medium complexion.[12]

Landstreet returned to his home in Leesburg, Virginia, where he resumed his ministerial duties on the Loudoun Circuit in Virginia. In 1869 he moved to Hillsboro, Virginia, where he spent four years. In 1874 he pastored in Piedmont, West Virginia, but after a year was transferred to the Baltimore Circuit. He remained with that circuit until 1877, when he became the agent for the Wesleyan Female Institute in Staunton, Virginia. From 1878 to 1880 he was in Arlington, Maryland. He had his second tenure at Martinsburg, West Virginia, from 1881 to 1883 and spent 1884 at Cumberland, Maryland. His last pastorate was at Piedmont in 1885. In 1886, at the Church's conference in Staunton, he asked to be retired. During this postwar period, he also acted as a trustee of Randolph Macon College.[13]

Landstreet chose to live the last years of his life in Martinsburg where he had made so many friends during his two terms as pastor. He died there on November 21, 1891. His son and namesake recalled that his father's last words were, "My son my time is very short. When the end comes, the Church, the Masons, and the old Confederate Soldiers will all want to do me honor. I want you to see that in all things the wishes of the old Confederates shall control."[14] He was buried in Green Hill Cemetery in Martinsburg.

Maj. Henry Brainerd McClellan

Assistant adjutant general
May 16, 1863, to May 12, 1864

> One cold day in the winter of 1863-64 while we were in winter quarters near the Rapidan River, below Orange, C.H. Va., and when I was one of many couriers of Major General J. E. B. Stuart, Major H. B. McClellan, Chief of Staff, came to me and said, "Gallaher, I want

you to fix yourself up, man and horse, and
go with me under a flag of truce. We
wish to make a good appearance you
know."

Complimented that he had selected
me out of so many fine boys who were
proud to be attached to the head quarters of Lee's cavalry, I got busy myself
and had my horse rubbed down nicely.

There were only three of us—Major
McClellan, the sergeant of couriers,
Ben Weller, and myself. That afternoon

*Maj. Henry Brainerd
McClellan*

we rode away from camp on our mission. It was a very cold
day and there was a slight snow on the ground and the
roads frozen hard. After riding some miles we came to our
infantry pickets. As usual we found North Carolinians
doing picket duty. These poor fellows fought as hard and
endured as much suffering as any others from any state.
And here on a bleak hill they were nearly frozen, no fires
allowed day or night, watching and guarding the more fortunate lying back miles away in camp and winter quarters.

They soon hailed us and inquired of our missions which
Major McClellan soon explained and they let us pass
beyond, wishing us good luck. After riding some miles
further on we came upon outpost pickets, the cavalry, who
had been there all the night before and as they were
required to be mounted all of the time for fear of being
surprised. After chatting awhile with these boys on outpost duty and learning all we could as to where we would
probably run into the enemy's out-posts, bade them good-
bye. We were in "No man's Land" and at once fixed a
white handkerchief (there were few in our army) upon a
sabre and holding it up to be seen, we rode on and on and
always with eyes and ears open. About sunset we suddenly heard the challenge "Halt!" We did so and soon
spied a couple of "blue coats" on top of a small hill in the
corner of some woods. They inquired our mission and told
us to advance. We did so and sat there talking with them
while one dashed back to their reserve for their captain,
who soon came up at a gallop. We explained matters.

Major McClellan desired to see his brother a captain or major on General George G. Meade's staff, who commanded the Army of the Potomac, and who had commanded at Gettysburg in 1863. General Meade's staff had some of General McClellan's old staff on it. General McClellan had been badly defeated by General Lee below Richmond and was deposed from the command of the great "Army of the Potomac." So they rode with us back a mile or two to the reserve, whom we found sitting around some fires trying to keep warm, but all saddled up and ready upon an instants alarm to go forth, whenever or wherever called.

A man was dispatched at once to Culpeper C.H. some ten miles away to bring Capt. McClellan to see his brother. We sat around the welcome fire in the woods talking with those boys. I say "boys," for we were all boys in both armies. They shared their canteens of brandy with us and we gave them all the tobacco we had. They had usually a hard time to get tobacco in the Northern Armies. I have taken several drinks of alcoholic nature in my life but if I lived a century I should never forget that brandy! We were nearly frozen and that brandy seemed like a nectar of the God's to us. But it apparently was no more welcome to us than our tobacco to those boys from the north. Along about midnight we heard horses galloping. They proved to be Captain McClellan and escort coming to see his brother, our Major McClellan, impatiently awaiting him. As the Captain hurriedly dismounted the Major rushed to him and soon they were locked in each others arms and weeping. We learned that a letter had come through our lines to Major McClellan telling him of a devoted sister's death in Philadelphia. And hence this flag of truce, whereby these brothers, one in each army fighting each other, could meet and talk over their grief and sorrowing loss of a sister!

They left us and went off to another fire some distance and sat there a long time talking by themselves with no one to disturb them. I shall never forget the pathetic sight of those two brothers sitting away off to themselves and sharing their sorrow at a sister's death and they situated

as they were. But the time came for them to bid each
other goodbye, and this was scarcely less emotional and
pathetic than their meeting there. Warmed somewhat with
the brandy we rode away and through their outpost pickets
again into "No Man's Land" on our return, and about
sunrise reached our camp again.[1]

Courier DeWitt Clinton Gallaher's account of McClellan's melancholy
reunion with his brother vividly pictures the tragedy that shadowed the lives
of the families of men in both armies. At the start of the war, McClellan
had received letters from his family and relatives in the North urging him
to return home. Disinheritance was threatened, but McClellan remained
with the Confederacy despite all their efforts.[2] He had been in the South
scarcely two years but had fallen in love with the region and its people.
His choice made, he never looked back. If he was disinherited, it did not
stop him from loving his family and grieving for his sister.

Henry Brainerd McClellan, known as "Harry" in his youth, came
from an old and distinguished Connecticut family. His great-grandfather,
Samuel McClellan, held the rank of general and commanded Connecticut
troops in the Revolutionary War. Harry's great-grandmother, Rachel Abbe,
Samuel McClellan's wife, was a descendant of William Bradford, the first
governor of Plymouth Colony, Massachusetts. McClellan's father, Dr.
Samuel McClellan, an eminent oculist, and Harry's uncle, Dr. George Mc-
Clellan, father of Gen. George B. McClellan, the future commander of the
Army of the Potomac, founded Jefferson Medical College in Philadelphia
on land that had been donated by Harry's grandfather, Rev. Ezra Stiles Ely.[3]

Harry was born October 17, 1840, in Philadelphia, Pennsylvania,
where he spent his childhood. He studied under the tutelage of Professor
Samuel Wiley Crawford and at age thirteen entered Williams College in
Williamstown, Massachusetts.[4] McClellan graduated in 1858 at age seven-
teen. He had wished to study for the ministry, but a family friend, Dr. Mark
Hopkins, persuaded him to postpone the decision because of his youth.
Through Dr. Hopkins, McClellan secured a teaching position in Stony Point
Mills, Cumberland County, Virginia. He stayed at the home of the William
Allen Perkins family, "Forkland," and taught in a log cabin schoolhouse that
stood in their yard.

In 1859, in answer to a query from his college, he responded with
the following:

I am in Virginia, not at Harpers Ferry, however, nor
Charles Town, but away in the country, on a tobacco

plantation, on the other side of the mountains . . . where I have learned to eat bacon and greens, corn-field peas, shoat, and many other delicacies you fellows who have never been south of the Mason and Dixon's line don't know anything about. This is my second year in the country. . . . I am teaching school, and have eleven of the future Presidents and Presidentesses under my charge. . . . I am comfortably situated in every respect, and only hope that all my classmates have had as pleasant times as I have had.[5]

The "pleasant times" ended abruptly with the coming of the war. McClellan enlisted in Ashland, Virginia, as a private in Company "G," 3rd Virginia Cavalry on June 14, 1861. His obvious talents did not escape the eyes of his superiors, and he received a lieutenancy and an appointment as adjutant to the regiment on May 18, 1862. President Jefferson Davis had been apprised of McClellan in a letter dated November 25, 1861. The unknown supporter wrote, "He [McClellan] was among the *first* to rush into the ranks and has been here in the Peninsula Army almost from the day of the war. He has, I learn from many sources, won the esteem, and respect, of all officers and men by his intelligence, activity and bravery. I trust it may be in your power to promote the wishes of this gallant gentleman."[6] The letter may have helped McClellan; it certainly did not hurt him. He actually needed no assistance. He had abilities enough to recommend him to anyone.

One of those who noticed McClellan was Gen. Fitzhugh Lee, who commended the then captain on his gallantry at the Battle of Kelly's Ford on March 17, 1863. Stuart, too, through the various reports that passed through his hands, had come to see McClellan's value, but he already had his quota of adjutants on his staff (Maj. Norman R. FitzHugh and Lt. R. Channing Price, who had replaced J. T. W. Hairston). Then on March 31 Maj. Samuel H. Hairston, Stuart's division quartermaster, resigned. The position had to be filled quickly, and Stuart assigned the post to FitzHugh. Price received a majority and became the cavalry's chief adjutant, and Stuart wasted little time requesting McClellan's services.

> Hd Qrs Cav Div A of N. Va.
> April 13th 1863

Lieutenant:

Reposing special confidence in your patriotism, fidelity and ability, and desiring to reward faithful and gallant service, I have determined, if agreeable to you to ask that

you be commissioned as Major & AAG to fill a vacancy on
my staff. Let me hear from you by the first opportunity, as
I must await your decision before making the application
to the Dept.

                                    Most Respectfully
                                    Your obt svt
                                    JEB Stuart
                                    Major Genl[7]

On May 16, just thirteen days after the Battle of Chancellorsville ended,
McClellan was a major, to rank from May 2, and Stuart's assistant adjutant
general. McClellan soon demonstrated his value to Stuart.

The Battle of Brandy Station, fought on June 9, 1863, may have had
an entirely different outcome had it not been for the cavalry's new adjutant.
Left by Stuart on Fleetwood Hill with a handful of couriers while the
general attended to the Yankee threat around St. James Church, McClellan
noticed an enemy flanking column approaching his position. Fleetwood
Hill, the key position on the battlefield, had to be held. McClellan dispatched one messenger after another to his chief to warn him of impending
disaster, then he looked about for anything that might be used to hamper
the Union forces' advance. Near the hill stood Lt. John Wright "Tuck"
Carter with a single howitzer of Capt. Roger Preston Chew's battery.
Carter had already expended most of his ammunition and had but a few
defective shells and some round shot left in his limber chest.

The major did not hesitate but called on Carter and his men to fire what
little they had at the enemy. As the howitzer boomed forth, McClellan
weighed his predicament. There seemed to be little else to do but wait for
rescue or capture. But fortunately the Federal commander, Gen. David
McM. Gregg, took the threat of the lone cannon seriously. He slowed his
troopers and deployed his own artillery. The delay proved fatal for the
Yankee cavalry but only by the narrowest of margins. The subsequent
fighting that covered Fleetwood saw the hill change hands several times.
In the end the hill belonged to the Confederates, and the few precious
minutes bought by McClellan's coolness and Carter's six-pounder howitzer
had made the difference.

The Gettysburg Campaign followed, from June 9 to July 14, 1863,
during which McClellan accompanied Stuart on the ride toward the
Susquehanna. He endured the hardships along with the rest of the cavalry.
In his later reports Stuart acknowledged McClellan's contributions to the
campaign. Years after the war the adjutant received the praise of another:
One of Stuart's couriers, James A. Buxton of the 2nd North Carolina

Cavalry, remembered McClellan as "a cultured and kind-hearted gentleman." Buxton recalled that McClellan "like General Stuart, was fond of singing, and on the marches it was common to hear 'Maryland, My Maryland,' 'Jine the Cavalry,' and other familiar songs sung by good leaders of the staff and escort, in which could be heard Major McClellan's tenor. . . ."[8]

McClellan continued to perform his duties throughout the summer and into the fall and winter. His mind may not have been completely occupied by thoughts of orders and reports, however. A young lady had entered his life. On December 12, 1863, he requested twenty days' leave so that he could be married. Stuart granted the petition, and Catherine Macon Matthews of Cumberland County, Virginia, became Mrs. Henry B. McClellan on December 31, 1863.[9] The union would produce nine children. The children were Ann Miller (September 1864–April 1, 1950); Margaret Ely (April 4, 1867–?); Georgia Matthews (?–September 30, 1920); Henry Stuart (May 15, 1870–1871); William Macon (December 1871–1872); Mary Carswell (?–December 21, 1936); John Hancock (January 21, 1876–July 9, 1931); Emily; and Robert Ely. In 1882, according to the Fayette County history, seven were still living. Only five children survived McClellan, however: Ann, John, Mary, Emily, and Georgia. The last two lived at home at the time of the major's death.

The resurgence of hostilities in May 1864 quickly precipitated Phil Sheridan's raid toward Richmond. The Battle of Yellow Tavern, which resulted in Stuart's mortal wounding and death, left McClellan without a position. He had been at Stuart's bedside the day the general died, and Stuart had given him his bay horse and asked the adjutant to perform a few final tasks for him. Stuart manifested the trust he had in McClellan, as well as his feelings for him, in the words he spoke during those final moments. Later, in writing of the scene, McClellan displayed his own sentiments through the solemn, almost reverent manner in which he recounted what had passed between him and his chief. The simplicity of McClellan's account illustrates the deep emotion he felt then and still felt years after.

McClellan was then called to the staff of Gen. Robert E. Lee, whom he served for three months, until he received an assignment to the staff of Gen. Wade Hampton, Stuart's eventual successor as commander of the cavalry. McClellan reported to Hampton on August 11, 1864, and remained with him when the South Carolinian joined Gen. Joseph E. Johnston's Army of Tennessee. McClellan surrendered at Greensboro, North Carolina, and was pardoned on April 26, 1865. He had been promoted to lieutenant colonel, but the commission did not reach him until after the surrender. He never claimed to be anything more than a major.

For about three years, McClellan resided at Ca Ira in Cumberland County, Virginia. His work during this time is not known. In 1869 he moved to Lexington, Kentucky, having accepted an assistant teaching position at the Sayre Female Institute. In 1870 he became principal of the school. During the next thirty-four years, McClellan practiced the profession for which he had been trained. His accomplishments were many, but one of his greatest was establishing one of the earliest kindergarten programs in the United States, assisted by his wife and their daughter, Georgia, who was named for Gen. George B. McClellan.

In 1885 McClellan published his book, *Life and Campaigns of Major General J. E. B. Stuart* (later retitled *I Rode with Jeb Stuart*), an excellent account of the Southern cavalry in the eastern theater of the war. In his description of Stuart he avoided much of the "color" that appears in the books of other staff officers. A complete understanding of Stuart cannot be attained without reading McClellan's book.

Between his writing, his duties at the institute, and his involvement in Confederate veteran activities, McClellan was kept quite busy. Early in 1904 he suffered a mild stroke, but his health apparently had returned by October 1 of that year when, while attending services at the First Presbyterian Church in Lexington, he suffered another stroke. This one proved to be fatal. He died at approximately 10:00 P.M. He was buried in Lexington Cemetery, Lexington, Kentucky.

Maj. John Pelham

Commander of the Stuart Horse Artillery
November 26, 1861, to March 17, 1863

Pelham and the Stuart Horse Artillery—the two are synonymous. Pelham formed and trained the 1st Stuart Horse Artillery under the eyes of the one whose name it bore, and he saw to it that the battery never disgraced that name. He forged a legendary fighting unit and made Stuart proud of his artillery and prouder still of its commander. Pelham, called the "Boy Major" and the "Gallant Pelham," was coveted by both Longstreet and Jackson, but Stuart would not part with him. His services were too valuable, his friendship too dear. Only death would break the bond.

Most of Stuart's staff members are unknown. A few have names recognizable from books about the war. Two or three might even be called famous. But only one became a legend. At least three full biographies have been written about the slender, blond youth from Alabama. Dozens of articles have appeared in print, and numerous poems have been penned in his honor.

On September 7, 1838, near Alexandria, Alabama, a third son was born to Dr. Atkinson and Martha McGehee Pelham. John grew up on the family's plantation outside of Jacksonville, Alabama, the town in which he received his early education. Pelham entered the United States Military Academy on July 1, 1856, one of only three of Stuart's future staff officers to attend West Point. (The others were H. S. Farley and R. F. Beckham. The latter would succeed Pelham in command of the horse artillery.)

The Alabamian roomed most of his five years at the academy with Thomas L. Rosser, a future major general of the Confederate cavalry. Pelham ranked in about the lower middle of his class. One year before he was scheduled to complete the five-year program of studies, he ranked thirty-fourth in a class of fifty. His best subject was cavalry tactics, in which he ranked nineteenth. He was thirty-first in artillery tactics. (One wonders what kind of grades his instructors would have given him a few years later.) His demerits totaled 552, most involving typical infractions such as the condition of his room or the appearance of his uniform.[1]

Pelham and many of his classmates never saw the graduation for which they labored so diligently. In 1861 states, politicians, soldiers, and cadets all faced the choice of allegiance to North or South. The following letter indicates Pelham's decision:

> His Excellency
> Jeff. Davis
>
> West Point, N.Y.
Feb 27th '61
>
> Dear Sir,
>   Being still a member of the Mily Acad'y, I don't think it would be exactly proper for me to offer my services to the new government but I am anxious to serve it to the best of my ability. If you think it would be better for me to resign now than to wait and graduate which will be in June a single word from you will cause me to resign and as soon as my resignation is accepted, I will consider myself under your orders and repair to Montgomery without delay.
>   I am a member of the 1st class which graduates in June next—you know the importance of that portion of the

course still to be completed, and also whether my services
are needed at present. May I expect recall if needed?

Most Respect'y
Your Ob't Serv't
Jno. Pelham
of
Alabama[2]

The letter was sent to President Davis through Pelham's father, and on
March 16 the cadet became a first lieutenant. Pelham waited as long as he
felt he dared, then on April 22, just a few weeks before graduation, he
resigned and headed for Alabama. Upon reaching his home state, he spent
a little time drilling militia before leaving for Virginia. After a few weeks
in Lynchburg, where he acted as an ordnance officer, he reported to Gen.
Joseph E. Johnston. On June 15 Johnston made Pelham a lieutenant and
the drill instructor of the Alburtis Battery, commanded by Capt. Ephraim
G. Alburtis.[3]

The battery consisted of four bronze, smooth-bore six-pounders.
The men lacked training, and there were no horses to pull the guns. Pelham
mounted a drilling campaign that soon had the men dragging their feet
with fatigue but expanding their chests with pride as they began to regard
themselves as a fighting unit. Horses materialized, as did powder and
shot. The "Boy Lieutenant" built the battery almost from the ground up.
It was excellent practice, for he had to do the same job again several
months later with the horse artillery.

The crucial test came at 1st Manassas. After standing in limber for five
hours, Pelham and the battery went into action alongside the Rockbridge
Artillery. Gen. Thomas J. Jackson, just having received the sobriquet
"Stonewall," watched Pelham display his fighting qualities for the first
time. With the help of Pelham's guns, the tide of battle turned and the
South claimed its first victory. In his report, Jackson mentioned Pelham
and acknowledged his contribution to the successful outcome of the battle.
This would not be the last time that words of praise would be written
about Pelham by "Stonewall."

The first step Pelham took toward the horse artillery occurred in
October 1861, when Col. William N. Pendleton transferred him to
Grove's Culpeper battery. At 1st Manassas a section of this battery under
Beckham had assisted Stuart in his attack on the Federal right. Now Pelham
inherited the battery, which had deteriorated considerably since the battle.
Part of the reason for its condition was the absence of Beckham, who had
moved on to the Reserve Artillery. The muster roll Pelham submitted on

October 31 reflected the battery's lack of pride and discipline. It contained but fifty-two names and listed twenty-one men as having deserted. Only twenty men were present and fit for duty.[4] But if Pelham felt discouraged, he kept it to himself. He went to work in Virginia, beginning to recruit almost immediately and continuing to do so for the next five months.

Meanwhile, Stuart had been campaigning for a battery of horse artillery. He even had an officer selected to command it—Lt. James Breathed. Then Joe Johnston and Pendleton entered the picture.

> Hdqrs. Army of the Potomac
> November 29, 1861
>
> Special Orders
> No. 557
> I. Captain Pelham will report with his Battery to Brig. Gen. J. E. B. Stuart for service as horse Artillery.
> By command of General Johnston
> Thomas G. Rhett
> A.A. General
>
> For
> Col. W. N. Pendleton
> Chief of Artillery
> Army of Potomac[5]

According to recruiting records, Lieutenant Pelham (his captain's commission had not yet materialized) visited Centreville, Culpeper, and Richmond. He also made a quick trip to his native state of Alabama and while there enlisted a few men.[6] Slowly the battery took shape.

Training began in earnest after a sufficient number of new names had been added to the roster. Smooth, quick transitions from limbered to unlimbered status and a rapid, accurate fire topped Pelham's list of goals for the battery. He would not settle for second best. He worked the men long hours, under conditions as close as possible to what would be encountered in the field. Toward the opening of the spring campaigning season, Pelham knew that he and the battery were ready. Then on May 1, 1862, Pelham was finally granted his captaincy, backdated to March 23.

During April 1862 Union general George B. McClellan's offensive had begun to make its way up the James River Peninsula. Progress was slow because McClellan feared he was outnumbered. The Confederate commander, Gen. Joseph E. Johnston, knew better and retreated toward Richmond. On May 5 a rear guard action that was fought near Williamsburg provided the horse artillery with an opportunity to show what it could accomplish. Called into action by Stuart in the vicinity of Fort Magruder, Pelham and his battery opened fire on the enemy in the woods along the road to Lebanon Church at approximately 2:00 P.M. For the next three hours, with one change of position to the Yorktown Road, Pelham demonstrated the effectiveness of his battery. His guns (two twelve-pound howitzers and one twelve-pound rifled Blakely, which was disabled when its elevation screw gave way), fired "286 rounds of spherical case and 4 of canister from the 12-pounder howitzers and 40 percussion shell and 30 solid shot from the Blakely gun. Total of 360."[7] With his ammunition finally depleted, Pelham withdrew.

In his report of the engagement, Stuart praised the performance of both Pelham and the horse artillery. His young captain's divining the need to go into action—and doing so before Stuart could issue the command—drew the special praise of the cavalry chieftain. Stuart's words in describing the incident (see page 9) show a certain amount of pleasant surprise at Pelham's actions. Pelham had displayed for the first time one of his most remarkable qualities. His ability to know exactly what to do and where to do it without waiting for written or verbal orders startled more than one Confederate general during the war, and the effect on the enemy can well be imagined. One of his other great strengths as a battlefield tactician was his ability to grasp the importance of terrain and post his guns accordingly.

Throughout the remainder of 1862, Pelham's name appeared ever more frequently in the record of Stuart's cavalry and the Army of Northern Virginia. During the Seven Days, 2nd Manassas, Sharpsburg, and countless minor encounters in between, he continually exhibited skills showing a maturity at war that belied his age and rank (he was a major as of August 9). Whether directing one gun or twenty, he was always master of the situation. He could also serve a gun when required, as he did on November 2 near "Welbourne" in Loudoun County. Selecting as his target a Union color bearer of the 7th Indiana Infantry a half mile away, Pelham fired a shell that killed and wounded a number of the enemy, including the color sergeant and a corporal of the color guard.[8]

One of the finest examples of Pelham's fighting prowess occurred just three days later when, with Capt. Mathias Henry's battery, he was attacked by Union cavalry north of Barbee's Crossroads in Fauquier County. Unlimbering his guns and opening fire, he threw back the Federal advance only to find that a regiment was preparing to attack him from the rear. Ordering his guns around 180 degrees, he fired at the new threat. Soon the action escalated, and the Confederate gunners found themselves firing both front and rear. Pelham, mounted in their midst, directed their fire until the blue troopers were so close it was no longer necessary. Fighting with pistols and sabers any of the enemy who had survived the hail of canister, he gave no thought of surrender. At last his old West Point roommate, Col. Tom Rosser, arrived to rescue the artillery.

Before the armies settled down into their winter encampments, the new commander of the Army of the Potomac, Gen. Ambrose Burnside, chose to make another effort to brush aside Lee's Army and get on to Richmond. The Battle of Fredericksburg, the result of Burnside's offensive drive, provided Pelham with a stage for his most famous act. Again Henry's battery played a role as Pelham, with one of its sections, galloped into position on the Union Army's left flank. His two guns, quickly reduced to one, a Napoleon, kept up a steady fire on Gen. George G. Meade's division. For two hours, with the artillery fire of an entire Federal corps crashing about him, he harassed the blue infantry. Ignoring Stuart's orders to withdraw, Pelham fell back only when he had nothing left to hurl at the long lines in his front. Later, Jackson put him in charge of fifteen guns with orders to halt another Union attack. Again the "Boy Major" rode to the front and fully confirmed Jackson's confidence in him. Pelham's actions earned him the plaudits of Lee, Jackson, Stuart, and other officers of lesser rank.

The Confederate victory at Fredericksburg ended the campaigning for 1862. Pelham spent the winter shuffling among Camp No Camp (as Stuart dubbed his winter headquarters), Richmond, and the homes of various Virginia families.

In March 1863 the Union cavalry again became active. On the seventeenth, a Federal cavalry force about three thousand strong under the command of Gen. William W. Averell crossed the Rappahannock River at Kelly's Ford. Confederate cavalry led by Gen. Fitz Lee moved to block Averell's route of march, not knowing that they were the target of the Union expedition. Stuart, Pelham, and Capt. Harry Gilmor rode from Culpeper toward the sound of the fighting. Pelham had no horse and almost missed his chance of accompanying his commander, but he managed to borrow one.

On reaching the battlefield, the trio became separated. Pelham spoke to Capt. James Breathed, telling him to keep up a steady fire with his guns. Then he galloped off to join the swirl of advancing gray cavalry. The accounts of what transpired next are confused and contradictory. Somewhere near a stone wall, Pelham was struck in the back of the head by a piece of a shell that had burst above him. He tumbled from his horse to the ground. Beyond these facts, little can be substantiated. Those present were caught up in the battle around them, with the result that testimony by eyewitnesses cannot be accepted unreservedly.

Still alive but thought to be dead, Pelham was thrown over the back of a horse by two troopers and taken off the field. Someone, very possibly Harry Gilmor, eventually noticed that he was still breathing and had him taken to the home of Judge Henry Shackelford, where he died quietly and without ever regaining consciousness. His body was first taken to Richmond, where it lay in state while hundreds paid their final respects. Stuart selected von Borcke to accompany the remains to Pelham's home in Alabama. Pelham was laid to rest in Jacksonville. On April 4, 1863, the Confederate Congress confirmed Pelham's nomination to the rank of lieutenant colonel to date from March 2. It was a final tribute to a remarkable young man.

Not without his faults as an officer (the lack of records indicates that he probably submitted very few reports of his actions), Pelham nevertheless possessed a gift for commanding artillery in battle. How far he could have advanced will never be known. The beardless youth's accomplishments were aptly summarized by Stuart in his General Orders No. 9.

> Headquarters Cavalry Division, Army Northern Va.,
> March 20, 1863.
>
> General Orders
> No. 9
>
> The Major General Commanding approaches with reluctance the painful duty of announcing to the Division its irreparable loss in the death of Major John Pelham, commanding the Horse Artillery.
>
> He fell mortally wounded in the battle of Kellysville, (March 17th,) with the battle cry on his lips, and the light of victory beaming from his eye.
>
> To you, his comrades, it is needless to dwell upon what you have so often witnessed—his prowess in action—already proverbial. You well know how, though young in years—a mere stripling in appearance—remarkable for his genuine modesty of deportment—he yet disclosed on the battlefield the conduct of a veteran, and displayed, in his handsome person, the most imperturbable coolness in danger.
>
> His eye had glanced over every battle-field of this army, from the first Manassas to the moment of his death, and he was, with a single exception, a brilliant actor in all.
>
> The memory of "THE GALLANT PELHAM," his many manly virtues, his noble nature and purity of

character, is enshrined as a sacred legacy in the hearts of all who knew him.

His record has been bright and spotless; his career brilliant and successful.

He fell—the noblest of sacrifices—on the altar of his country, to whose glorious service he had dedicated his life from the beginning of the war.

In token of respect for his cherished memory, the Horse Artillery and Division Staff will wear the military badge of mourning for thirty days—and the senior officer of Staff, Major Von Borcke, will place his remains in the possession of his bereaved family—to whom is tendered in behalf of the Division the assurance of heartfelt sympathy in this deep tribulation.

In mourning his departure from his accustomed post of honor on the field, let us strive to imitate his virtues, and trust that what is loss to us, may be more than gain to him.

By command of Major General J. E. B. Stuart,

R. Channing Price,
Major and A.A.G.[9]

The passing of such a gifted officer was a serious blow to the army, which duly mourned the fallen hero. Pelham's death was also a deep personal loss for Stuart. He truly loved the Alabamian as a brother and later named his last child Virginia Pelham in memory of his friend. Stuart desired that his son, Jimmie, should grow up to be just like Pelham.[10] Stuart's grief is apparent in the following letter he wrote to the bereaved family:

> Hd Qrs Cav Division A. of N.Va.
> March 29, 1863
>
> My dear Sir—
> With the deepest grief, I approach a subject which has doubtless brought to your household sorrowful wailing. I refer to the death of your son—my comrade—<u>friend all</u> but brother,—John Pelham who was to me as a younger brother—whose place on my staff—at my fireside—in my Division—but most of all at the head of the corps to which his genius has imparted so much efficiency and fame—the Horse Artillery—is vacant,—and the vacancy sends pangs to my heart that knew him, and in the space elapsed, a nation's wail is heard from out yon capitol,

mourning her lost hero—so noble—so chivalrous—so pure—<u>so beloved</u>.

I know that man's sympathy is emptiness, to one who has lost as you have, the promise and hope of a noble son—but when I tell you, <u>I loved him as a brother</u>, you will permit me to share with you a grief so sacred, so consoling.

He has won a name immortal on earth, and in heaven he will reap the rewards of a pure and guileless heart. I attended church with him the sabbath preceding his death, and marked his close attention to the Word: often have I seen him reading the Sacred volume, and I doubt not in its Sacred truths the young soldier founded a hope of a bright immortality above.

If you would know his military exploits, (and I know he was too modest ever to have informed you) read my official reports since the commencement of the war, <u>these are his biography</u>, and had he lived he would have risen to the highest honors in the nation.

Major Pelham lost his life in the battle of Kellysville on the 17th inst in the <u>strict</u> and <u>legitimate</u> discharge of his duty—with no display of <u>rashness</u> and <u>excessive zeal</u> as some have insinuated—but displaying the same coolness and selfpossession for which he had always been distinguished.

I enclose his ring for his mother, it was taken from his finger at the time of his death, and as he has often made allusion to this ring, I am anxious to commit it to her charge.

A tribute to his memory, sent by my staff, who loved him dearly, to the Richmond papers will I trust accompany this letter—together with some verse, and General Division orders announcing his death. His remains were sent to you in charge of his cousin and I hope have reached you.

His trunk with its contents just as he left it, his sabre, two servants, and two horses, awaiting your orders as to their disposition.

In conclusion let me beg of you a favor to send over any photograph or daguerreotype you may have of our dear departed comrade and friend, in order that I may have it copied, to keep as a precious token, to recall in future years his noble face.

I shall be glad to hear from you, and will cheerfully render you any service in my power.

Most Respectfully
and truly yours
J. E. B. Stuart
Major Gen'l
Commanding[11]

Maj. Philip Henry Powers

Quartermaster
March 18, 1862, to June 5, 1862

Officially, the period of time Powers served with Stuart was quite brief, which explains his anonymity in conjunction with the general's staff. But had the authorities in Richmond acted earlier, or had Power's health withstood the rigors of campaigning, his name may have appeared alongside those of the better known staff members.

Little information is available concerning Powers's early life. He was born on April 10, 1828, but his place of birth is unknown. The earliest records indicate that at twenty he became a tutor for the six children of Lorenzo Lewis at "Audley" near Berryville, Virginia. On December 28, 1852, he married Roberta Macky Smith at her home, "Smithfield," in Clarke County, Virginia. The couple's first child was born in 1854 in Charles Town, Virginia, now West Virginia. Eventually nine more children would be added to the family: Alice Burnett (1854–1934); Elizabeth Macky (1856–1939); Jaquelin Smith (1857–97); William Smith (1860–1955); twins, Katherine Stuart (March 8, 1864–1946) and Fanny Ballard (March 8, 1864–?); Philip Henry II (1866–1914); Roberta (1868–69); Mary Hazard (1870–1916); and Edmonia Ware (1876–1971).

Before the war Powers joined a militia company known as the Clarke Cavalry. When Virginia seceded he enlisted as a private, along with the rest of his company, on April 18, 1861. Early that year the Clarke Cavalry became Company "D" of the 1st Virginia Cavalry. This association with the 1st Virginia would have brought Powers into contact with Stuart, who commanded the regiment. Powers must have soon demonstrated his usefulness, as he rose to the rank of sergeant major in his company by late July. He passed through the cavalry skirmishes in the Shenandoah Valley and participated in the Battle of 1st Manassas. On July 23, 1861, he wrote a letter to his wife describing the battle's aftermath.

> Yesterday we had a drenching rain all day and most of last night, and being without our tents we could not escape the rain and mud. We broke our camp however about midnight and marched to this place [Fairfax Courthouse] accompanied by two regiments of infantry and one battery of artillery. I was glad to leave, for as I wrote you we were near by a hospital of the enemy where [there were] over three hundred of their wounded, dead and dying. many of them necessarily left out in all the inclemency of weathers to die. To pass by it was enough to soften and sicken the hardest heart. I will not dwell upon the awful scene.
>
> The battle was nothing to this after piece. The excitement of the contest, the cheering of the soldiers, the triumph of victory and the whole field of many of its terrors—nothing could lessen the horrors of the field by moonlight. Enough—I cannot, I will not describe it. May God, in his infinite mercy, avert a second such calamity. Our march after we got beyond the scenes of the fight was rather cheering than otherwise. For twelve miles the road was literally strewn with every description of baggage, wagons, ambulances, barrels of sugar, crackers, ground coffee and thousands of axes, spades, shovels, picks, arms by the thousands, clothing of every description, cooking utensils—in fact, everything—and all left behind to expedite their flight, which was never stopped until they reached Washington.
>
> Our troops have been busily engaged in appropriating everything they might possibly need, from a pin cushion to the finest army tent. In this place we found in several houses clothing enough to fill every room in our house. Their army was splendidly equipped with every possible convenience and comfort. But I cannot account for their utter confusion and panic. Their own papers give our regiment [1st Virginia Cavalry] the credit for turning the tide of victory on our side. The papers if you can see them will give you all particulars. . . .[1]

In September 1861, just two months after Powers wrote the above letter, the Clarke Cavalry transferred from the 1st Virginia to the 6th Virginia Cavalry. Whether Powers accompanied it is unclear. He may have remained with Stuart's headquarters in some capacity. At this point Powers's career becomes blurry. Roger W. Steger was appointed assistant quartermaster on October 2 by Stuart but resigned in November. Stuart then submitted Powers's name to the Secretary of War, who refused to grant the appointment to Powers or to anyone else.[2] On November 19, Stuart and Powers were informed the appointment was ordered but then countermanded because the law did not allow for a commissary and a quartermaster at the brigade level. This obviously does not coincide with the fact that Steger had held the post or that Dabney Ball was then performing as the cavalry brigade's commissary officer. In a letter to his wife, Flora, on November 24, Stuart mentioned his fear that Powers would not receive the appointment.

The situation remained stalemated until March 18, 1862, when Powers was commissioned major to rank from March 6 and ordered to report to Stuart as quartermaster. Plunging into his work, the cavalry's new quartermaster quickly discovered that his rank and position had both good and bad aspects. On April 27, 1862, Powers shared some of what he was experiencing with his sister, Mary, from an encampment he had named "Camp Forlorn."

> As I cannot write to her [Powers's wife, whom he feared was cut off behind enemy lines], I turn my pen to you. Knowing that you alas will be glad to hear of my condition in this the most forlorn of all places. Well I am as yet neither <u>entirely</u> devoured by <u>ticks</u> nor swamped in mire, though I have been in eminent and repeated peril from both. I had supposed that Manassas excelled the world in the depth and filth of its mud. I had not then experienced the soil of [illegible] County.
>
> The weather has been despicable since our sojourn in this encampment. Cold rains nearly every day. And our men have not a tent. I have managed to make myself passably comfortable. Sleeping in a neighboring farm house when the weather was very bad, and at other times in a very comfortable tent which is only allowed to Quartermasters and Commissaries. They ought to have some perquisites to compensate for the incessant worry incident to their duties.[3]

In the same letter, Powers expressed his concern over the approaching campaign.

> We are expecting a battle, the lines of the two Armies stretching across the Peninsula, in many places not more than 500 yards apart, from which an interchange of shots is continually going on night and day. But still the fight does not come off. I am almost afraid this is only a feint, that a heavy force will hold us here, while the advance upon Richmond will be made elsewhere.[4]

Shortly after Powers wrote his sister, the Peninsula Campaign commenced. During the weeks of strenuous activity that followed, Powers's health began to fail. He was not alone, as the conditions on the James River Peninsula caused widespread sickness in both armies. He could have requested a furlough, but he did not feel that he should hold on to his position if he could not perform the duties required of him. On June 5, 1862, he submitted his resignation, stating, "Owing to the condition of my health which has been fading for some time, rendering me [illegible] incapable of discharging the duties of my office with justice to the Gov't, or advantage to the service, I have the honor to tender the resignation of my commission as Brigade Q.M.; and respectfully urge that it be accepted at once."[5]

Though he had terminated his association with Stuart's headquarters and the army by his resignation, Powers had no intention of remaining out of the military any longer than necessary. On April 26, 1863, after he had regained his health sufficiently, he reenlisted in the 1st Virginia Cavalry. He was immediately detailed to the cavalry's quartermaster corps and ordered to report to Stuart's headquarters. From August 18, 1863, to May 12, 1864, he served as a courier. In June 1864 he received a transfer to the commissary department of the cavalry and eventually reached the rank of captain. He continued in this role for the remainder of the war.[6]

Powers was greatly affected by Stuart's death. On May 15, 1864, he wrote the following to his wife from Spotsylvania.

> My dear Wife:
> The Sabbath morn opens upon us sadly this morning, and with a heart depressed with deep and bitter grief I long to commune with some heart which can sympathize with me. We heard yesterday of the death of our noble

leader, Genl. Stuart and the news has thrown a gloom upon us all. Since the death of the lamented Jackson, no event, no disaster, has so affected me. Jackson was a great loss to his country and to the cause. Genl. Stuart is a great loss to his country. But to us, who have been intimately associated with him—and to me in particular—his loss is irreparable, for in him, I have lost my best Friend in the army.

I cannot realize that he is <u>gone</u>, that I am to see his gallant figure nor hear his cheering voice, no more. "God's will be done," a great man has fallen, and his faults are now swallowed up and forgotten in the recollection of his eminent virtues—his glorious valor and patriotism. May God in his mercy comfort his poor widow. My heart sorrows for her, as for one very near to me.[7]

After the surrender at Appomattox, Powers rode to Scottsville, Virginia, where he had rented a house for his family. Their home, "Auburn," which had been located adjacent to "Smithfield," had burned in 1863. They returned to Clarke County, Virginia, and lived at "Smithfield" until "Auburn" was rebuilt. As soon as his family was settled Powers began to teach at Wickliffe Academy. In 1868 he built Auburn School, where he taught until 1876. He became active in state politics and served a number of times at congressional conventions as a representative for Clarke and Warren counties. In addition to teaching, Powers farmed "Auburn's" four hundred acres and was a representative in the Farmers Assembly of Virginia. He became active in the Wickliffe Church and remained a loyal and contributing member until his death.

In 1887 Powers contracted typhoid during a trip involving one of his many positions. His health began to deteriorate to such an extent that he felt obligated to do as he had done previously when quartermaster under Stuart. Fearing that he would be unable to perform the duties connected with the office of representative, he withdrew his name as candidate for Virginia's House of Delegates. Hope was expressed that he would recover his health, but on September 18 he died at his residence. He was buried in Green Hill Cemetery in Berryville, Virginia.

Maj. Richard Channing Price

Aide-de-camp and assistant adjutant general
August 8, 1862, to May 1, 1863

The letters Channing Price wrote home to his
mother and sister during his period of service with
Stuart are among the most valuable of documents
to anyone attempting to grasp an understanding
of what transpired behind the scenes at cavalry
headquarters. The dull routine of camp life, the
ever-changing weather, the depression and anxiety
caused by both the stress of combat and the boredom of
inactivity are all shared by Price with complete honesty. He hid nothing:
not his anger with his comrades when he felt they were shirking their duties,
not his joy that he might become a major on the staff. Price permits the
reader to walk among the tents of Stuart's camps and to catch a revealing
glimpse of those who followed the plume in a domestic setting. When these
peaceful scenes were interrupted by the enemy, however, Price gives a
vivid picture of the men at war.

Richard Channing Price was born in Richmond on February 24,
1843, to Thomas Randolph Price, Sr., a fairly affluent merchant, and the
former Christian Elizabeth Hall. Channing and his older brother,
Thomas, were cousins of Stuart's, and the families were quite close.

When on Stuart's staff, Price demonstrated a remarkable trait that he
had developed while working with his father. The elder Price's eyesight
had deteriorated to the point that he could no longer see well enough to
maintain the correspondence necessary to conduct his business, so he called
on his son to write for him. Channing's father had the tendency to dictate
his letters quite rapidly, one after another. Channing, who had attended
Robbins' School in Richmond, quickly mastered the art of virtually
complete and immediate auditory memorization. He managed not only
to write out his father's letters correctly, but also to do so without taking
notes. Obviously such a talent in an adjutant would be invaluable to a general. Channing was able to ride at Stuart's side, listen to the general give
orders for several different officers, and then during a halt write out all
the orders. W. W. Blackford expressed his amazement at Price's gift in his
memoirs and stated that the young adjutant rarely made an error.[1]

At the start of the war, Price joined the 3rd Company of Richmond
Howitzers on October 10, 1861. He participated in all the actions of that
unit, including those on the peninsula. In a letter written to his mother

on March 9, 1863, Price divulged some of his feelings concerning his service with the Howitzers. He recognized that his brother, Thomas, believed his life had become quite difficult, and he resented that Thomas had asked Stuart for a furlough to attend a wedding. Channing would have welcomed the opportunity to get just one leave during the entire time he was on the peninsula but was denied one. Having fought in the ranks, Channing was very grateful to Stuart for taking him on the staff and thought his brother should have felt the same.[2]

Stuart brought Channing Price to his staff on August 8, 1862, and made him one of his aides-de-camp.[3] Almost from the beginning, however, he also employed Channing as an adjutant. In at least one letter, Price complained that he was inundated with work, as he performed the duties of both positions. Stuart had discovered his cousin's talents as a writer quite early. He wrote to Flora on October 26 that "Price is such a ready and correct writer."[4] Paperwork did not occupy all of the young lieutenant's time, though. He accompanied Stuart and the cavalry on many of their most famous expeditions, including the Chambersburg Raid, known also as the Second Ride Around McClellan, in October 1862; and the Dumfries Raid, which took place during the Christmas season of 1862.

As things settled down a bit, Price managed to visit his home on furlough in January 1863. When he returned to camp, he dutifully wrote to his mother to inform her of his arrival. His letter, dated January 28, presents a taste of camp life.

> I rode to camp then & found all well & making themselves as comfortable as possible under the circumstances. We had a merry party at dinner, considering the weather, as Chiswell [Dabney] and I had the General [Stuart] and Von Borcke with us, and dinner consisting of cold bread, cold turkey, corn-beef, tongue, pickle, and oysters which we cooked in our tent. Everything except the oysters was brought from home by Chiswell or myself. The General has gone . . . and we are in his tent, having an uproarious time with the Banjo, Violin, & Tambourine, but in the midst of it all, I am writing this scrawl.
>
> . . . I fear for the next few days, when the snow begins to melt. Now it is cheerless & desolate enough, especially to those of us who have just returned from the gay scenes of last week, but getting around a comfortable fire, we try our best to forget the cold and discomfort.[5]

With the coming of spring, Stuart began to realize that J. T. W. Hairston's health would not permit him to carry out his duties as adjutant much longer. Accordingly, Stuart asked for Hairston's resignation, which was duly tendered, and almost immediately, with the following letter, requested that Price be appointed to replace Hairston as assistant adjutant general.

> HdQrs Stuart's Division Cavalry
> Army of NVa March 4, 1863
>
> General:
>
> I have the honor to request that R. Channing Price, my present valued and efficient Aide-de-camp be commissioned as Major, AAG on my staff vice major J. T. W. Hairston whose resignation on account of ill health has been already forwarded. I desire the appointment to take effect Mar 1st. I have the honor to be
>
> Mo Respectfully
> Your obt svt
> JEB Stuart
> Major Genl
> Comdg
>
> Gen. S. Cooper
> A & I Genl
> CSA[6]

Price continued in his duties as aide-de-camp until the promotion was approved. Though proud of the promotion, he expressed some concern over it in a letter to his mother. He felt that Stuart should have given him a trial period before requesting him as his assistant adjutant general. Price did not want the appointment unless he was truly deserving. But Stuart knew his man.[7] As mentioned earlier, Price had already begun to function as an adjutant shortly after joining the staff and had displayed his eminent qualifications for the post, so his feelings that Stuart had promoted him without knowing whether he could handle the job might just have been a case of nerves.

Unhappily, one of Price's first tasks as adjutant involved announcing to the cavalry the death of Maj. John Pelham. Price had the sad duty of writing out General Orders No. 9. His personal feelings toward Pelham reflect those of almost all who met the "Boy Major." Price acknowledged that though Pelham had his faults, as does every man, he "was one of the noblest specimens I ever had the pleasure of meeting with."[8] Along with the cavalry in general, Price wondered how Pelham's place could ever be filled.

Stuart, ever proud of his staff and their accomplishments, presented Price with a beautiful pair of major's stars for his uniform. Price nevertheless admitted he was not nearly as thrilled at becoming a major as he had been at being brought out of the ranks and pronounced a lieutenant. He also had difficulty in adjusting to his clerks and others calling him "Major Price." Characteristically, he acknowledged that the opportunity for further promotion while he remained on the staff was virtually nonexistent, and he stated that he would not aspire to a line commission, not being worthy, in his opinion, of such a position nor desiring one.[9]

When Maj. Norman FitzHugh left his position as adjutant to assume the duties of quartermaster for the cavalry, Price was prepared for the shock. Whereas Stuart had kept the two of them busy as adjutants, all the work now fell to Price. The general, highly pleased with Price's work, placed most of the burden on his shoulders rather than delegating some of it to other officers. The new major voiced his chagrin over the situation and received some sympathy from surgeon John Fontaine, but Price continued to work in his usual competent manner.[10]

The arrival of spring signaled the opening of hostilities between the two great armies in the eastern theater of the war. Union and Confederate cavalry sparred with each other along the Rappahannock River. During one of these small fights, Stuart and his staff barely avoided a tragedy. Channing wrote of the incident to his mother on April 16.

> Gen. [Fitzhugh] Lee soon returned & reported all well at Kelly's & we were all lying in an open field with our horses grazing nearby, looking on at an artillery duel which had been going on sometime to our right & left and wondering why they did not fire at us as we were 40 or 50 & much lower & easier to hit than the batteries firing at them. Suddenly I as well as others noticed that there was a stir at the Yankee lines & several exclaimed that they are going to give us a shot. I was half reclining on the grass with Capt. [James Louis] Clark's head resting on Capt. [Benjamin Stephen] White's gloves lying on my knee. I got up and walked into the woods to untie my horse who had gotten himself twisted in the bushes: hearing a shot I looked & a shell lit exactly where I had been lying & right into the centre of the group, throwing dirt over a good many, but not exploding and consequently not touching a man or horse. Capt. White had just picked up his gloves & assured me that it hit just

where they laid: altogether it was the most wonderful
escape I ever knew.[11]

The new Federal commander of the Army of the Potomac, Gen. "Fighting
Joe" Hooker, soon brought the precampaign skirmishing to a halt and
launched another drive on Richmond by demonstrating against the
Confederate position at Fredericksburg while marching the bulk of his
army up the north side of the Rapidan River. Into the Wilderness he led
ninety thousand men. Then he stopped leading and planted his headquarters
flag at the small crossroads known as Chancellorsville. This proved to be a
fatal mistake for Hooker. Robert E. Lee was not one to allow such an
opportunity to slip by. With his brilliant lieutenant, "Stonewall" Jackson,
Lee struck the Union forces.

On May 1, 1863, in an attempt to find a vulnerable spot in the
Union defensive position, Jackson and Stuart, accompanied by their
staffs, made a scout of the Federal right flank in the vicinity of the iron
works. Jackson, believing he had found the enemy's flank, asked Stuart to
bring up some guns and enfilade the Yankee line. Stuart ordered Maj. R. F.
Beckham to advance. The new commander of the Stuart Horse Artillery
brought up four guns: three from Capt. William M. McGregor's battery
and one from Capt. James Breathed's battery. The guns had no sooner
opened fire when the Federals responded with between eight and ten
pieces of artillery. One of McGregor's guns had every member of its crew
killed or wounded. The horse artillery was withdrawn, but the enemy
had so quickly found the range that their shells continued to rain down
upon the Confederate battery.

Jackson and Stuart quickly recognized that the Union position was
well defended and began to retire out of range. As the generals and their
staffs fell back, a shell exploded near the party and a fragment struck Price
behind the knee. He at first thought the wound was only a minor one
and insisted on remaining with Stuart. An artery had been severed, however, and his boot quickly filled with blood. The loss of blood was great
and caused him to faint. No surgeon was present, nor did any of the staff
members have a tourniquet. Price was carried back about a mile to the
home of Charles Welford on the Furnace Road. His brother, Thomas,
arrived and was with him at the end, which came sometime around midnight. Stuart, stunned by the loss, bought tourniquets for every member
of his staff so that such a tragedy could be averted in the future.[12]

The Confederate forces did manage to defeat Hooker, but they also
lost Jackson, whose arm was shattered by a bullet. He died May 10, 1863,
of pneumonia as a result of being weakened by the amputation of his arm.

On May 11, when the turmoil of the Battle of Chancellorsville was over, Stuart wrote the following letter to Price's mother.

> Hd Qrs Cavalry Division A of N Va.
> Orange C.H. May 11, 1863

My Dear Cousin:

Let me share with you the deep grief for the fate of your dear boy, whose loss to me is scarcely less than to you.—Let one share with you the fond recollections of his many noble qualities, and the sincere prayer that this sad affliction may be sanctified to our eternal welfare.

The dear boy fell at my side, displaying the same devotion to duty, and abnegation of self which signalized his whole career.

As an Adjt General—he had no superior, and his reputation as an able and efficient staff officer had already spread through the army. Many have been the expressions of regret and sympathy from officers of all grades, ever the highest. He was known most favorably to Gen' Lee who knew and appreciated his worth. His career though brief was so spotless and successful that it is well to consider whether, amid the mutations of human events, it is not better to have a career ended nobly, as his was than to risk the fluctuations of fortune in an uncertain future—At all events let such considerations help us to bow in submission to the decree of an allwise God—and say in our humble supplications "Thy will be done."

Channing was so reserved that it is hard to tell what his religious impressions were, but his bible and prayer book were often objects of his attention and his conduct while with me was as exemplary as a Christian's could have been.

He was an universal favorite, and was cheerful and happy in his occupation—I have no hesitancy in saying no one about me could have been less spared, and I miss him hourly now. His ready pen and fine perception saved me much labor, and contributed amazingly to the success of operations under my control—

We all deeply regret that his remains did not reach you in time for interment, but hope that Thomas had furnished you with the circumstances of his death.

The Division staff will wear mourning for 30 days—
every member feeling that in our hearts Channing's
place can never be filled—Give my love to all the family,
with assurances of lasting esteem.

                                    Most affectionately
                                               Yours
                                       J. E. B. Stuart
                                      Major Genl[13]

Price was buried in Hollywood Cemetery in Richmond.

Lt. Thomas Randolph Price, Jr.

Assistant engineer
February 10, 1863, to June 1863

Though Thomas R. Price, Jr., became one of the
most well-known philologists of his time, he is
remembered today not for his study of language
but rather for some excerpts from a diary he had
the misfortune to lose while on a bridge-building
expedition near Germanna Ford in April 1863.
History has judged him almost solely on a few lines
that writers have selected from that portion of his diary
published by *The New York Times.* His life is worthy of a fairer assessment.

Thomas, the older brother of Channing Price, was born in Richmond
on March 18, 1839. Of his early years little is known, but they were probably
similar to that of most young men of his time. He graduated from the
University of Virginia in 1858 and entered into the study of law. His choosing to study law may not have been entirely his own decision, for he left it
after just one year when his father gave him permission to study literature.
He may have been influenced in his choice of a career by his friendship
with University of Virginia professor Basil Lanneau Gildersleeve.[1]

Price journeyed to Europe and settled in Berlin in 1859. There he
studied Latin, Greek, and Sanskrit with some of the most brilliant scholars
in the field of language. The spring of 1861 found him in Greece studying
archaeology, topography, and the modern Greek language. After another
six months in Paris investigating French literature, he was on the verge of
receiving his doctorate when he decided that he had remained out of the war
in America long enough. On Christmas eve of 1862, Price ran the blockade
and returned to Richmond. His immediate concern was attaching himself

to some branch of service, and in that he was aided by his family's relationship with Stuart. On January 12, 1863, Stuart requested that Price be assigned to his staff.

> Hd Qrs Cav Division A of N V.
> Jany 12th 1863
>
> Col.
>
> I would be glad to have three lieutenants of Engineers assigned to my Division. I think their service would be valuable to the Dept and to the country.
>
> Thos. R. Price, Jr. who I understand is an applicant for such a position would be <u>very acceptable</u> to me, and I hope you will appoint and assign him to my command.
>
> JEB Stuart
> Major Genl
> Comdg
>
> Col J. F. Gilmore
> Chief Engineers CS[2]

Stuart's request was granted, and Thomas Price joined his staff. Commissioned a lieutenant in the engineers on April 5, 1863, to rank from March 17, Price reported to Stuart sometime in mid-February. Almost immediately, Price regretted his decision to join the army. He longed for the life he had been living in Europe and for the studies he had left. He performed his duties, but he had no joy in it.

In early April Price was assigned to help rebuild a bridge that had been destroyed by the enemy. Capt. Charles Read Collins was in charge of the expedition, temporarily filling in for Capt. W. W. Blackford, who was ill. Along with Price went the staff's other lieutenant of engineers, Frank Robertson. They had to delay their departure for at least a day because of a snowstorm but finally arrived at their destination and commenced working on the bridge. Before too long a Federal reconnaissance force attacked the Confederates, capturing all but the engineers and the men on the south side of the river.[3] Price escaped unscathed, but in the frantic dash to safety he lost his diary, which was recovered by one of the pursuing Yankees.

Recognizing the diary for what it was, someone in the military turned it over to an agent of *The New York Times,* who also noticed its potential as propaganda. On May 21, 1863, selected portions of the diary appeared in the *Times.*

AN INSIDE VIEW OF THE REBEL ARMY
Interesting Extracts From the Diary of an
Officer on Stuart's Staff.

[At the time of the arrival of our army at Chancellorsville, among other things found in the Chancellor house was a diary of an officer on the staff of Gen. Jeb. Stuart, which we have had in our possession. The individuality of the writer is masked under a pseudonym, which we have penetrated, but do not care to reveal. The diary is exceedingly interesting and well written, and bears the impress of a refined and cultivated mind. It extends over several months, and is exceedingly minute and detailed. We give below a few extracts, omitting such passages as might unpleasantly implicate the writer.—Ed. Times.]

Feb. 10, 1863—Mounted my uniform yesterday morning, buckled on my sabre and pistol, and after a farewell at home, started off on the train to begin my new life as a soldier. The day fine and mild—arrived at Hamilton Crossing, and was put down along with my baggage in a lake of mud; no conveyance at hand. Sent word by courier to [word illegible], and after waiting for several hours at the Quartermaster's cabin I was sent for and carried away baggage and all. Paid my respects to Gen. J. E. B. Stuart, and was introduced ★ ★ ★ to the various members of the staff. Major FitzHugh is his adjutant; Chiswell Dabney his Aid-de-Camp. Gen. Stuart came to headquarters about midnight; had a great romp with his two aides, and roused up the whole camp by his singing and shouting. His conduct was held by his familiars to be the prelude to some important event; he is said to be always very gay when he is resolved upon any dashing achievement. ★ ★ ★ Mrs. Gen. Stuart [illegible] camp with her little son; she goes to Richmond to-morrow.

Feb. 12—Nothing of importance in camp. Went to work in my new profession by tracing a map of Spotsylvania and Caroline. ★ ★ ★ Our fare is at present very bad— nothing but heavy biscuits and molasses ★ ★ ★ Oh! to be back at my favorite studies! Oh! for Berlin, or Paris, or Athens. I long so to hear again literary conversation, and have my thoughts once more directed to agreeable topics.

Feb. 13— ★ ★ ★ Dined with Gen. Stuart—his mess not much better than ours. He joked about his "stalled beef." It seems that the oxen in stall are condemned to die, and *their meat finds its way to the tables even of major generals.*

Feb. 17— ★ ★ ★ After breakfast, Maj. Von B, Maj. Pelham and I mounted, rode through the woods and fields across the country to strike the main road at Chancellorsville. ★ ★ ★ We crossed the Rapidan at Ely's Ford. ★ ★ ★ No food for man or horse in this barren wilderness, where the ferocity of man has conspired with an unkindly nature to render the entire country a scene of desolation. ★ ★ ★

Feb 18—Important news from headquarters. Two of the grand divisions of the Yankee army have left the Rappahannock on the 30, and are in motion. Gen. R. E. Lee says they have gone to Washington and Fortress Monroe. [This was at the time the Ninth Corps moved to Fortress Monroe.—Ed. Times] Our army is in consequence being dispersed. Gen. Longstreet's corps is the first to move. Gen. Pickett's division has already reached Richmond, and we passed Gen. Hood's to-day at Hanover Junction.

Feb. 27— ★ ★ ★ ★ Toward evening Gen. Stuart came into [name not given]'s tent, and we passed a tolerably pleasant evening. The General tickled his staff and threw them down in the mud. Then we had hard-boiled eggs and stories about his different raids. He said [two words illegible] that the Chickahominy raid was the most perilous and the most successful of all; that if, in his Pennsylvania raid, the enemy or the depth of water had prevented his recrossing of the Potomac, it was his intention to have boldly penetrated into the interior of Pennsylvania—to have wandered about through the country, and finally, if compelled, to have returned to Northwest Virginia. The scheme he said he had reported to Gen. Lee and the

Secretary of War and if they would give him 10,000 men, *he desired nothing better than to execute it in the coming spring.* During my absence Gen. Fitz Hugh Lee has executed a brilliant attack upon the Yankee cavalry. He crossed the north fork of the Rappahannock high up, at Kelly's Ford, attacked the cavalry picket at United States Ford in the rear and captured them all—fourteen killed, wounded and taken on our side. About [number illegible] prisoners and a large number of horses taken.

March 1— ★ ★ ★ News received to-day that the railroad bridge over the North Anna has been washed away. All communication with Richmond has been thus cut off.

March 2—Rode in afternoon with [name not given] to Gen. R. E. Lee's headquarters. His quarters not more comfortable than our own—he's on the main road near the Telegraph Road—pitched in a little grove of pine saplings and half buried in the mud. A host of negro servants in his camp, washing, cooking, tending the horses, etc.

March 4—Gen. Stuart called me into his tent this evening and asked me if I had nothing better than the *Fairy Queen* to pass my evenings—offered me thereupon the use of Jomini's *Practice of War,* and a translation of an article on last Summer's campaign by the Prince de Joinville. The latter I had previously read whilst in London. ★ ★ ★ His style is clear and graphic, but his opinions are hopelessly biased and incorrect.

 ★ ★ ★ Gen. Stuart was with us and prattled on all the evening in his garrulous way—described how he commenced the war by capturing 50 of Patterson's advance guard on the day preceding Bull Run.

March 18—(In Richmond.) Arose before day and hurried up to the station—found there a great crowd and intense excitement. The trains had been seized by military authority, and I despaired at first of finding means of going. Gen. R. E. Lee was there in person directing the movements of troops. I heard a thousand rumors of a Yankee raid to Gordonsville and of an impending fight near Fredericksburg. ★ ★

March 22— ★ ★ ★ Rode to pay a visit to Oby Price. He is a private in the First howitzers, and his camp is not far from us in the pines back of the field where Gen. Stuart held his review of Fitzhugh Lee's brigade. Found him well, and surprisingly happy and content. I have not seen him since the day I sailed from New York for Europe. He was then a neat, dapper little gentleman, with a decided *penchant* for the dressing and comfortable living. Now, what a change—a broad-shouldered, black-bearded, coarsely-dressed man, used to hard living and privation. His transformation is almost as singular as my own. Both show strikingly the power of circumstances and foreign influences in molding the character and pursuits of men—he the neat, precise New York merchant, converted into the artilleryman. I the retired, bookish student of philology, into a cavalry officer.

March 25—Breakfasted by invitation with Gen. Stuart. We were alone, and he was especially kind and talkative. He recounted with glee a scene which passed with Mr. Seddon on the General's recent visit to Richmond. He had requested an audience with the Secretary and the usher announced him simply as Gen. Stuart, without initials. Mr. Seddon was seated at his desk and did not rise nor look up as the General entered the room. At last the General advanced and spoke. At the sound of his voice up bounced the Secretary, all confused, and stammered out that he had taken him to be the other Gen. Steuart, of Maryland.

March 25— ★ ★ About dinner-time Stonewall Jackson came over to make a visit to the General. I went out to ride and met him going away in the road between headquarters and Mr. Garnett's. He was sweeping along at an easy gallop on a large handsome bay. Passed so quickly that I had not time to distinguish his features; nothing in him to recall the caricatures which popular veneration has delighted to make of the popular hero; handsomely dressed in [illegible] General's uniform—a jaunty cap, a full black beard and a fine horse; altogether a rather dazzling vision for one used to our slovenly headquarters.

March 28— ★ ★ ★ The talk increased of a speedy raid to Loudoun.

April 5— ★ ★ Capt. [name not given] came over in the evening—was present at an interesting conversation between him and Gen. Stuart. *Both agreed that the next attempt of the enemy to cross would be opposite the mouth of Mine River. [U.S. Ford.] The General predicted that the next battle would be fought near Chancellorsville.*

April 19—I think the staff made the narrowest escape Tuesday I ever saw. A shell, fired from the hills across from Rappahannock Knob, struck exactly in the midst of us, (some standing and others reclining on the ground,) but fortunately did not explode, though throwing dirt over five or six men and horses. Gens. Stuart and W. H. F. Lee were in the group, *and had it exploded, one or both of them would have gone under.*[4]

Quite obviously, the editor of *The New York Times* carefully chose those passages that appeared in print. The entries under the dates February 10 and March 4 are those most frequently quoted by writers to show Stuart in a bad light. Price's imprudent recording of his opinion of Stuart caused great embarrassment for himself, Stuart, and the Price family. Occurring as it did so soon after Channing's death, the publishing of the diary must have added to the sorrow both Stuart and the Prices were feeling. In Thomas's defense, the paper certainly would not have published anything to put Stuart in a good light. The entry for March 25, however, gives some indication that Price's opinion of Stuart was mellowing.

What emerges most from the diary extracts is Price's distaste for the war in general. Enough is written to make it seem doubtful that he would have enjoyed any other position in the army. He was sobered by a visit to Oby Price, whom he last remembered as a finely dressed gentleman waving good-bye to him from the dock in New York. The shock of Oby's transformation was compared to his own, and in recognizing that he was not the only one to have had his life turned inside out by the war, Price may have begun to accept his fate a bit more gracefully. In the second entry written on March 25, he does not comment about Stuart or about Stuart's story concerning Secretary Seddon. Instead, from that point on, Price avoided making any criticism about Stuart or the war. Perhaps he was beginning to see his general and the conflict from a different viewpoint.

Sadly, the damage had been done. Stuart, for all his love of the Prices, realized that Thomas could no longer remain a member in good standing on the staff. Price was ordered to leave and report to the engineer department in Richmond. Difficult as the situation was, at least one member of the staff made an effort to help Price. W. W. Blackford wrote the following about his assistant:

> June 7th 1863
> Head Qrs Cav Div
> Near Brandy Station
>
> Colonel
>   Lt. T. R. Price Jr. assigned to Eng'r duty at this head qrs. has been relieved and ordered to report to you. It affords me pleasure to state that the causes leading to this were in no way connected with his professional duties but of a character wholly personal between Gen. Stuart and himself. While with me Lt. Price has discharged his duties satisfactorily and would after a little [illegible], make a most valuable officer. I am sir
>
> Yours respectfully
> Wm W. Blackford
> Capt. Corps Eng'r
>
> Col. J. F. Gilmore
> Chief Eng'r ANV[5]

The letter gives the impression that Blackford and Price worked together closely. This was a stretching of the truth, however. Price, according to his brother, Channing, had two, possibly three, furloughs, one of which lasted for eight days, during his stay with Stuart. In addition, Blackford was sick for an entire month and could not have observed Price discharge his duties satisfactorily or otherwise. And there is considerable doubt that Blackford would have written such a letter of recommendation without Stuart's knowledge. No evidence exists that Stuart asked Blackford to write to Colonel Gilmore about Price, but the idea that Stuart may have done so should not be discounted, given the grief of the Price family at the time, Stuart's feelings toward them, and the character of Lee's cavalry chieftain.

After Price arrived in Richmond, he reported to the Engineer Department and was assigned to the headquarters in Richmond. As far as can be determined, he never again served in the field. At the war's end, he was paroled on May 4, 1865. His commission as major had been submitted but not approved prior to Lee's surrender.

After the war, Price managed to find a teaching job at the University School in Richmond. While working there he met Lizzie Triplett, whom he married on December 26, 1867. He became professor of Greek and Latin at Randolph-Macon College from 1869 to 1876, when he accepted the position of professor of Greek and English at the University of Virginia, succeeding his mentor, Dr. Gildersleeve. In 1882 Price assumed the professorship of English at Columbia University in New York. He remained there until his death in 1903.

Price was completely dedicated to his field of study and did everything in his power to draw students into a study of philology. His commitment to teaching overshadowed his writing to such an extent that his influence was misjudged during his lifetime and later. His work led him to travel to parts of the world seldom visited at that time. He spent 1891 in Denmark, and in 1895 and 1898 he went to the Frisian Islands to study the Frisian language. Before his death he had mastered six modern languages, as well as Latin, Greek, and Hebrew. He deserves considerable credit for challenging his students to further their education to the point that many returned to the South and became professors and college presidents. His contribution to the educational rebuilding of the South after the war was significant.

On May 30, 1884, Heros von Borcke arrived in Hoboken, New Jersey. The mighty Prussian had returned to make a tour of the South and meet again the men of the Confederate cavalry. Greeting him on the dock was none other than Thomas Randolph Price. Had Price been truly ostracized by the rest of the staff, he would not have been there to welcome von Borcke. The relationship he had with the staff had not been destroyed by the publishing of his diary. He was still one of the family.

On May 7, 1903, after a three-week illness, Price died at his home in New York. He was survived by his widow and one daughter.

2nd Lt. Francis Smith Robertson

Assistant engineer
March 1863 to May 12, 1864

Had anyone told Frank Robertson, as he lay in his bed trying to recuperate from what had been diagnosed as pericarditis, that he would one day be galloping beside his visitor as an officer on his staff, chances are the sickly youth would not have believed it. Gen. "Jeb" Stuart had come to call on Capt. W. W. Blackford and extended his visit to Blackford's brother-in-law, Frank Robertson. Stepping into Robertson's bedchamber, Stuart found him reading a medical journal and promptly told him to throw it in the fire. Stuart asked the youth questions about the campaign in western Virginia, to which Robertson was able to reply because he had been involved in the disaster.[1] The interview, for such it turned out to be, ended with Stuart wishing Robertson a quick recovery as he exited the room.

2nd Lt. Francis Smith Robertson

Robertson, deeply affected by Stuart's kindness, never forgot his first meeting with the great cavalry leader, who had taken a brief moment out of his busy schedule to speak to the ailing relative of a friend. A week later Robertson received an even greater surprise: A letter from Stuart arrived offering him a staff position. Stunned, Robertson, who had been thinking about taking a sea voyage to regain his health, began instead to make plans to join Blackford as an assistant engineer at cavalry headquarters. Months would pass before he would again be able to withstand the strain of campaigning, but Stuart had established a goal toward which the young man could strive.

A descendant of Pocahontas, Francis Smith Robertson, better known as Frank, could trace his ancestry back to his state's earliest times. He was born in Richmond on January 3, 1841. His father, Wyndham Robertson, had been governor of Virginia from March 1836 to March 1837 (he filled out the unexpired term of Littleton Waller Tazewell), and his mother, the former Mary Frances Trigg Smith, had been heiress to a fortune in land in Virginia and Louisiana. Frank's childhood as part of a somewhat affluent family mirrored that of his neighbors. His early years were marked by a consuming interest in horses. In a letter dated October 9, 1844, two months before Frank's fourth birthday, his father wrote, "Frank shows no precocity except for the art & mystery of a jockey. He is destined certainly to bring the art of [word illegible] to a point of perfection not yet dreamed of. He knows 'A' & crooked 'S' but not 'B' from a bull's foot—and this is the sum of his literary achievements."[2] This practice in the saddle at an early age was what enabled many a Southern cavalryman to ride circles around his Union counterpart in the early years of the war when horses were plentiful.

Frank began his education in earnest at the Hanover Academy. In September 1859 he entered the University of Virginia, where war was the paramount topic of conversation. Robertson did not favor secession, but he felt it was his duty to remain loyal to Virginia whatever course was followed.[3]

In December 1860 Robertson and two of his intimate friends, William B. Tabb and W. Page McCarthy, decided to form a military company. It became known as the "Sons of Liberty."[4] The company drilled in preparation for a war that Robertson hoped would never come. After the firing on Sumter and Lincoln's call for troops, Virginia seceded, and the "Sons of Liberty" were soon marching off to Harpers Ferry. Along with the rest of the boys in the company, Robertson carried a flintlock musket without a flint and a cartridge box with no cartridges. The company arrived at Harpers Ferry just in time to watch the arsenal burn. After only four days, the governor ordered the "Sons of Liberty" back to the university.

But Robertson soon left the university and traveled to Richmond, where he attempted to join the Richmond Howitzers. When his father discovered his son's intentions, he made him remove his name from the roll. Robertson instead received a commission as a second lieutenant in the regular army of Virginia. His new rank entitled him to be drilled at the Virginia Military Institute until fit to be called an officer. Robertson lasted two months; then his fear that the war would end without him led him to leave and enlist in the 48th Virginia Infantry. He became a first lieutenant and attempted to put his knowledge of what he had learned at VMI to work in June 1861. By his own accounting, he was not much of a success.

The 48th Virginia was ordered to western Virginia. There Robertson contracted "camp fever" and, prostrated by the illness, had to be taken home by his father to recover. Overly eager to rejoin his regiment, the young lieutenant rushed back to his duties too soon and suffered a relapse, which affected his heart. The doctors in Richmond diagnosed pericarditis and sent him home. It was during this time that Stuart visited him.

It was not until March 1863 that Robertson's health would at last permit him to accept Stuart's offer. On March 3 he wrote his father, in part:

> Dear Pa
> I am once more safely ensconced in a tent as a member of the Army & the consciousness of being once more on duty in the field brings with it a pleasure even greater than I had anticipated & for the first time in 12 months I feel comparatively happy.[5]

Upon his arrival at cavalry headquarters, Second Lieutenant Robertson was quickly introduced to the other staff officers and put to work coloring one of Blackford's maps. Progress proved slow, but his perseverance won out. With that assignment behind him, Robertson awaited a more difficult task. In late April 1863 the higher command decided that a bridge that had been destroyed—at Germanna Ford on the Rapidan River—should be rebuilt. The task fell to the engineers of the cavalry. Blackford was ill, however, and could not take charge of the project. Since Robertson and T. R. Price were both viewed as being too inexperienced to assume full command, a replacement for Blackford was necessary. Capt. Charles Read Collins of the 15th Virginia Cavalry became the chief engineer for the bridge-building expedition.

The three engineers, along with eighty workers, set out for Germanna Ford. They arrived around April 21 and immediately began to cut timber and make the other necessary preparations for the bridge's construction. About one week's work had been completed when, on April 29, Vespasian Chancellor, one of Stuart's couriers, informed Collins that he had received a report of a Union force advancing on the ford.[6] Captain Collins could not bring himself to believe the report, since it came from a civilian source and not the Confederates picketing the Rappahannock River to the north. Robertson volunteered to verify the rumor and crossed the Rapidan. He passed by a Confederate woodcutting detail and rode on for about a mile. All seemed peaceful and quiet.

Reining in his horse, Robertson paused to talk with an elderly gentleman whose home was next to the road. Scarcely had they begun their conversation when the old man shouted a warning. Robertson turned to see Union skirmishers barely seventy-five yards away. He quickly spurred his horse and galloped back toward the ford amid curses and bullets. Robertson was well mounted, on his favorite and fastest horse, Miranda,[7] but though he was able to escape, his warning arrived too late to save the woodcutters north of the ford who were on foot. These forty Confederates, who were cut off from the river, had to surrender. Robertson, who had been sent by Collins to a small knoll after giving his report, saw the whole unpleasant incident.

The work detail on the south side of Germanna took refuge in a road cut that hid them from the view of the advancing Federal column. Robertson, now the only Confederate in sight because of his exposed position on the knoll, soon heard bullets whistling through the air close by. Realizing his vulnerability, the young lieutenant rode back down the hill, seeking shelter behind a small cabin. This quickly became the target of the Union skirmishers on the opposite side of the river. One of the enemy's bullets kicked dust into Robertson's eyes, temporarily blinding him. When he could see again, the captured Confederates had been marched rearward, and a column of Federal cavalry was crossing the ford, unaware of the remaining forty Confederates concealed in the road cut.

As the blue troopers approached the south bank, the Confederates rose and fired into the head of the column. Those Federal soldiers who were not killed scattered for whatever cover was available. For the next few hours, a handful of Rebels held up several thousand Federals until eventually the remaining bridge builders were forced to surrender. Robertson, who had been watching all the action from behind the cabin, did not wish to spend the next several months in a Yankee prison. His only escape route lay up over the hill, which was in full view of about five thousand of the enemy. Undaunted, he mounted Miranda and galloped off, and though the ground around him was torn up by bullets, he somehow managed to make it over the crest of the hill to safety. Collins and Price also escaped, though the latter lost his now famous diary in his haste to avoid capture.

At the Battle of Chancellorsville, Robertson adopted a different role from that of engineer. Basically acting as a guide and courier, he passed through numerous dangers during the three days. He talked and joked with a dying Channing Price, believing that his friend had received a wound that would merely send him home for a few months. He was shocked to learn from Dr. Eliason that Price had only about fifteen minutes to live. Eliason proved correct, as Price died of blood loss and shock shortly after speaking with Robertson.[8]

By the battle's second day, Jackson had been wounded and Stuart commanded the 2nd Corps. Robertson was kept busy as a courier, several times braving heavy enemy fire to carry orders to Jackson's division and brigade commanders. On one occasion, he had just returned to Stuart when an artillery shell or solid shot passed so close to him that he was knocked from his horse. The effect, called "winding," gave Robertson a headache but caused no physical injury more serious than a few scrapes and bruises. Stuart and the rest of the staff thought that Robertson had been killed or wounded, but his quick return to the saddle relieved their fears.

Robertson was greatly concerned with the possible relapse of his heart trouble, but the strenuous life in the cavalry seemed to agree with him and he grew stronger. He was thrilled with the cavalry reviews held at Brandy Station in late May and early June 1863. Proud of his small part as a member of the staff, his only negative feeling grew out of his encounter with Brig. Gen. William E. "Grumble" Jones. Robertson was ordered by Stuart to tell Jones to prepare his men to pass in review, upon which

"Grumble" assailed Robertson with numerous strong expletives, thereby revealing the reason for his strange pseudonym.

On June 9, 1863, Robertson took part in the Battle of Brandy Station. Once again he served as a courier and transmitted a number of his commander's most important orders, including the one that brought Wade Hampton's brigade galloping to Fleetwood Hill when the hill was in danger of being captured by the Union cavalry. Robertson had a number of close calls, as revealed in this portion of a letter he wrote on June 12, 1863.

> I was considerably puzzled to know where to go or what to do, but concluded the Gen' must be making for the hill [Fleetwood] with the rest. I galloped on but on getting nearly to the top met a large body of Yankees who were sweeping everything before them. [Lt. Chiswell] Dabney (who was with me) as soon as we had recovered from our precipitate retreat, told me the Gen' was on the right and we rode in that direction and reached the top of the hill several hundred yards further on. When we reached the top we saw a regiment or two of our men, who had charged round the left of the hill, pursuing a large body of Yankees who were flying toward Brandy Station. I supposed at once that the hill was in our possession, on seeing our men on the opposite side and put up my pistol and rode very composedly right into the head of the Eighth Illinois who came charging and yelling around a skirt of trees on the heels of a portion of the Twelfth Va Cav, who had taken to most inglorious flight.
>
> With my usual good luck I was obliged to run once more for my life, with a Yankee Orderly Sergeant right at my heels popping away at my back every jump of his horse—how he happened to miss me I can't imagine, for a fairer mark or a more helpless one was never presented. I was riding Bostona and do what I could I could neither turn her to the right or left—nor could I draw my pistol. Every time I attempted to unbutton the pistol holster, she commenced blundering, absolutely it seemed on purpose, and I was forced to withdraw my hand to grasp the rein and hold her up—for at least two hundred yards this race kept up and I could see the fellow raise his pistol between his horses ears and take deliberate aim, but

fortunately I was not even grazed, tho' one of the balls
cut a slight furrow in Bostona's leg.[9]

The Yankee sergeant either ran out of bullets or was discouraged by other
Confederates from pursuing Robertson any farther. The lieutenant never
revealed the means of his salvation. He had one other narrow escape that
day. While resting beneath a cherry tree with several other staff members,
an enemy shell landed within ten yards of the group and bounced within
a yard and a half of Robertson's head. Luckily the shell failed to explode,
or there would have been others of the staff to bury alongside Farley.

The Army of Northern Virginia's movement north was well under
way by the time the battles of Aldie, Middleburg, and Upperville, Virginia,
were fought. At Middleburg, Robertson, sent as a courier by Stuart to
Munford, again had to race for his life from a pistol-firing pursuer. This
time the young engineer rode Miranda, and a pistol shot of his own
wounded either the horse or rider chasing him.[10] Munford received Stuart's
message, thanks to Robertson, and withdrew from what could have been
an unpleasant predicament.

Robertson's experiences during the march north included helping a
wounded von Borcke from the field near Upperville, crossing the Potomac
at Rowser's Ford, chasing the Federal supply train, fencing with Judson
Kilpatrick's cavalry at Hanover, and comforting a frightened Carlisle family
during the cannonade on the city. For this last "adventure" he was rewarded
with a cool drink and a small banquet.[11] Once he arrived at Gettysburg,
Robertson became involved in the events that led up to the cavalry engagement on July 3. He distinctly remembered carrying an order from Stuart to
Hampton in which the South Carolinian was told to avoid an engagement.
Frustratingly, despite having ridden at top speed, Robertson arrived too
late. The cavalry fight was on by the time he reached Hampton's line.[12]

On the retreat, a much fatigued assistant engineer had one more
remarkable adventure before he crossed the Potomac into Virginia.

> The general [Stuart] and his staff rode to Williamsport.
> It was raining and very dark. We had barely reached the
> suburbs when he ordered me to go to the Lower Ford
> with some message to our Headquarters ambulance. It
> was important, but to this day [Robertson wrote this in
> the early 1920s] I have never remembered what it was. I
> had never been in Williamsport before, nor had any idea
> where the Lower Ford was, but rode down its dark street
> at a fast gallop. I saw a big fire ahead that flashed upon

the river. It blinded both Miranda and myself, so without a pause we went off the abutment of a bridge across the canal. I felt myself flying in space, and expected I would land on the sides of the river bank. The next thing I remembered I was lying on my back digging mud out of my mouth. The mare was standing by me, and I remained there, I suppose, for an hour as everything seemed whirling around, and wasn't sure I was alive. I went to the Ford and found the ambulance. I bore patiently the jeers and laughter of a lot of soldiers round the fire "where the hell have yuse come from." I was a mass of mud, Miranda ditto. I led her out into the river, and soaked for some time. I had all my equipment except my hat.

(May mention here that some years after the war, I wrote the postmaster at Williamsport, Md. to ask if he could tell me the distance from the top of this bridge abutment to the water of the canal. He wrote me that he was a Confederate soldier, had gone and measured distance desired and found it to be 23 feet, so with 4 or 5 feet of water withdrawn, my fall to the mud bottom must have been about 27 or 28 feet.)

After my bath I rode back another way to town. I saw some Cavalry in the furniture shop, and they allowed me to make one move. I pulled out the lower drawer of a bureau and went to sleep in it. The next morning I called for help to get out of it, an inch of muddy water left in it. I also had to be lifted on Miranda, very stiff, and my right shoulder hurting. I reported to the General whom I found at the Upper Ford.[13]

The strain of the entire campaign proved too much for Robertson's constitution. Upon the cavalry's encamping at "The Bower," Stuart had his assistant engineer put to bed. Surgeon Talcott Eliason examined him and found that his shoulder was severely injured. He immediately issued Robertson a two-month furlough. Two days later, accompanied by Dabney Ball and his wife, who were traveling to Salem, Virginia, and riding in a hair-covered rocking chair sitting in an ambulance, Robertson began his journey home. According to his account of the trip, he and his companions ate well. He shot partridges with his pistol as the birds were sitting on fences along the route.[14]

A resurgence of his old physical problem, which this time was diagnosed as rheumatic endocarditis, prohibited Robertson from ever rejoining

Stuart on the front lines, though he probably did visit cavalry headquarters a few times. In spite of this, he did not cease to be connected with the general or his staff. Stuart wrote his absent engineer at least twice, once on September 21, 1863, and again on April 18, 1864. The general also asked "The" Garnett to write Robertson on April 30 to keep him abreast of what was transpiring and to inform him that Stuart was attempting to secure a promotion for him.

By January 1864 Robertson was in Richmond and recovered enough that he could accept map-drawing assignments from Stuart. From that time until Stuart fell at Yellow Tavern, Robertson was engaged in creating maps of areas Stuart felt were important. One section of Virginia that received the engineer's attention was the terrain along the Rapidan River. Robertson's only brush with danger occurred when Sheridan came close to Richmond. The engineer made an attempt to reach the skirmish line outside the city but turned back. When he returned, he was stunned to hear of Stuart's wounding. Robertson arrived at Dr. Brewer's house in time to bid farewell to his chief and friend.

Soon after Stuart's death, Robertson was assigned to the staff of W. H. F. Lee. He served with Lee to the war's end. His duties were strenuous at times, but he managed to keep his health, thanks to short respites in Richmond. One such occasion was prompted by the unfortunate condition of his commander.

> General Lee as you have already heard is my guest and with all due regard for his precious health, I would like his remaining so for at least a week longer—alas! his head which three days ago was about the size of a half bushel, is fast assuming its natural dimensions, which even then compares to Tom Brender's as a mountain to a mouse. The swelling has unfortunately ceased,—he declares Richard is himself again and will return Tuesday to the Army. I have most earnestly cited several instances of relapse occurring from too early exposure of poison oak sufferers but it availeth nothing,—and my arduous duties as ADC on extra duty in Richmond are fast drawing to a close. I am however thankful for what I have had, and shall ever regard Poison Oak as a favorite plant. I have enjoyed my short stay exceedingly, the more so as I was considerably jaded down by the previous ten days of hard service, and was sorely in need of rest. I am

> thinner than I ever was before in good health,—weighing
> only 136 pounds, when it ought to be 150.[15]

When the war's end came at Appomattox, Robertson returned to his family home, "The Meadows," near Abingdon, Virginia. In 1868 he married Stella Wheeler of Rockville, Maryland. They had four children, all girls: Mary Reade, Katy Booker, Nellie Motley, and Stella. He was engaged in farming until his death on August 10, 1926. He is buried in Abingdon.

Maj. Garland Mitchell Ryals

Provost marshal
June 1863 to May 12, 1864

The career of Garland M. Ryals contained its share of unique twists and turns. His service in the Confederacy's armies took him from Louisiana to Pennsylvania, and at various times he was a color sergeant in the cavalry, a lieutenant of cavalry, an aide-de-camp, an ordnance officer, and a provost marshal. After the war, he became involved in the mercantile business, truck farming, and politics. Versatile, like W. W. Blackford, Ryals rarely failed at any venture he undertook.

A native Virginian, Garland Ryals, the son of Vincent C. and Hardenia Mitchell Ryals, was born on May 27, 1839, in Cumberland County. He received his formal education in his home county, but no record exists of his having attended a college. At the commencement of the war, Ryals enlisted for one year on May 14, 1861, in the Cumberland Light Dragoons. This unit became Company "G" of the 3rd Virginia Cavalry. He served as color sergeant with the company until it was mustered in at Ashland, when he became second sergeant. At one time he was attached to Gen. John B. Magruder's headquarters, but it is not known in what capacity, though one source indicates that it may have been as a courier.[1]

On December 24, 1861, Ryals was commissioned a second lieutenant to rank from November 23. Assigned to a Kentucky cavalry regiment, he somehow ended up as ordnance officer in a brigade commanded by Brig. Gen. John C. Breckinridge. On August 5, 1862, Ryals participated in the Battle of Baton Rouge, but his unit is unknown. At the time he was an aide-de-camp on the staff of Gen. Benjamin H. Helm, but Helm did not command his troops in the battle, having been injured in a fall from his horse. Because of Helm's fall and temporary disability, Ryals's career took one of its characteristic twists when on August 25, 1862, while stationed at Jackson, Mississippi, he was relieved as aide to Helm. His new assignment did not arrive until September 10, when he was ordered to report to General R. E. Lee.[2]

Upon reaching the Army of Northern Virginia, Lee sent Ryals to Stuart, who sent the lieutenant on to Gen. Fitzhugh Lee. From about September 10, 1862, to April 1863, Ryals served first as ordnance officer and then as provost marshal with Lee. On several occasions Lee commended Ryals for his conduct in the face of the enemy, specifically during the Dumfries Raid in December 1862, a raid across the Rappahannock in February 1863, and at the battle of Kelly's Ford on March 17, 1863. Lee wrote that in the last affair, Ryals "rendered great service" by the "accurate transmission of orders" and by his "conduct under fire."[3] While with Lee, Ryals renewed his relationship with the 3rd Virginia by taking Sgt. John Winn Talley to assist him with his duties in the ordnance department.

Just how, when, or why Ryals ended up as the cavalry's provost marshal remains unclear. His conduct at Kelly's Ford, however, may have played a very important part in his assignment to Stuart's staff. His actions in that battle definitely had something to do with his being commissioned a first lieutenant on April 8, 1863. Stuart mentioned Ryals as being attached to his staff and acting as the cavalry's provost marshal on June 24, 1863, but the possibility that he was on the staff as early as late April should not be ignored. In any event, the position of provost marshal in the cavalry during the waning years of the Confederacy would not have been an enviable one. One of his "expeditions" produced the following report.

> HdQrs Office Provost Marshal
> Cavalry Corps
> Orange CH Nov. 11, 1863
>
> General,
>   In accordance with orders received from your HdQrs,
> I have visited the counties of Rappahannock, Fauquier,
> and Loudoun for the purpose of arresting deserters,
> conscripts, and absentees from their various commands.
>   I have the honour to report that I have arrested
> thirty-four in number. Of these a large number were
> conscripts. Much good was accomplished by the trip, as
> a large number were driven to their commands by my

being in the vicinity. I remained as long as I thought any good could be done.

I learned that a large number went to Maryland and Prince William County to avoid me. They will return I suppose as soon as they hear of my having left the country and can be caught by making another [illegible] upon them.

> I am General Very Respectfully
> Your Obt Servt
> G. M. Ryals
> Provost Marshal

Maj Genl J. E. B. Stuart
Comdg Cavalry A.N.Va.[4]

Performing his duty was one thing, but receiving recognition for it was another. Though all of his superior officers—Stuart included—were greatly satisfied by his work, Ryals felt ignored by Richmond, which he obviously was. He wrote a letter to Samuel Cooper, adjutant and inspector general, informing him of the fact that every other corps-level provost marshal in the army held the rank of major, while he was still but a lowly lieutenant.[5] Joining him in the fight were Generals Fitz Lee, Lunsford Lomax, Williams Wickham, and Stuart. The latter added the following endorsement:

> Hd Qrs Cav Corps
> Dec, 4th 1863.
>
> Lt. Ryals is zealous, faithful, extremely brave and cool in action, always distinguishes himself in action by his conspicuous gallantry. Well versed in his duties as an officer, has been in a great number of battles. His own promotion has been the last thing to receive his attention. Universally regarded where known as a most deserving officer. Is 2nd Lt. in the regular army and as he is Provost Marshal of the Corps his appointment as Major Prol. army is legitimate under the law.
>
> J. E. B. Stuart
> Major Genl[6]

The barrage of "fan mail" worked to some extent. On December 8, 1863, Ryals received his commission as captain. Surprisingly, considering how long some officers waited for advancement, he became a major on January 5, 1864.[7] Just the fact that Stuart managed to get Ryals from a first lieutenant to a major in less than a month while he could not get Cooke a majority or Pelham or Beckham a lieutenant colonelcy over months of trying demonstrates the fickle manner in which the Confederate government at times worked. This is not to say that Ryals was undeserving, for he had performed his duties well under the most trying of circumstances, but it does illustrate the unfair treatment of some individuals and branches of service by the officials in Richmond.[8]

During the winter months, much of the army settled into a state of relative inactivity. Ryals was not as lucky. His business of rounding up AWOL officers and men continued unabated. One of his assignments was to give an accounting of personnel turned over to the provost at various locations. Ryals's report of the operation will serve as an example of his duties as the cavalry's provost marshal. It was to be one of the last he submitted to his chief.

> Headquarters Provost-Marshal Cavalry Corps
>   Army of Northern Virginia
>   Charlottesville, February 4, 1864
> Maj. Gen. J. E. B. Stuart
>   Commanding Cavalry Corps
> General: In obedience to your order per telegraph I have the honor to report as follows:

October.

From Madison Court-House to mountain near James City (first day)	109
From mountain to Culpeper Court-House	105
Culpeper Court-House and Brandy Station	41
Brigadier-General Young reported sent to rear	67
Brandy Station (Sunday evening)	233
Brandy Station	119
Brandy Station (citizen, James Lacy, Baltimore)	1
Turned over to guard at Warrenton	74
Brigadier-Generals Young and Rosser report sent to rear	36
Turned over to infantry guard at and near Manassas	79

General Gordon reported sent to guard at Warrenton	17
Captured by cavalry and turned over at Warrenton under guard	83
Captured on reconnaissance to Sudley Church	27
Sudley Church (citizens)	2
Captured at Gainesville, New Baltimore, and Buckland	368
New Baltimore and Buckland	9
Total	1,370

The foregoing list embraces officers and men. A liberal addition may be allowed for prisoners captured by men and turned over to the infantry guards and not credited to the cavalry. One negro escaped from the guard while getting on the cars at Culpeper Court-House. The fact was reported at the time.

One hundred and seven long-range guns turned over at Madison Court-House to provost-marshal, 96 turned over at James City, 42 at Culpeper Court-House. Another lot (number not known) was collected near Culpeper Court-House and sent to depot. Nine horses turned over to me were turned over to horse artillery.

I have the honor to be, very respectfully, general, your most obedient servant,

G. M. Ryals
Major, and Provost-Marshal

[P.S.]—This report includes only the prisoners that were reported to the provost-marshal. It is believed, however, that the number captured by the cavalry will reach 1,600 when we include those turned over to the infantry and others sent back without coming to the provost-marshal.[9]

The provost marshal's job could be difficult and complicated. Ryals's performance must have pleased Stuart as well as the general's eventual successor, Wade Hampton, for Ryals was never replaced.

Somehow amidst reports and letters, Ryals found the opportunity to court and win the hand of Elizabeth Kennedy, daughter of Mr. D. W. Kennedy. The couple was wed in Charlottesville, Virginia, on February 14,

1864. After returning to the army, Ryals made preparations for the opening of the 1864 campaign, not knowing that his career was about to take another turn. As with the rest of the staff, Stuart's death left Ryals without a position. His record at this period reflects the confusion he must have been feeling regarding his future role in the army. His past accomplishments, however, were not overlooked.

Ryals was announced as Gen. Wade Hampton's provost marshal on August 11, 1864, though he actually had probably been assigned to the general sometime in late May. In July Ryals became quite ill. He fell into the care of Charles Grattan, who attempted to find a suitable place for his fellow officer to recuperate.[10] Ryals's record shows that he took a fifteen-day leave on July 21, 1864, apparently to recover his health. After returning to duty, he served as provost marshal until the war's end. He escaped through the lines at Appomattox and was paroled in Charlottesville six weeks after the surrender, but this was backdated to April 9, 1865. He had not accompanied Hampton to North Carolina but had remained behind with Fitz Lee's cavalry, though there is no record that he was transferred to Lee's staff.

Immediately after the war, Ryals settled in Nelson County, Virginia, where he engaged in farming and the mercantile business. In 1868 he moved with his family, which at this time consisted of his wife and daughter, to Savannah, Georgia. The year 1869 brought tragedy: Ryals's wife of five years died. Ryals, though grieved, had become involved in truck farming and already had begun to make a reputation for himself in his new home. Now he threw himself into his work. His life again entered a happy period when he met Anne B. Ware, daughter of Mr. and Mrs. Thomas E. Ware, from Greenville, South Carolina. The couple was married on October 21, 1870, and had four children: three sons, James Warren, Edward C., and Sidney G.; and one daughter, Mary Louise. This same year marked Ryals's initial involvement in Savannah politics. He was appointed a member of the nominating committee for the Democratic Party for the offices of mayor and alderman.

The growth of his truck-farming business provided Ryals with an income that allowed him to serve his city and state in new ways. In 1880 he was placed on the executive committee for the Democratic Party for two years. In 1882 he served as a delegate to the Georgia State Sunday School Association, as a delegate to the gubernatorial convention, and as a president of the Chatham County Vegetable and Fruit Growers Association. He maintained affiliations with his fellow Confederate veterans and attended the unveiling of Lee's statue in Richmond in 1887. He had received a special invitation from Gov. Fitz Lee, one of his old commanders. Ryals was also a member of the Confederate Veterans Association and the Georgia Hussars.

Ryals ran for state legislature in 1888 and was elected. While in the state government he introduced several bills, one of which dealt with the abolishing of the convict lease system, and also functioned as chairman on the special committee on agriculture. He was reelected in 1890 to another term. Following his second term, Ryals ran for county treasurer but lost by just 186 votes. He does not appear to have sought any other public offices after this, though he frequently was appointed to various committees.

In his personal life, Ryals's hard work had made him financially secure. Except for problems with an arsonist who burned several of Ryals's properties (a barn in December 1889 and a large stable, a house, and a pumping house in January 1890), Ryals lived the rest of his life in what might be termed undisturbed retirement.[11]

Ryals's health began to deteriorate after the turn of the century. He developed diabetes, and in September 1904 his condition worsened to the point that the amputation of his right leg became necessary. He never recovered from the operation. Gangrene set in, and Ryals died on September 13, 1904.[12] He is buried in Bonaventure Cemetery in Savannah along with his wife, Anna, who died on May 17, 1912.

Capt. Samuel Granville Staples

Volunteer aide-de-camp
April 1862 to July 1862

Samuel Granville Staples escaped from the battlefields unscathed. He spent not a single day on sick call. He should have served Stuart long and well, but he did not. His entire wartime service lasted only about two months, though this time was filled with considerable activity. He was involved in the Peninsula Campaign, in which the Confederate forces, at first under Joe Johnston and later under Robert E. Lee, opposed Maj. Gen. George B. McClellan, who was leading his army up the peninsula. Sometime in early July 1862, not long after the battles had ended, somewhere along the roads just east of the Confederate capital, Staples suffered a fall from his horse. His injuries compelled him to resign from the staff and sit out the remaining years of the conflict.

If Staples failed to make his mark in the military, the same cannot be said of his civilian life, either before or after the war. Born at the family home, "Stonewall," in Patrick Courthouse (now Stuart), Virginia, on November 29, 1821, Staples was the eldest son of Abram Penn Staples and Mary Stovall Penn.[1] His higher education began at age fourteen, when he entered Patrick Henry Academy in Henry County. The school's principal, Joseph P. Godfrey, was known throughout lower Virginia as an excellent educator. Two years later Staples enrolled at Randolph Macon College. He spent almost three years at that institution before his father caused him to transfer to the University of Virginia for the latter part of his junior and then his senior year.

After completing his final year, Staples decided to study law and began attending classes at the university. Shockingly, his professor was killed by a deranged student, and Staples, realizing that some time might pass before the college secured the services of another professor, again transferred—this time to William and Mary College. He graduated with a degree in law in June 1842 and returned home, hoping to begin his practice. His father had other plans, and Staples was persuaded to enter the county clerk's office with the view of becoming his father's successor. He followed his father as deputy clerk of the county and clerk of the superior court in April 1844. He held these offices until 1851.

Virginia's Constitution underwent changes in 1849 and 1850. As a result, the offices Staples held would no longer be appointed positions but rather elected ones. Staples decided to resign his clerkships and take up the practice of law. The people he had served since 1844 called upon him to run for the House of Delegates in the general election to be held in October 1851. He agreed, ran, and was elected. During his terms in office, for he ran again and was reelected, he was placed on the committee for courts of justice. He continued as a member of the house until 1855, when, because of his father's illness, he withdrew from the election. With the death of his father, Staples entered into a few years of private life. But as war threatened, the public again called on him to run for office. He was subsequently elected as a delegate to Virginia's secession convention, where he pronounced himself and his constituency as being antisecessionist.

President Abraham Lincoln's call for seventy-five thousand troops to put down the rebellion in those states having already seceded altered the situation entirely, and Staples voted for the ordinance of secession, which took Virginia out of the Union. He also voted for the measure that attached the fortunes of Virginia to those of the Confederacy. Having done its work, the convention adjourned sometime in May 1861. According to one account, Staples immediately joined Stuart's staff, but this is not sustained by other sources. No record, official or otherwise, attaches Staples to Stuart before May 1862. While consideration must be given to the fact that he may have joined the staff in the last days of April 1862, nothing supports an earlier date. In Stuart's report of the fighting on May 3, 1862, he specifically mentioned that Staples had joined him "but a day or two before," which would mean May 1 or 2.[2]

If the date Staples joined the staff is somewhat conjectural, the length of his service and the date of his leaving are equally uncertain. Again, accounts conflict on both these points, and the discrepancies are not minor. One asserts that he remained with Stuart for a year; another claims that he suffered his injury sometime immediately after the Seven Days Battles.[3] The latter view would appear to be correct, as Stuart failed to mention Staples in any reports after the one he submitted describing the action of May 5. Had Staples stayed with the staff until 1863, his name certainly would have found its way into the records. The only other solution would involve his obtaining a furlough in an attempt to regain his health and, failing to do so, leaving the staff at a later date. Though it is doubtful that an entire year would be required to determine his permanent incapacity for further service, such a circumstance is not beyond the realm of possibility.

Staples's rank is also something of a mystery. His name does not appear on the roll of Confederate staff officers in the National Archives, nor does he appear to have been attached to any company or regiment of cavalry. Stuart referred to him as a captain in the reports already mentioned, but there may not have been a commission making the rank official. Staples was probably a captain in the same sense that W. D. Farley and W. E. Towles were captains. Stuart pronounced them of captain's rank on his staff and they were recognized throughout the army as such, though they never received a commission.

The war dragged on for three more years, but Staples played no part in it, or if he did, no records were left telling of his role. After the war, he placed his name on the ballot for judge in Patrick County and was unanimously elected. After serving a second term, he failed to win election to a third and left office in January 1880. His record during his tenure as judge was excellent, since he had only three of his rulings overturned in ten years.[4] He later worked in Washington, D.C., in the Department of the Interior. Staples's final years were spent in Roanoke, Virginia, where he died on August 6, 1895, at the home of his son Daniel. He was buried in Fairview Cemetery in Roanoke. His wife, Caroline Harris DeJarnette, whom he had married on June 12, 1855, had preceded him in death on January 1, 1892. They had seven children: four boys, Abram Penn, Daniel DeJarnette, Samuel Granville, and Waller Redd; and three girls, Caroline DeJarnette, Lucy, and Mary Huldah.[5]

Capt. Roger Williams Steger

Assistant quartermaster
October 2, 1861, to November 11, 1861

Roger W. Steger holds the honor of being one of the first three officers selected by Stuart when the new brigadier general initially began to organize his staff. Steger also holds the distinction of being the first regular officer to resign from Stuart's staff. Quite possibly, if absolutely accurate dates could be established, he set the record for the shortest duration of any officially appointed officer on the staff. Stuart's reasons for selecting Steger are unknown, and Steger's reasons for resigning are equally a mystery. In fact, very little is known about the cavalry's first quartermaster.

Born to John H. and Jane Gaines Steger in Amelia County, Virginia, in 1834, Roger Steger spent his early years on the 1,140-acre family farm known as "Kennons."[1] He entered the Virginia Military Institute on January 15, 1851, but the life of a cadet did not suit him, and he left the school in July 1852.[2] Steger then enrolled at the Amelia Academy to complete his education under W. H. Harrison, who was the school's principal. After graduation, Steger taught school for a while and also tried his hand at farming. He married Georgianna Carlton prior to the war. There were no children from the marriage.

In May 1861 Steger enlisted in the Amelia Dragoons, which became Company "G" of the 1st Virginia Cavalry. His association with the 1st Virginia would have brought him into contact with Stuart, who must have recognized Steger as having qualities that would make him a good staff officer. When Stuart became commander of the Army of Northern Virginia's first cavalry brigade, he called on Steger to be his quartermaster. Steger was appointed captain and assistant quartermaster with orders to report to Stuart on October 2, 1861. He barely could have settled into his job when, on November 11, he tendered his resignation and returned to his company.[3] His record indicates that at the time of his being commissioned he held the rank of sergeant, but as his place in the company had been filled, he dropped to the rank of private.

Steger continued to serve with the 1st Virginia until he was captured sometime during the winter of 1863 near Fredericksburg. He was held as a prisoner of war until early in 1865, when he was exchanged.[4] Rejoining the 1st Virginia, he served until the war's end.

After the war he resumed farming, probably in Amelia County. He died at his brother's home in Richmond on November 24, 1877, and is buried in Hollywood Cemetery Section M, Lot 25. His grave has no marker.

Capt. James Hardeman Stuart

Volunteer aide-de-camp and signal officer
June 26, 1862, to August 30, 1862

Hardeman Stuart has the distinction of being one of three officers from Stuart's staff (Pelham and Will Farley are the other two) to have a short chapter dedicated to him in John Esten Cooke's *Wearing of the Gray.* Cooke's short eulogy conveys the courage and spirit of Hardeman, whom Cooke first saw at Gaines' Mill in late June 1862. Cooke unfortunately knew little of the personal side of the youthful signal officer, who would be the first of the staff killed in the war. Cooke's omission is regrettable, since the passing years have further obscured Hardeman's life.

Depending on which source is consulted, Hardeman was born in Mississippi in either 1839 or 1841.[1] His father was Oscar J. E. Stuart, who owned a plantation near Jackson. Hardeman studied law at the school that became the University of Mississippi, graduating in 1859. His records at the university indicate that he was from Jackson and returned there to establish his law practice. There is also evidence to suggest that he opened a law office for a short time in Lake Village, Chicot County, Arkansas, but had moved back to Jackson before the war.[2] At the start of the war, Hardeman enlisted as a private for one year on May 24, 1861. He joined a local infantry company known as the "Burt Rifles," which became Company "K" of the 18th Regiment Mississippi Infantry. He was mustered into the Confederate Army at Corinth, Mississippi, on June 7, 1861.

Hardeman and the rest of his regiment traveled to Virginia, where he was assigned to the signal corps. His records show him on duty during the months of September and October 1861 on the signal line near Centreville, Virginia.[3] In a letter to his aunt dated September 8, 1861, Hardeman stated that he was permanently detached from his regiment to the signal corps of the army.[4] The status of the signal corps at this time was an unofficial one as far as Richmond was concerned. The corps existed in the field, but the Confederate Congress had not made it an actual branch of the armed forces. On December 23, Hardeman wrote to his father:

> I have not heard yet whether Congress will authorize a Signal Corps or not. Capt. Alexander [Edward Porter Alexander, later a brigadier general, was acting as Gen. P. G. T. Beauregard's signal officer at this time] thinks it will. Gen. J.E.B. Stuart promised without solicitation on my part to write to Capt. Alexander and get him to

recommend me for a commission. I have not heard from
him yet, hope to do so in a few days.[5]

The intervention of General Stuart on behalf of Hardeman could not
have been all that surprising to the Mississippian. They were double third
cousins, and their families had corresponded prior to the war.

Despite his high hopes, nothing changed over the next several
weeks, and Hardeman settled into the routine of life in winter quarters.
He informed his sister Bettie on January 14, 1862, that he had contracted
the mumps and that he was quite swollen but otherwise doing well.[6]
Having previously been stationed near Centreville, Hardeman was now
located at Signal Station No. 2 near Hague in Westmoreland County. He
described his quarters to his aunt in a letter dated January 26.

> I left Maj. Beale's [later Brig. Gen. Richard Lee Turber-
> ville Beale of the 9th Virginia Cavalry] HdQrs on the
> 8th and came to the signal station. I am very easily fixed.
> The furniture consists of two tables, three chairs, one
> sofa and two "bunks." There is a leak in the roof just
> over mine, but it does not trouble me much as I have an
> oil cloth. The floor is of sand so I do not have the trouble
> of sweeping.[7]

Hardeman continued to be active with the signal corps throughout the
winter and into the spring of 1862, spending a considerable amount of
his time reading. "K" Company's muster roll for March and April 1862
listed Hardeman as being absent and detached to the signal corps. His rank
was still that of private, and he was continuing his training for a permanent
position in the signal corps. At times he became disillusioned with the
uncertainty of his position and considered joining either the artillery or
the cavalry.

In March Hardeman received orders moving him to Rapidan Station
in Culpeper County. The proposed signal corps had not yet been authorized,
leaving Hardeman still attached to an unofficial organization, a circumstance
that his letters show frustrated him. April saw him moved yet again, this
time to Clark's Mountain in Orange County. Capt. Edward P. Alexander
informed him that President Davis was at last aware of the signal corps.
All of Alexander's letters to the president apparently had gone no further
than Secretary of War Judah P. Benjamin's desk, a situation that had not
pleased Davis, much less Alexander and Hardeman.[8]

On June 5, 1862, Hardeman was discharged from the 18th Mississippi, as his year's enlistment had expired. Within a few days he conveyed some good news to his aunt.

> Richmond, Va. June 11th '62
>
> Dear Aunt Ann,
>
> I have this day rec'd my appointment as Captain in the Signal Corps. . . . I have been sick for some days past. I think I am improving now. Nothing new. Yankees in a few miles of Richmond, but they will <u>never</u> take the city. Oscar [Hardeman's brother] is well. Love to all at home. . . . I am ordered to report to Genl Stuart—will be attached to his staff. I am
>
> Affectionately
> Yr Nephew
> J. Hardeman Stuart[9]

By mid-June Stuart was a member of his cousin's staff and was involved in throwing back the Yankees from Richmond. John Esten Cooke mentioned that when he first met Hardeman at Gaines' Mill, Hardeman was a volunteer aide-de-camp, not the signal officer of the staff. Hardeman rode through the entire Peninsula Campaign with the cavalry, joining with Pelham in the fun of chasing gunboats with the horse artillery. Before the end of the Seven Days fighting, General Stuart was convinced that his young cousin had talents he could use.

Though appointed the cavalry's signal officer, Hardeman did indeed perform more like an aide-de-camp during and immediately after the Peninsula Campaign. On the morning of July 2, General Stuart had his young cousin riding all over the countryside. On this date, Hardeman recorded in his diary that he had traveled twenty-three miles that morning and stopped around noon to dry his clothes, as it had been raining heavily all the while. He had carried messages to and from "Stonewall" Jackson and had led General Stuart to a rendezvous with the hero of the Valley. Hardeman finally rejoined Stuart that evening.[10]

The cavalry had a chance to rest, refit, and reorganize after McClellan had been safely bottled up around Harrison's Landing. Captain Stuart recorded that he was trying to get his signal corps "rigged out" from July 22 to 26. He then reported to cavalry headquarters at Hanover Court House. On the twenty-eighth, Hardeman, along with General Stuart, von Borcke, and others, was visiting "Dundee," the home of Dr. Lucien

Bonaparte Price. A fire broke out in the doctor's barn. Hardeman wrote that he was the first at the scene and assisted in saving numerous items.[11]

The period of peace and quiet, interrupted from time to time by reviews and gala festivities, came to a halt with a new threat from the north. John Pope was on the march, and Lee determined to chastise him. Stuart and the cavalry left the homelike atmosphere of Hanover Court House and moved toward the enemy. Following the brief setback at Verdiersville on August 18, in which Maj. Norman R. FitzHugh was captured, General Stuart and the cavalry readied themselves to put General Lee's plan into operation. Hardeman Stuart was to have an important role in the opening stages of the campaign. His involvement can best be understood through the words of his diary.

> [August] 20th [1862]—Crossed the Rapidan at Mitchell's Ford. Went to Kelly's Ford on the Rappahannock. Saw a great number of Yankees on the hill on the other side. Went to Gen. Stuart, passing through Stevensburg. Genl sent me after some mules—caught & turned them over to Col. T. L. Rosser of the 5th Va. Cav. HdQrs at James Barbours [near Brandy Station]. There were several brilliant cav. charges on the road from Stevensburg by Brandy Station to Cunningham's [Beverley's] Ford on the Rappahannock.
>
> 21st—Went to Cunningham's [Beverley's] Ford. Had a fight of the artillery. We exploded a Yankee caisson. Used my signals for the first time. Adams was present, the rest (except Lawrence) with the wagon. Sent Lawrence to bring them up. Was out all night hunting for Gen. Jackson—found him early in the morning. Gen. [Stuart] stayed at Dr. Welford's.
>
> 22nd—Crossed at Welford's Ford over the south branch of the Rappahannock [the Hazel River]. Had an artillery duel—some of our men wounded. Went through Jeffersonton in Culpeper Cty. Crossed Waterloo bridge. Part of the Cav. Div. at Hart's Mill. Gen. [Stuart] sent me to the view tree on watery mount. It rained heavily & I was completely drenched. Spent the night at Mrs. Scott's—enjoyed myself very much conversing with the young ladies, the Misses Scott.
>
> 23rd—Was scarcely out of bed in the morning when a negro ran into the room & told me the Yankees were

coming. I dressed hastily & mounting my horse rode off to the top of the mountain. Sergts. Bestor & Lawrence of my Signal Corps accompanying me. I sent a servt to inform Sergt. Adams that the enemy were upon us. Went a mile into the country & sent a negro to ascertain whether any Yankees were about. He returned & reported there were none, that a party of our men had alarmed us. In the evening saw two regts of Yankee cav. come into Warrenton. I watched them until dark, when I went into the country across fields, tearing down fences & crossing bogs until I came to Mrs. Meredith's, where I stayed all night. Was most hospitably entertained.

24th—Early in the morning before I got up a courier came in with instructions for the "Signal Corps" captured from the Yankees. I could gather nothing new from them & handed them to Sergt. Adams to keep. Dressed & went out & another courier rode up to the gate inquiring for Capt. Stuart—told me that the Genl said I must return as the Yankees were advancing. I ate my breakfast & set out. When I got on the turnpike saw the Yankees a half mile off advancing. Crossed Waterloo bridge & in 3/4 of an hour the Yankees came up. Our skirmishers had a fight with them. We found 18 rounds of shell on them, & having no more withdrew our guns. Several Regts of infantry marched down to burn the bridge.[12]

This was Hardeman's last entry, except for a notation in the margin that read:

Learned from the country people that a Yankee force five or six thousand strong had passed down the Telegraph road. Inf. cav. & artillery—Gen. [Christopher C.] Augur's Brigade.[13]

On the following day, August 25, General Stuart dispatched Hardeman and a few men to capture the Union signal station on a hill known as View Tree. The hill overlooked Warrenton, and Hardeman recorded in his diary he had had possession of it on the twenty-third. Proudly wearing his new captain's coat with its dual rows of braiding on each sleeve, Hardeman set out to execute his orders. The mission failed. Upon reaching View Tree, Hardeman found that the enemy's numbers were too great for his small band of men. He scouted the position thoroughly on foot, leaving his horse and his new coat in the care of one of his men. J. E. Cooke reported that Hardeman's party was attacked and the horse holder, whose name has mercifully been lost, fled the scene. In the ensuing chase, Hardeman's horse and coat were captured, but the captain managed to make his escape.

Moving in the direction of Manassas, Hardeman came upon his old companions of the 18th Mississippi. Since they were going to the same place as he, and knowing that his mission was impossible to complete, he joined them. This turned out to be a fatal error. When he had not been able to carry out General Stuart's orders, he should have sought out the general and reported to him, but he did not. He remained with the infantry through August 29 and into the next day, when Cooke saw him. A short time after Cooke left, Hardeman participated with either the 4th or 5th Texas in the final attack of the day. Hardeman was killed charging in their midst.[14] One source stated that he was shot through the neck and lived but a short time.[15] His body was later recognized by an old schoolmate, who reported that Hardeman had been stripped by scoundrels to his undershirt and drawers.[16]

General Stuart was shocked on hearing of his cousin's death. He had expected him to be on View Tree or, failing in that, to report back to him. When the latter had not happened, he had assumed that the former had. For Hardeman the deciding factor had been the loss of his horse. His exuberance in meeting his old company led him to join with them in one more battle. He was buried where he fell. His horse, coat, and captain's commission, which had been in his coat pocket, were recaptured by General Stuart's cavalry the following Sunday.[17]

Edward Stuart spent three days searching for his brother's grave. Near dusk on the third day, he discovered it already marked with a crude wooden headboard. Dismounting, Edward constructed a rail pen around the grave. As far as is known, Hardeman Stuart still rests today somewhere on the Manassas Battlefield.

Maj. Lewis Frank Terrell

Inspector
October 7, 1862, to June 7, 1863

Trying to explain Frank Terrell's position on Stuart's staff borders on the impossible. He was an artillery officer without any artillery. He fought with the guns but did not really command them. He spent the greater part of his time on courts-martial duty—drudgery for one who craves action. His pent-up zeal for a combat role led to a break with Stuart. Terrell ended his days on the staff with some bitterness toward his commander. He had expected a more active role in the horse artillery, and when it did not materialize, he chose to leave.

Lewis Frank Terrell (he preferred to be called Frank) was born in Hanover County, Virginia, on September 12, 1836, to Nicholas and Marie B. Terrell. He was the youngest of the family. His father, a physician, provided well for his family, and Frank never really wanted for anything.

Maj. Lewis Frank Terrell

Though not exactly affluent like their neighbors at "Dundee," the Prices, Dr. Terrell managed to give his children if not the best of everything, the nearest thing to it.

Frank received his higher education at the University of Virginia. He chose to enter the legal profession and was fortunate enough to study under Arthur A. Morson, one of the leading lawyers of his day.[1] Terrell even had the opportunity to travel to Europe twice in order to further his education. While he was in Paris, South Carolina seceded from the Union. Terrell, understanding what lay ahead, abandoned his studies and hurried back to Hanover, Virginia. He arrived just as his native state began to gather forces for the coming storm.

Terrell helped raise and organize a company of artillery and was elected lieutenant. The unit, formed in April 1861, became known as Capt. William Nelson's Company, Virginia Light Artillery.[2] Terrell was with his company all through the early weeks of the Peninsula Campaign and earned plaudits from many of his superiors, including Gen. "Prince" John Magruder. Terrell was absent when his company reorganized in April 1862, however, and failed to gain reelection. For the moment he found himself unemployed. His period of uncertainty ended on July 17, 1862, when he received an appointment as first lieutenant of artillery from Virginia with orders to report to General Magruder.[3]

Fortune had smiled on Terrell, for Magruder had noticed the young lieutenant from Hanover and saw to it that the artillery did not lose a fine officer. Terrell's records are not clear as to what duty he was assigned by Magruder (one source states that he was on Magruder's staff). He could not have remained there long, however.[4] "Prince" John failed to perform up to Robert E. Lee's standards and was soon gone from the newly christened Army of Northern Virginia. Terrell somehow managed to attach himself to Brig. Gen. Beverly H. Robertson as a voluntary aide sometime in June

1862, and in this capacity at the Battle of 2nd Manassas, while fighting with captured enemy guns, he fabricated lanyards and turned infantrymen into cannoneers.[5]

Terrell's gallant performance attracted Stuart's attention, and when the Sharpsburg Campaign ended, Stuart had Terrell promoted to a majority in the artillery and brought him onto the staff as an inspector.[6] According to von Borcke, Terrell joined the headquarters on October 10, 1862, while Stuart was encamped at "The Bower."[7]

Almost immediately, Stuart unconsciously set into motion the chain of events that would end in Terrell's leaving the staff. If Terrell thought his commission in the artillery would earn for him a place in the Stuart Horse Artillery, he was sadly mistaken. Stuart, wishing to utilize Terrell's legal training, assigned him to courts-martial duty, and by October 20 Terrell was signing his pay voucher as a judge advocate.[8] Having studied the law, Terrell was eminently qualified to serve in this position, but it was not what he had had in mind, though he went to his work without a complaint.

The winter months passed with Terrell still tied to a desk. Toward the end of the winter, a faint possibility arose for Terrell to become actively involved in the war, though whether he ever knew of it is uncertain. Lt. Gen. James Longstreet, along with most of the other generals in the army, had long coveted the services of John Pelham. In February 1863 he proposed a plan that would have transferred Pelham to the 1st Corps as chief of artillery. The whole idea hinged on "Stonewall" Jackson's request to make Col. E. Porter Alexander a brigadier general of infantry. Such a promotion would have left Longstreet without an artillery chief, as Alexander held that position in Longstreet's Corps. To soften the blow to Stuart, Longstreet further suggested that Terrell replace Pelham upon that officer's promotion.[9] The commander of the 2nd Corps must have known something about Terrell and of Stuart's respect for his fighting qualities. He obviously felt that Stuart would not bar Pelham's promotion to such an important post.

This plan went as far as R. E. Lee's asking for Alexander's promotion, and with such strong support Longstreet may have hoped to have Pelham before the opening of the campaign season. Nothing happened, however, most likely because Alexander, not wishing to leave the artillery where he had some seniority for the infantry where he would have been low man, raised his voice against it. Meanwhile, Terrell kept drawing his pay as a judge advocate.

The inactivity of the army probably helped Terrell endure the long months of courtroom duty, but with the coming of spring he began to seek every opportunity to escape the boredom of the courtroom. Such an opportunity came on March 17, 1863. The Battle of Kelly's Ford offered a break in the tedium, and Terrell took complete advantage of it. Rushing to the scene, he assisted Capt. James Breathed's horse artillery and also served as a staff officer. He received a commendation in both Stuart's and Fitz Lee's reports, which also contained the sorrowful news of Pelham's death.[10]

Stuart, though grief stricken, had to attend to the business of replacing his fallen artillery chief. Terrell had reason to believe that he stood an excellent chance to secure the appointment. Instead, Stuart chose outside the horse artillery and his staff and selected Maj. R. F. Beckham, who was appointed April 7, 1863. Terrell's immediate reaction was not recorded, but about a month later, on May 9, Terrell requested and received a ten-day furlough.[11] He never returned to cavalry headquarters.

An attempt was made, most likely on Stuart's orders, to keep Terrell with the cavalry's artillery arm. On June 2, 1863, Beckham issued orders stating, "Major Lewis F. Terrell having been assigned to duty with the Horse Artillery, he will be obeyed and respected accordingly."[12] The individual who "assigned" Terrell to the horse artillery could only have been Stuart. The effort was too little too late. Words were exchanged. Terrell felt he had earned the post, and Stuart had not given it to him. He requested to be relieved of duty with Stuart because "unfortunate disagreements arose" and he was "heartily sick" of his place on Stuart's staff. He further asked for a separate command.[13] On June 7, 1863, just five days after he was assigned to the horse artillery, Terrell was relieved of duty with Stuart.

With the Army of Northern Virginia's second invasion of the north looming in the immediate future, Terrell was not long unemployed. Every man was needed, and his particular merits had not been noticed by Stuart alone. Orders dated June 13, 1863, sent Terrell to Maj. Gen. Isaac R. Trimble. By one account, Trimble made Terrell his chief of artillery, which would have been quite a feat considering that the general had no command when the campaign opened. Whatever position he filled with Trimble, once the army had returned to the soil of Virginia, Terrell was ready to move and did so on August 14.

After a ten-day furlough, Terrell, leaving Lee's army for good, headed toward Charleston, South Carolina. His new orders dated August 27, 1863, assigned him to Gen. P. G. T. Beauregard, who appointed him commander of the Light Artillery Brigade, Department of South Carolina, Georgia, and Florida on November 1, 1863. For some unknown reason Terrell secured another furlough—this one for thirty days—on December 31, 1863. He journeyed to Richmond, where on January 25, 1864, he requested and received a ten-day extension to begin January 31.

Terrell's record now becomes confusing. He was appointed inspector of the 7th Military District, South Carolina on February 18, but either immediately before or after this, Brig. Gen. William B. Taliaferro requested that Terrell be made his artillery commander. Terrell accepted and journeyed to Florida, where he arrived too late to participate in the Battle of Olustee (Ocean Pond) on February 20, 1864. The records state that though he was not involved in the battle, "he rendered good service by the energy and experience he displayed in the skirmishes which succeeded."[14] While engaged in these duties, Terrell contracted typhoid fever. He was moved to James Island, South Carolina, where his condition worsened. He died on April 14, 1864. His body was returned to Virginia, and he was buried in Hollywood Cemetery in Richmond. His gravestone reads:

> *Major*
> *Lewis Frank Terrell*
> *Born Hanover Co. Va.*
> *Sept. 12, 1836*
> *Died on St. James Island*
> *April 14, 1864*
> *A Gallant Confederate Soldier*
> *"No thought of self or fears*
> *with never a duty shirked"*

Capt. William Eskridge Towles

Volunteer aide-de-camp and acting assistant adjutant general
December 1, 1861, to July 1862

The eldest son of Maj. John T. and Frances Peyton Towles of Bayou Sara, Louisiana, William Eskridge Towles was born in Staunton, Virginia, on March 15, 1837, in the home of his grandfather, William S. Eskridge. When he was but a few months old, the family returned to Louisiana. At age nine he was sent to live with his grandfather, who had moved to Lexington, Virginia. Two years later William began to attend the school of his uncle, R. T. W. Duke, in Lewisburg. His uncle's relocation forced him to return to Staunton until 1854, when he entered the University of Virginia. He proved to be an apt student and earned a bachelor of arts in 1857, master of arts in 1858, and bachelor of law in 1860.[1]

In 1860 William and his brother, John Turnbull Towles, who had also attended the university, left Virginia for Louisiana. They settled in New

Orleans where William studied Louisiana state law until the war's start. William joined the "Crescent City Rifles," an infantry company that became part of the 7th Louisiana Regiment. His brother, John, joined "The Jeff Davis Guards." Desiring to be with his brother, William transferred to that group. The company received orders to proceed to Richmond on May 24, 1861. After arriving in early June, it was incorporated with other Mississippi companies into the 1st Battalion of Mississippi Volunteers.

Throughout the rest of June and into July the battalion worked at becoming an efficient military organization. Soon two other companies were added, and the battalion was ordered to Manassas. Arriving the day after the Battle of the 1st Manassas, the Mississippians established their camp. Their disappointment over the missed opportunity to fight the enemy was softened by the addition of four new companies, which gave them enough to form a regiment, the 21st Mississippi Infantry. The camp at Manassas proved to be an unhealthy one, however. Typhoid fever broke out among the troops. Among the first to contract the disease was John Towles. William watched his brother slowly become weaker and die on September 5, 1861.[2]

After his brother's death, William no longer felt at home in the regiment and requested a transfer to the Washington Artillery of New Orleans, which he joined on December 1, 1861. He did not remain with his new unit for very long. Gen. P. G. T. Beauregard had Towles assigned to Stuart's headquarters as a voluntary aide.[3] Stuart and Towles were related (Towles was another nephew of Stuart's uncle, J. E. Brown, after whom Stuart was named), and in all probability, Stuart had asked Beauregard to make the assignment. Towles quickly went from a private in the artillery to a "captain" on the staff. The rank was mostly honorary, as no commission was forthcoming to make it official.

Stuart put Towles to work immediately as aide and adjutant. In a letter to Flora on February 23, 1862, Stuart indicated that he was quite pleased with his relative's performance.[4] Towles accompanied the cavalry through all the preliminary operations preceding the Peninsula Campaign, including the Chickahominy Raid. During the campaign itself he displayed both courage and efficiency. At Williamsburg, in particular, he won Stuart's praise. In his report of the action, Stuart recorded the following:

> At daylight, the 5th instant [May 5, 1862], I rode down to reconnoiter the ground, and beyond it, from which the enemy had been repulsed the evening before. I directed a company (Captain Hobson's) of the Fourth Virginia Cavalry, near by, to proceed cautiously down the Telegraph road and reconnoiter the position and movements of the

enemy. It had not proceeded far before meeting with one
of the enemy, who surrendered on the spot, and I returned
to question him. I had scarcely emerged from the woods
when a brisk fire was opened by the enemy's skirmishers
along the edge of the woods to my left. Appreciating at
once the danger of the company which had just started
down the Telegraph road, diverging from the other at this
point, I asked who would volunteer to run the gauntlet to
bring back Captain Hobson's company. Capt. W. E. Towles
my volunteer aide, promptly accepted the service and
performed it with credit and success. As he returned
with the company he found the enemy's infantry in his
road, but, nothing daunted, he seized the musket of the
nearest one and bore it off in triumph, with an entire
regiment of the enemy's infantry close to his left.[5]

In his other reports recounting the campaign against McClellan on the
peninsula, Stuart also mentioned Towles, but during the same period a
problem had arisen. Stuart evidently had promised to secure a commission
for Towles but was either unsuccessful or did not have the opportunity to
make the application due to the military situation.[6] Towles, after having
served a number of months as a volunteer, may have realized that his position
had little security and requested a permanent place on the staff. He felt that
Stuart was overlooking him even though no other volunteer staff member
had received an increase in rank or a commission at this time. Becoming
impatient, he left the staff and returned to the Washington Artillery in
July 1862.

   He continued to serve as a private with the artillery until January
1863, when he secured a furlough. He decided to return to Louisiana to
visit his home. On February 19, 1863, Towles was killed when the train
he was riding ran off the abutments of a bridge that had been destroyed
by floodwaters over Chunkey's Creek, a tributary of the Chickasawha
River just west of Meridian, Mississippi. The accident happened at night
while the guard who was stationed to warn the train left his post. Towles's
body was recovered by a family servant.[7] He is buried in the Towles
Cemetery, West Feliciana Parish, Louisiana.[8]

Lt. Thomas Baynton Turner

Aide-de-camp
September 4, 1862, to March 1863

The stories of a charming maiden's redemption by a dashing hero may have crossed the minds of the two cavalry officers as they sat quietly in the canoe taking them across the Rappahannock River into enemy territory. They had offered to conduct the scouting and rescue mission, and their commanding general had assented. Lieutenants Thomas B. Turner and Walter Q. Hullihen had much in common. Both were young, ages nineteen and twenty-one; both recently had been appointed cadets from Virginia, Turner in June and Hullihen in July; and both served as aides to Gen. "Jeb" Stuart. Doubtless Turner and Hullihen had weighed the dangers involved but had felt that they could overcome anything that might interfere with their goals. Events almost proved them wrong.

The incident that prompted Turner and Hullihen's rescue mission had occurred in early December when Gen. Robert E. Lee's daughter Mary became trapped behind enemy lines as the Federals advanced and pushed back Lee's Army of Northern Virginia. Mary had been visiting friends, most likely Dr. and Mrs. Richard Stuart of "Cedar Grove" plantation in King George County, and had not had time to escape.

Upon landing on the river's northern bank, Turner and Hullihen traveled cautiously on foot until they reached the plantation. They offered to escort Mary back to her father, but her friends persuaded Mary not to attempt the journey. Their fears proved to be justified. The two scouts concluded their mission by locating and identifying several Federal units. Then they made their way back to the river, where they constructed a makeshift raft of logs held together with their suspenders. With the launching of the shaky craft, safety seemed only a few paddle strokes away. Unfortunately, the suspenders came loose, and the raft reverted to a shapeless mass of logs.

Returning to the shore, the two adventurers incautiously walked directly into a Union cavalry patrol. Turner's answers satisfied the patrol's commander and they were allowed to go, but the officer in charge sent a trooper along to escort the two "stragglers" back to their camp.

To all appearances the war for both Turner and Hullihen seemed about to be over, but their cool heads and dauntless courage saved them. On the pretext of admiring their Union guard's horse, Hullihen moved closer to the pistol-wielding trooper. The Federal cavalryman, distracted by the conversation, was unprepared when Hullihen made a grab for his revolver. The brave lieutenant was quick but not quick enough. He missed and had the pistol shoved into his face. But the shock of his prisoner's action must have disconcerted the Yank, for though he fired several times, he failed to hit Hullihen even once.

Meanwhile, Turner directed his own carbine on the trooper, who now turned his attention to his other prisoner. With the mounted man charging down upon him, Turner calmly took aim and pulled the trigger. Turner never knew for sure whether he had hit the Federal, but the man wheeled his horse around and galloped off down the road, only to fall or jump from his mount after traveling about fifty yards. Whether this was because of fear or a wound the two lieutenants did not know, nor did they wait to find out. Managing to avoid other Union patrols, they stopped over at the home of one of Turner's relatives, finally secured a canoe, and returned to the Confederate side of the river.

Lt. Thomas Baynton Turner, the younger of these two daring aides-de-camp, was born in May 8, 1843, in Fauquier County, Virginia. His father, Edward Carter Turner, was the owner of "Kinloch" near The Plains. The name of the family plantation is often associated with Tom to distinguish him from a plethora of Turners with the same first name. "Kinloch" Tom is frequently confused with "Prince George" Tom Turner (named after his native county, Prince George, Maryland), who was mortally wounded as a lieutenant riding with Mosby during the famous Loudoun Heights raid of January 10, 1864. This latter Turner served in Company "K" of the 1st Virginia Cavalry under Stuart but was never attached to Stuart's staff or headquarters.[1]

"Kinloch" Tom was reared in Fauquier County, but at age sixteen or seventeen moved to Alexandria, Virginia, where he obtained work as a clerk. While there he joined a militia company known as the "Alexandria Riflemen," which had been organized on March 10, 1856. With the outbreak of the war, Turner and the rest of the Riflemen enlisted on April 17, 1861, for one year. On May 24, 1861, the Alexandria company and several others from northern Virginia were organized at Manassas Junction to create the 17th Virginia Infantry.

Led by their colonel, Montgomery D. Corse, the 17th participated in the Battle of 1st Manassas, though it was not heavily engaged. Turner passed through the battle and stayed with the regiment until January 1862, when he became ill and returned to "Kinloch." Temporarily regaining his health, he attempted to rejoin his company, only to be admitted to

Chimborazo Hospital on March 12, 1862, with dysentery. His condition was such that he was allowed to take a room at the Monumental Hotel and only report to the hospital three times a week for examination. He also appears to have spent some time with his regiment at Camp Taylor, near Orange Court House, Virginia, in late March and possibly early April. This was most likely in conjunction with his plans for his future in the army. Turner's actual discharge from Chimborazo did not occur until May 26, 1862.

During his absence, Turner missed the engagement at Williamsburg, where Col. James L. Kemper's brigade, to which the 17th had been attached, suffered 326 casualties. He would have returned in time for the Battle of Seven Pines on May 31 to June 1, but in all probability he was no longer with the regiment. The muster roll for May–June was marked "transferred." The reason for this is revealed in the following letter:

> Camp Taylor
> Near Orange C.H.
> Apl 2, 1862
>
> To Hon. G. W. Randolph
> Sir,
> I have the honor to make application for a Cadet Warrant wishing to be in the C.S. Army. I remain your humble servant.
>
> Thomas Turner
> Co. A, 17 Ret. Va. Vol.[2]

Turner received at least three hearty endorsements of his application. The first two came from within his regiment.

> Camp Taylor Mar 31st, 1862
> Private Thomas B. Turner desiring to obtain a cadet Warrant in the Confederate States Service, it gives me pleasure to state that he is a gentleman of good sense, pleasant address, unexceptionable deportment & the highest character. He has performed the duties of a soldier in my company since April last to the entire satisfaction of myself & the other officers of the A [Company]. I trust he will receive the desired appointment.
>
> Morton Marye
> Capt. Comdg Co. A 17th Regt. Va. Vols.

I cordially endorse the above statement of Capt. Marye referring to Private Turner & respectfully recommend his appointment to the position he seeks.

M. D. Corse
Col. Comg 17 Regt. Va. Vols.[3]

Additionally, Turner secured a third recommendation from a powerful source.

Richmond, Va.
April 7, 1862
Respectfully forwarded to the Hon'ble Secty of War. Mr. Thomas B. Turner who has been serving since the commencement of the War as a private in a company of rifles from Alexandria, and who has reenlisted for the war, is of good character, family deportment, and appearance. His brother is a private in the C.S. Army and has reenlisted for the war, I am told. This is the case with all of his male relatives as far as I know, who are of the proper age for military duty. He is about 18 years old.

G. W. C. Lee
Col. & Adj. to the
President[4]

With such influential men supporting him, Turner secured the cadet warrant and probably left his regiment sometime in late May or early June to make preparations for his new assignment. The first indication of what that assignment was comes from a letter Stuart wrote to his wife, Flora, on September 4, 1862. In the letter he asked Flora to pass a message on to Gen. R. E. Lee's daughter Mary. Part of the message referred to Turner and stated that he was with Stuart. On August 26 Turner's father recorded in his diary that his sons visited and ate with him that day.[5] Most likely Turner was already attached to Stuart as an aide-de-camp at this time and had obtained permission to visit his home. On the twenty-sixth Stuart was at Gainesville, which was not too far from "Kinloch."

Passing through the Battle of 2nd Manassas unscathed, Turner moved with the cavalry into Maryland. Though Stuart's cavalry was kept busy protecting Lee's infantry columns prior to the Battle of Sharpsburg, it had little to do during the engagement itself. Afterward the cavalry assisted in the army's retreat into Virginia. Stuart crossed the Potomac behind the

Federals to distract McClellan and draw his attention away from Lee. Stuart's foray proved successful, and he returned safely to the south side of the river on September 22. Turner was not as lucky as his chief. Sometime, quite probably during the cavalry's activity behind the Union Army, he was captured when his horse was shot beneath him. J. E. Cooke recounted that Turner had an interview with Gen. George B. McClellan during his short period of captivity. He fortunately spent no time in a Northern prison camp. He was paroled on September 22, 1862, giving his rank as lieutenant and his position as aide-de-camp to Stuart.

Out of the war temporarily, Turner spent several weeks at home before returning to the army around November 18. He undoubtedly participated in the numerous cavalry clashes as the two armies maneuvered toward Fredericksburg. Gen. Ambrose Burnside succeeded McClellan on December 7, 1862, setting the stage for the Battle of Fredericksburg on December 13. A few days before the battle, Turner and Hullihen left on their knightly errand behind enemy lines. To their chagrin they missed the fight. One version of the story stated that they returned the day after the battle.[6]

The usually dreary winter encampment was enlivened by Stuart's Dumfries Raid. From December 26 to 31, Stuart made life for the Federals quite unpleasant as he galloped about in the rear of Burnside's army destroying supplies and taking prisoners. Turner probably rode along with his general, unless the aide-de-camp had no horse. This expedition would have been his last as one of Stuart's aides.

By the spring of 1863, Turner again seems to have desired a change of scene. From all accounts he and the majority of the staff had missed the Battle of Kelly's Ford, which had claimed Pelham's life. Turner apparently approached Stuart soon afterward, asking to be allowed to join John S. Mosby's Partisan Rangers. Stuart, who never would have sent Mosby someone in whom he lacked faith, gave Turner permission to go and even wrote out a letter of introduction.

> I can cheerfully recommend Turner as of the right sort of stuff for such daring enterprises. He has served with distinction in the infantry, had his horse killed under him in Maryland, and had on several occasions shown great courage, coolness, and gallantry. Give him a chance.[7]

Turner left Stuart's staff in late March 1863 and traveled to his home, arriving there on the twenty-eighth. His father was not very happy about his son's decision to ride with the famous guerrilla chieftain, but he could scarcely stand in his way. The young lieutenant began operations with Mosby almost immediately. Within a month he was dead.

The circumstances that led to his death began with a scouting mission to Warrenton on April 25, 1863. At approximately eight that evening, Turner, Walter E. Frankland, William L. Hunter, and possibly two other rangers arrived at the home of Charles H. Utterback, about three miles from Warrenton.[8] While engaged in conversation with Utterback, the small party was attacked by Capt. E. J. Farnsworth of Gettysburg fame and members of the 8th Illinois Cavalry.

Accounts differ as to what happened next. According to Turner's father, his son was shot at the same moment that the Federals were discovered and did not have an opportunity to escape.[9] James J. Williamson's version states that Turner tried to fight his way out and was struck while attempting to escape.[10] In either case, Turner was the only Confederate casualty and was shot by Captain Farnsworth himself.

The wound proved quite serious. The ball entered near the left shoulder and penetrated into a lung or lungs, where it was later believed to have lodged. Carried first into Utterback's house, Turner was moved the following afternoon to the house of a Mr. Skinker. The next morning the friends and neighbors who had carried him to Skinker's returned to convey him to "Kinloch." Turner was partially paralyzed, and the possibility of his recovery remained slim. The doctor had already prepared the family for the worst, as he believed the wound to be mortal. Turner's condition, though not very good, worsened after he was visited twice on the afternoon of April 28 by a Union cavalry patrol. He was roughly handled during the first visit by the patrol's commander, who felt that Turner might be shamming. On the second visit, a Federal surgeon examined Turner's wound and pronounced him too ill to move. The manhandling he had received weakened Turner considerably, and any chance of his recuperation was lost. On April 29 at 6:15 A.M., just nine days short of his twentieth birthday, Turner died. He was buried at "Kinloch."[11]

Maj. Andrew Reid Venable

Assistant adjutant and inspector general
May 5, 1863, to May 12, 1864

For a number of Stuart's staff officers, the flower of romance bloomed during the years of the war. Several were married after seeking and obtaining the necessary furlough in order to share a few days with their lovely brides.

The marriage of Maj. A. R. Venable, however, was of a different nature. He was probably the only Confederate soldier to have a Philadelphia wedding while the war was still being fought.

This strange episode in the life of one of Stuart's finest staff officers began on October 27, 1864, when Venable rode into enemy lines during the fighting along Hatcher's Run south of Petersburg, Virginia. Entrusted with dispatches from Brig. James Dearing to Lt. Gen. Wade Hampton, on whose staff he was then serving, Venable, riding in heavily wooded terrain, too late found himself

Maj. Andrew Reid Venable

among troops belonging to the command of Federal brigadier general Thomas W. Egan. The Union general had no luck extracting information from Venable, who according to one source had many words to say to his captor but all of a rather scornful nature.[1] Egan sent Venable on his way, and before long the young adjutant was on a train north to Old Capitol Prison in Washington, where he spent a short period of confinement. His stay there was only temporary, as his final stop was to be Fort Delaware in Pennsylvania. He never arrived.

Once again Venable traveled by train, but on this trip he remained alert looking for an opportunity to escape. With evening approaching, the engine slowed upon reaching the outskirts of Philadelphia. At that moment, Venable bolted through an open window and disappeared into the night. He sought and found refuge with Southern sympathizers in Philadelphia, who put their home and money at his service. Venable adopted the role of a promoter from the oil fields of Pennsylvania and even made a few trips to the western part of the state to acquire additional knowledge so that he could better play his role.

While in Philadelphia, he wrote his fiancée, Ariadne Hackney Stevens (niece of Maryland's governor), who was staying in Baltimore, that she should make marriage plans and join him.[2] She rushed north, and the couple was married by Rev. Dr. W. S. Plummer, a college friend of Venable's father. Shortly after the wedding, Venable bade his wife farewell and headed west. His new bride returned to Baltimore while he slowly made his way back to the Confederacy, where he fought until Appomattox.

Andrew Reid Venable was born at "Vineyard" in Prince Edward County, Virginia, on December 2, 1832. His father, Samuel Woodson Venable, Jr., was a planter, and his mother was Jane Reid, daughter of Andrew Reid, for whom Venable was named. Venable entered Hampden-Sidney College in 1849 and graduated in 1852. He elected to leave the plantation and farming, choosing instead to settle in St. Louis, where he became involved in the commission business. While in St. Louis he met two people who were to play important roles in his life. One was his future wife, Ariadne Stevens, and the other was 2nd Lt. "Jeb" Stuart, who was stationed at Jefferson Barracks, Missouri, where his new regiment, the 1st U.S. Cavalry, was organized.[3] In those few months during the spring of 1855, Stuart and Venable began a friendship that lasted until Yellow Tavern.

Venable, a successful businessman, remained in St. Louis through all the turmoil that preceded the war. A states' rights advocate, he somehow managed to avoid controversy and build up a respectable clientele. Nevertheless, when Lincoln called for troops and Virginia's path became clear, he abandoned everything he had gained, rushed home, and joined the 3rd Battery of Richmond Howitzers. His association with this company was brief. On December 24, 1861, Venable received a captain's commission and was assigned as assistant commissary of subsistence in the 1st Regiment of Virginia Artillery.[4] In this capacity he served with Col. John Thompson Brown, the distinguished artillerist. Brown soon noticed that on numerous occasions when the enemy was encountered, his commissary officer had a tendency to arrange matters in order that he might join in the fray in whatever position Brown could use him. Commissary officers were not supposed to be combat officers, but no one could convince Venable of that.

The friendship between Stuart and Venable was renewed when their paths crossed during the early months of the war. In late November and early December 1862, the two were together along the Rappahannock as Stuart watched for any attempt at a crossing of the river above Port Royal by Ambrose Burnside's Army of the Potomac. Stuart and Venable, who was still with Thompson Brown, were guests at "Gay Mont" in Caroline County, home of some of Mrs. W. W. Blackford's relatives, on several occasions between November 24 and December 10. Venable, Stuart, Brown, and others dined together at "Gay Mont" on December 6.[5] The visits continued until Burnside made his intentions clear and the Battle of Fredericksburg was fought.

From at least December 30, 1862, to February 18, 1863, Venable was stationed at Milford Depot south of Fredericksburg. His duties as commissary officer may have kept him busy, but they probably were not quite what he desired to be doing.

His opportunity to meet the enemy again came at the Battle of Chancellorsville. On May 2, after Stuart had assumed command of the wounded Jackson's corps, Venable, while seeking Colonel Brown, encountered Stuart, who had just dispatched his last officer on a mission. The meeting was fortuitous for both. Venable offered to act as a voluntary aide-de-camp, and Stuart immediately gave him an urgent message to carry. For the rest of the day Venable was either by his old friend's side or riding over the battlefield bearing one order after another. When the day ended, Venable had won a place on the staff.[6]

On May 16, 1863, Venable was appointed major and assistant adjutant general to rank from May 11. He was ordered to report to Stuart, who had been able to have him added to the staff because of Channing Price's death. Venable's service to Stuart was such that he frequently gained mention in the general's reports. During the Gettysburg Campaign, and again at Auburn, when Stuart's cavalry was cut off from the rest of Lee's army, Venable performed in an exceptional manner. In the latter action, Stuart sent Venable to Lee with vital information about an enemy movement. Venable rode into Auburn only to find his way blocked. He exited the place under a hail of bullets and made his way to Lee through enemy-held territory. This brave action resulted in praise from Stuart.[7]

The winter of 1863–64 passed uneventfully for Venable, though he did receive a fifteen-day furlough on October 30, 1863. When the spring brought another Federal "On to Richmond" campaign, Venable rode with his chief through the early days of May in the Wilderness and then accompanied him as he galloped in pursuit of Sheridan's men. Venable was with Stuart on the morning of May 10 when the general visited his wife at Beaver Dam. As they rode away, Stuart confided in his friend that he did not want to survive the war if the South lost. The next day Stuart received his death wound. Among those who assisted Stuart from the field at Yellow Tavern, Venable saw his commander to safety before returning to the front. He never saw Stuart again. His chieftain left Venable one of his horses—the gray, named General—as he lay dying.[8]

For a short time after Stuart's death, Venable was attached to W. H. F. Lee's staff. In early June Venable had a brush with death near Haw's Shop. "The" Garnett was accompanying him and recorded the incident.

> The enemy skirmishers drove me out of Haw's Shop and riding with Major Venable (Andrew R.) I ascended a steep little hill to get a better view of them. Just as we reached the crest we were fired on by several of them, and beat a hasty retreat down a rocky and very steep slope. Reaching the foot of the hill, and thinking that I had heard the stroke of a bullet, I turned to Maj. Venable and asked if he was hit. "I think not," he said, "Are you?" He wore a heavy frock coat the tails of which had been pressed thick by the sagging of his sabre-belt. To this fortunate accident he owed his life. A

bullet had struck him just above the cantle of his saddle—*a posteriori,* so to speak, going through the thick folds of his coat tails piercing every garment he had on; he found it in the seat of his drawers and withdrew it rather triumphantly and with great satisfaction that it had gone no further.[9]

On August 11 Venable became Wade Hampton's adjutant.[10] In less than a month he became involved in the famous "Beefsteak Raid" ordered by Hampton to supply Lee's famished army with fresh meat. Venable and another of Stuart's former staff officers, G. M. Ryals, were placed in charge of the escort that was to take the cattle back to Confederate lines. How much cow-punching experience the two had is unknown, but their efforts earned the following accolade in Hampton's report of the venture.

> Major Venable, of my staff, was ordered to superintend this movement of the cattle, and, with Major Ryals, Provost Marshal, who had been very efficient in conducting it up to this time, to place them quickly across the Nottoway River at Freeman's Ford. These officers discharged their duty admirably, and the successful manner in which the cattle were brought off is due very much to their zeal and enterprise.[11]

Within a month of the raid, Venable was a prisoner and was beginning the adventure that culminated in his escape and marriage. After he returned to the army, he was granted a twenty-day leave beginning February 8, 1865. On March 16 he was assigned as assistant adjutant and inspector general to Brig. Gen. John Echols and sent to southwestern Virginia.[12] He was still there when Lee's army surrendered at Appomattox. Soon thereafter Venable capitulated in Charlotte, North Carolina.

After the war, Venable settled down on his estate, "Milnwood," near Farmville, Virginia, to the type of life he had earlier moved to St. Louis to avoid. He proved to be a success as a farmer just as he had been as a businessman. Active in the Farmer's Alliance, secretary and treasurer of the State Fair Association, Venable was a pioneer of sorts in the dairy industry. He was the first to introduce a high class of dairy cows in southwest Virginia. He was a participant in community and church activities. When the Confederate veterans organization began, he initiated the movement to construct a statue to Stuart. His goal was achieved with the unveiling of Stuart's monument in Richmond on May 30, 1907.

Venable once spoke to a friend of his life: "I was born with a spirit hard to control, and the struggle of my life has been to conquer it."[13] His struggle began to come to an end during the first half of 1909, when his health started to deteriorate. Following a brief illness, he passed away quietly at his home on October 15. He was buried in Hampden-Sidney the next day.

A tribute to his memory appeared in the October 22 issue of the Farmville *Herald*. It said, in part:

> He was a man of abounding charity. Never rich in this world's goods he contributed more to the comfort and practical support of others than any other one man we have known of. He had a wealthy friend who authorized him to find out the worthy ones in need of help and to draw upon him to meet their wants. This he did judiciously and well, and at the same time drew upon his own resources to meet the demands largely and liberally. And he not only gave to the needy and sick, but he carried the gifts in person and often kneeled at the bedside of the sick and humbly, earnestly asked for those things which the world can neither give nor take away.[14]

Maj. Johann August Heinrich Heros von Borcke

Aide-de-camp, assistant adjutant general, and inspector
June 1862 to June 17, 1863 (end of effective service)

The difficulty in dealing with the personage of Heros von Borcke stems from his now famous *Memoirs of the Confederate War,* in which he unabashedly claimed for himself deeds that had been performed by other members of Stuart's staff. Nevertheless, to dismiss von Borcke as a braggart and a charlatan would be a terrible injustice to a man who was recognized throughout the Army of Northern Virginia for his gallantry and steadfast devotion to Stuart and the Southern cause. That he was greatly admired and respected despite his tendency of self-glorification is witnessed to by the welcome he received upon his return to America in 1884. Von Borcke was loved and appreciated by those who knew him, and as true friends do, they graciously overlooked his faults.

The image of the six-foot-four 240-pound von Borcke, dragoon sword in hand, mounted and charging toward the ranks of the enemy must have been a sight to behold. Most interesting would have been the countenances of those awaiting his fearsome onslaught. Whatever might have been said for or against him, no one ever would have denied von Borcke's courage.

Johann August Heinrich Heros von Borcke was born on July 23, 1835, in Ehrenbreitstein, Prussia.[1] His family, one of the oldest in Prussia, could trace its lineage back to 1186 and claimed a proud heritage of nobility. Von Borcke's father, Otto Theodor Heros von Borcke, was a soldier, so it was not surprising that Johann also chose a military career. After attending schools in Berlin and at Halle, von Borcke received a commission as an ensign on June 14, 1853. His first service was in the Cuirassier Regiment of the Guards. After seven years he was transferred to the Second Brandenburg Regiment of Dragoons.

It has been speculated that von Borcke left Europe to come to the Confederacy because, though he was a soldier, he was not obtaining firsthand experience at war. To a young man of von Borcke's age and temperament, the fact that he had yet to participate in a battle would be cause enough to find a war in which to join the fight. Another factor may have also played a role. One source stated that von Borcke and his father had had a disagreement over financial matters; thus trouble within the family may have contributed to the Prussian's decision to enter into the conflict taking place in America.[2]

Von Borcke disembarked from the steamer *Kate* in Charleston, South Carolina, on the morning of May 24, 1862.[3] His trip across the Atlantic had not been uneventful, his first ship, the *Hero,* having been boarded by sailors from one of the Federal ships patrolling Southern waters as part of a massive blockade designed to strangle the South's foreign commerce. After his first view of Southern soldiers on the city streets, the Prussian was unsure whether he had chosen wisely. But his judgment was based on the European ideal of soldiers, and he would soon come to appreciate the Confederacy's troops for what they were: fighters.

Much to his regret, von Borcke had been forced to destroy his letters of introduction when his ship had been inspected at sea, so he traveled from Charleston to Richmond filled with doubt about how he might be received. This difficulty quickly disappeared, however, after an interview with Confederate secretary of war George Wythe Randolph, who supplied von Borcke with a letter of introduction to Brig. Gen. "Jeb" Stuart, who was then on duty with the cavalry forces attached to the army defending the Confederate capital. A fully accoutred von Borcke left Richmond in search of Stuart on May 30, 1862. He had wasted no time finding the war.

The relationship between "Von," as he was called at cavalry headquarters, and Stuart began on a positive note and spiraled upward from there. Von Borcke's performance in the Battle of Seven Pines on May 31,

1862, demonstrated to Stuart that Secretary Randolph had not sent him an inexperienced foreigner. The Prussian watched his new commanding officer closely and came away totally committed to Stuart as a man and a soldier. While von Borcke may have stretched the truth when he wrote that a dying Stuart told him, "I never loved a man as much as yourself," there can be little doubt that their friendship ran strong and deep.[4]

On June 20 von Borcke accepted his commission as captain of cavalry from the hands of Secretary of War Randolph. Stuart, knowing that von Borcke's commission was ready, had sent the Prussian to Richmond with a report. Von Borcke wrote in his memoirs, "I returned to headquarters with a sense of hearty satisfaction such as I had not known for a long time." Surprisingly, considering the slow rate of advancement for junior officers in the Confederate Army, "Von" remained a captain for just a few weeks. While encamped at Hanover Court House following the Seven Days Campaign, Stuart was promoted to major general and several of his headquarters entourage also received promotions. Von Borcke was made a major on the staff to date from July 25, though the date of appointment was August 8, with the date of confirmation being October 7. The actual position he held on the staff was assistant adjutant and inspector general. He was never, as he claimed, chief of staff.

Recounting the Prussian's exploits while serving with Stuart would be impossible within such limited space. To ignore his career completely, however, would be an injustice. One of von Borcke's proudest moments came when Stuart asked him to deliver a beautiful dress frock coat to Gen. "Stonewall" Jackson. Famous for his plain attire, Jackson had to be cajoled into donning the coat in von Borcke's presence. "Von" wrote that Jackson's staff was ecstatic over their general's dashing appearance.

Von Borcke's legendary dragoon sword and the manner in which he used it earned him a number of sobriquets, including "Long Blade" and "Major Armstrong." On more than one occasion, however, "Von" was forced to retreat along with other staff members. At Verdiersville Stuart and a small number of the staff, including von Borcke, had to flee a Federal cavalry patrol. And during the Battle of Brandy Station on June 9, 1863, Lt. Frank S. Robertson recalled seeing von Borcke and Capt. Benjamin S. White in precipitate retreat. The Prussian's mighty blade was no match for a Yankee cavalry regiment in full charge. On this occasion, Captain White had been wounded in the face and neck, and von Borcke had been assisting him from the field when the enemy made their charge. This was the second time von Borcke helped one of Stuart's wounded staff. On August 20, 1862, he had come to the aid of Capt. Redmond Burke, who had suffered a leg wound while charging at von Borcke's side.

Less than two weeks after White's wounding, von Borcke himself was wounded during the Battle of Middleburg on June 19, 1863. The site of von Borcke's wounding has been reported variously as Middleburg and Upperville. The Union forces under Gen. Alfred Pleasonton, attempting to penetrate Stuart's cavalry curtain and ascertain the whereabouts of Lee's army, struck at the Southern horsemen, who were occupying a position on a wooded ridge about a half mile west of Middleburg. The battle opened about 7:00 A.M., but the main Federal thrust did not develop until 9:30 A.M. The engagement lasted almost all day, until Stuart at last began to fall back to another ridge a half mile to his rear. Von Borcke helped rally some disordered regiments, then rejoined Stuart and the other staff officers. As the small group of officers rode together across the open field, they became the target of Union sharpshooters. While "Von" was speaking to Stuart, one ball clipped the gold braid from von Borcke's pants leg, then another ball struck him in the throat.[5]

Capt. W. W. Blackford, who was riding close to von Borcke, saw that the wounded man was slowly falling from his saddle and that his spur was about to catch on his blanket strap behind the saddle. Spurring his own mount alongside the Prussian's, he threw the leg clear, and von Borcke, his hands losing their grip on the horse's mane, fell onto his back on the grass. Blackford and his brother-in-law, Lt. Frank S. Robertson, rushed to von Borcke's assistance, and with a trick "Von" himself had shown Blackford, helped the wounded man remount his horse and escorted him off the field to an ambulance.[6]

At first von Borcke's wound was diagnosed by surgeon Talcott Eliason as being mortal, but the huge Prussian rallied during the night and over the next several months made a remarkable recovery. Though he attempted to rejoin Stuart on various occasions, the severity of his wound had so weakened his constitution that he was never again fit for field service, at least for the Confederacy. What has been neglected concerning von Borcke's recovery period are the numerous letters written on his behalf by Stuart and others to secure another position for the Prussian. Stuart began his campaign on August 10, 1863, with the following letter:

Hd Qrs Cavalry Div A of NV.
Aug. 10th 1863

Mr. President;

One of your Excellency's nature, will pardon *my* addressing you a communication, when you understand, it is in the interest of the *brave* and the *suffering* that I write.

Major Heros von Borcke of my staff—a Prussian Cavalry officer of high social position at home, early espoused our cause, ran the blockade when it was a matter of great risk, and tendered his services to our govt. I was so fortunate as to have him assigned to me for duty. He has served with great distinction, and has impressed all with the value of his services, and his thorough mastery of his profession.

After the most miraculous escapes, he was very seriously wounded near Middleburg, during the recent advance to Penn. and it is feared he will not be able to take the field for months.

In order to give him the advantage of a sea voyage recommended by his Surgeon, as well as to derive benefit to ourselves, from his enlarged experience in the Cavalry Service, I am desirous that he should be sent to Europe, to procure a better pattern of fire arms & equipments for our Cavalry Service, and if practicable cause their shipment to us. In the twofold capacity of Prussian of distinction and a Confederate officer of high rank I think he can be of great service in furthering our interests in Europe.

If these suggestions meet your approval I would respectfully recommend that the rank of Brig. Gen'l be conferred upon him not only because of his high merit, but to give him more consequence abroad.—I believe in a case somewhat similar Prince Polignac of Gen'l Beauregard's staff was com'd, Brig. Gen'l.

I have the honor to be
> Dear Sir—
>> Your obt svt
>> J. E. B. Stuart
>> Major Gen'l[7]

This effort on von Borcke's behalf failed, but Stuart continued to petition Richmond, writing again in January and April 1864. He was aided in his campaign by Gens. Wade Hampton and Fitzhugh Lee, both of whom testified to von Borcke's "high soldierly qualities, his capacity, and his military perception of transacting events upon the field of battle."[8] When it became known that a brigade of cavalry was to be organized specifically for the defense of Richmond, an attempt was made by Stuart, Hampton, and Fitz Lee to secure a brigadier generalship and command of the brigade for von Borcke. Again the War Department rejected the suggestion and instead, on May 28, 1864, ordered von Borcke to southwestern Virginia and eastern Tennessee to inspect mounted troops serving in that area under Gen. W. E. "Grumble" Jones.

The War Department had not been entirely oblivious to von Borcke's contributions to the army and the cause. In appreciation for his efforts, a resolution of thanks was drafted and entered into the record.

> Whereas Maj. Heros von Borcke, of Prussia, assistant adjutant and inspector general of the cavalry corps of the Army of Northern Virginia, having left his own country to assist in securing the independence of ours, and by his personal gallantry in the field having won the admiration of his comrades as well as that of his commanding general, all of whom deeply sympathize with him in his present sufferings from wounds received in battle: Therefore,
>
> *Resolved by the Congress of the Confederate States of America,* That the thanks of Congress are due, and the same are hereby tendered, to Major von Borcke, for his self-sacrificing devotion to our Confederacy, and for his distinguished services in support of its cause. *Resolved,* That a copy of the foregoing resolution be transmitted to Major von Borcke by the President of the Confederate States.
>
> Approved January 30, 1864.[9]

Despite this commendable action, the government was not inclined to give von Borcke an increase in rank, so the struggle on his behalf continued. On August 13, 1864, Hampton wrote yet another letter asking that von Borcke be appointed inspector general of all the cavalry with the rank of colonel, citing the Prussian's service record with the cavalry as excellent grounds for the position. The request was denied, and von Borcke continued through a period of uncertainty. In his memoirs he revealed little about this time, jumping ahead to his accepting a mission to Europe as a "representative" of his adopted nation. In one final letter written on December 18, 1864, Hampton urged that von Borcke be granted a colonelcy, "as he has been charged with a very important mission abroad."[10] This plea at last gained something, even though it was not the full colonelcy for which Hampton had asked. On December 20, 1864, Heros von Borcke became a lieutenant colonel. Before the new year he ran the blockade on the ship *Tallahassee,* sailing from Wilmington, North Carolina, under the guns of Fort Fisher. He reached England and there eventually learned of Lee's surrender.

After the war von Borcke turned to writing his memoirs, which appeared in 1866 and have since become famous. He had not, however, permanently turned in his sword. When war erupted between Prussia and Austria in 1866, he returned home to be recommissioned as a second lieutenant in the Third Neumarkt Regiment of Dragoons. He was present at the Battle of Koniggratz on July 3, 1866. After the battle he was presented to Helmuth von Moltke, who greeted von Borcke, much to the Prussian's pleasure, by saying, "Are you not the American?" The bullet he still carried in his lung continued to trouble him and finally forced his retirement from military service in 1867, though by one account he served as personal adjutant to Field Marshal Prince Frederick Charles from 1875 to 1880.

On September 16, 1867, von Borcke married Magdalene Honig of Gralow. They had three sons: Wolf Henning Erich, born in Berlin on May 6, 1873; Wulf Werner, born at Zychce on June 5, 1874; and Henning Wulf Rudiger, born at Giesenbrugge on September 14, 1881. Von Borcke's father died at Giesenbrugge on November 12, 1878, leaving Heros the East Prussian estate. Von Borcke's wife, Magdalene, died on August 26, 1883.[11]

While in residence at Giesenbrugge, von Borcke had two visitors from America. One was Capt. William Gordon McCabe, who watched as "Von" ran the German flag up the flagpole of one of the castle's towers and the Confederate flag up the other. The second visitor was Col. Charles Venable, formerly of Robert E. Lee's staff. Venable was on sabbatical from the University of Virginia when he visited von Borcke in 1883. He secured the Prussian's promise to revisit Virginia in 1884.

Von Borcke's return to Virginia was quite a success, despite the fact that the mighty Prussian had added another two hundred pounds. Arriving at Hoboken, New Jersey, on May 30, 1884, he was greeted by Tom Price, a former member of Stuart's staff and at that time a professor at Columbia University. The trip to Richmond was highlighted by stops at Baltimore, Washington, Alexandria, and Fredericksburg. On reaching the city that had been the Confederacy's capital, von Borcke experienced a great reunion of many of his cavalry companions from the war. During the festivities, von Borcke's mighty blade, which he had left behind when he journeyed to England almost twenty years earlier, was produced by the Price family, who had held it all those long years. "Von" presented the sword to his adopted state, Virginia, and again left it behind when he returned to Germany. He made a side trip to Staunton to visit Stuart's widow before embarking for Germany on August 15, 1884.[12]

After his return to Giesenbrugge, von Borcke married Magdalene's sister, Tony Honig, on July 31, 1885. The couple had one child, Caroline Virginia Magdalene, born at Giesenbrugge on May 5, 1887. Sometime after von Borcke's return from America, he moved to Berlin. He died there on May 10, 1895. Gen. Williams C. Wickham said that von Borcke "was ever in the front rank of the charge and always in the rear of the retreat. No man in the Confederate Army did more faithful service than Heros von Borcke!"[13]

Maj. Benjamin Stephen White

Aide-de-camp
October 21, 1862, to July 14, 1863 (end of effective service)

On June 9, 1863, Stuart's cavalry faced an almost unprecedented challenge from the rapidly improving Union horse in what became known as the Battle of Brandy Station. Like so many others that day, Capt. B. S. White, one of Stuart's aides, met the enemy with pistol and saber. In the mass of confusion he was recognized by a fellow staff officer, Frank Robertson, who, years after the war, recorded the following:

> There was a general mix-up of battle lines, indeed there were none. Every Regiment seems to be doing its own fighting regardless of other Regiments. Still trying to locate General Stuart, I rode this strip of pines and emerged directly in front of a charging Regiment of Yanks in hot pursuit of a part of our 12th Virginia. Major Von Borcke and Capt. White, I saw speeding in front of me, the latter shot through the neck, it seemed limber and useful in watching the rear, but an hour or so afterward it seemed very stiff and useless. I joked him about it frequently.[1]

Robertson joined von Borcke and White in their flight, which might have ended in their capture had it not been for a gallant countercharge by the 11th Virginia. White's wound might have been inflicted shortly before Robertson saw him galloping for his life, which could explain White's ability to look back at his pursuers. The wound was very serious, however, and once out of danger von Borcke quickly found a courier to take White from the field.[2] After the Gettysburg Campaign, White never rode with Stuart again, but his chief never forgot the contributions he had made while a member of the staff.

Benjamin Stephen White was born in Montgomery County, Maryland, on March 11, 1828, the son of Nathan Smith White II and Evelina Wailes. Only a few facts are known about his early life. In 1851 he married Sarah Ellen Nichols, who died in 1856. White eventually remarried, though the date is unknown. His second wife was Mary Elizabeth Meade of Virginia. Before the war he ran a store in Poolesville, Maryland.

At the outbreak of the war he offered his services to the Confederacy and was commissioned as a second lieutenant in the Confederate States cavalry on November 16, 1861.[3] His assignment from this date until he joined Stuart's staff is unclear, but he played a major part in the success of Stuart's Chambersburg Raid, on October 9–12, 1862. White's detailed knowledge of the terrain immediately north of the Potomac River in Maryland brought him an appointment as guide for that portion of the raid. Stuart needed an escape route from the Union forces that were rapidly closing in on his column. Having been reared in the area, White was quite familiar with all the roads and trails in the vicinity. He also knew of a ford in the river and directed the columns to it. The enemy guarding it was duped into abandoning their position, and the Confederates crossed the river under the eyes of their frustrated and exhausted pursuers.

During the raid White rode his favorite horse, Maggie Mitchell. According to an interview he gave a reporter in 1883, the horse performed beyond the call of duty by marching 186 miles with White in the saddle. He stated that the beautiful black mare responded whenever there was a crisis, often outrunning her more well-rested comrades. The horse survived the war after carrying her master through three years of the conflict and passing through numerous actions unscathed.[4]

In his report of the excursion into Pennsylvania, Stuart mentioned White and his importance to the mission. The cavalry chief sent White to Richmond in charge of the prisoners captured on the raid. Around the same time Stuart also requested that the Marylander be transferred to his staff. This was accomplished on October 21, 1862. Over the next few months White filled the position of aide-de-camp and did some independent scouting for Stuart in Loudoun and neighboring counties. The fact that he was entrusted with such missions confirms Stuart's faith in his abilities.

Though badly wounded at Brandy Station, White forced himself to endure the exhausting summer campaign in Pennsylvania.[5] He reached Gettysburg and returned, but once the cavalry was safely back in Virginia, his condition forced Stuart to employ him in a totally different manner. No attempt was made to remove him from the staff, although such a move would have been entirely justified. Instead, in early July 1863, Stuart placed White in charge of the cavalry corps horse infirmary in the Tye River Valley, halfway between Charlottesville and Lynchburg.[6] Though far removed from cavalry headquarters, White would not be forgotten by his commander-in-chief, who tried to obtain a majority for his aide. On July 15, 1863, Stuart wrote that White "distinguished himself for gallantry and efficiency—energy and skill—particularly at Fleetwood . . . where he received a painful wound leading a charge. Capt. White has command of the Horse Infirmary Corps of the Cav. Corps and has constantly under his control about 500 men and 2000 horses."[7]

The letter failed to gain the desired result, but Stuart kept trying. On December 15, 1863, he reported the following regarding Captain White:

> Cmdg. Infirmary Corps of the Cavalry Corps in Tye River Valley reports having sent back to the ranks in a serviceable condition 1210 horses since the establishment of the camp in August last, all of which, he is very positive, would have been entirely lost to the services, but for the facilities afforded by the H.I. for their recuperation.[8]

This endorsement was also accompanied by a request for a majority for White. Finally, on January 5, 1864, White became a major with orders to report to Stuart, who continued to employ him at the horse infirmary.

Following Stuart's death White continued at his post, but his records do not disclose how long he remained there. His wound must have healed to the point where he could again perform more actively, for on November 29, 1864, Lt. Col. John S. Mosby received the following order:

> Hdqrs. Cavalry Corps, Army of Northern Virginia,
> November 29, 1864
> Lieut. Col. John S. Mosby.
> Comdg. 43rd Virginia Partisan Rangers battalion cavalry:
> Colonel: Maj. B. S. White is directed by orders from army headquarters to proceed to the section of country in which you operate to collect and bring out for use of our cavalry here such cavalry arms, particularly carbines, as he may find in the hands of citizens—arms which have been captured from the enemy and deposited in the country by our soldiers or others. He is directed to call upon you for a detail of men to assist him in this work, and for such other assistance as you may feel able to extend to him. He will show you the orders under

which he is acting. General Hampton directs me to inform you of these facts and to represent to you the urgent necessity for arms which now exists in the command. Our numbers are largely increasing, increasing daily. Many of our men are without proper cavalry arms, and many of them have no guns at all. It is necessary for us to put on foot some extraordinary measures to supply this want, and at Captain Grattan's suggestion Major White is sent to you for this purpose. Will you please give to him such assistance as may be in your power, and such men and information as he may need. By doing so you will confer great benefit upon the service.

Very respectfully, your obedient servant,

H. B. McClellan

Assistant Adjutant-General[9]

The assignment was a difficult one, and its success is unknown. White's position at this time is equally a mystery. Capt. Charles Grattan of Stuart's staff was attached to the ordnance department under Hampton's command. White may have been affiliated with Hampton's staff or the ordnance service, but he may have been selected because of his knowledge of the area in which he was to collect the arms.

At the war's end White was paroled as a major in Winchester on April 24, 1865. At the time of his parole he was thirty-five years old and five feet, nine inches tall, with a fair complexion, light hair, and hazel eyes. He gave his destination as Baltimore and his former residence as Montgomery County, Maryland.[10]

After the war White lived and worked in Baltimore. In 1883 he moved to Laytonsville, Maryland, and later to Barnesville, Maryland. He died on March 21, 1891, and was buried in Monocacy Cemetery in Beallsville, Maryland.

PART THREE

Stuart's Headquarters Personnel

His men believed in him heartily, and it was a common saying among them that "Jeb never says 'Go, boys,' but always says 'Come, boys.'" We felt sure, too, that there was little prospect of excitement on any expedition of which he was not leader. If scouting was to be merely a matter of form, promising nothing in the way of adventure, he would let us go by ourselves; but if there were prospect of "a fight or a race," as he expressed it, we were sure to see his long plume at the head of the column before we had passed outside our own line of pickets.

—George Cary Eggleston[1]

The story of Stuart's headquarters would not be complete without recognizing the many men who served in posts that, though often behind the scenes, were vital to the efficiency of the cavalry corps. No matter how talented the general and his staff, unless they numbered in the hundreds the work that was required of them never would have been accomplished. Mounds of paperwork necessitated many hands to copy, sort, discard, or file orders, requests for furloughs, medical reports, inventories, ad infinitum. Messages needed to be carried from one location to another. The movements and plans of the enemy had to be discovered, and headquarters security had to be maintained. The clerks, couriers, escort troopers, and most of the scouts who performed these tasks have seldom received the attention of historians. A few of the scouts became famous, but many others are virtually unknown.

The clerks of the various departments churned out reams of paper that were as much the lifeblood of the cavalry as were the men who faced the enemy. Without electric lights, typewriters, or computers, these men kept the troopers saddled, armed, clothed, and fed as best they could in a country that began to run short of materiel very early in the conflict. Their job was a thankless one, and for the most part they have been forgotten.

The couriers of Stuart's headquarters performed a task vital to the mounted arm. The transmission of orders was necessary for the successful accomplishment of any military movement. The courier was frequently required to brave the fire of the enemy or outrun an unfriendly patrol bent on his capture and thus needed a fast horse and a cool head. In some cases a courier also needed an appetite for paper to save secret dispatches from the enemy.

Stuart's daring scouts have been among the most celebrated of Southern cavalrymen. Mosby, Stringfellow, and a handful of others became famous for their courageous feats. Their fame has unfortunately overshadowed many other bold men. Of all who rode with Stuart, the scouts ran the greatest risks. If captured, a quick death often awaited them. Stuart demanded much from these men. Many of his exploits depended on acquiring accurate information about the enemy. Regular cavalry patrols could supply some of what was needed, but only the scouts could probe deep enough behind enemy lines to uncover the kind of intelligence that was really necessary. On many occasions, their success contributed extensively to the success of Stuart and the entire cavalry.

The cavalry chieftain's escort often found themselves where the lead flew the thickest. Determined to protect their leader, many of these men ran greater risks than they would have taken had they remained with their regiments. Nevertheless, many felt that the honor of being in Stuart's escort far outweighed the additional dangers to which such duty exposed them.

The large number of men who filled the roles of clerk, courier, escort trooper, and scout for Stuart's headquarters throughout the war renders it impossible to provide even a short biography for each man. The best that can be done is to record their names and a few facts about their service with Stuart. As representative of this group, however, the lives of four of these men are explored and their stories recorded. They are typical of all those who "followed the plume."

Pvt. George W. Freed

Bugler
May or June 1861 to May 12, 1864

Many of the men who rode in the long, gray-clad column on the night of August 22, 1862, remembered it as one of the darkest they had ever experienced. Sheets of blinding rain would soon reduce the visibility even more. The clouds were gathering as the troopers were positioned around the enemy encampment. The officers were told to have the men give their wildest "Rebel yell" and charge when they heard the sound of the bugle. All eyes strained to catch a glimpse of the target that lay before them. Campfires flickered among the tents, and here and there figures could be seen moving about with a calmness that came from the belief that the enemy was miles and miles away. The quiet solitude would last but a few moments longer.

Maj. Gen. "Jeb" Stuart had led his men to Catlett's Station in order to gather important information for his commander, Gen. R. E. Lee, and to shake up the Union commander Gen. John Pope. There was also the little matter of a lost hat and cape for which Stuart had vowed revenge.[1]

When all was ready, Stuart turned to a man sitting astride a horse and spoke a brief order: "Sound the charge, Freed." Pvt. George W. Freed lifted his bugle to his lips. Scarcely had the first notes broken than bugles were echoing the call from what seemed every direction, and with a thunderous "Rebel yell," the Confederates swept into the Union camp.

This experience was not an unfamiliar one for George Freed. He had been following Stuart from almost the beginning of the brilliant cavalryman's career. Freed was born on December 24, 1834, in or near Waynesboro, Virginia. Not much is known about his early life, but he was probably involved in what was his postwar occupation, farming. He enlisted in the Valley Rangers from Waynesboro on April 19, 1861, and rode north with the company to Harpers Ferry. Soon after their arrival, the Rangers became Company "E" of the 1st Virginia Cavalry, which was commanded by Col. "Jeb" Stuart. One of Stuart's first orders was to attach Freed to his headquarters as bugler.[2] Freed remained in this position throughout the war until Stuart's death.

Freed was present with Stuart on the fateful journey to Yellow Tavern. "The" Garnett recorded an exchange between Stuart and Freed as the gray cavalry set out in pursuit of Sheridan on the afternoon of May 9, 1864.

> About 3 o'clock P.M. General Stuart left the church [near Spotsylvania Court House] and commenced that long and toilsome journey which terminated in his death. It might be worthwhile to dwell here for a moment on some sad thoughts which will rise in the mind in contemplation of the circumstances I am about to relate. He bade Gen. Lee "goodbye" and summoning a few of his staff officers rode off from the army. To a believer in the theory of "presentiments" it would have been easy to infer from Gen. Stuart's manner that he felt deeply and seriously the awful crisis that was at hand. The cheerful smile, the hearty laugh, the merry hum of his voice as he ran over and over some favorite song—"Her Bright Smile Haunts Me Still" or "Ever of Thee I'm Fondly Dreaming," one or the other of which he was continually humming even in the midst of battle,—all this was changed. His mind was at work with graver matters. Who can tell what the inner communings of his dauntless soul were then? It was on this very march that one of the men, our bugler, a man named Freed, who was riding just behind him remarked, "General, I believe you are happy in a fight." The General turned on him suddenly and said, "You're mistaken, Freed, I don't love

bullets any better than you do. It is my duty to go where
they are sometimes, but I don't expect to survive this war."[3]

Stuart would voice this same feeling to Maj. A. R. Venable on the following
day as they rode away from Beaver Dam after Stuart saw his wife for the
last time. The major never forgot Stuart's prophetic words, and Freed
doubtless remembered them as well.

After Stuart's death, Freed served with Gen. Fitz Lee for the remainder
of the war. He then returned to Waynesboro, where he farmed until his
death on May 30, 1908. A few days after Freed died, the following letter
appeared in the Staunton *Spectator & Vindicator.* It will serve as a fitting
epitaph to the gallant bugler.

> To the survivors of Company E:
> Dear Comrades,
> Again we are called to follow the remains of one of
> the old company to his final resting place, and one that
> so often by the blast of his bugle called us to mount our
> horses, go to the front and meet the enemy in the not to
> be forgotten past. George W. Freed, after a few days
> sickness of pneumonia, died on May 30th, 1908, aged
> 73 years. His remains were followed toward the grave by
> nine members of the old company and quite a number
> from other commands, and buried in Waynesboro.
> It will be remembered by many of you that George
> was one of the original members of the old volunteer
> cavalry company that left Waynesboro on the 19th of
> April, 1861, under the command of the lamented Captain
> William Patrick, and marched down the Valley to
> Harper's Ferry, where we were, with the other companies,
> formed into the 1st Va. cavalry regiment, and J. E. B.
> Stuart was appointed our colonel, and one of the first
> orders issued by him was to have "Freed" (as old Jeb ever
> after called him) permanently detailed as his headquarters
> bugler.
> While George always claimed his membership of the
> company, he remained with Gen. Stuart until the day of
> Stuart's death in the city of Richmond, when he reported
> to Gen. Fitz Lee, and remained with him to the surrender
> at Appomattox.

I now recall an incident that occurred at Slatersville, New Kent County. Our company was run into by a stampeded regiment, and George's horse was knocked down and a greater portion of the horses passed over him. George, himself being an active man, kept his feet by pushing himself from one horse to the other until they all had passed. When Col. Fitz came up he said, "Freed, that was a close call," and George answered very emphatically, "Yes, and you were among them, for I saw you." Fitz laughed heartily. Both Gen. Stuart and Gen. Fitz Lee became very fond of and very much attracted to George, and in camp as well as on the battle field, he was ever at their side ready to carry their orders to any point, regardless of danger, or distance. I write this letter knowing that not only the regiment, but many in the brigade, or even the division, will remember Freed the bugler.

Waynesboro, Va.

Luther[4]

Pvt. DeWitt Clinton Gallaher

Courier
October 27, 1863, to March 1864

Fear that the war would end before they could witness the "great adventure" prompted many young men to leave home, school, and sweetheart to join the army. One such young man was DeWitt Clinton Gallaher, who turned his back on his studies at Hampden-Sidney College in June 1863 to accept an aide-de-camp appointment on the staff of Gen. John D. Imboden. Commissioned a captain, Gallaher should have been set for the duration of the war. The young officer's position and the luck he had in obtaining it undoubtedly aroused the envy of many who aspired to similar status. Yet within four months, Gallaher resigned for exactly the same reason he had left Hampden-Sidney College: The war was passing him by, and he wanted to be a part of it. On October 8, 1863, Gallaher enlisted in Company "E" of the 1st Virginia Cavalry as a private. Nineteen days later he was detailed to Stuart's headquarters as a courier. His "great adventure" was about to begin.

Gallaher was born in Jefferson County, Virginia, now West Virginia, on August 2, 1845. He was the son of Hugh Lafferty and Elizabeth Catherine Gallaher.[1] While he was still quite young, his family moved to

Waynesboro, Virginia. At thirteen he attended Georgetown College. Three years later he entered Washington College, moving after only one year to Hampden-Sidney, which he left to join Imboden's staff.

During his period of service with Stuart, Gallaher participated in the previously recounted expedition (see pages 197–200) behind enemy lines, during which he accompanied Maj. H. B. McClellan to a mournful meeting with the major's brother. His service with Stuart was curtailed because of an unidentified illness that struck him in January 1864. Another difficulty arose when he had to report himself without a mount, a condition in which no self-respecting courier wished to be found. Unable to carry out his duties, Gallaher was sent back to his regiment.

By March Gallaher was well and had secured another horse. He fought a number of actions with his company as Grant pushed toward Richmond. On June 25 a piece of shell struck him in his left boot but fortunately failed to inflict a wound. He remained with his regiment until October, when he accepted an invitation to join Gen. Thomas Rosser's command. Once again he was detached as a courier, this time for Rosser. Gallaher suffered through the demoralizing Shenandoah Valley Campaign in the fall of 1864, and at the time of Lee's surrender at Appomattox, he was back in the Valley carrying out Rosser's orders to call in all soldiers on furlough. He was included in Lee's surrender, but not knowing this, he applied for parole in Staunton on May 1, 1865. At this time he was described as being nineteen years old, and five feet, seven inches tall, with dark hair and brown eyes.

Picking up his education where he had left off, Gallaher entered the University of Virginia in the fall of 1865. He graduated in 1868, then taught for a year before traveling to the Universities of Berlin and Munich, where he spent two years in study. Returning to the United States in 1872, he settled in Charleston, West Virginia. He was admitted to the bar and practiced law for more than fifty years. He married Florence Miller in July 1876. The couple had three sons and two daughters. Gallaher died on December 25, 1927, at his home in Charleston.

Pvt. Leopold Levy

Courier and clerk (Commissary Department)
May 4–5, 1861; July 21, 1861; February 1, 1862, to May 3, 1863

Born in Aldenstadt, Bavaria, on May 6, 1828, Leopold Leow immigrated to the United States in 1848 with his sister and two brothers.[1] The customs agent at the port of Baltimore changed the name of the family from Leow to Levy for reasons known only to him. Settling in Amelia County, Virginia,

Levy worked as a clerk until he saved enough money
to open a store himself. In 1858 Levy married
Rosena Hutzler. The couple would eventually
have seven children: Joseph, an unnamed infant
who died in 1861, Isaac, Amelia, Monro,
Florence, and Marion. Levy became a member
of the Amelia County Troop, a cavalry company
that had been organized in 1846. In 1859 the
troop offered its services to Virginia's governor at
the time of John Brown's raid on Harpers Ferry.
The governor did not call up the company,
however, which was fortunate for Levy, who was ill with typhoid fever.

Pvt. Leopold Levy

      With the coming of the war, Virginia mobilized her men. All three
Levy brothers volunteered their services to the state. Solomon joined the
infantry and was mortally wounded at the Battle of McDowell. Sampson
entered the cavalry and served in Company "G" of the 1st Virginia throughout the war. Leopold went to war when Capt. Samuel S. Weisiger called
the Amelia Dragoons into camp at Amelia Court House. The camp was
located about three hundred yards from Levy's home, but he was kept in
camp like everyone else, even though his only son, Joseph, was quite ill and
his wife feared that the baby might die.[2] The men spent their time drilling
and sharpening their swords. On May 9 the company was enlisted at the
court house before starting for Richmond. The Dragoons passed through
the Confederate capital and encamped at Ashland, where they remained
for about six weeks.

      Levy and the rest of the Amelia Troop had their first experience at war
near Berryville, Virginia. Several of the men came close to being captured
but managed to escape. A few days later, on July 10, 1861, the troop became
Company "G" of the 1st Virginia Cavalry. Almost immediately Stuart,
now their commanding officer, had them out screening the movement of
Joe Johnston's army. The Battle of 1st Manassas followed. Levy served as a
special courier for Stuart during the engagement.

      After the battle came months of picket duty. Levy wrote letters home
from Falls Church, Munson's Hill, and Centreville, but he never received
a furlough to go home until March 1862. The furlough was actually a
business trip. Levy, with the rank of acting sergeant, and Lt. William Wilson
journeyed to Amelia County on recruiting duty. The leave proved of short
duration, and Levy was soon back with his regiment. Levy's wife visited
him sometime in April.

      By this time Levy had actually become a member of the cavalry's
Commissary Department. On February 1 he had been assigned to Maj.

Dabney Ball,[3] but his work for the major did not relieve him of other duties. At the Battle of Williamsburg on May 4–5 he again carried messages for Stuart. Over the next few weeks, the Confederate Army under Johnston had been forced back to the outskirts of Richmond. In June Stuart made his famous circuit of McClellan's army, but Levy had bilious fever and was left behind.

Passing through the 2nd Manassas, Sharpsburg, and Fredericksburg campaigns, Levy continued his work in the Commissary Department. Major Ball had resigned, and Levy was now serving under Maj. William J. Johnson. In the third week of April 1863, Levy received a pass that allowed him to return home and collect supplies for the use of the cavalry. He was enjoying his leave when on May 1 he received orders to report back to headquarters, as the enemy had taken the offensive. He set out to rejoin the cavalry. Crossing the James River somewhere between Columbia to the west and Goochland to the east, he arrived in the vicinity of Yanceyville on May 3. Here his luck ran out.

A Union cavalry raid under the direction of Maj. Gen. George Stoneman had slipped around the Confederate Army's left flank and headed south. The raiders had swept through Louisa Court House and pushed on toward Yanceyville. Levy, heading north, ran into them. He, along with his traveling companion, John T. Southall of Company "G," 1st Virginia, were captured. Also taken prisoner in the same area was Major Johnson. Levy was now to enter upon his greatest trial of the war.

Not wanting to carry all the prisoners with them, the Federals paroled some, including Levy. Unfortunately, before he was able to leave for home to await exchange, the Yanks changed their mind and decided to take all the prisoners along for the ride. Levy was placed on a horse without a saddle or bridle and was kept on the march for four days, until he fainted from fatigue and physical strain. He was a large man, weighing close to two hundred pounds. Without stirrups, Levy was unable to hold up his weight and could not support himself. The valves in the veins of his legs were destroyed. He would never recover from the damage his four-day ride caused him. He eventually reached Old Capitol Prison in Washington, where he was paroled a second time and sent south.[4]

Upon his arrival in Richmond, he was admitted to General Hospital No. 9. He was later transferred to Chimborazo Hospital No. 2, where his condition was diagnosed as varicose veins.[5] Though he made repeated efforts to return to duty, he was unable to ride or walk for very long periods. Finally, in the spring of 1864, he was allowed to return home. For the rest of his life, Levy would have to bandage his legs from the ankles to above the knees to be able to walk.[6] During the last year of the war, he ran his store and cared for the families of his comrades in his old company. When the enemy broke through Lee's lines at Petersburg in April 1865, Amelia Court House stood in the path of the retreating Confederates heading west and the pursuing Federals under Grant. Though his store was looted, Levy was not disturbed, but between the Yankees and the debts owed to him by his neighbors, who could not repay him, he was penniless and ruined at war's end.

Undaunted, Levy moved to Richmond and began anew. He at first dealt in government supplies but later entered the retail grocery business. Success in these ventures led him into the commission business, for which he displayed great talent. He recouped his fortune and became an influential businessman. For twenty-five years he was a member of the Chamber of Commerce and for ten years one of the directors of the First National Bank. He was also one of the first members of the Grain and Cotton Exchange and the Tobacco Exchange. Active in the Confederate Veterans' organization, Levy became one of the earliest members of the Lee Camp, No. 1, as well as a director in the Veteran Cavalry Association of Northern Virginia. He was instrumental in raising the funds and acquiring the land for the Confederate Home for Veterans in Richmond. Levy died on November 15, 1897.

Pvt. Channing Meade Smith

Scout
July 1863 to April 1864

Lexington 6 Nov 1865
Pvt Channing M. Smith served in the Cav of the Confederate Army & was one of Genl J. E. B. Stuart's most trusted scouts. He was frequently sent in charge of detached parties to watch the enemy, gain information of his movements, & always acquitted himself well. He sometimes acted under my special directions. I found him active, bold, faithful & intelligent in the discharge of his duties & very reliable.

R E Lee[1]

The man about whom this letter was written was born on May 22, 1842, at "Llangollen," northwest of Upperville, in Loudoun County, Virginia.

Channing Meade Smith, named after Bishops Channing Moore and William Meade, was the fifth child of Dr. Adolphus Cornelius and Ellen Powell Smith. Much of Channing's early life remains obscure, though there is some speculation that Dr. Smith took his family to Louisiana for a time and then returned to Virginia shortly before the war.[2]

At the outbreak of the war, a very young Channing Smith enlisted on April 25, 1861, in the "Black Horse Troop" from Warrenton, Virginia.[3] This legendary unit later became Company "H" of the 4th Virginia Cavalry. With the rest of his company, Smith participated in the Battle of 1st Manassas. Shortly after the battle, the "Black Horse" was honored by being selected as Gen. Joe Johnston's personal bodyguard. On September 4, 1861, the company became part of the 4th Virginia. Through all this, Smith performed the duties that fell to him. He had one close call on October 4, 1861, when the regiment was surprised while in the vicinity of Pohick Church. The Union attack was repulsed without the loss of a man, but Smith's horse and four others were casualties.

During November and December 1861 Smith served as a regimental clerk. With the coming of 1862 he returned to his company, and with it he passed through the campaigns and raids in which Stuart's cavalry was engaged. At the battle of Fredericksburg he was selected to be a courier for Gen. R. E. Lee. Up to this time, Smith either had not begun his scouting career or had kept it a secret. Evidence of his being a scout prior to September 1862 cannot be found, and even after this date the records do not show him detached from his company. Sometime in early 1863, however, he attracted the attention of Stuart, who on May 10 detailed Smith as a special scout to work behind enemy lines. Smith must have performed in some manner that caught Stuart's eye, but regrettably, what he did went unrecorded.

Stuart began to rely more heavily on Smith in the fall of 1863. Maj. Gen. George G. Meade's Army of the Potomac crossed the Rapidan River planning to surprise Lee and interpose the Federal forces between the Southern army and Richmond. While the movement was in progress, Smith penetrated the Union lines and rode all through Meade's army. Taking his time, he stopped briefly at Gen. Gouverneur K. Warren's headquarters and talked with the staff officers. Afterward, he rode through the reserve artillery before returning to Lee's army. Along the way, Smith had gathered vital information; captured a supply wagon, which he later had to abandon; and somehow managed to carry off a flag belonging to Gen. John Sedgwick's corps, which he presented to General Lee. His companion on this daring venture was Richard H. Lewis, another of Stuart's many scouts.

During the winter and spring of 1863–64, Smith was placed in charge of a number of scouts who operated behind Gen. Ulysses S. Grant's lines between Manassas and Culpeper Court House. On April 10, 1864, Smith sent the following to Stuart from Jeffersonton in Culpeper County:

General

I send you the following information, which comes from a source perfectly reliable. I am indebted to a lady in Culpeper Court-House, who is very prudent, vivacious, &c and whose opportunities for hearing are good as she has been a good deal at Grant's Headquarters.

The sutlers, traders, & everything of the kind are ordered to pack up, and leave within ten days. All extra baggage has been sent to Washington, and all persons not connected with the army ordered to leave.

The Eleventh and Twelfth Army Corps have been ordered here and are daily expected. The three consolidated corps are estimated at 75,000–25,000 each. Meade is expected to have 100,000 men when all re-enforcements come up.

Guards and deserters report a large number of artillerymen as having arrived.

Gen Grant has been to Fortress Monroe to confer with Butler, but has returned to the army. I can hear of no road in construction to Germanna. No fortifications about the Court-House or Stevensburg.

The roads are in shocking condition. Corduroy roads have been made all through the army. I will try to learn which way they will move. This can only be done from leakage from staff officers—General Grant's. You can judge of its merit. Desertions are very frequent. Forty are said to have escaped the other night. They all confirm these reports.

This lady gathered the information from confidential conversations with officers. You know her, but I am requested to give no name. I will do my best at watching, and will try and advise you at an early period of movements, &c.

Lewis [most likely Sgt. Richard H. Lewis of the 4th Virginia Cavalry] went to Fauquier last week. I expect to have heard from him ere this. Will go then myself tomorrow, and see what arrangements he has made to watch the railroad. I shall leave a man in Culpeper with instructions to notify you of any movement, however. I will be gone only a few days. One of the men with me I have sent to his regiment—the bearer of this. I wrote to Colonel Randolph [Col. Robert Randolph, 4th Virginia Cavalry] for another. I suppose there will be no difficulty about it.

I will direct the courier to go through as quickly as possible, though he will have the river to swim.

Will you do me the favor to ask Major McClellan [Maj. Henry B. McClellan of Stuart's staff] to keep my letters until I send for them.

I am very truly

Yours Most Respfly
Channing M. Smith

Enclosed are some stamps for Major Venable [Maj. Andrew R. Venable of Stuart's staff][4]

Smith continued to roam around behind enemy lines gathering vital information for Stuart. He joined Richard H. Lewis and another 4th Virginia trooper in Fauquier County soon after writing the above letter. On April 16, near Catlett's Station, the three scouts attacked a party of five Federals of which they killed four, while the fifth escaped. Stuart wrote of the incident to Lee and praised the three men. Before forwarding the letter to Richmond, Lee endorsed it, stating, "I have on several previous occasions called the attention of the Secretary of War to the gallantry of Channing M. Smith and the other young scouts of the army."[5]

On May 11, as Stuart prepared to engage Sheridan at Yellow Tavern, Smith reentered Confederate lines somewhere in the Wilderness. He was totally exhausted and sought a few hours of sleep. Awakened before midnight, he received orders directly from Lee sending him back across the lines to discover Grant's intentions. Accompanied by Fred Moore, the courier who had brought his orders, Smith rode among masses of men and wagons crowding the roads in the rear of the Union Army. The two finally headed back undisturbed to their own army.

In August 1864 Smith transferred from the 4th Virginia to Mosby's 43rd Battalion of Partisan Rangers. Little time was required for Smith to demonstrate to the "Gray Ghost" that he was a man who could be trusted implicitly. On December 6, 1864, Mosby wrote to the Secretary of War requesting that Smith be breveted a lieutenant. R. E. Lee's endorsement strongly echoed Mosby's recommendation.

> Head Qrs ANV
>
>   6 Dec 1864
>   Res. forwarded & recommend under the provisions of the law for appointment for valor and skill. This young man has been so often recommended for appointment by the late Maj. Gen. Stuart and myself that it is deemed unnecessary to state more explicitly in this communication the facts upon which the recommendation is based.
>
>   R E Lee
>   Gen[6]

The repeated efforts of Stuart, Lee, and Mosby at last brought Smith the commission he deserved. He received his lieutenancy and was still serving with the famous guerrilla chieftain when Lee surrendered at Appomattox. When Mosby heard of the surrender, he sent Smith to Lee to inquire if he should continue the fight. Meeting Lee at the home of Gen. R. H. Chilton in Richmond, Smith asked the gallant soldier what Mosby should do. Lee, true to his parole, refused to issue any orders to Mosby. Smith then inquired what he personally should do. Lee told him to go home, which Smith did after first returning to Mosby with Lee's words of advice. The "Gray Ghost" promptly disbanded his Rangers and all went home.

Smith returned to Upperville, Virginia, and began farming. On December 12, 1867, he married Lucy Davenport Smith, the daughter of William and Mary Glascock Smith, of "Chelsea" in Fauquier County. The couple lived in Upperville until 1875, when they moved to "Montana" near Delaplane in Fauquier County. They had eight children: William Adolphus, Robert Channing, Mary Elizabeth, Ellen Powell, David Blackwell, Roberta Chilton, Sarah Catherine, and Harry Lee. Smith died on November 8, 1932. His wife had preceded him in death on November 25, 1923.

Roster

THE ROSTER THAT follows lists the men who were detached from their units or assigned directly to Stuart's headquarters. No claim is made that the roster is complete. Several sources (among them the *Official Records,* National Archives, state records, and personal accounts) were checked to assemble this list. The men whose names appear were definitely attached to cavalry headquarters sometime during Stuart's tenure of command. Some names may have been inadvertently omitted, however, because of missing or unclear records and the writer's failure to check each and every source, an almost impossible task. Certainly there will be additions in the future. In most instances, references to those men whose last name only is given came from a single source. Efforts to locate additional information concerning them failed. It is hoped that this lack of detailed records can be corrected in the future.

Adams, ——————
> Sergeant   Signal Corps
> Assigned to cavalry's signal corps under J. Hardeman Stuart; exact dates of service unknown.

Aldrich, ——————
> Sergeant
> Assigned to cavalry's ordnance department as clerk to J. E. Cooke; exact dates of service unknown.

Ammen, Marcus
> Private   2nd VA Cav, Co "G"
> Enl. May 17, 1861, at Fincastle. Detached as scout; dates of service unknown.

Armistead, Walker Keith
> Private   5th VA Cav
> Enl. May 10, 1862, at Richmond. Detached to Stuart's HQ August 18, 1862, to January 1863; applied for cadet warrant; endorsed by Stuart; lieutenant, aide-de-camp for his father, Gen. Lewis Armistead.

Armstrong, William
> Private   2nd VA Cav, Co. "E"
> Enl. June 20, 1862, at Harrisonburg. Was substitute for W. J. Rucker;
> detached as scout December 24, 1862; length of service unknown.

Ashby, George Robert
> Private   9th VA Cav, Co "A"
> Enl. July 20, 1861. Detailed with Major FitzHugh on QM duty
> July 1863 to October 6, 1864.

Barnes, Andrew J.
> Private   2nd VA Cav, Co "B"
> Enl. May 30, 1862, at Lynchburg. Detailed to Stuart's HQ; dates
> and type of service unknown.

Barrett, Robert L.
> Private   2nd VA Cav, Co "E"
> Enl. May 23, 1861, at Amherst CH. Detached as scout December 24,
> 1862; length of service unknown.

Barrow, Robert A.
> Private   3rd VA Cav, Co "D"
> Enl. July 5, 1861, at Jamestown. Detailed as wagoner July to
> November 1863.

Barton, Green H.
> Private   9th VA Cav, Co "E"
> Enl. September 15, 1862. In escort at Dranesville & Mine Run
> November 26 to December 3, 1863; killed in action at Mine Run.

Barton, Robert R.
> Private   1st VA Cav
> Enl. April 18, 1861, at Lexington. Detached as courier from September
> 1861 to April 17, 1862.

Bassett, Robert Lewis
> Private   4th VA Cav, Co "E"
> Enl. May 27, 1861, in Hanover County. Detached with Stuart May to
> June 1862; type of service unknown; appointed to Virginia Military
> Institute.

Batis, Norral Willis
Private   1st VA Cav
Detailed as Stuart's HQ blacksmith from May 1863 to May 12, 1864.

Baylor, Richard Channing
Private   12th VA Cav
Enl. June 25, 1862, at Charles Town. Courier; volunteered to pass through enemy lines with message when Stuart trapped at Auburn in October 1863; mortally wounded in action on November 29, 1863; died the next day.

Beall, Henry D.
Private   12th VA Cav, Co "B"
Enl. September 17, 1862, at Conrads Store. Detached as scout November 1863 to May 1864; captured at Lexington June 11, 1864.

Beckham, John
First Sergeant   17th VA Inf, Co "K"
Detached as scout; transferred to Stuart April 7, 1864; length of service unknown.

Berkeley, William R.
Private   3rd VA Cav, Co "K"
Enl. August 12, 1863, at Fredericksburg. Detailed as clerk September 1863 to May 1864.

Bestor, Daniel P.
Sergeant   Signal Corps
Assigned to cavalry's signal corps under J. Hardeman Stuart; served from June to September 1862.

Booth, ———
Sergeant
Assigned to cavalry's ordnance department as clerk to J. E. Cooke; exact dates of service unknown.

Boteler, Charles Peale
Private   12th VA Cav, Co "F"
Enl. April 29, 1862, in Rockingham Co. First enlistment (October 23, 1861) had been in the Rockbridge Artillery; served in Stuart's signal corps June 1863 to May 1864.

Brawford, James
Private   10th VA Cav, Co "B"
Enl. May 1, 1862, at Richmond. Detached as courier July 1863 to April 30, 1864.

Bridges, Hardage
Private   2nd VA Cav, Co "A"
Enl. July 13, 1861, at Frying Pan Church. Detached as courier December 20, 1862; length of service unknown.

Brigman, ———
Private
Part of escort at Dranesville December 20, 1861.

Brown, Daniel H.
Private   3rd VA Cav
Enl. March 21, 1862, at Young's Mill. Detailed with G. M. Ryals as provost marshal September 1863 to May 1864.

Brown, James F.
Civilian aide, later courier   1st VA Cav
Was with Stuart at 1st Manassas; transferred from 1st VA to Breathed's Battery Stuart Horse Artillery.

Brown, John Whitehead
Private   2nd VA Cav, Co "E"
Enl. February 24, 1861, at Amherst CH. Detached as scout September 1862 to March 1863.

Brown, Robert A.
Private   4th VA Cav, Co "B"
Enl. August 25, 1863, in Caroline County. Detached as scout; dates of service unknown.

Burke, John Redmond
Private   1st VA Cav
Transferred from 2nd VA Inf, Co "K" on August 8, 1861; detached with Capt. Redmond Burke of Stuart's staff on October 20, 1861; captured November 24, 1862; detached to Stuart's HQ January 29, 1863.

Burke, Matthew P.

Private   1st VA Cav

Detached with Capt. Redmond Burke of Stuart's staff on October 20, 1861; captured November 24, 1862; detached to Stuart's HQ on January 29, 1863; deserted April 16, 1863.

Burke, Redmond

Private   1st VA Cav

Part of escort at Dranesville December 20, 1861.

Buxton, James A.

Private   2nd NC

Detailed as courier June 9 to September 1863.

Carpenter, A. H.

Private   4th VA Cav, Co "C"

Enl. April 24, 1861. Detailed as courier with Stuart October 7, 1863, to April 1864; with Stuart at Yellow Tavern.

Carroll, Robert Goodloe Harper

Private   1st VA Cav, Co "K"

Part of escort at Dranesville December 20, 1861.

Carson, J. H.

Private   Jeff Davis Legion

Part of escort on Chickahominy Raid June 12–15, 1862.

Catlett, Henry C.

Private   6th VA Cav, Co "D"

Enl. April 18, 1861, at Berryville. Detached to Stuart's HQ November–December 1863; type and length of service unknown.

Chancellor, Thomas Frazer

Private   9th VA Cav, Co "E"

Enl. March 1, 1862. Detached as courier December 1862 to April 1863; mortally wounded in action; died of wounds July 15, 1863.

Chancellor, Vespasian

Private   9th VA Cav, Co "E"

Enl. February 1, 1864. Detached as scout; exact dates of service unknown.

Chewning, Marcus A.
> Private   9th VA Cav, Co "E"
> Enl. April 25, 1861, at Fredericksburg. Detached as scout with Channing M. Smith.

Childress, Henry Patton
> Bugler   6th VA Cav, Co "I"
> Enl. May 4, 1861, in Orange County. Detached as courier December 24, 1862; detailed as bugler August 15, 1863, to at least October 1864.

Clingan, R. T.
> Private   Cobb's Legion
> Detached as courier; exact dates of service unknown; killed in action September 17, 1862, while acting as a courier for Stuart.

Cole, E. D.
> Private   15th VA Cav, Co "H"
> Served in Stuart's escort during Gettysburg Campaign.

Colvin, George W.
> Third Sergeant   4th VA Cav, Co "A"
> Enl. March 13, 1862, in Stafford County. Detached as scout March to April 1864.

Conroy, Dennis
> Private   Breathed's Batt, Stuart Horse Arty
> Enl. November 5, 1861, at Richmond. Served as Pelham's orderly; exact dates unknown.

Cooke, Nathaniel Burwell
> Private   6th VA Cav, Co "D"
> Enl. October 20, 1862, in Jefferson County. Detached as courier October 1862 to February 1863.

Coyle, James W.
> Private   12th VA Cav, Co "B"
> Enl. September 25, 1862, at Charles Town. Detached as scout April 15, 1864; length of service unknown but probably until May 12, 1864.

Curtis, Charles P.
Private   4th VA Cav, Co "H"
Enl. August 15, 1861, at Manassas. Detached as scout in Fauquier County February to October 1863.

Cushen, Randolph D.
Private   1st VA Cav
Enl. August 12, 1861, at Fairfax CH. Detached to Stuart's HQ October 1861 to February 1862; type of service unknown.

Daniel, John M.
Private   2nd VA Cav, Co "K"
Enl. May 13, 1861, at Culpeper CH. Detailed at Stuart's HQ in 1863; type and length of service unknown.

Davis, ———
Served in Stuart's escort during Gettysburg Campaign.

Davis, W. B.
Served as courier; son of Col. James Lucius Davis of the 10th VA Cav.

Dawson, Benjamin F.
Private   6th VA Cav, Co "H"
Enl. October 18, 1862, at Salem. Detached December 27, 1863; type of service unknown; later served as scout with Frank Stringfellow.

Deane, Francis Henry
Private   4th VA Cav, Cos "I" & "E"
Enl. June 10, 1862. From Richmond; served as courier to Stuart and clerk to Major McClellan; carried message from McClellan to Stuart at Brandy Station; became cadet February 11, 1864.

Denton, George W.
Private   2nd VA Cav, Co "C"
Enl. May 17, 1861, at Fincastle. Detached as scout in 1862; wounded in action in side June 11, 1863, at Culpeper CH.

Dickenson, James Cooper
Private   9th VA Cav, Co "B"
Enl. May 7, 1861. Detailed by Stuart to run seine fishery on Rappahannock March to June 1863.

Dolman, Miles P.

Private   2nd VA Cav, Co "C"

Enl. May 16, 1862, at Fincastle. Detached as scout November 1862; length of service unknown; wounded in action in chest June 9, 1863.

Doswell, Benjamin T.

Private, Corporal   4th VA Cav, Co "G"

Enl. May 9, 1861. Detached as courier during Chickahominy Raid June 12–15, 1862; detailed as clerk to Maj. Norman R. FitzHugh January–April 1864.

Driskell, John L.

Private   2nd VA Cav, Co "C"

Enl. May 17, 1861 at Fincastle. Detached as scout November– December 1862; captured in Maryland July 5, 1863.

Eddins, H. Hillery

Private   12th VA Cav

Transferred August 7, 1863. First enlistment (April 20, 1861) had been in Percell Artillery; reenlisted on September 1, 1863; courier; volunteered to pass through enemy lines when Stuart was trapped at Auburn in October 1863.

Edmonds, Phillip M.

Private   6th VA Cav, Co "H"

Enl. March 16, 1862, at Salem. Detailed as courier September– October 1862; marked as deserter January 1, 1863.

Eggleston, William Archer

Private   1st VA Cav, Co "G"

Enl. May 9, 1861, at Amelia CH. Detached to Stuart's signal corps November 28, 1863; length of service unknown.

Eliason, Rutledge Homes

Private   6th VA Cav, Co "A"

Enl. July 24, 1861, at Union. Detached as courier August 21–31, 1863; detached to medical dept., cavalry corps August 31– December 5, 1863; wounded in action May 5, 1864.

Ellis, Augustine Henry
Private   13th VA Cav, Co "H"
Enl. April 24, 1861, at Waverly. Detached as courier; exact dates of service unknown; was present at cavalry headquarters in February 1864 and was with Stuart at Yellow Tavern.

Estill, Robert Kyle
Private   1st VA Cav, Co "C"
Enl. April 18, 1861, at Lexington. Detached as courier July 1863 to May 12, 1864; wounded in action at Haw's Shop May 29, 1864.

Evans, Maurice
Private   4th VA Cav, Co "A"
Enl. April 23, 1861. Detached as scout May to July 1862.

Farish, Benjamin Bruce
Private   9th VA Cav, Co "E"
Enl. March 5, 1862. Detached as courier May to August 1862.

Farish, Robert Toombs
Private   9th VA Cav, Co "E"
Enl. March 5, 1862. Detached as courier September 1862 to April 1863; killed in action September 1863 while on scout for Stuart in Culpeper County.

Farrar, Benjamin J.
Private   2nd VA Cav, Co "E"
Enl. May 23, 1861, at Amherst CH. Detached as scout September 1862 to March 1863; discharged August 1863, having acquired mail contract from CS government.

Fewell, ———
Served in Stuart's escort during Gettysburg Campaign.

Findlay, Frank Smith
Private   1st VA Cav
Enl. May 14, 1861, at Abingdon. Detached as courier October 3, 1861, to April 1862; part of escort at Williamsburg May 5, 1862.

Fisher, Joel T.
> Private   2nd VA Cav, Co "D"
> Enl. May 20, 1861, in Franklin County. Detached as courier March to July 3, 1863; captured at Gettysburg July 3, 1863, while on duty as Stuart's courier; POW in Point Lookout, MD; exchanged February 10, 1865.

Flint, Edward S.
> Private   9th VA Cav, Co "K"
> Enl. April 18, 1862. Detached as courier April 18, 1862, to May 1864.

Flournoy, George H.
> Private   13th VA Cav, Co "G"
> Enl. October 16, 1861, at Camp Maurice. Detached as courier; exact dates of service unknown.

Fontaine, Charles
> Private   5th VA Cav, Co "H"
> Enl. February 1, 1864, at Richmond. Detached February 1864 to Stuart's HQ as clerk.

Fowlkes, Adrian
> Private   1st VA Cav, Co "F"
> Enl. May 9, 1861, at Amelia CH. Detached as courier September to November 1861.

Frayser, Richard Edgar
> Private   3rd VA Cav, Co "F"
> Enl. June 28, 1861. Detached as scout during Chickahominy Raid June 12-15 1862; promoted to captain in signal corps and assigned to Stuart's staff.

Freed, George W.
> Private and bugler   1st VA Cav, Co "E"
> Enl. April 19, 1861, at Waynesboro. Served as bugler for regiment; detached to Stuart; exact dates of service unknown but was with Stuart in May 1864.

Fuqua, William H.
> Private   3rd VA Cav, Co "F"
> Enl. March 9, 1862, at Jamestown. Detailed as wagoner July 1863 to May 1864.

Gallaher, DeWitt Clinton
Private   1st VA Cav, Co "E"
Enl. October 8, 1863, at Orange Springs. Detached as courier on October 27, 1863, through at least March 1864.

Garnett, Theodore Stanford
Private   9th VA Cav, Co "F"
Enl. May 15, 1863. Detached as clerk-courier almost immediately after enlistment; promoted to lieutenant and aide-de-camp on Stuart's staff February 17, 1864.

Garrett, William L.
Private   10th VA Cav, Co "G"
Enl. January 1, 1862, in Russell County. Detached to Stuart's HQ April 1864; type and length of service unknown.

George, Alexander Speirs
Private   10th VA Cav, Co "A"
Enl. May 28, 1863, in Culpeper. Served in escort (length of service unknown); detached as courier November–December 1863 to at least February 1864.

George, Wingfield Scott
Private   4th VA Cav, Co "A"
Enl. April 23, 1861. Detached as scout; exact dates of service unknown; captured September 30, 1863, on Potomac River; POW at Old Capitol Prison, Washington, D.C.; exchanged February 18, 1864; killed in action at Trevilian Station, June 11 or 12, 1864.

Gibson, Gilbert B.
Private   6th VA Cav, Co "A"
Enl. September 17, 1861, at Leesburg. Detached to Stuart's HQ September–October 1862; type and length of service unknown.

Gleason, John W.
Private, sergeant   9th VA Cav, Co "F"
Enl. June 10, 1861. Detached as courier July 20, 1862; length of service unknown; promoted to sergeant and assigned as clerk to J. E. Cooke at cavalry HQ.

Goode, Robert W.
> Private   1st VA Cav, Co "G"
> Detached as courier from October 1, 1862, to May 12, 1864.

Goodwin, Jr., Littleton
> Private   9th VA Cav, Co "E"
> Transferred from Fredericksburg Artillery November 5, 1861; detached as courier January 1863 to March 1864.

Graham, J. M.
> Private   4th VA Cav, Co "A"
> Enl. 1861. Detached as scout; exact dates of service unknown.

Grant, James
> Private   10th VA Cav, Co "A"
> Enl. May 28, 1863, at Culpeper. Detailed as clerk November or December 1863; length of service unknown. Grant also served in escort.

Graves, John F.
> Private   3rd VA Cav, Co "G"
> Enl. May 18, 1861, at Charles City CH. Detached as courier July to September 1863.

Graves, William Cornelias
> Private   3rd VA Cav, Co "D"
> Enl. May 9, 1861, at Charles City CH. Detached to Stuart's HQ July–September 1863; type of service unknown.

Green, Moses M.
> Private   4th VA Cav, Co "H"
> Enl. March 15, 1862, at Brandy Station. Detached as scout January–February 1864.

Griffith, John
> Private   6th VA Cav, Co "H"
> Enl. September 14, 1862, at Salem. Detached to Stuart's HQ November 27, 1863; type and length of service unknown.

Hagan, William Henry
Private, corporal   1st VA Cav, Co "F"
Enl. April 18, 1861. Detailed to Stuart's HQ July 24, 1861; commanded escort on numerous occasions; promoted to lieutenant on staff May 1862.

Hansborough, James Farish
Private   4th VA Cav, Co "H"
Enl. March 15, 1862, at Brandy Station. Detached as scout April 1864; length of service unknown.

Harbaugh, Ignatious
Civilian volunteer
Acted as guide during Chambersburg Raid October 9–12, 1862; from Silverburg, Washington Co., Md.

Harris, William
Private   2nd VA Cav, Co "K"
Enl. May 24, 1861, at Culpeper CH. Detached as courier November 1862 to at least July 1863; exact length of service unknown.

Harrison, Rev. Edmund
Private   4th VA Cav, Co "E"
Enl. July 10, 1861, at Richmond. Detached with Stuart November 1861 to February 1862; type of service unknown.

Hazlewood, John A.
Private   2nd VA Cav, Co "C"
Enl. May 17, 1861, at Fincastle. Detached as scout November 1862 to April 1863; captured July 3, 1863, in Maryland; POW at Point Lookout, Md.; exchanged February 13, 1865.

Henson, George W.
Private   6th VA Cav, Co "H"
Enl. June 9, 1861, at Salem. Detached as courier May–June 1862; wounded in action June 29, 1864.

Hickman, R. M.
Private
Served in escort at Williamsburg May 5, 1862; horse killed while he was carrying orders.

Hollingsworth, Thomas

Private

Served in escort at Williamsburg May 5, 1862.

House, ———

Served in Stuart's escort during Gettysburg Campaign.

Hudson, Robert J.

Private   2nd VA Cav

Enl. April 17, 1862, at Gordonsville. Detached as scout December 24, 1862, to March 1863.

Hull, Richard Gascoigne

Private   9th VA Cav, Co "B"

Enl. April 3, 1862. Detached as scout November 1863 to April 1864.

Hume, Charles

Private   1st VA Cav, Co "G"

Enl. August 6, 1862, at Ashland. Detached to Stuart's signal corps October 1, 1862; length of service unknown.

Hume, Frank

Private   1st MD Cav

Detached as scout; exact dates of service unknown.

Hunt, John C.

Private   3rd VA Cav, Co "K"

Enl. March 12, 1862. Detached as orderly to General Stuart; dates of service unknown; mortally wounded in action at Gettysburg July 3, 1863, and died the same day.

Jackson, ———

Lieutenant

Served as a volunteer; was aide to a General Jones (probably David R.).

Janney, William Walter B.

Private   6th VA Cav, Co "D"

Enl. April 23, 1861. Detached as courier September–October 1861.

Jenkins, Junius

Private 13th VA Cav, Co "A"
Enl. August 31, 1861, at Camp Cook. Detached as courier July 1863; length of service unknown.

Johnston, Samuel R.

Second lieutenant 6th VA Cav, Co "F"
Enl. April 20, 1861. Served as special aide to Stuart at Dranesville December 20, 1861; detached by Stuart for outpost service from January to April 1862.

Jones, James Wesley

Private 3rd VA Cav, Co "C"
Enl. May 20, 1861. Detached as clerk in 1863; exact dates of service unknown.

Jones, William Preston

Private 9th VA Cav, Co "E"
Enl. September 18, 1861. Detached as courier September 1862 to September 1863 (for either Stuart or Fitz Lee).

Judkins, Robert Linnear

Private 13th VA Cav, Co "G"
Enl. October 10, 1862, at Culpeper CH. Detached as courier August 1, 1863; length of service unknown.

Keeling, James Milnor

Sergeant
Detached as courier at Yellow Tavern May 11, 1864.

Keene, F. D.

Private 2nd VA Cav, Co "I"
Enl. November 1, 1862, at Leesburg. Detached as courier January 1, 1863; length of service unknown; wounded in action June 12, 1864.

Kelly, Charles H.

Private 13th VA Cav, Co "C"
Enl. March 1, 1862, in Suffolk County. Detailed as clerk at Stuart's HQ January–February 1863.

Kephart, Jacob M.
> Private   12th VA Cav, Co "D"
> Enl. April 19, 1862, at Charles Town. Detached for "special duty" with Stuart September–October 1862; died of typhoid fever December 20, 1863.

Knight, Paul M.
> Private   2nd VA Cav, Co "E"
> Enl. May 23, 1861, at Amherst CH. Detached to Stuart's HQ; type and length of service unknown; wounded in action at Spotsylvania CH May 8, 1864.

Landram, Henry W.
> Private   9th VA Cav, Co "B"
> Enl. April 17, 1862. Detailed as clerk in division ordnance May 1863 to September 30, 1864; probably served first with Capt. J. E. Cooke and then with Capt. Charles Grattan.

Landstreet, Edward
> Private   1st VA Cav, Co "A"
> Enl. September 22, 1861, at Fairfax CH. Detached to Stuart's HQ November 10, 1861, to August 1862; type of service unknown; was in escort at Dranesville December 20, 1861, and Williamsburg May 5, 1862.

Lawrence, ———
> Sergeant   Signal Corps
> Assigned to cavalry's signal corps under J. Hardeman Stuart; exact dates of service unknown.

Leopold, Andrew T.
> Private   12th VA Cav, Co "D"
> Detached for "special duty" with Stuart September–October 1862; captured at Shepherdstown November 28, 1862; executed by hanging at Fort McHenry on May 25, 1863, on orders of Gen. John A. Dix.

Levy, Leopold
> Private   1st VA Cav, Co "G"
> Enl. May 1861 at Amelia CH. Courier for Stuart at 1st Manassas; served in commissary dept with Maj. Dabney Ball and Maj. William J. Johnson from February 1, 1862, to May 3, 1863.

Lewis, Henry L. Dangerfield

Private   6th VA Cav, Co "D"

Enl. August 11, 1861, at Fairfax CH. Detached as courier from September 1861 to December 1863; possibly same Lewis as served in Stuart's escort at Dranesville in December 1861.

Lewis, Richard H.

Sergeant   4th VA Cav, Co "H"

Enl. April 25, 1861. Detached as scout January–April 1864.

Lipscomb, Alexander C.

Private   10th VA Cav, Co "F"

Enl. May 13, 1862, at Richmond. Detached as courier July 1863 to April 1, 1864.

Logan, Hugh

Civilian volunteer

Acted as guide on Chambersburg Raid October 9–12, 1862.

Loughborough, James H.

Private   10th VA Cav, Co "L"

Enl. June 9, 1861, at Richmond. Detached to Stuart's signal corps September 1862 to October 1863.

Loury, Cephas V.

Private   2nd VA Cav, Co "A"

Enl. May 13, 1861, at Liberty. Detached as courier March 4, 1862; length of service unknown.

Lownes, Charles D.

Private   4th VA Cav, Co "E"

Enl. February 9, 1864. Detailed as courier to Stuart's HQ March to May 12, 1864.

Mastilla, A. A.

Private   4th VA Cav, Co "H"

Enl. February 11, 1862. Detached as scout for Stuart April 1864; length of service unknown.

McCombs, William Alexander B.

Private   1st VA Cav, Co "E"

Detached as courier December 14, 1862; length of service unknown.

McDonald, J.
> Private
> Served in escort at Williamsburg May 5, 1862.

McMurray, John P.
> Private   6th VA Cav, Co "D"
> Enl. March 18, 1862, at Warrenton Junction. Detailed to Stuart's
> HQ from August 31 to December 1863; type of service unknown.

Meador, L. Tazewell
> Private   2nd VA Cav, Co "D"
> Enl. May 20, 1861, in Franklin County. Detached to Stuart's HQ
> September 1861 to February 1862; type of service unknown.

Miller, George B.
> Private   4th VA Cav, Co "D"
> Enl. March 10, 1862. Detached as scout with Channing M. Smith
> March to May 12, 1864.

Minghini, Joseph Lee
> Private   12th VA Cav, Co "D"
> Enl. September 21, 1862, at Shepherdstown. Detached as courier from
> at least March to October 1863; assisted in taking the wounded Maj.
> John Pelham off the field at the Battle of Kelly's Ford March 17,
> 1863.

Mitchell, Philip E. Cary
> Private   6th VA Cav, Co "D"
> Enl. April 20, 1861. Detached as courier November 1861.

Mitchell, William Robert
> Private   4th VA Cav, Co "C"
> Enl. March 10, 1862. Detached with Stuart January–April 1864;
> type of service unknown.

Moffett, John T.
> Private   6th VA Cav, Co "H"
> Enl. September 10, 1862, at Salem (Fauquier County). Detached to
> Stuart's HQ as scout November 27, 1863, to April 10, 1864; worked
> with Frank Stringfellow.

Mosby, John Singleton
> Private   1st VA Cav, Co "D"
> Enl. May 14, 1861. Detailed by Stuart as scout (placed with couriers) April to December 1862.

Myers, David H.
> Private   1st VA Cav, Co "F"
> Enl. October 13, 1862, at Strider's Mill. Detached to Stuart's HQ July 20 to September 1863; type of service unknown; detached again February 5, 1864; type and length of service unknown.

Nelson, Samuel A.
> Private, sergeant   4th VA Cav, Co "B"
> Enl. August 1, 1862, at Centreville. Detached as courier April 30 to July 30, 1862, and again in October 1863; served in escort during Gettysburg Campaign; wounded in action October 11, 1863.

O'Brien (O'Bryan), John
> Private   10th VA Cav, Co "F"
> Enl. May 13, 1862, at Richmond. Detached to Stuart's HQ March to May 1863; type of service unknown.

Owens, Jr., Cuthbert
> Private   6th VA Cav, Co "H"
> Enl. March 9, 1862. Detached as courier August 1 to December 1863; killed in action May 11, 1864.

Padgett, Charles P.
> Private   6th VA Cav, Co "H"
> Enl. February 21, 1862, at Camp Smith. Detached as courier May–June 1862; was buried June 10, 1862; cause of death unknown.

Page, Charles C.
> Sergeant   13th VA Cav, Co "B"
> Enl. May 17, 1861, at Petersburg. Detached to Stuart's signal corps August 31, 1863; length of service unknown.

Page, William Byrd
> Private   6th VA Cav, Co "D"
> Enl. May 17, 1861. Detached as courier November 1861.

Parker, E. L.
> Private
> Served in escort at Williamsburg May 5, 1862.

Patterson, Solomon H.
> Private   1st VA Cav
> Enl. May 22, 1861, at Harrisonburg. Detached as courier January to May 12, 1864.

Patterson, William H.
> Private   1st VA Cav
> Enl. July 24, 1862, at Fairfax CH. Detached as courier September 1861 to February 1863.

Pegram, William M.
> Private   4th VA Cav, Co "H"
> Enl. May 1, 1863, in Fauquier County. Detached as clerk with Maj. H. B. McClellan from September 1863 to at least April 1864.

Pettigrew, Lucian B.
> Private   2nd VA Cav, Co "C"
> Enl. May 17, 1861, at Fincastle. Ordered to report to Stuart sometime in 1862; exact dates and type of service unknown.

Pettit, James C.
> Private   2nd VA Cav, Co "E"
> Enl. March 1, 1862, at Stone Bridge. Detached as scout December 24, 1862; length of service unknown.

Pierson, John C.
> Private   4th VA Cav, Co "D"
> Enl. March 11, 1862. Detached with Stuart January–April 1864; served in escort during Chickahominy Raid June 12-15, 1862; killed in action at Five Forks April 1, 1865.

Powers, Philip Henry
> Private   1st VA Cav
> Enl. April 26, 1863. Detailed in QM dept. immediately after enlistment; had served on Stuart's staff; served as courier from August 18, 1863, to May 12, 1864; paroled at Appomattox; first enlistment April 18, 1861, in 1st VA Cav.

Purdie, A.
Private   5th VA Cav, Co "K"
Enl. April 4, 1862, at Petersburg. Ordered November 1863 to report to Stuart as courier.

Quarles, J. Thompson
Private
Chief of field telegraph; served in escort at Gettysburg and acted as courier.

Rader, Zebulon C.
Private   1st VA Cav, Co "C"
Enl. April 18, 1861, in Lexington. Detailed to Maj. Dabney Ball in commissary dept. November 1861 to April 1862.

Ranson, Thomas Davis
Private   12th VA Cav, Co "B"
Enl. November 25, 1862, at Charles Town. Had previously served in the 2nd and 57th VA Inf; detached as scout; dates of service unknown; became captain in charge of scouts in secret service and reported directly to Stuart and R. E. Lee.

Reid, Joseph Samuel
Sergeant   4th VA Cav, Co "H"
Enl. April 25, 1861. Detached as scout January–February 1864.

Ripley, Charles P.
Private   6th VA Cav, Co "A"
Enl. September 1, 1861, at Ashland. Served in escort at Williamsburg May 5, 1862; detached as courier September 1862; length of service unknown.

Roberts, John W.
Fourth corporal   1st VA Cav, Co "F"
Enl. September 17, 1862, at Striders Mill. Detached as scout; dates of service unknown.

Robertson, John William
Private   1st VA Cav, Co "C"
Enl. April 18, 1861, in Lexington. Detached as courier November–December 1861.

Routh, S. M.
Private
Served in escort at Dranesville December 20, 1861, and Williamsburg May 5, 1862.

Rowe, George W.
Private   6th VA Cav, Co "I"
Enl. March 15, 1862, in Orange Co. Detached as courier December 24, 1862; length of service unknown.

Rucker, Paul B.
Private   2nd VA Cav, Co "E"
Enl. March 10, 1862, at Amherst CH. Detached as scout December 24, 1862; length of service unknown; wounded in action at Haw's Shop.

Rust, James
Private   6th VA Cav, Co "H"
Enl. March 18, 1862, at Salem. Detached as courier September–November 1862.

Sale, William M.
Captain   Commissary Dept
Appointed July 14, 1862. Assigned as assistant commissary officer to Maj. Dabney Ball and Maj. William J. Johnson.

Shepherd, Joseph H.
Private   6th VA Cav, Co "D"
Enl. April 20, 1861. Detached as courier November 1862.

Sheppard, ———
Served as Stuart's telegraph operator.

Shippey, William F.
Sergeant   1st VA Cav, Co "A"
Enl. April 19, 1861, at Newtown. Detailed as sergeant of quartermaster guard at Stuart's HQ September to November 1861.

Shotwell, Ellis M.
Private   2nd VA Cav, Co "E"
Enl. September 1, 1862, in Greene Co. Detached as scout December 24, 1862; length of service unknown.

Shriver, Thomas Herbert
> Private   1st VA Cav, Co "K" (2nd)
> Enl. June 27, 1863, in Union Mills, Md. Served as guide in Gettysburg Campaign.

Smith, Allen
> Private   12th VA Cav, Co "H"
> Enl. August 27, 1862, at Harrisonburg. Detached to Stuart's HQ March–April 1864; type and length of service unknown.

Smith, Boyd M.
> Private   4th VA Cav, Co "H"
> Enl. January 23, 1863. Detached with Stuart through all of 1863; type of service unknown.

Smith, Channing Meade
> Private   4th VA Cav, Co "H"
> Enl. April 25, 1861. Detached as scout July 1863 to April 1864.

Smith, Zedekiah Wesley
> Private   1st VA Cav, Co "A"
> Enl. July 16, 1861, in Berkeley Co. Detached as courier January to August 1862.

Staley, William
> Private   12th VA Cav, Co "D"
> Enl. September 2, 1862, at Shepherdstown. Detached for "special duty" for Stuart September–October 1862.

Steele, Stewart R.
> Chief bugler   1st VA Cav, Co "F"
> Enl. May 5, 1861, at Harpers Ferry by Stuart. Detached to Stuart's HQ as bugler.

Steger, James A.
> Private   4th VA Cav, Co "K"
> Enl. March 10, 1862. Detailed to Stuart's HQ May–June 1863; type of service unknown.

Stringfellow, Benjamin Franklin

Private   4th VA Cav, Co "E"

Enl. May 22, 1861, at Culpeper CH. Detailed as scout May–June 1862; served to at least January 1864; captured in Middleburg June 12, 1863; later served as scout for R. E. Lee.

Stuart, Edward

Private   Signal Corps

Assigned to cavalry's signal corps under his brother, J. Hardeman Stuart; exact dates of service unknown; also may have served as courier.

Sweeney, Robert M.

Private   2nd VA Cav, Co "H"

Enl. August 25, 1863, at Williamsburg. Detailed to Stuart's HQ from January to May 12, 1864; type of service unknown.

Sweeney, Sampson D.

Private   2nd VA Cav, Co "H"

Enl. January 1, 1862, at Centreville. Detached to Stuart's HQ November 1862 to January 13, 1864; type of service unknown; died of smallpox in hospital at Orange CH January 13, 1864.

Talliaferro, William G.

Private   Breathed's Batt, Stuart Horse Arty

Enl. June 17, 1862, at Richmond. Attached to cavalry's signal corps under Captains J. H. Stuart and R. E. Frayser from June 17 to October 23, 1862.

Templeman, Robert

Private   7th VA Cav, Co "A"

Detached as courier; dates of service unknown.

Terry, N. R.

Private   10th VA Cav, Co "C"

Enl. August 12, 1862, at Richmond. Detached as ambulance driver December 31, 1863, to April 1, 1864.

Thompson, William T.

Private   13th VA Cav, Co "G"

Enl. August 15, 1861, at Camp Maurice. Detached as courier January 1863; served in Stuart's escort during Gettysburg Campaign; with Stuart at Yellow Tavern.

Thomson, James Hammer
Private   6th VA Cav, Co "D"
Enl. September 4, 1861, at Camp Bee. Detached as courier December 1861 to June 1862.

Throckmorton, John Ariss
Lieutenant   6th VA Cav, Co "F"
Enl. April 20, 1861. Served as special aide to Stuart at Dranesville December 20, 1861.

Timberlake, David Algenon
First lieutenant   4th VA Cav, Co "G"
Enl. May 9, 1861. Detached as scout during Chickahominy Raid June 12–15, 1862; served as guide during Seven Days Campaign.

Timberlake, John Henry
Private   4th VA Cav, Co "G"
Enl. March 3, 1862. Detached as scout during Chickahominy Raid June 12–15, 1862.

Timberlake, Richard Lewis
Private   12th VA Cav, Co "B"
Enl. October 17, 1862, at Charles Town. Detached as scout April 1, 1864; length of service unknown but probably until May 12, 1864; killed in action at Sycamore Church September 16, 1864.

Toler, Washington Nelson
Private   6th VA Cav, Co "K"
Enl. May 22, 1861, at Alexandria. Detached as scout February 12, 1862, to December 27, 1864.

Tomlin, R. C.
Private
Served in escort at Williamsburg May 5, 1862.

Towles, Robert C.
Sergeant   4th VA Cav, Co "A"
Enl. April 23, 1861. Detached as scout May–June 1863.

Van Pelt, Benjamin S.
   Private   1st VA Cav, Co "I"
   Enl. May 22, 1861, in Harrisonburg. Detached to Stuart's HQ;
   length and type of service unknown.

Vass, James
   Private   4th VA Cav, Co "H"
   Enl. March 15, 1862, at Bealeton. Detached as scout July to
   October 1863.

Waldon, ――――
   Private
   Served in escort at Mine Run November 26 to December 3, 1863;
   wounded in action at Mine Run.

Walker, George W.
   Lieutenant   Breathed's Batt, Stuart Horse Arty
   Served as Pelham's aide; exact dates of service unknown.

Walker, J. P.
   Private   2nd VA Cav, Co "I"
   Enl. June 9, 1862, in Campbell County. Detached as scout March 27,
   1864; length of service unknown; captured September 1, 1864, in
   Fairfax County; POW at Elmira, N.Y.; paroled March 2, 1865.

Walker, J. S. L.
   Private   2nd VA Cav, Co "I"
   Enl. June 9, 1862, in Campbell County. Detached as courier March 29
   to November 1863.

Walter, Frederick William
   Bugler   Cobb's Legion
   Detached as division bugler December 1, 1862, to April 21, 1863.

Walton, Thomas R.
   Private   13th VA Cav, Co "B"
   Enl. March 21, 1862, at Chuckatuck. Detached as courier July 1863;
   remained at cavalry HQ after Stuart's death until November 1864.

Weaver, Horace
>Private   6th VA Cav, Co "H"
>Enl. March 16, 1862, at Weaversville. Detached as courier July to December 1863.

Weaver, Mortimer
>Private
>Served in escort at Williamsburg May 5, 1862.

Weaver, Virgil
>Private   6th VA Cav, Co "H"
>Enl. March 16, 1862. Detached as courier July–August 1863.

Webb, James E.
>Lieutenant
>From Alabama; assigned as assistant ordnance officer to Capt. Charles Grattan on April 4, 1864; relieved and assigned to James Dearing's brigade on September 19, 1864.

Weller, Benjamin Franklin
>Private, sergeant   1st VA Cav, Co "E"
>Enl. May 2, 1861, at Waynesboro. Detached as courier November 1862 to May 12, 1864; as sergeant commanded couriers at Mine Run November 26, 1863, to December 3, 1863; wounded in action November 27, 1863.

Whiting, Clarence C.
>Private   6th VA Cav, Co "A"
>Enl. March 1, 1862, at Warrenton Junction. Served in escort at Williamsburg May 5, 1862; detached as courier September to November 1862.

Williams, Z. F.
>Private   Breathed's Batt, Stuart's Horse Arty
>Enl. May 14, 1862, at Orange CH. Detached by order of General Stuart on April 1, 1864; type of service unknown.

Willis, William Byrd
>Private   6th VA Cav, Co "I"
>Detached as courier December 24, 1861; length of service unknown.

Wilson, William Randolph

Lieutenant, assistant surgeon   1st VA Cav, Co "G"

Enl. May 9, 1861, in Amelia CH. As lieutenant, detached to Stuart's HQ; type and length of service unknown; assigned as assistant surgeon under surgeon Talcott Eliason; POW September 18, 1862.

Woodbridge, George

Private   4th VA Cav, Co "E"

Enl. May 8, 1861, at Richmond. Detached as courier; dates of service unknown.

Woodbridge, George N.

Private   4th VA Cav, Co "I"

Enl. July 28, 1861, at Union Mills. Detailed to Stuart's HQ; dates and type of service unknown.

Woodward, Thomas E.

Private   12th VA Cav, Co "I"

Enl. June 30, 1863, at Brandy Station. Attached to cavalry corps HQ November 1863 to February 1864; detached as courier March–April 1864.

APPENDIXES

STAFF OFFICERS' PERIODS OF SERVICE

NAME	1861			1862												1863												1864				
	O	N	D	J	F	M	A	M	J	J	A	S	O	N	D	J	F	M	A	M	J	J	A	S	O	N	D	J	F	M	A	M
Ball	●	●	●	●	●	●	●	●	●	●	●	●	●	●	●	●	●	●	●	●	●	●	●	●	●	●	●	●	●	●	●	●
Beckham									●	●										●	●	●	●	●	●	●	●	●	●			
Blackford									●	●										●	●	●	●	●	●	●	●	●	●			
Boteler																●	●	●	●	●	●	●	●					●	●	●	●	●
Brien	●	●				●	●		●																							
Burke						●	●																									
Chew										●																			●		●	
Christian									●	●																						
Clark																			●	●	●	●	●	●	●							
Cooke				●	●	●	●		●	●	●	●	●	●	●	●	●	●	●	●	●	●	●	●		●	●	●	●	●	●	●
Dabney		●		●	●	●	●		●	●	●	●	●	●	●	●	●	●	●	●	●	●	●	●	●	●						
Eliason				●	●	●	●		●	●	●	●	●	●	●	●	●	●	●	●	●	●	●									
Farley, H.										●																						
Farley, W.																			●	●	●	●	●									
FitzHugh									●	●	●	●	●	●	●	●	●	●	●	●	●	●	●	●	●	●	●	●	●	●	●	●
Fontaine																					●	●	●	●	●	●	●	●	●	●	●	●
Frayser									●	●	●																	●	●	●	●	●
Freaner																												●	●	●	●	●
Garnett																												●	●	●	●	●
Gilmor																		●														
Goldsborough																					●	●										
Grattan																								●				●	●	●	●	●
Grenfell																								●		●	●					
Hagan											●	●												●	●	●	●	●	●	●	●	●

	1861			1862												1863												1864				
	O	N	D	J	F	M	A	M	J	J	A	S	O	N	D	J	F	M	A	M	J	J	A	S	O	N	D	J	F	M	A	M
Hairston, J.				•	•	•	•	•	•	•	•	•	•	•	•	•	•	•														
Hairston, P.	•																															
Hairston, S.			•	•	•	•	•	•	•	•	•	•	•	•	•	•	•	•														
Hanger											•	•	•	•	•	•	•	•	•	•	•	•	•	•	•	•	•	•	•	•	•	•
Hullihen								•	•	•	•	•	•	•	•	•	•	•	•	•	•	•	•	•	•	•	•	•	•	•	•	•
Johnson																																
Kennon																																
Landstreet									•	•																						
McClellan			•	•	•	•	•	•	•	•	•	•	•	•	•	•	•	•	•	•	•	•	•	•								
Pelham	•		•	•	•	•	•	•	•	•	•	•	•	•	•	•	•	•	•	•	•	•	•	•	•	•	•	•	•	•	•	•
Powers						•	•																									
Price, C.								•	•	•	•	•						•	•	•	•	•	•	•								
Price, T.										•	•	•						•	•	•	•											
Robertson																		•	•	•	•	•	•	•								
Ryals																																
Staples							•	•	•	•	•																					
Steger		•	•																													
Stuart, J. H.											•	•	•																			
Terrell					•	•	•	•				•	•																			
Towles					•	•	•	•													•											
Turner																			•													
Venable													•	•	•	•	•	•	•	•	•	•	•	•	•	•	•	•	•	•	•	•
von Borcke													•	•	•	•	•	•	•	•	•	•	•									
White, B.													•	•	•	•	•	•	•	•	•	•										

Note: A month has been indicated for service regardless of the amount of time served in that month.

Confederate Regulations Regarding Staff Officers' Duties

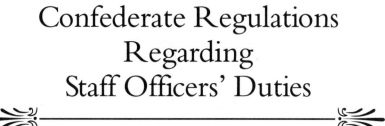

THE CONFEDERATE GOVERNMENT issued regulations regarding the officers of a staff and the various duties they were to perform. Most of the generals used their staff personnel in ways other than those established by the government. Nevertheless, the importance of the government's guidelines should not be overlooked. The excerpts that follow appeared in two books issued for the Confederate Army. "The Staff" is from the *Manual of Instruction for the Volunteers and Militia of the Confederate States,* and Articles II, IV, VII, and XXXVI are from the *Regulations for the Army of the Confederate States, 1863.*

THE STAFF

32. The well-being and efficiency of an army must depend in a large degree upon the thorough organization of the various departments of the *Staff.*

These are:

An Adjutant-General's Department.

An Inspector-General's Department.

A Quartermaster's Department.

A Commissary Department.

An Engineer Department.

An Ordnance Department.

A Pay Department.

A Medical Department.

33. The officers of the adjutant-general's department are, an adjutant-general, with such rank as may be assigned him by legislative enactment, usually that of colonel or brigadier-general, with as many assistant adjutant-generals as the exigencies of the service may require.

The adjutant-general should be the chief of staff of the commander-in-chief. He is the regular channel through which commanders of corps and chiefs of departments communicate with the commander-in-chief; and all orders, special instructions and general regulations, issued by the commander-in-chief relative to the organization, discipline and instruction of the forces, are prepared and published by the adjutant-general, conformably to the direction of the commander-in-chief.

When the commander-in-chief takes the field the adjutant-general should accompany him; when an army in the field is in command of any general not the general-in-chief, an assistant adjutant-general is assigned to him as chief of his staff.

An assistant adjutant-general, with the rank of "captain," is assigned to the commander of each brigade, and one with the rank of "major" is assigned to the general of every division. In each case the assistant adjutant-general is the chief of staff of his general, and his duties are of the same general nature as those of the adjutant-general.

An adjutant is the chief of staff of his regiment.

34. The officers of the inspector-general's department are one or more inspector-generals, with a division inspector for each division, and a brigade inspector for each brigade.

To the inspector-general, and the division and brigade inspectors, are assigned the duties of inspecting the troops, fortifications, camps, etc., at stated times; and division and brigade inspectors are specially entrusted with the instruction of regimental officers. The militia laws of Virginia, and some of the other States, impose all the duties of this department upon that of the adjutant-general, in which case the division and brigade inspectors become the chiefs of staff of their divisions and brigades, and discharge all the duties which usually devolve upon the assistant inspector-general.

35. The officers of the quartermaster's department are, a quartermaster-general, who has the control of the department; one or more assistant quartermaster-generals, quartermasters and assistant quartermasters.

The duties of this department are, to provide quarters and transportation for the troop; storage and transportation for all army supplies; clothing for the troops; camp and garrison equipage; cavalry and artillery horses; fuel; forage; straw, and stationery.

36. The officers of the commissary department are, a commissary-general, one or more assistant commissary-generals, and as many commissaries and assistant commissaries as the exigencies of the service may require.

To this department are assigned the duties of providing all the supplies necessary for the subsistence of the troops.

37. The officers of the engineer department are, a chief engineer, and as many officers of engineers as may be necessary to give efficiency to the department.

The duties of this department usually relate to the construction of permanent and field fortifications; works for the attack and defense of places;

for the passage of rivers; for the movements and operations of troops in the field, such as reconnaissances and surveys as may be required for these objects.

38. The ordnance department is officered in the same manner as that of the engineers.

This department has charge of all arsenals and armories; all cannon and artillery carriages and equipments; all apparatus and machines for the service and maneuvers of artillery; all small arms and accoutrements and horse equipments; all ammunition, and all materials for the construction of munitions of war.

39. The officers of the pay department are, a paymaster-general, one or more deputy paymaster-generals, and one paymaster, ordinarily to every regiment. When large bodies of troops are serving together, the number of paymasters may be very much reduced without detriment to the service.

To this department belong all the duties pertaining to the payment of the troops when they are in the service of the State.

40. The officers of the medical department are a surgeon-general, with one surgeon to each regiment, and such other surgeons and assistant surgeons as a proper attention to the health of the troops may require.

The senior medical officer, on duty with any corps in the field, unless otherwise specially ordered by the commanding officer, will be, ex officio, the medical director, and will have the general control of the medical officers and supervision of the hospitals under their charge.

ARTICLE II
Succession in Command or Duty

11. The officers of engineers are not to assume nor be ordered on any duty beyond the line of their immediate profession, except by the special order of the President.

12. An officer of the Medical Department cannot exercise command except in his own department, or over enlisted men, as a commissioned officer.

13. Officers of the Quartermasters or Subsistence Departments, though eligible to command according to the rank they hold in the army of the Confederate States, not subject to the orders of a junior officer, shall not assume the command of troops unless put on duty under orders which specially so direct by authority of the President.

ARTICLE IV
Appointment and Promotion of Commission Officers

21. Cadets appointed under Confederate law, shall be assigned to such duties, governed by exigencies of the service, as will best promote their military experience and improvement, until a military school shall be established by the Government for their instruction.

ARTICLE VII
Appointments on the Staff

31. General Officers appoint their own Aides-de-camp.

ARTICLE XXXVI
Troops in Campaign
Organization of an Army in the Field

475. Staff officers and officers of engineers, and artillery, according to the nature of the service, are assigned to the headquarters of armies and divisions, and detached brigades, by order of the general commanding-in-chief, when the distribution of these officers has not been regulated by the War Department. The necessary staff will be assigned to commanders of brigades.

476. When an Engineer or other officer is charged with directing an expedition or making a reconnaissance, without having command of the escort, the commander of the escort shall consult him on all arrangements necessary to secure the success of the operation.

477. Staff officers, and commanders of engineers, and artillery, report to their immediate commanders the state of supplies, and whatever concerns the service under their direction, and receive their orders, and communicate to them those they receive from their superiors in their own corps.

478. The senior officer of engineers, of artillery, and the departments of the general staff serving at the chief headquarters in the field, will transmit to the bureau of his department at Richmond, at the close of the campaign, and such other times as the commander in the field may approve, a full report of the operations of his department, and whatever information to improve its service he may be able to furnish.

The report of the officer of engineers will embrace plans of military works executed during the campaign, and, in case of siege, a journal of the attack or defense.

Confederate Regulations Regarding Staff Officers' Uniforms

THE CONFEDERATE GOVERNMENT also published guidelines regarding staff officers' uniforms. The *Uniform and Dress of the Army of the Confederate States,* issued by the adjutant and inspector general's office in September 1861, delineated what was to be worn by all ranks in all branches of the service. Though these regulations were not completely ignored, compliance quickly became difficult. For the enlisted man, practicality and availability often ruled. The officer corps, however, did make an effort to adhere to the regulations, though they were not always successful. The official regulations pertaining to staff personnel were as follows:

TUNIC
For Commissioned Officers

1. All Officers shall wear a tunic of gray cloth, known as cadet gray; the skirt to extend halfway between the hip and the knee; double breasted for all grades.

2. For a Brigadier General—Two rows of buttons on the breast, eight in each row, placed in pairs . . .; stand-up collar . . .; cuffs two and a half inches deep on the underside, there to be buttoned with three small buttons, and sloped upwards to a point at a distance of four inches from the end of the sleeve; pockets in the fold of the skirt, with one button at the hip and one at the end of each pocket, making four buttons on the back of the tunic, the hip buttons to range with the lowest breast buttons.

3. For a Colonel—the same as for a Brigadier General, except that there will be only seven buttons in each row on the breast, placed at equal distance.

4. For a Lieutenant Colonel, Major, Captain, and Lieutenant —the same as for a Colonel.

Facings

6. The facings for General Officers, and for Officers of the Adjutant General's Department, the Quartermaster General's Department, the

Commissary General's Department, and the Engineers—buff. The tunic for all officers to be edged throughout with the facings designated.

7. For the Medical Department—black.

8. For the Artillery—red.

9. For the Cavalry—yellow.

BUTTONS

13. For General Officers and Officers of the General Staff—bright gilt, rounded at the edge, convex, raised eagle in the centre, with stars surrounding it; large size, one inch in exterior diameter; small size, half an inch.

14. For Officers of the Corps of Engineers, the same as for General Staff, except that, in place of the eagle and stars, there will be a raised E in German text.

15. For Officers of Artillery, . . . and Cavalry—gilt, convex, plain, with large raised letter in the centre: A, for the Artillery; . . . C, for the Cavalry; large size, seven-eighths of an inch in exterior diameter; small size, half an inch.

16. Aides-de-Camp may wear the button of the General Staff, or of their regiments or Corps, at their option.

TROUSERS

19. The uniform trousers for both officers and enlisted men will be of cloth throughout the year; made loose, and to spread well over the foot; of light (or sky) blue color for regimental officers and enlisted men; and of dark blue cloth for all other officers; reinforced for the Cavalry.

21. For Officers of the Adjutant General's Department, the Quartermaster General's Department, the Commissary General's Department, and the Corps of Engineers—one stripe of gold lace on the outer seam, one inch and a quarter in width.

22. For the Medical Department—a black velvet stripe, one inch and a quarter in width, with a gold cord on each edge of the stripe.

23. For regimental Officers—a stripe of cloth on the outer seam, one inch and a quarter in width; color according to corps: for Artillery, red; Cavalry, yellow. . . .

CHAPEAU, OR COCKED HAT

26. A chapeau, or cocked hat, will be worn by General Officers and Officers of the General Staff and Corps of Engineers, of what is called the French pattern. . . .

27. Forage cap for officers—a cap similar in form to that known as the French kepi. . . .

CRAVAT, OR STOCK

32. For all officers—black.

BOOTS

34. For all officers—ankle or Jefferson.

SASH

42. For officers of the General Staff and Engineers, and of the Artillery . . . —red silk net. For officers of the Cavalry—yellow silk net. For medical officers—green silk net. All with bullion fringe ends; to go around the waist, and to tie as for General Officers [behind the left hip].

BADGES TO DISTINGUISH RANK

51. On the sleeve of the tunic, rank will be distinguished by an ornament of gold braid . . . extending around the seam of the cuff, and up the outside of the arm to the bend of the elbow. To be of one braid for lieutenants; two for captains; three for field officers [major, lieutenant colonel, and colonel]; and four for general officers. The braid to be one-eighth of an inch in width.

52. On the front part of the collar of the tunic, the rank of officers will be distinguished as follows:

55. Lieutenant Colonel—Two stars of same material, size and arrangement as for colonel [that being embroidered in gold, arranged horizontally, and dividing equally the vertical space of the collar; each star to be one and one-fourth inches in exterior diameter; front star to be three-fourths of an inch from the edge of the collar].

56. Major—One star of same material and size as for a colonel; to be placed three-fourths of an inch from the edge of the collar, and dividing equally the vertical space.

57. Captain—Three horizontal bars, embroidered in gold; each one-half inch in width; the upper bar to be three inches in length; the front edge of the bars to incline to correspond with the angle of the collar, and to be three-fourths of an inch from the edge; the line of the back edges to be vertical.

58. First Lieutenant—Two horizontal bars of the same material and size as for captains, and dividing equally the vertical space of the collar.

59. Second Lieutenant—One horizontal bar of the same material and size as for the centre bar of captain, and dividing equally the vertical space of the collar.

HAIR AND BEARD

69. The hair to be short; the beard to be worn at the pleasure of the individual; but when worn, to be kept short and neatly trimmed.

Further guidelines regarding kepis were issued by the War Department on January 24, 1862, in General Orders No. 4. Noted below are those that applied to Stuart's staff.

Forage Cap for the Army of the Confederate States

Pattern—Of the form known as the French kepi; to be made of cloth.

For General Officers, and Officers of the General Staff and Engineers—Dark blue band, sides and crown.

For the Artillery—Dark blue band; sides and crown red.

For the Cavalry—Dark blue band; sides and crown yellow.

Marks to Distinguish Rank

Four gold braids for General Officers; three for Field Officers; two for Captains; and one for Lieutenants, to extend from the band on the front, back and both sides to the top of the cap—and the centre of the crown to be embroidered with the same number of braids.

Men on active duty in the field could not be held accountable if they were not able to comply with these minutely detailed regulations. Stuart's staff, however, made gallant efforts to be as finely attired as possible, and Blackford commented on how much better dressed was Stuart's staff than "Stonewall" Jackson's when they rendezvoused at Ashland prior to the Seven Days.[1] Soon after joining the staff, Frank Robertson, Blackford's assistant, found that his fellow officers liked to present a dashing image. A letter to his sister reflected his discovery that a plain uniform would just not do.

> If my jacket is still unfinished, I should like the arms to be trimmed with buff and gold lace. I directed otherwise, but the staff have all fixed up to such an alarming extent that I shall have to follow suit, or be taken for a courier. Cousin William [Blackford] will have it done if you will get Wyndham to tell him I want a cord of buff run around the sleeve marking the edge of the cuff if there were any.[2]

The staff members' concern about their appearance mirrored their chieftain's concern for his. Stuart took liberties with the regulations basically regarding three items: his coat, his hat, and his boots. Though Stuart owned a frock coat (tunic), he much preferred the shell jacket. Four out of the five photographs of him taken during the war show him wearing a shell jacket. He also chose to wear a slouched hat rather than a kepi and favored high-top boots over the Jefferson or ankle boot. These breaks with the regulations reveal Stuart's practical nature: He was a man always on the move, and his uniforms reflected this.

Photographs of staff members in uniform, though limited in number, reveal that the men took some of the same liberties as their commander. Both frock coats and shell jackets can be seen. Chiswell Dabney wore a kepi, while von Borcke and G. M. Ryals sported slouched hats.[3] Ryals wore the regulation ankle boots, but Dabney and L. F. Terrell apparently preferred high boots.[4]

Portions of at least three staff members' uniforms survive. Capt. R. B. Kennon's frock coat and Capt. James L. Clark's frock coat, shell jacket, and vest rest in the Museum of the Confederacy. Lt. Col. Roger P. Chew's shell jacket is housed at the Harpers Ferry National Historical Park. These uniforms are beautifully preserved and give ample evidence that while Stuart and his staff followed the army's uniform regulations to a degree, the individual tastes of the men and their gallant leader also governed what was worn by the men who "followed the plume."

NOTES

LIST OF ABBREVIATIONS

CSR: *Compiled Service Records of Confederate General and Staff Officers, and Non-Regimental Enlisted Men*

CWT: *Civil War Times*

CWTI: *Civil War Times Illustrated*

CV: *Confederate Veteran*

DU: Duke University

HL: The Huntington Library

HSWCB: *The Historical Society of Washington County, Va., Bulletin*

JCM: The Jefferson County Museum of West Virginia

MACMEC: *Minutes of the Annual Conferences of the Methodist Episcopal Church, South*

MDAH: Mississippi Department of Archives and History

MDLC: Manuscript Department of the Library of Congress

MHM: *Maryland Historical Magazine*

OR: *The War of the Rebellion: The Official Records of the Union and Confederate Armies*

SHC/UNC: Southern Historical Collection, Library of the University of North Carolina at Chapel Hill

SHSP: *Southern Historical Society Papers*

UCL: University of Chicago Library

UP: *Unfiled Papers and Slips Belonging to Confederate Compiled Service Records*

USAMHI: U.S. Army Military History Institute

UVAL: University of Virginia Library

VCCWQ: *Virginia Country's Civil War Quarterly*

VHS: Virginia Historical Society

VMIA: The Virginia Military Institute Archives

VSL: Virginia State Library

STUART AND HIS STAFF
History

1. Sgt. B. J. Haden, *Reminiscences of J. E. B. Stuart's Cavalry* (Charlottesville, Va.: Progress Publishing Co., n.d.), p. 11.

2. U.S. War Department, *The War of the Rebellion: The Official Records of the Union and Confederate Armies* (Washington, D.C.: U.S. Government Printing Office, 1880–1901), V, pp. 183–84.

3. OR, V, pp. 490–94.

4. OR, XI, 1, pp. 444–45.

5. OR, XI, 1, p. 573.

6. OR, XI, 1, p. 1040.

7. OR, XI, 1, p. 1041.

8. OR, XI, 1, p. 522.

9. OR, XII, 2, pp. 733–39.

10. OR, XII, 2, pp. 734–35.

11. OR, XIX, 1, p. 821.

12. OR, XIX, 1, p. 54.

13. OR, XXV, 2, p. 862.

14. OR, XXVII, 2, pp. 679–87.

15. OR, XXVII, 2, pp. 679–87.

16. OR, XXVII, 2, pp. 709–10.

17. OR, XXIX, 1, p. 453.

18. OR, XXIX, 1, p. 901.

Selection and Duties

1. "Jeb" Stuart to Flora Stuart, March 24, 1863, James Ewell Brown Stuart Papers, Virginia Historical Society.

2. W. W. Blackford, *War Years with Jeb Stuart* (New York: Charles Scribner's Sons, 1945), p. 90.

3. Norman R. FitzHugh, National Archives and Record Service, comp., *Compiled Service Records of Confederate General and Staff Officers, and Non-Regimental Enlisted Men,* (Washington, D.C., 1961), Microcopy No. 331, Roll 94.

4. Harry J. Warthen, Jr., "Family Ties," *Civil War Times Illustrated,* Vol. XXII, 6, (October 1983), p. 34. The individuals Stuart asked to stand behind FitzHugh were Thomas Randolph Price (father of staff members Channing and Tom Price) and Stuart's brother Alexander.

5. Stuart to Flora, October 22, 1862, James Ewell Brown Stuart Papers, VHS.

6. Heros von Borcke to R. Channing Price, July 29, 1862, R. Channing Price Papers, Southern Historical Collection, Library of the University of North Carolina at Chapel Hill.

7. John Esten Cooke, *Outlines from the Outpost* (Chicago: R. R. Donnelley & Sons Co., 1961), pp. 15–16.

8. Garnett Family Papers (#38–45–B), *Continuation of War Sketches,* unpublished manuscript, Manuscripts Division, Special Collections Department, University of Virginia Library.

9. Blackford, *War Years with Jeb Stuart,* p. 309.

Stuart and the Men

1. Jedediah Hotchkiss to his wife, January 11, 1863, Hotchkiss Papers, Manuscript Department of the Library of Congress, Roll 4, Frame 484–85.

2. R. Channing Price to his sister, December 4, 1863, R. Channing Price Papers, SHC/UNC.

3. "Jeb" Stuart to Frank Robertson, September 21, 1863, Wyndham Robertson Papers, Department of Special Collections, University of Chicago Library.

4. John Esten Cooke, "General Stuart in Camp and Field," *Annals of the War* (Philadelphia: The Times Publishing Company, 1879), p. 672.

5. Maud Carter Clement, "Sketch of the Life of Chiswell Dabney," *Writings of Maud Carter Clement* (Chatham, Va.: Pittsylvania Historical Society, 1982), p. 8.

6. Blackford, *War Years with Jeb Stuart,* pp. 160–61.

7. R. Channing Price to his mother, April 5, 1863, R. Channing Price Papers, SHC/UNC.

8. In Garnett, *Continuation of War Sketches,* UV, Theodore Garnett recounted that in the early days of March 1863, he and the rest of the staff were invited to a "Grand Ball and Tournament" given by the officers of A. P. Hill's 3rd Corps. The event left an indelible impression on the young lieutenant's mind.

9. Garnett, *Continuation of War Sketches,* UV.

10. Maud Carter Clement, "A Letter from the Reverend Chiswell Dabney to His Wife in 1907 on the Occasion of the Unveiling of a Statue of General J. E. B. Stuart," *Writings of Maud Carter Clement* (Chatham, Va.: Pittsylvania Historical Society, 1982), p. 31.

STUART'S STAFF OFFICERS

1. John Esten Cooke, *Wearing of the Gray* (Bloomington: Kraus Reprint Co., 1977), pp. 17–18.

Ball, D.

1. "Rev. Dabney Ball," *Minutes of the Annual Conferences of the Methodist Episcopal Church, South* for the year 1878 (Nashville: Southern Methodist Publishing House, 1884), pp. 10–11.

2. Patricia L. Faust, ed., *Historical Times Illustrated Encyclopedia of the Civil War* (New York: Harper & Row, 1986), p. 37.

3. Dabney Ball to Ward Hill Lamon, April 21, 1861, Lamon Collection, The Huntington Library.

4. Peter W. Hairston to his wife, September 20, 1861, Peter Wilson Hairston Papers, SHC/UNC.

5. Peter W. Hairston to his wife, September 22, 1861, Hairston Papers, SHC/UNC.

6. Dabney Ball to Stuart, July 15, 1862, J. E. B. Stuart Collection, HL.

7. Dabney Ball, *CSR,* (Washington, D.C., 1961), Microcopy No. 324, Roll 49.

8. At this time there were two towns in Virginia named Salem. One, now called Marshall, was located northwest of Warrenton, while the other lay on the Virginia and Tennessee Railroad southwest of Lynchburg. Ball accompanied Lt. F. S. Robertson on Robertson's trip home to recuperate from injuries incurred during the Gettysburg Campaign. Robertson recorded that the parson was returning to his wife in Salem, making perfectly clear that his destination was the latter Salem. Capt. Frank S. Robertson, "Reminiscence of the Years 1861–1865," *The Historical Society of Washington County, Va. Bulletin,* Series II, 23 (1986): p. 30.

9. "Jeb" Stuart to Dabney Ball, July 20, 1863, Dabney Ball, *CSR,* (Washington, D.C., 1961), Microcopy No. 324, Roll 49.

10. At least one reference indicates that Ball may have joined Stuart as chaplain in mid-September 1863. Pvt. Henry D. Beall wrote that about September 14, after acting as a courier for Stuart, he returned to the general to report the success of his mission. Exhausted from thirty-six hours of riding with little rest and no food, Beall ate and, after another conversation with Stuart, lay down on a robe by the fire. He distinctly remembered Ball spreading the robe for him, bidding him to lie down upon it. H. D. Beale [Beall], "An Allnight Ride and Its Reward," *Confederate Veteran* XXXVI, 1928, p. 259.

11. "Rev. Dabney Ball," MACMEC for the year 1878, pp. 10–11.

12. *Ibid.,* p. 11.

Beckham, R. F.

1. "Jeb" Stuart to Gen. Samuel Cooper, March 26, 1863, Robert F. Beckham, *CSR,* (Washington, D.C., 1961), Microcopy No. 331, Roll 20.

2. Samuel H. Lockett to Hon. L. P. Walker, March 6, 1861, Robert F. Beckham, *CSR,* (Washington, D.C., 1961), Microcopy No. 331, Roll 20.

3. Robert F. Beckham to Hon. Jeremiah Morton, June 23, 1861, Robert F. Beckham, *CSR,* (Washington, D.C., 1961), Microcopy 331, Roll 20.

4. According to one source, Beckham may have reported unofficially to Smith much earlier, on October 1, 1861. Nimrod Hunter Steele, "The Nimrod Hunter Steele Diary and Letters," *Diaries, Letters, and Recollections of the War Between the States* (Winchester, Va.: Winchester-Frederick County Historical Society Papers, 1955), Vol. III, p. 57.

5. Gustavus W. Smith, *Confederate War Papers* (New York: Atlantic Publishing and Engraving Company, 1884), p. 164.

6. H. B. McClellan, *I Rode with Jeb Stuart* (Bloomington, Ind.: Indiana University Press, 1958), p. 234.

7. "Jeb" Stuart to Gen. Samuel Cooper, May 21, 1863, Robert F. Beckham, *CSR,* (Washington, D.C., 1961), Microcopy 313, Roll 20.

8. OR, XXIX, 2, pp. 839–42.

9. "Jeb" Stuart to R. F. Beckham, February 15, 1864, Robert F. Beckham, *CSR,* (Washington, D.C., 1961), Microcopy No. 331, Roll 20.

Blackford, W. W.

1. Blackford, *War Years with Jeb Stuart,* p. 11.

2. Jones's caustic personality, which biographers trace to the drowning of his wife just shortly after they were married, rightfully earned him the nickname of "Grumble." He maintained a running feud with virtually everyone, including Stuart. The bad feelings eventually led to his removal from Stuart's direct command. He was killed at the Battle of Piedmont on June 5, 1864.

3. William W. Blackford to his Uncle John, July 27, 1861, Blackford Family Papers, SHC/UNC.

4. Charles F. M. Garnett to Gen. G. W. Randolph, May 13, 1862, William W. Blackford, *CSR,* (Washington, D.C., 1961), Microcopy No. 324, Roll 1.

5. Heros von Borcke, *Memoirs of the Confederate War for Independence* (Dayton: Morningside, 1985), Vol. I, p. 321.

6. Blackford, *War Years with Jeb Stuart,* pp. 176–78.

7. Letter to author from Virginia Polytechnic Institute, March 25, 1988.

8. In his introduction to Blackford's *War Years with Jeb Stuart,* Douglas Southall Freeman gives Blackford's date of death as May 1, 1905. The reason for the discrepancy is unknown.

Boteler, A. R.

1. OR, IV, 2, p. 718.

2. "Jeb" Stuart to Jefferson Davis, February 6, 1864, Alexander R. Boteler, *CSR,* (Washington, D.C., 1961), Microcopy No. 331, Roll 28.

Brien, L. T.

1. Peter W. Hairston to his wife, May 5, 1861, Hairston Papers, SHC/UNC.

2. "Cooleemee" records in Brien's handwriting end on March 15, 1864.

3. David Cardwell, *The State Columbia* (S.C.), n.d.

4. *The Daily News* (Frederick, Md.), November 26, 1912.

Burke, R.

1. From a copy of a manuscript in the author's files titled *Murder at Midnight* by Thomas J. Evans, who states that Burke's great-great-great grandson, Robert C. Burke, has done research showing Ireland to be Burke's birthplace.

2. Peter W. Hairston to his wife, September 26, 1861, Hairston Papers, SHC/UNC.

3. Redmond Burke, *CSR,* (Washington, D.C., 1961), Microcopy No. 324, Roll 2.

4. OR, V, pp. 493–94.

5. Stuart Wright, *Colonel Heros von Borcke's Journal,* p. 114.

6. "Jeb" Stuart to Flora Stuart, October 22, 1862, James Ewell Brown Stuart Papers, VHS.

7. Thomas J. Evans, *Murder at Midnight,* manuscript in the author's files.

8. *Ibid.,* p. 7.

9. Stuart's General Orders No. 14, December 3, 1862, James Ewell Brown Stuart Papers, Duke University.

Chew, R. P.

1. Jennings Cropper Wise, *The Long Arm of Lee* (New York: Oxford University Press, 1959), p. 163.

2. Chew, Rouse, and Thomson left the Virginia Military Institute before graduating but later were declared graduates. Chew would have graduated in 1862, Rouse in 1863, and Thomson in 1864 had not the war interrupted their studies.

3. Chew's actual birthplace remains a mystery. His father had been born on a farm near Round Hill in Loudoun County, but sometime after the death of Roger Sr.'s father, John, in 1838, he moved to a house in Snickersville (now Bluemont), also in Loudoun County. The farm, now known as "Locust Grove," still stands.

4. Milton Rouse to Joseph R. Anderson, November 19, 1903, Milton Rouse File, the Virginia Military Institute Archives, Lexington, Va.

5. *Ibid.,* Rouse File, VMIA.

6. *Ibid.,* Rouse File, VMIA.

7. Wise, *The Long Arm of Lee,* p. 166.

8. George M. Neese, *Three Years in the Confederate Horse Artillery* (Dayton, Ohio: Press of Morningside Bookshop, 1983), p. 179; Ada Bruce Desper Bradshaw, ed., *Civil War Diary of Charles William McVicar* (limited edition, n.d.), p. 11.

9. George M. Neese to Roger P. Chew, October 22, 1900, Roger Preston Chew Papers, the Jefferson County Museum.

10. Wade Hampton to Kenna, March 13, 1888; Matthew C. Butler to Thornton T. Perry, March 7, 1904; and Thomas Rosser to T. T. Perry, March 16, 1904, Chew Papers, JCM.

Christian, J. R.

1. In his book *A Guide to Virginia Military Organizations: 1861–1865,* Lee Wallace gives Christian's name as Jones Richardson Christian. According to the Christian family genealogy, however, he was named after his father, Capt. Jones Rivers Christian, who had been captain of the New Kent cavalry in the War of 1812. Lee Wallace, *A Guide to Virginia Military Organizations: 1861–1865* (Lynchburg: H. E. Howard, 1986), pp. 42, 352.

2. OR, XI, 1, pp. 513–23, 1036–40.

3. Jones R. Christian, *CSR,* (Washington, D.C., 1961), Microcopy No. 324, Roll 27.

4. The May 8 date is found in Jones R. Christian, *CSR,* (Washington, D.C., 1961), Microcopy No. 324, Roll 27; Martin F. Graham, "The Immortal 600: Their Long Journey to Freedom," *Virginia Country's Civil War Quarterly* X (September 1987): p. 59.

Clark, J. L.

1. James L. Clark, *CSR,* (Washington, D.C., 1961), Microcopy No. 331, Roll 56.

2. The letter was printed in an article entitled "The Gallant Pelham: True Details of the Great Cannoneer's Death, now first told, in words of his tentmate, Captain James Louis Clark." The magazine from which the article comes is unknown, but a copy of the article is located in the Alabama Department of History and Archives in Montgomery.

3. Dennes E. Frye, *12th Virginia Cavalry* (Lynchburg: H. E. Howard, Inc., 1988), p. 116.

Cooke, J. E.

1. John O. Beaty, Ph.D., *John Esten Cooke, Virginian* (Port Washington: Kennikat Press, n.d.), p. 6.

2. *Ibid.,* p. 76.

3. *Ibid.,* pp. 79–80.

4. OR, XXVII, 2, pp. 679–87.

5. Beaty, *John Esten Cooke, Virginian,* pp. 108–9.

6. Stuart E. Brown, Jr., *The Old Chapel, Clarke County, Virginia* (pamphlet, n.d.).

7. Beaty, *John Esten Cooke, Virginian,* p. 161.

8. Jay B. Hubbell, ed., "The War Diary of John Esten Cooke," *The Journal of Southern History,* VII (1941): pp. 526–40.

Dabney, C.

1. The gauntlets that Dabney lost on this occasion were returned to him after the war. According to an account written by Sgt. B. J. Haden, Stuart's wife, Flora, had learned through an unnamed source that a gentleman in New Jersey was in possession of the hat her husband had lost at Verdiersville. She wrote to him and found that though he did not have Stuart's hat, he did have a pair of gauntlets that bore the name C. H. Dabney. Mrs. Stuart evidently informed Dabney, who immediately wrote to the gentleman, and the gloves were returned. Haden stated that he saw the gloves and was told the story by Dabney himself.

2. Von Borcke, *Memoirs of the Confederate War for Independence,* Vol. I, pp. 105–8.

3. Chiswell Dabney, *CSR,* (Washington, D.C., 1961), Microcopy No. 331, Roll 70.

4. Chiswell Dabney, "The Battle of Brandy Station," *Writings of Maud Carter Clement* (Chatham, Va.: Pittsylvania Historical Society, 1982), p. 59.

5. *Ibid.,* pp. 59–60.

6. *Ibid.,* p. 60.

7. *Pittsylvania County Paper,* "The Reverend Chiswell Dabney," *Writings of Maud Carter Clement* (Chatham, Va.: Pittsylvania Historical Society, 1982), p. 14.

Eliason, T.

1. Von Borcke, *Memoirs of the Confederate War for Independence,* Vol. II, p. 295.

2. *Ibid.,* pp. 298–99.

3. Though records are sketchy, it is believed that Eliason's father was stationed at Fort Macon, which is opposite Beaufort, North Carolina, in 1826. In the census of 1860 Eliason gave Beaufort as his birthplace, but in the census of 1880 he declined to name a town, stating only that he was born in North Carolina.

4. Letter to author from Thomas Jefferson University dated November 9, 1989.

5. Sarah W. Chunn was the daughter of John M. Chunn and Ann M. (Cocke) Chunn. Both of Sarah's parents died young—her father on April 22 or October 27, 1838, and her mother on March 11, 1840—and she had to live with her guardian, Marshall Ashby.

6. Von Borcke, *Memoirs of the Confederate War,* Vol. II, p. 8.

7. OR, V, p. 442.

8. Talcott Eliason, *CSR,* (Washington, D.C., 1961), Microcopy No. 331, Roll 85.

9. "Jeb" Stuart to Flora Stuart, July, 18, 1863, James Ewell Brown Stuart Papers, VHS.

10. "Jeb" Stuart to Flora Stuart, October 3, 1863, James Ewell Brown Stuart Papers, VHS.

11. Talcott Eliason, *CSR,* (Washington, D.C., 1961), Microcopy No. 331, Roll 85.

12. *The True Index,* December 23, 1865.

13. *Morning Herald* (Hagerstown, Md.), October 25 and 26, 1896.

Farley, H. S.

1. Ashley Halsey Jr., *Who Fired the First Shot?* (New York: Hawthorne Books, 1963), pp. 27–36.

2. Randolph W. Farley, *The Farley, Fairlie, Farlo Family* (Hollis, N.H.: Times Press, 1902).

3. John Crane and James F. Kieley, *West Point: "The Key to America"* (New York: Whittlesey House, 1947), p. 230.

4. Robert Lebby, "The First Shot on Fort Sumter," *The South Carolina Historical and Genealogical Magazine* (Charleston: South Carolina Historical Society, July 1911), p. 144.

5. Henry S. Farley, *CSR,* (Washington, D.C., 1961), Microcopy No. 331, Roll 90.

6. Richard J. Sommers, *Richmond Redeemed* (Garden City: Doubleday & Company, 1981), p. 194.

7. *Ibid.,* p. 351.

8. Henry S. Farley, *CSR,* (Washington, D.C., 1961), Microcopy No. 331, Roll 90.

Farley, W. D.

1. William D. Farley, *CSR,* (Washington, D.C., 1961), Microcopy No. 331, Roll 90.

2. Family information supplied by Isobel S. Stewart.

3. William Watts Ball, "Captain William C. [*sic*] Farley, Part II," *The Laurens Advertiser,* December 3, 1936.

4. "Capt. Wm. Downs Farley," *Tri-Weekly Mercury,* July 7, 1863.

5. Transcript of this letter supplied by Isobel S. Stewart.

6. "Sword Captured during War of Confederacy Is Returned," *News & Courier,* November 26, 1923.

7. "Capt. Wm. Downs Farley," *Tri-Weekly Mercury,* July 7, 1863.

8. *Ibid.*

9. Robertson, "Reminiscence of the Years 1861–1865," HSWCB, p. 21.

10. *Ibid.,* p. 20.

11. This passage was taken from a newspaper article; the name of the newspaper and the title of the article unfortunately are not known. Captain Blocker's account provides more detail than any other account of Farley's death. Note, however, that Francis W. Pickens was not the governor of South Carolina when the Battle of Brandy Station was fought; Milledge L. Bonham was then in office.

12. Transcript of this letter supplied by Isobel S. Stewart.

FitzHugh, N. R.

1. Louis A. Sigaud, *Belle Boyd: Confederate Spy* (Richmond: The Dietz Press, 1944), p. 89.

2. From information supplied by Sandra O'Keefe.

3. Blackford, *War Years with Jeb Stuart,* p. 90.

4. From information supplied by Robert K. Krick.

5. Norman R. FitzHugh, *CSR,* (Washington, D.C., 1961), Micro-copy No. 331, Roll 94.

6. From a diary of James Hardeman Stuart, James Hardeman Stuart Papers, Mississippi Department of Archives and History.

7. OR, II, 4, p. 578; Sigaud, *Belle Boyd: Confederate Spy,* p. 103.

8. R. Channing Price to his mother, October 15, 1862, R. Channing Price Papers, SHC/UNC.

9. William Willis Blackford Papers (#5859), UVAL.

10. R. Channing Price to his mother, March 30, 1863, R. Channing Price Papers, SHC/UNC.

11. Norman R. FitzHugh, *CSR,* (Washington, D.C., 1961), Micro-copy No. 331, Roll 94.

12. "Jeb" Stuart to Flora Stuart, March 4, 1863, James Ewell Brown Stuart Papers, VHS.

13. Norman R. FitzHugh, *CSR,* (Washington, D.C., 1961), Microcopy No. 331, Roll 94.

14. *Ibid.*

15. 1880 Census of St. Johns County, Florida.

16. 1880 Census of St. Johns County, Florida; 1910 Census of St. Johns County, Florida.

17. 1880 Census of St. Johns County, Florida; John R. Richards, comp., *Florida State Gazetteer* (New York: The South Publishing Company, 1886–87), Vol. I, p. 368.

18. Soldier's Pension Claim of Norman R. FitzHugh, Florida State Archives.

Fontaine, J. B.

1. This account of the circumstances that precipitated the death of John B. Fontaine was summarized from Sommers, *Richmond Redeemed,* pp. 342–45.

2. George Freaner to Elizabeth Winston Price Fontaine Haw, October 6, 1864, VHS.

3. John B. Fontaine, *CSR,* (Washington, D.C., 1961), Microcopy No. 331, Roll 96.

4. Von Borcke, *Memoirs of the Confederate War for Independence,* Vol. II, pp. 174–76.

5. John B. Fontaine, *CSR,* (Washington, D.C., 1961), Microcopy No. 331, Roll 96.

Frayser, R. E.

1. Richard E. Frayser, *CSR,* (Washington, D.C., 1961), Microcopy No. 324, Roll 29.

2. Richard E. Frayser, "A Narrative of Stuart's Raid in the Rear of the Army of the Potomac," *Southern Historical Society Papers,* XI (1883), pp. 505–17.

3. *Ibid.,* p. 513.

4. Richard E. Frayser, *CSR,* (Washington, D.C., 1961), Microcopy No. 324, Roll 29.

5. Edward Stuart to his uncle, September 3, 1862, Oscar J. E. Stuart and Family Papers, MDAH.

6. OR, XIX, 1, p. 821.

7. Clifford Dowdey, ed., *The Wartime Papers of R. E. Lee* (New York: Bramhall House, 1961), p. 502.

8. Richard E. Frayser, *CSR,* (Washington, D.C., 1961), Microcopy No. 258, Roll 117.

9. Graham, "The Immortal 600: Their Long Journey to Freedom," *VCCWQ,* Vol. X, September 1987, p. 59.

Freaner, G.

1. George Freaner, *CSR,* (Washington, D.C., 1961), Microcopy No. 331, Roll 98.

2. Hagerstown, Md., *Mail* (weekly), November 15, 1878.

3. George Freaner to Christian Philip Humrich, August 1851. Special Collections, Boyd Lee Spahr Library, Dickinson College.

4. George Freaner, *CSR,* (Washington, D.C., 1961), Microcopy No. 331, Roll 98.

5. *Ibid.*

6. J. Thomas Scharf, *History of Western Maryland* (Baltimore: Regional Publishing Company, 1968), Vol. 2, pp. 1102–3.

Garnett, T. S.

1. Capt. W. Gordon McCabe, "The Honorable Theodore S. Garnett," *SHSP,* Series III, No. XLI, September 1916, pp. 68–81.

2. Frank S. Robertson, "Reminiscence of the Years 1861–1865," *HSWCB,* p. 16.

3. *Ibid.,* p. 25

4. Garnett, *Continuation of War Sketches,* UV.

5. *Ibid.*

6. *Ibid.*

7. Theodore S. Garnett, *CSR,* (Washington, D.C., 1961), Microcopy No. 331, Roll 103.

8. *Virginian-Pilot and the Norfolk Landmark,* April 28, 1915.

Gilmor, H. W.

1. Virgil Carrington Jones, *Gray Ghosts and Rebel Raiders* (McLean: EMP Publications, 1984), pp. 114, 170.

2. *Evening News* (Baltimore), July 18, 1979.

3. W. W. Goldsborough, *The Maryland Line in the Confederate Army* (Gaithersburg: Olde Soldier Books, 1987), p. 242.

4. *Ibid.,* p. 242.

5. Jones, *Gray Ghosts and Rebel Raiders,* p. 114.

6. There are many different versions of Pelham's death. Several men have stated they helped take the wounded Pelham off the field. What is given here is Gilmor's version, not necessarily the correct one.

7. Robert K. Krick, *Lee's Colonels* (Dayton, Ohio: Morningside Bookshop, 1984), p. 135.

8. Jones, *Gray Ghosts and Rebel Raiders,* p. 215.

9. *Ibid.,* pp. 217–18

10. Goldsborough, *The Maryland Line in the Confederate Army,* pp. 243–44

11. Geoffrey W. Fielding, ed., "Gilmor's Field Report of His Raid in Baltimore County," *Maryland Historical Magazine* (September 1952): pp. 234–40; Jones, *Gray Ghosts and Rebel Raiders,* pp. 263–64.

12. Mosby was spending the night at the home of James H. Hathaway just east of Rectortown. Asleep and in his nightshirt when the Federals appeared, Mosby awoke and quietly slipped out the window of his second story bedroom. He perched on the limb of a tree that almost touched the house and remained there throughout the futile search that followed. As the frustrated Boyd and his men rode away, Mosby climbed back through the window and resumed his interrupted sleep. Virgil Carrington Jones, *Ranger Mosby* (Chapel Hill: The University of North Carolina Press: 1944), pp. 9–10; Jones, *Gray Ghosts and Rebel Raiders,* pp. 178–79.

13. Jones, *Gray Ghosts and Rebel Raiders,* pp. 287–92.

14. John Bakeless, "Catching Harry Gilmor," *CWTI,* Vol. X, No. 1, April 1971, pp. 34–40

15. Baltimore *Sun,* March 6, 1883.

Goldsborough, R. H.

1. Goldsborough's home was most likely "Myrtle Grove," near Easton, Maryland, until October 1849, when his mother died. The 1850 census indicates that he was still living in the county but not necessarily at "Myrtle Grove." The 1860 census has him living with a Jane Feddeman, who may have been a relative. His father lived until 1890.

2. Wise, *The Long Arm of Lee,* pp. 335, 338.

3. Robert H. Goldsborough, *CSR,* (Washington, D.C., 1961), Microcopy No. 331, Roll 108.

4. Lee A. Wallace, *A Guide to Virginia Military Organizations: 1861–1865,* p. 68.

5. Robert H. Goldsborough, *CSR,* (Washington, D.C., 1961), Microcopy No. 331, Roll 108.

6. *Ibid.*

7. R. Channing Price to his mother, March 30, 1863, R. Channing Price Papers, SHC/UNC.

8. W. W. Blackford stated that Goldsborough was sent to Col. Matthew C. Butler, but in his report of the battle Stuart wrote that he had dispatched his aide to Wickham with an urgent message. Blackford, *War Years with Jeb Stuart,* p. 214; OR, XXVII, 2, p. 687.

9. Blackford, *War Years with Jeb Stuart,* p. 214.

10. Robert H. Goldsborough, *CSR,* (Washington, D.C., 1961), Microcopy No. 331, Roll 108.

11. *Ibid.*

Grattan, C.

1. Information concerning Charles Grattan's three brothers was supplied by Martha T. Grattan.

2. From "The Manuscript of Robert Grattan," p. 30. Other sources stated that Charles was born at "Contentment" on December 18, but his father's statement is impossible to refute. Excerpts from Robert Grattan's manuscript were supplied by Martha T. Grattan.

3. From information supplied by Col. George Grattan Weston, Ret., grandson of Charles Grattan.

4. Charles Grattan, *Some Reminiscences of Camp Life with Stonewall Jackson—Before He Was Known to Fame.* A copy of the manuscript was supplied by Col. George Grattan Weston, Ret.

5. *Ibid.*

6. *Ibid.*

7. *Ibid.*

8. Charles Grattan, *CSR,* (Washington, D.C., 1961), Microcopy No. 331, Roll 110.

9. *Ibid.*

10. OR, XXV, p. 841.

11. *Ibid.,* p. 845.

12. Quoted from the original in the possession of Col. George Grattan Weston, Ret.

13. Garnett, *Continuation of War Sketches,* UV.

14. Charles Grattan to his wife, July 19, 1864, Mary E. Grattan Papers, SHC/UNC.

15. *Staunton Spectator* (Va.), June 27, 1902.

Grenfell, G. St.L. O.

1. One source states that his name was Ommnacy. Mabel Clare Weaks, "Colonel George St. Leger Grenfell," *The Filson Club History Quarterly* (Louisville: The Standard Printing Company, 1959), Vol. XXXIV, p. 8.

2. Stephen Z. Starr, *Colonel Grenfell's Wars: The Life of a Soldier of Fortune* (Baton Rouge, 1971), p. 17.

3. Don. C. Seitz, *Braxton Bragg: General of the Confederacy* (Columbia: The State Company, 1924), p. 269.

4. Garnett, *Continuation of War Sketches,* UV.

5. Grenfell did accuse Stuart of scheming to get rid of him, but as with much of what Grenfell said and wrote, there is no evidence to support his accusation. Starr, *Colonel Grenfell's Wars: The Life of a Soldier of Fortune,* pp. 111–12.

6. James D. Horan, *Confederate Agent: A Discovery in History* (New York: Crown Publishers, 1954), p. 108.

7. *Ibid.,* p. 191.

Hagan, W. H.

1. The dates given for Hagan's period of service with Stuart include only the time after he was commissioned a lieutenant.

2. George Cary Eggleston, *A Rebel's Recollections* (New York: Hurd and Houghton, 1875), pp. 128–29.

3. Henry Hagan, *CSR,* (Washington, D.C., 1961), Microcopy No. 324, Roll 6.

4. *Ibid.*

5. The rank of major became associated with Hagan after the war and had no connection with his war service, as he attained only the rank of lieutenant during the war.

6. *The Shepherdstown Register* (W.Va.), November 6, 1875.

7. A newspaper reference states that Hagan was proprietor of the hotel. The date of the reference was April 26, 1879.

Hairston, J. T. W.

1. James Thomas Watt Hairston File, VMIA.

2. Peter W. Hairston, *The Cooleemee Plantation and Its People* (Winston-Salem: Hunter Publishing Company, 1986), pp. 139–40.

3. Col. W. A. Love, "Company Records," *CV,* XXX, p. 50.

4. OR, V, p. 184.

5. Hairston File, VMIA.

6. James T. W. Hairston, *CSR,* (Washington, D.C., 1961), Microcopy No. 331, Roll 114.

7. OR, XI, 3, p. 522.

8. James T. W. Hairston, *CSR,* (Washington, D.C., 1961), Microcopy No. 331, Roll 114.

9. OR, XIX, p. 56.

10. James T. W. Hairston, *CSR,* (Washington, D.C., 1961), Microcopy No. 331, Roll 114.

11. J. T. W. Hairston to Gen. Francis H. Smith, January 28, 1867, Records of the Superintendent, Incoming Correspondence, VMIA.

12. Elizabeth Seawell Hairston, *The Hairstons and Penns and Their Relations* (Roanoke, Va.: 1940), p. 28.

Hairston, P. W.

1. Hairston Papers, SHC/UNC.

2. Hairston, *The Cooleemee Plantation and Its People,* pp. 57–58. (Note: The author, Peter W. Hairston, is a descendant of Peter Wilson Hairston of Stuart's staff.)

3. Peter W. Hairston to his wife, September 28, 1861, Hairston Papers, SHC/UNC.

4. Peter W. Hairston to his wife, various dates, Hairston Papers, SHC/UNC.

5. Hairston, *The Cooleemee Plantation and Its People,* pp. 59, 67.

6. Hairston, *Diary of Peter W. Hairston,* Hairston Papers, SHC/UNC.

7. Hairston, *The Cooleemee Plantation and Its People,* p. 72.

Hairston, S. H.

1. Hairston, *The Hairstons and Penns and Their Relations,* p. 25. Another source stated Samuel was born in Patrick County, Va.: Judith Parks America Hill, *A History of Henry County, Virginia* (Baltimore: Regional Publishing Company, 1983), p. 192.

2. Letter in author's files from Laura Frances Parrish, Assistant College Archivist, The College of William and Mary in Virginia.

3. Hairston, *The Hairstons and Penns and Their Relations,* p. 26.

4. Samuel H. Hairston, *CSR,* (Washington, D.C., 1961), Microcopy No. 331, Roll 114.

5. *Ibid.*

Hanger, J. M.

1. Peggy S. Joyner, *Frederich & Peter Hanger of Virginia: 1740 Immigrants, Some Ancestors & Descendants* (typed manuscript, n.d.), p. 1.

2. J. Marshall Hanger, *CSR,* (Washington, D.C., 1961), Microcopy No. 331, Roll 116.

3. *Ibid.*

4. *Ibid.*

5. *Ibid.*

6. E. Griffith Dodson, *Clerk of the House of Delegates and Keeper of the Rolls of the Senate Speakers and Clerks of the Virginia House of Delegates, 1776–1955* (Richmond: 1956), p. 93.

Hullihen, W. Q.

1. E. Hullihen to John T. L. Preston, Esq., September 3, 1858, Records of the Superintendent, Incoming Correspondence, VMIA.

2. From a newspaper article in the files of Trinity Church; the name of the paper and the date of publication are unknown.

3. Walter Q. Hullihen, *CSR,* (Washington, D.C., 1961), Microcopy No. 331, Roll 134.

4. From a newspaper article in the files of Trinity Church; the name of the paper and the date of publication are unknown.

5. Von Borcke, *Memoirs of the Confederate War for Independence,* Vol. II, p. 232.

6. Walter Q. Hullihen, *CSR,* (Washington, D.C., 1961), Microcopy No. 331, Roll 134.

7. *Ibid.*

8. *Ibid.*

9. One source stated that he was assigned to Payne in December 1864, but the records are unclear. Joseph H. Crute, Jr., *Confederate Staff Officers* (Powhatan: Derwent Books, 1982), p. 146. (Crute lists Hullihen as Walter F. Hullehen.)

10. W. Q. Hullihen to W. Gordon McCabe, November 21, 1916, William Gordon McCabe Papers, VHS.

11. Hullihen File, VMIA.

12. ———, *Thornrose: Beautiful Thornrose Cemetery* (Staunton, 1907).

13. *Ibid.,* p. 61.

14. Clement, "A Letter from the Reverend Chiswell Dabney to His Wife in 1907 on the Occasion of the Unveiling of a Statue of General J. E. B. Stuart," *Writings of Maud Carter Clement* (Chatham, Va.: Pittsylvania Historical Society, 1982) p. 31.

Johnson, W. J.

1. Blackford, *War Years with Jeb Stuart,* Appendix.

2. Charles Grattan to his wife, (July 19, 1864), Mary E. Grattan Papers, SHC/UNC.

3. OR, XXV, pp. 1062, 1064–65. Stoneman first seemed to credit Harrison with the capture but later in his report named Tupper as the capturing officer.

4. In all probability, Privates Leopold Levy, one of Johnson's commissary clerks, and John T. Southall of Company "G," 1st Virginia Cavalry were two of the men captured along with Johnson.

5. William J. Johnson, *CSR,* (Washington, D.C., 1961), Microcopy No. 331, Roll 141.

Kennon, R. B.

1. Dr. W. M. Pritchett, "Our Civil War Soldiers," *Brunswick Times-Dispatch* (Va.), October 14, 1976.

2. Unfortunately, while depressed, General Cocke took his own life. Ezra J. Warner, *Generals in Gray* (Baton Rouge: Louisiana State University Press, 1959), p. 57.

3. Clara V. Kennon, comp., *An Experience of Capt. and Assistant Adjutant General Richard Byrd Kennon of Gen. Stuart's Staff (then Colonel Stuart) at First Manassas as Related by Capt. Kennon to His Children Years Later,* n.d., Richard B. Kennon Papers, Virginia State Library, p. 2.

4. Richard B. Kennon, *CSR,* (Washington, D.C., 1961), Microcopy No. 331, Roll 147.

5. Clara V. Kennon, comp., *A Narrative of Capt. and Assistant Adjutant General Richard Byrd Kennon of Gen. Stuart's Staff of the Time Gen. Stuart Crossed the Potomac into Maryland on His Way to Gettysburg,* n.d., Richard B. Kennon Papers, VSL, pp. 1–2.

6. *Ibid.,* p. 7.

7. *Ibid.,* pp. 3, 8.

8. Richard B. Kennon, *CSR,* (Washington, D.C., 1961), Microcopy No. 331, Roll 147.

9. Pritchett, "Our Civil War Soldiers," *Brunswick Times-Dispatch* (Va.), October 14, 1976.

Landstreet, J.

1. The exact dates of Landstreet's service with Stuart certainly cover a lengthier period, but they could not be ascertained from Landstreet's records.

2. OR, XI, 1, p. 1040.

3. "John Landstreet," MACMEC for the year 1892, p. 7.

4. "Who have Withdrawn from the Connection this year?" MACMEC for the year 1862, p. 10.

5. John Landstreet, *CSR,* (Washington, D.C., 1961), Microcopy No. 324, Roll 8. This same source also gives April 9, 1862, as Landstreet's date of appointment.

6. Landstreet to his wife, August 12, 1862, John Landstreet Papers, VHS.

7. Haden, *Reminiscences of J. E. B. Stuart's Cavalry,* p. 6.

8. John W. Thomason, Jr., *Jeb Stuart* (New York: Charles Scribner's Sons, 1930), p. 257.

9. Col. Wm. A. Morgan, "Rev. John Landstreet," *Martinsburg Statesman,* November, 24, 1891.

10. *Ibid.*

11. John Landstreet (son of Rev. Landstreet), *Presentation of Portrait of Chaplain John Landstreet to R. E. Lee Camp Portrait Gallery, Battle Abbey,* January 19, 1925, United Confederate Veterans, Virginia Division, R. E. Lee Camp No. 1, Soldier's Home records, VHS.

12. John Landstreet, *CSR,* (Washington, D.C., 1961), Microcopy No. 324, Roll 8.

13. "John Landstreet," MACMEC for the year 1892, p. 7.

14. Landstreet, *Presentation of Portrait of Chaplain John Landstreet to R. E. Lee Camp Portrait Gallery, Battle Abbey,* January 19, 1925, VHS.

McClellan, H. B.

1. Wade T. Parker, Jr., ed., "A Flag of Truce," *A Diary: Depicting the Experiences of DeWitt Clinton Gallaher in the War Between the States While Serving in the Confederate Army* (n.p., n.d.), pp. 27–28.

2. H. B. McClellan, *CSR,* (Washington, D.C., 1961), Microcopy No. 331, Roll 169.

3. McClellan, *I Rode with Jeb Stuart,* p. v; "Major H. B. McClellan," Lexington *Morning Herald* (Ky.), April 2, 1900.

4. William Henry Perrin, ed., "Maj. H. B. McClellan," *History of Fayette County, Kentucky* (Chicago: O. L. Baskin & Co., Historical Publishers, 1882), p. 651.

5. *Williams Report of the Class of 'Fifty-Eight* (n.p., 1859), p. 9.

6. H. B. McClellan, *CSR,* (Washington, D.C., 1961), Microcopy No. 331, Roll 169.

7. *Ibid.*

8. J. A. Buxton, "One of Stuart's Couriers," *Confederate Veteran,* Vol. XXX, pp. 343–44.

9. One source stated that his wife was from Buckingham County, Va. Perrin, ed., "Maj. H. B. McClellan," *History of Fayette County, Kentucky,* p. 651.

Pelham, J.

1. Charles G. Milham, *Gallant Pelham: American Extraordinary* (Washington, D.C.: Public Affairs Press, 1985), p. 23.

2. John Pelham to Jefferson Davis, February 27, 1861, National Archives and Record Service, comp., *Unfiled Papers and Slips Belonging to Confederate Compiled Service Records,* (Washington, D.C., 1961), Microcopy No. 347, Roll 310.

3. Originally known as the Wise Battery because it was sponsored by Gov. Henry A. Wise, the battery later became Capt. James S. Brown's

Company, Virginia Light Artillery. It was disbanded on October 4, 1862, because of severe losses.

4. Laura C. Perkinson, "Grove's Culpeper Battery: The Building Block of the Stuart Horse Artillery," *The Cannoneer: Newsletter of the John Pelham Historical Association,* Vol. I, No. 1, July 1982, pp. 5–6.

5. Milham, *Gallant Pelham: American Extraordinary,* p. 59.

6. According to their service records, Privates Jesse A. Adams and W. Bollinger were enlisted in Alabama by Pelham on February 2, 1862. Other individuals' records show that Pelham was recruiting, at least, between December 11, 1861, and April 15, 1862.

7. OR, XI, 1, p. 575.

8. Milham, *Gallant Pelham: American Extraordinary,* p. 197.

9. OR, XXV, p. 60.

10. "Jeb" Stuart to Flora Stuart, March 19, 1863, James Ewell Brown Stuart Papers, VHS.

11. "Jeb" Stuart to Dr. Atkinson Pelham, March 29, 1863, Anniston and Calhoun County Public Library.

Powers, P. H.

1. Philip H. Powers to his wife, July 23, 1861, Philip H. Powers Papers, courtesy of Lewis Leigh, Jr., and U.S. Army Military History Institute.

2. Philip H. Powers, *CSR,* (Washington, D.C., 1961), Microcopy No. 331, Roll 201.

3. Philip H. Powers to his sister Mary, April 27, 1862, Philip H. Powers Papers, courtesy of Lewis Leigh, Jr., and USAMHI.

4. *Ibid.*

5. Philip H. Powers, *CSR,* (Washington, D.C., 1961), Microcopy No. 331, Roll 201.

6. Philip H. Powers, *CSR,* (Washington, D.C., 1961), Microcopy No. 324, Roll 11.

7. Philip H. Powers to his wife, May 15, 1864, Philip H. Powers Papers, courtesy of Lewis Leigh, Jr., and USAMHI.

Price, R. C.

1. Blackford, *War Years with Jeb Stuart,* pp. 204–5.

2. R. Channing Price to his mother, March 9, 1863, R. Channing Price Papers, SHC/UNC.

3. R. Channing Price, *CSR,* (Washington, D.C., 1961), Microcopy No. 331, Roll 202.

4. Stuart to Flora, October 26, 1862, James Ewell Brown Stuart Papers, VHS.

5. R. Channing Price to his mother, January 28, 1863, R. Channing Price Papers, SHC/UNC.

6. R. Channing Price, *CSR,* (Washington, D.C., 1961), Microcopy No. 331, Roll 202.

7. R. Channing Price to his mother, March 9, 1863, R. Channing Price Papers, SHC/UNC.

8. R. Channing Price to his mother, March 21, 1863, R. Channing Price Papers, SHC/UNC.

9. R. Channing Price to his mother, March 25, 1863, R. Channing Price Papers, SHC/UNC.

10. R. Channing Price to his mother, April 5, 1863, R. Channing Price Papers, SHC/UNC.

11. R. Channing Price to his mother, April 16, 1863, R. Channing Price Papers, SHC/UNC.

12. Robertson, "Reminiscence of the Years 1861–1865," *HSWCB,* p. 11.

13. "Jeb" Stuart to his cousin Mrs. Thomas Randolph Price, Sr., May 11, 1863, by permission of Adele Mitchell.

Price, T. R.

1. "Price, Thomas Randolph," *Dictionary of American Biography* (New York: Charles Scribner's Sons, 1943), Vol. 15, pp. 219–20.

2. Thomas R. Price, *CSR,* (Washington, D.C., 1961), Microcopy No. 331, Roll 202.

3. R. Channing Price to his mother, April 5 and 16, 1863, R. Channing Price Papers, SHC/UNC; Robertson, "Reminiscence of the Years 1861–1865," *HSWCB,* p. 9; Robert K. Krick, *Lee's Colonels* (Dayton: Morningside Press, 1984), pp. 82–83.

4. *New York Times,* May 21, 1863.

5. W. W. Blackford to Col. J. F. Gilmore, June 7, 1863, Thomas R. Price, *CSR,* (Washington, D.C., 1961), Microcopy No. 331, Roll 202.

Robertson, F. S.

1. Frank Robertson Reade, *In the Saddle with Stuart* (unpublished manuscript), Frank Robertson Reade Papers, UV.

2. Wyndham Robertson to his sister, October 9, 1844, courtesy of James S. Patton.

3. Reade, *In the Saddle with Stuart,* Frank Robertson Reade Papers, UV, p. 10.

4. *Ibid.,* pp. 10–11.

5. Frank S. Robertson to his father (Wyndham Robertson), March 3, 1863, Wyndham Robertson Papers, UCL.

6. Reade, *In the Saddle with Stuart,* Frank Robertson Reade Papers, UV, p. 36.

7. Miranda proved a remarkable animal, with the unique talent of avoiding enemy fire by aligning herself behind the largest tree nearby. She apparently had more sense than the vast majority of the soldiers, who repeatedly exposed themselves to the hail of lead, which killed and maimed indiscriminately.

8. Reade, *In the Saddle with Stuart,* Frank Robertson Reade Papers, UV, p. 51.

9. Frank S. Robertson to his sister, Kate, June 12, 1863, Wyndham Robertson Papers, UCL.

10. Robertson, "Reminiscence of the Years 1861-1865," *HSWCB,* pp. 22–23.

11. *Ibid.,* p. 26.

12. *Ibid.,* p. 27; Reade, *In the Saddle with Stuart,* Frank Robertson Reade Papers, UV, p. 105.

13. Robertson, "Reminiscence of the Years 1861–1865," *HSWCB,* pp. 28–29.

14. *Ibid.,* p. 30.

15. Frank S. Robertson to his sister, Kate, August 28, 1863, Wyndham Robertson Papers, UCL.

Ryals, G. M.

1. Garland M. Ryals, *CSR,* (Washington, D.C., 1961), Microcopy No. 324, Roll 34.

2. Garland M. Ryals, *CSR,* (Washington, D.C., 1961), Microcopy No. 331, Roll 217.

3. OR, XXV, p. 62.

4. Garland M. Ryals, *CSR,* (Washington, D.C., 1961), Microcopy No. 331, Roll 217.

5. *Ibid.*

6. *Ibid.*

7. The campaign to make Ryals a major did not end with his promotion to captain. On December 10, 1863, Brig. Gen. Pierce M. B. Young entered the fray on Ryals's behalf by addressing yet another letter to General Cooper.

8. General Cooper may have intended from the beginning to grant Ryals his majority but may not have felt that he could justify a jump of three ranks (first lieutenant, captain, major) all at once. He therefore may have chosen to do it gradually over a period of two months.

9. OR, XXIX, 2, pp. 453–54.

10. Charles Grattan to his wife, Mary (July 19, 1864), Mary E. Grattan Papers, SHC/UNC.

11. Savannah *Morning News,* December 8, 1889; Savannah *Morning News,* January 31, 1890.

12. Savannah *Evening Press,* September 14, 1904.

Staples, S. G.

1. From information supplied by Edwin M. Wilson, great-grandson of Samuel G. Staples.

2. OR, XI, 1, p. 445.

3. *History of Virginia* (New York: The American Historical Society, 1924), p. 225; Staples autobiography, D. W. Persinger Papers, UVAL.

4. Staples autobiography, D. W. Persinger Papers, UVAL.

5. From information supplied by Edwin M. Wilson, including "Staples Memoranda," by Jean Watts Staples.

Steger, R. W.

1. Mary Armstrong Jefferson, *Old Homes and Buildings of Amelia County,* Virginia, Vol. I (Berryville: Virginia Book Co., 1964), pp. 81–83.

2. Roger Williams Steger, Archives, VMIA.

3. Roger W. Steger, *CSR,* (Washington, D.C., 1961), Microcopy No. 331, Roll 236.

4. Roger Williams Steger, Archives Alumni Files, VMIA.

Stuart, J. H.

1. J. H. Stuart's records with the 18th Mississippi agree as to his date of enlistment, May 24, 1861, but his age at the time of his enlistment is given as twenty on one form and twenty-two on another; James H. Stuart, *CSR,* (Washington, D.C., 1961), Microcopy No. 269, Roll 274.

2. Support for this possibility comes from a letter Hardeman wrote to his father on March 27, 1862. He stated that if the organization of the signal corps failed to materialize, he would "return home and join a cavalry company from Chicot City Ark." His connection to the community could have come from his law practice there before the war. J. Hardeman Stuart to his father, March 27, 1862, James Hardeman Stuart Papers, MDAH.

3. James H. Stuart, *CSR,* (Washington, D.C., 1961), Microcopy No. 269, Roll 274.

4. J. Hardeman Stuart to his Aunt Ann, September 8, 1861, James Hardeman Stuart Papers, MDAH.

5. J. Hardeman Stuart to his father, December 23, 1861, James Hardeman Stuart Papers, MDAH.

6. J. Hardeman Stuart to his sister, Bettie, January 14, 1862, James Hardeman Stuart Papers, MDAH.

7. J. Hardeman Stuart to his Aunt Ann, January 26, 1862, James Hardeman Stuart Papers, MDAH.

8. J. Hardeman Stuart to his father, April 1862, James Hardeman Stuart Papers, MDAH.

9. J. Hardeman Stuart to Aunt Ann, June 11, 1862, James Hardeman Stuart Papers, MDAH.

10. From a diary of J. Hardeman Stuart, James Hardeman Stuart Papers, MDAH.

11. *Ibid.*

12. *Ibid.*

13. *Ibid.*

14. According to some sources Hardeman Stuart was supposed to have charged with his old regiment, the 18th Mississippi. This regiment was not engaged at 2nd Manassas, however. Two letters written to Hardeman's brother, Oscar, from two different individuals state that he fell in with one of these Texas regiments and was killed charging with them. C. M. Parker to Oscar Stuart, September 2, 1862, and G. B. Green to Oscar Stuart, September 1, 1862, Oscar J. E. Stuart and Family Papers, MDAH.

15. C. M. Parker to Oscar Stuart, September 2, 1862, Oscar J. E. Stuart and Family Papers, MDAH.

16. G. B. Green to Oscar Stuart, September 1, 1862, Oscar J. E. Stuart and Family Papers, MDAH.

17. Cooke, *Wearing of the Gray,* p. 146.

Terrell, L. F.

1. John Randolph Tucker, *A Tribute to the Memory of Maj. Lewis Frank Terrell* (n.p., n.d.), VHS.

2. Wallace, *A Guide to Virginia Military Organizations: 1861–1865,* p. 27.

3. Lewis F. Terrell, *CSR,* (Washington, D.C., 1961), Microcopy No. 331, Roll 244.

4. Tucker, *A Tribute to the Memory of Maj. Lewis Frank Terrell,* VHS.

5. Lewis F. Terrell, *CSR,* (Washington, D.C., 1961), Microcopy No. 331, Roll 244.

6. *Ibid.*

7. Von Borcke, *Memoirs of the Confederate War for Independence,* Vol. I, p. 299.

8. Lewis F. Terrell, *CSR,* (Washington, D.C., 1961), Microcopy No. 331, Roll 244.

9. Wise, *The Long Arm of Lee,* p. 424.

10. Tucker, *A Tribute to the Memory of Maj. Lewis Frank Terrell,* VHS; OR, XXV, pp. 58, 63.

11. Lewis F. Terrell, *CSR,* (Washington, D.C., 1961), Microcopy No. 331, Roll 244.

12. Stuart Horse Artillery, *CSR,* (Washington, D.C., 1961), Microcopy No. 258, Roll 51.

13. Lewis F. Terrell, *CSR,* (Washington, D.C., 1961), Microcopy No. 331, Roll 244.

14. Tucker, *A Tribute to the Memory of Maj. Lewis Frank Terrell,* VHS.

Towles, W. E.

1. Rev. John Lipscomb Johnson, *The University Memorial Biographical Sketches* (Baltimore: Turnbull Brothers, 1871), p. 341.

2. *Ibid.,* p. 343.

3. Andrew Booth, *Records of Louisiana Soldiers* (Spartanburg: The Reprint Company, 1988), Vol. III, p. 856.

4. "Jeb" Stuart to Flora Stuart, March 24, 1863, James Ewell Brown Stuart Papers, VHS.

5. OR, XI, 1, p. 570.

6. Johnson, *The University Memorial Biographical Sketches,* p. 344.

7. *Ibid.,* p. 345.

8. From a letter written to the author by Michael F. Howell.

Turner, T. B.

1. Besides these two "Tom" Turners, there was Thomas Shirley Turner (known as "Baltimore Tom"), Thomas Theodore Turner (known as "St. Louis Tom"), Thomas B. Turner (known as "Rectortown Tom," from the 8th Virginia Infantry and the 7th Virginia Cavalry), Thomas H. Turner (known as "Essex County Tom," from McGregor's battery of the Stuart Horse Artillery), and Thomas Turner (no sobriquet; a Marylander from Breathed's battery of the Stuart Horse Artillery).

2. Thomas B. Turner, *CSR,* (Washington, D.C., 1961), Microcopy No. 324, Roll 595.

3. *Ibid.*

4. *Ibid.*

5. Edward Carter Turner's other son was named Bradshaw Beverley Turner.

6. Burke Davis, *Jeb Stuart: The Last Cavalier* (New York: Bonanza Books, 1957), pp. 257–58.

7. Major John Scott, *Partisan Life with Col. John S. Mosby* (New York: Harpers & Brothers, 1867), p. 73.

8. The exact number of men in the party differs according to which account is consulted. The names given here are from James J. Williamson, *Mosby's Rangers* (New York: Time-Life Books, 1982), p. 231, which states that only three men were involved. In his diary, Edward Carter Turner wrote that his son was accompanied by four men. Edward Carter Turner, "The Border Between," *The Years of Anguish: Fauquier County, Virginia 1861–1865* (Annandale, Va.: Bacon Race Books, 1987), p. 40.

9. Turner, *The Years of Anguish,* p. 40

10. Williamson, *Mosby's Rangers,* p. 231

11. Turner, *The Years of Anguish,* pp. 15–40; this account is summarized from Turner's diary.

Venable, A. R.

1. W. Gordon McCabe, "Major Andrew Reid Venable, Jr.," *SHSP,* Vol. XXXVII, p. 70.

2. This is the name that appears on the Venable's gravestone. Another source stated that Mrs. Venable's name was Adeline.

3. McCabe, "Major Andrew Reid Venable, Jr.," *SHSP,* Vol. XXXVII, p. 62.

4. Andrew R. Venable, *CSR,* (Washington, D.C., 1961), Microcopy No. 331, Roll 254.

5. The visits are chronicled in the diaries of William Robertson Bernard and Helen Struan Bernard Robb. Other members of Stuart's headquarters mentioned as having visited "Gay Mont" during this period were Capt. W. W. Blackford, Maj. Heros von Borcke, Maj. John Pelham, Maj. Lewis F. Terrell, Capt. Richard E. Frayser, Capt. William D. Farley, Lt. Chiswell Dabney, Lt. Walter Q. Hullihen, Pvt. Frank Deane (courier), and Pvt. Benjamin Franklin "Frank" Stringfellow (scout); excerpts from these diaries courtesy of James S. Patton.

6. McCabe, "Major Andrew Reid Venable, Jr.," *SHSP,* Vol. XXXVII, p. 64.

7. OR, XXIX, 1, pp. 447, 453.

8. McClellan, *I Rode with Jeb Stuart,* p. 416.

9. Garnett, *Continuation of War Sketches,* UV.

10. Crute, *Confederate Staff Officers,* pp. 119–20; Andrew R. Venable, *CSR,* (Washington, D.C., 1961), Microcopy No. 331, Roll 254.

11. OR, XLII, 1, p. 946.

12. Andrew R. Venable, *CSR,* (Washington, D.C., 1961), Microcopy No. 331, Roll 254.

13. *Farmville Herald* (Va.), October 22, 1909.

14. *Ibid.*

Von Borcke, H.

1. Mr. Adrian H. von Borcke of Hamburg, West Germany, presented evidence that von Borcke's name was Johann Heinrich August Heros von Borcke.

2. Ralph Jerome Cannaday, "The Prussian Rebel," *Civil War Times,* Vol. III, No. 8, December 1961, p. 15.

3. R. F. S. Starr, "A Prussian for Virginia," *CWTI,* Vol. XIX, No. 10, February 1981, p. 34. Because the *Hero* was unloading cargo at Nassau, von Borcke was forced to change to the *Kate.*

4. Von Borcke, *Memoirs of the Confederate War for Independence,* Vol. II, p. 293.

5. *Ibid.,* p. 293.

6. Blackford, *War Years with Jeb Stuart,* p. 219. The trick was to twist and hold down the horse's ear, which distracted the animal, allowing Blackford and Robertson to assist von Borcke back into the saddle. Von Borcke had learned the trick in Europe, and during one of the numerous conversations among campmates, he shared it with Blackford, never suspecting that it would one day save his life. Blackford's recollection of this information while under enemy fire is a tribute to his coolness and intelligence.

7. "Jeb" Stuart to Jefferson Davis, August 10, 1863; Heros von Borcke, *CSR,* (Washington, D.C., 1961), Microcopy No. 331, Roll 27.

8. Wade Hampton to Hon. Jas. A. Seddon, March 20, 1864, and Fitz Lee to Hon. James A. Seddon, March 29, 1864; Heros von Borcke, *CSR,* (Washington, D.C., 1961), Microcopy No. 331, Roll 27.

9. OR, XXVII, 2, p. 712.

10. Wade Hampton to Gen. S. Cooper, December 18, 1864; Heros von Borcke, *CSR,* (Washington, D.C., 1961), Microcopy No. 332, Roll 27.

11. Names and dates regarding von Borcke's children supplied by Adrian H. von Borcke of Hamburg, West Germany.

12. Stuart Wright, *Colonel Heros von Borcke's Journal* (Palaemon Press Limited, 1981), pp. 42–47.

13. Maj. Edgar Erskine Hume, *Colonel Heros von Borcke: A Famous Prussian Volunteer in the Confederate States Army* (The Historical Publishing Co., Inc., 1935), p. 21.

White, B. S.

1. Robertson, "Reminiscence of the Years 1861–1865," *HSWCB,* p. 21

2. Von Borcke, *Memoirs of the Confederate War for Independence,* Vol. II, p. 274.

3. Benjamin White, *CSR,* (Washington, D.C., 1961), Microcopy No. 331, Roll 265.

4. *Montgomery County Sentinel* (Md.), May 18, 1883.

5. OR, XXVII, 2, p. 710.

6. White did remain on Stuart's staff after this date, but his situation was similar to that of von Borcke's in that his effective service with Stuart virtually ended with his wounding. In a letter written in August 1863, Stuart stated that White was assigned to the infirmary "while acting as an assigned officer upon my staff." Benjamin White, *CSR,* (Washington, D.C., 1961), Microcopy No. 331, Roll 265.

7. "Jeb" Stuart to General J. R.Cooke, July 15, 1863, Benjamin White, *CSR,* (Washington, D.C., 1961), Microcopy No. 331, Roll 265.

8. Benjamin White, *CSR,* (Washington, D.C., 1961), Microcopy No. 331, Roll 265.

9. OR, XLIII, 2, p. 926.

10. Benjamin White, *CSR,* (Washington, D.C., 1961), Microcopy No. 331, Roll 265.

STUART'S HEADQUARTERS PERSONNEL

1. Eggleston, *A Rebel's Recollections,* pp. 135–36.

Freed, G. W.

1. When Stuart was surprised and almost captured at Verdiersville on August 18, 1862, he had to leap the back fence of the property to escape, leaving behind his haversack, blanket, talma (overcoat), cloak, and hat.

2. Luther, "In Memory of Geo. W. Freed," *Staunton Spectator & Vindicator* (Va.), June 5, 1908.

3. Garnett, *Continuation of War Sketches,* UV.

4. Luther, "In Memory of Geo. W. Freed," *Staunton Spectator & Vindicator* (Va.), June 5, 1908.

Gallaher, D. C.

1. "The Last Roll," DeWitt Clinton Gallaher, *CV,* XXXV, p. 66.

Levy, L.

1. *Richmond Dispatch,* November 16, 1897; from information supplied by Mrs. Warren West, a descendant of Private Levy.

2. Mrs. Leopold Levy to her children, May 31, 1907, courtesy of Mrs. Warren West.

3. Leopold Levy, *CSR,* (Washington, D.C., 1961), Microcopy No. 324, Roll 8.

4. *Richmond Dispatch,* November 16, 1897; Mrs. Leopold Levy to her children, May 31, 1907.

5. Leopold Levy, *CSR,* (Washington, D.C., 1961), Microcopy No. 324, Roll 8.

6. Mrs. Leopold Levy to her children, May 31, 1907.

Smith, C. M.

1. From a copy of Lee's letter, courtesy of Samuel Hopkins, grandson of Channing M. Smith.

2. From family material courtesy of Samuel Hopkins.

3. Channing M. Smith, *CSR,* (Washington, D.C., 1961), Microcopy No. 324, Roll 46.

4. From a copy of Lee's letter courtesy of Samuel Hopkins.

5. From a copy of Lee's letter courtesy of Samuel Hopkins.

6. Channing M. Smith, *CSR,* (Washington, D.C., 1961), Microcopy No. 324, Roll 209.

APPENDIXES

1. Blackford, *War Years with Jeb Stuart,* p. 71.

2. Frank S. Robertson to his sister Kate, May 24, 1863, Wyndham Robertson Papers, UCL.

3. An enlarged and more inclusive view of R. Channing Price's photograph shows him also holding a kepi in much the same pose as Chiswell Dabney. Thomas Turner wears a kepi in his photograph, but since the picture was taken before the war, it cannot be included in the survey of what the staff wore.

4. In the famous photograph of von Borcke in his lieutenant colonel's shell jacket, the giant Prussian wears high boots.

BIBLIOGRAPHY

MANUSCRIPTS

Anniston and Calhoun County Public Library, Alabama
　　Stuart to Dr. Atkinson Pelham, March 29, 1863
Dickinson College, Boyd Lee Spahr Library
　　George Freaner to Christian Philip Humrich, August 1851
Duke University
　　John Esten Cooke Papers
　　James Ewell Brown Stuart Papers
Florida State Archives
　　Soldier's Pension Claim of Norman R. FitzHugh
The Huntington Library, California
　　Dabney Ball Papers
Jefferson County Museum, West Virginia
　　Roger Preston Chew Papers
Library of Congress
　　Jedediah Hotchkiss Papers
Mississippi Department of Archives and History
　　James Hardeman Stuart Papers
　　Oscar J. E. Stuart and Family Papers
National Archives (Compiled Service Records)
　　Compiled Service Records of Confederate Soldiers Who Served in Organizations
　　　Raised Directly by the Confederate Government
　　Compiled Service Records of Confederate Soldiers Who Served in Organizations
　　　from the State of Mississippi
　　Compiled Service Records of Confederate Soldiers Who Served in Organizations
　　　from the State of Virginia
　　Compiled Service Records of Confederate General and Staff Officers, and Non-
　　　Regimental Enlisted Men
　　Unfiled Papers and Slips Belonging to Confederate Compiled Service Records

Letters Quoted from National Archives
　　Dabney Ball File
　　Robert F. Beckham File
　　William W. Blackford File
　　Heros von Borcke File
　　Alexander R. Boteler File
　　Thomas R. Price File
　　Benjamin S. White File
　　Unfiled Papers and Slips
Southern Historical Collection, Library of the University of North Carolina at Chapel Hill
　　R. Channing Price Papers
　　Peter Wilson Hairston Papers
　　Blackford Family Papers
　　Mary E. Grattan Papers
Virginia Historical Society
　　James Ewell Brown Stuart Papers

John Landstreet Papers
George Freaner to Mrs. E. W. Fontaine, October 6, 1864
William Gordon McCabe Papers
United Confederate Veterans, Virginia Division, R. E. Lee Camp No.1, Richmond,
  Soldier's Home Records, ca. 1885–1940
The Virginia Military Institute Archives, Lexington, Va.
  Roger P. Chew File
  James Thomas Watt Hairston File
  Walter Q. Hullihen File
  Milton Rouse File
  Roger W. Steger File
Virginia State Library
  Richard B. Kennon Papers
United States Army Military History Institute
  Philip H. Powers Papers
University of Chicago Library (Department of Special Collections)
  Wyndham Robertson Papers
University of Virginia
  William Willis Blackford Papers
  Garnett Family Papers
  Frank Robertson Reade Papers
  D. W. Persinger Papers
Williams College
  H. B. McClellan File

PRIVATELY OWNED PAPERS

Mrs. George G. Grattan IV
  Excerpts from *Manuscript of Major Robert Grattan*
Maria Hood
  Theodore Stanford Garnett Papers
Samuel Hopkins
  Channing M. Smith Family History
Robert deT. Lawrence IV
  Thomas B. Turner Papers
Lewis Leigh, Jr.
  Philip H. Powers Papers
Adele Mitchell
  "Jeb" Stuart to Mrs. Thomas Randolph Price,
    Sr., May 11, 1863
James S. Patton
  Wyndham Robertson to sister, October 9, 1844
  William Robertson Bernard Diary
  Helen Struan Bernard Robb Diary
Isabel Smith Stewart
  William D. and Henry S. Farley Family Papers and History
Mrs. Warren West
  Leopold Levy Family Papers
George Grattan Weston
  Charles Grattan Papers
Edwin M. Wilson
  Samuel G. Staples Family History

NEWSPAPERS

Baltimore *Evening Sun*
Brunswick, Va., *Times-Dispatch*
Clarke, Va., *Courier*
Columbia, S.C., *State Columbia*
Farmville, Va., *Herald*
Frederick, Md., *Daily News*
Hagerstown, Md., *Mail* (weekly)
Hagerstown, Md., *Morning Herald*
Martinsburg, W.Va., *Herald*
Martinsburg, W.Va., *Independent*
Martinsburg, W.Va., *Statesman*
Montgomery County, Md., *Sentinel*
News & Courier
New York Times
Norfolk, Va., *Norfolk Landmark*
Norfolk, Va., *Virginian-Pilot*
Richmond, Va., *Dispatch*
Roanoke, Va., *Times*
Savannah, Ga., *Morning News*
Savannah, Ga., *Evening Press*
Shepherdstown, W.Va., *Shepherdstown Register*
Staunton, Va., *Daily News*
Staunton, Va., *Spectator*
Staunton, Va., *Spectator & Vindicator*
Tri-Weekly Mercury
True Index

ARTICLES AND UNPUBLISHED MANUSCRIPTS

Bakeless, John. "Catching Harry Gilmor." *Civil War Times Illustrated* X, no. 1 (April 1971): pp. 34–40.

Ball, William Watts. "Captain William C. [*sic*] Farley, Part II." *The Laurens Advertiser* (S.C.), December 3, 1936.

Buxton, J. A. "One of Stuart's Couriers." *Confederate Veteran* XXX (1931): p. 343.

Cannaday, Ralph Jerome. "The Prussian Rebel." *Civil War Times* III, no. 8 (December 1961): p. 15.

"Capt. Wm. Downs Farley." *Tri-Weekly Mercury*, July 7, 1863.

Clement, Maud Carter. "Sketch of the Life of Chiswell Dabney," *Writings of Maud Carter Clement*. Chatham, Va.: Pittsylvania Historical Society, 1982, pp. 7–13.

Clement, Maud Carter. "A Letter from the Reverend Chiswell Dabney to His Wife in 1907 on the Occasion of the Unveiling of a Statue of General J. E. B. Stuart," *Writings of Maud Carter Clement*. Chatham, Va.: Pittsylvania Historical Society, 1982, pp. 31–33.

Dabney, Chiswell. "The Battle of Brandy Station," *Writings of Maud Carter Clement*. Chatham, Va.: Pittsylvania Historical Society, 1982, pp. 56–61.

Davis, Erick F. "A Pikesville Diary of 1864," *History Trails*. Baltimore: Baltimore County Historical Society, 1979, pp. 9–13.

Fielding, Geoffrey W., ed. "Gilmor's Field Report of His Raid in Baltimore County." *Maryland Historical Magazine*, September 1952.

Frayser, Richard E. "A Narrative of Stuart's Raid in the Rear of the Army of the Potomac." *Southern Historical Society Papers* XI (1883): pp. 505–17.

Goldsborough, Eleonora Goldsborough (Winter). *The House of Goldsborough* IV, 1932.

Graham, Martin F. "The Immortal 600: Their Long Journey to Freedom." *Virginia Country's Civil War Quarterly* X (September 1987): pp. 50–53.

Hubbell, Jay B., ed. "The War Diary of John Esten Cooke." *The Journal of Southern History* VII (1941): pp. 526–40.

"John Landstreet." *Minutes of the Annual Conferences of the Methodist Episcopal Church, South,* for the year 1892.

Joyner, Peggy S. *"Frederich & Peter Hanger of Virginia: 1740 Immigrants, Some Ancestors & Descendants."* N.p., n.d.

Lebby, Robert. "The First Shot on Fort Sumter." *The South Carolina Historical and Genealogical Magazine* (July 1911): pp. 142–45.

Love, W. A. "Company Records." *Confederate Veteran* XXX (1931): p. 50.

McCabe, W. Gordon. "The Honorable Theodore S. Garnett." *Southern Historical Society Papers* Series III, no. XLI, (September 1916): pp. 68–81.

McCabe, W. Gordon. "Major Andrew Reid Venable, Jr.," *Southern Historical Society Papers* XXXVII (1938): pp. 61–73.

Morgan, Wm. A. "Rev. John Landstreet." *Martinsburg Statesman* (W.Va.). November 24, 1891.

Parker, Wade T., Jr., ed. "A Flag of Truce." *A Diary: Depicting the Experiences of DeWitt Clinton Gallaher in the War Between the States While Serving in the Confederate Army.* N.p., n.d.

Perkinson, Laura C. "Grove's Culpeper Battery: The Building Block of the Stuart Horse Artillery." *The Cannoneer: Newsletter of the John Pelham Historical Association* I, no.1 (July 1982): pp. 5–6.

Pritchett, Dr. W. M. "Our Civil War Soldiers." *Brunswick Times-Dispatch* (Va.), October 14, 1976.

"The Reverend Chiswell Dabney." *Pittsylvania County Paper, Writings of Maud Carter Clement.* Chatham: Pittsylvania Historical Society, 1982.

"Rev. Dabney Ball." *Minutes of the Annual Conferences of the Methodist Episcopal Church, South.* Nashville: Southern Methodist Publishing House, 1884, pp. 10–11.

Starr, R. F. S. "A Prussian for Virginia," *Civil War Times Illustrated* XIX, no. 10 (February 1981): pp. 33–39.

Steele, Nimrod Hunter. "The Nimrod Hunter Steele Diary and Letters." *Diaries, Letters, and Recollections of the War Between the States III.* Winchester: Winchester-Frederick County Historical Society Papers, 1955.

"Sword Captured during War of Confederacy Is Returned." *News & Courier,* November 26, 1923.

Warthen, Harry J., Jr. "Family Ties," *Civil War Times Illustrated* XXII, no. 6 (October 1983): pp. 34–35.

Weaks, Mabel Clare. "Colonel George St. Leger Grenfell." *The Filson Club History Quarterly* XXXIV (January 1960): pp.5–23.

"Who have Withdrawn from the Connection this year?" *Minutes of the Annual Conferences of the Methodist Episcopal Church, South,* for the year 1862. New York: Carlton and Porter, p. 10.

Williams Report of the Class of 'Fifty-Eight. N.p., 1859.

BOOKS

The Annals of the War, by Leading Participants, North and South. Philadelphia: The Times Publishing Company, 1879.

Augusta Parish and Trinity Episcopal Church 1746–1946. Staunton, Va., 1946.

Balfour, Daniel T. *13th Virginia Cavalry.* Lynchburg, Va.: H. E. Howard, 1986.

Beaty, John O. *John Esten Cooke.* Port Washington, N.Y.: Kennikat Press, N.d.

Blackford, W. W. *War Years with Jeb Stuart.* New York: Charles Scribner's Sons, 1945.

Boatner III, Mark M. *The Civil War Dictionary.* New York: David McKay Company, 1959.

Booth, Andrew. *Records of Louisiana Soldiers.* Spartanburg, S.C.:The Reprint Company, 1988.

Bradshaw, Ada Bruce Desper. *Civil War Diary of Charles McVivar.* N.p., n.d.

Brown, Stuart E., Jr. *The Old Chapel, Clarke County, Virginia.* N.p., n.d.

Calfee, Mrs. Berkeley G. *Confederate History of Culpeper County.* N.p., n.d.

Cooke, John Esten. *Outlines from the Outpost.* Chicago: The Lakeside Press, 1961.

Cooke, John Esten. *Wearing of the Gray.* Bloomington, Ind.: Indiana University Press, 1977.

Crane, John, and James F. Keiley. *West Point: "The Key to America."* New York: Whittlesey House, 1947.

Crute, Joseph H., Jr. *Confederate Staff Officers.* Powhatan, Va.: Derwent Books, 1982.

Davis, Burke. *Jeb Stuart: The Last Cavalier.* New York: Bonanza Books, 1957.

———. *They Called Him Stonewall.* New York: Rinehart & Company, 1954.

Dawson, John Harper. *Wildcat Cavalry.* Dayton, Ohio: Morningside House, 1982.

Delauter, Roger U. *18th Virginia Cavalry.* Lynchburg, Va.: H. E. Howard, 1985.

Dickinson, Jack L. *8th Virginia Cavalry.* Lynchburg, Va.: H. E. Howard, 1986.

Dictionary of American Biography. New York: Charles Scribner's Sons, 1943.

Divine, John E. *35th Battalion Virginia Cavalry.* Lynchburg, Va.: H. E. Howard, 1985.

Dodson, E. Griffith. *Clerk of the House of Delegates and Keeper of the Rolls of the Senate Speakers and Clerks of the Virginia House of Delegates, 1776–1955.* Richmond, 1956.

Douglas, Henry Kyd. *I Rode with Stonewall.* Greenwich, Conn.: Fawcett Publications, 1961.

Downey, Fairfax. *Clash of Cavalry: The Battle of Brandy Station.* New York: David McKay Company, 1959.

Driver, Robert J., Jr. *1st Virginia Cavalry.* Lynchburg, Va.: H. E. Howard, 1991.

———. *14th Virginia Cavalry.* Lynchburg, Va.: H. E. Howard, 1988.

Eggleston, George Cary. *A Rebel's Recollections.* New York: Hurd and Houghton, 1875.

Farley, Randolph W. *The Farley, Fairlie, Farlo Family.* Hollis, N.H.: Times Press, 1902.

Faust, Patricia L., ed. *Encyclopedia of the Civil War.* New York: Harper & Row, 1986.

Freeman, Douglas Southall. *Lee's Lieutenants.* New York: Charles Scribner's Sons, 1942.

———. *R. E. Lee: A Biography.* New York: Charles Scribner's Sons, 1962.

Frye, Dennis E. *12th Virginia Cavalry.* Lynchburg, Va.: H. E. Howard, 1988.

Glass, Robert C., and Carter Glass, Jr. *Virginia Democracy: A History of the Achievements of the Party and Its Leaders in the Mother of Commonwealths, The Old Dominion.* Springfield, Va.: Democratic Historical Association, 1937.

Goldsborough, W. W. *The Maryland Line in the Confederate Army.* Gaithersburg, Md.: Olde Soldier Books, 1987.

Hackley, Woodford B. *The Little Fork Rangers: A Sketch of Company "D" Fourth Virginia Cavalry.* Richmond: Press of the Dietz Printing Company, 1927.

Haden, B. J. *Reminiscences of J. E. B. Stuart's Cavalry.* Charlottesville, Va.: Progress Publishing Co., n.d.

Hairston, Elizabeth Seawell. *The Hairstons and Penns and Their Relations.* Roanoke, Va., 1940.

Hairston, Peter Wilson. *The Cooleemee Plantation and Its People.* Winston-Salem, N.C.: Hunter Publishing Company, 1986.

Halsey, Ashley, Jr. *Who Fired the First Shot.* New York: Hawthorne Books, 1963.

Hassler, William Woods, *Colonel John Pelham: Lee's Boy Artillerist.* Chapel Hill, N.C.: The University of North Carolina Press, 1960.

Hill, Judith Parks America. *A History of Henry County, Virginia.* Baltimore: Regional Publishing Company, 1983.

History of Virginia. New York: The American Historical Society, 1924.

Horan, James D. *Confederate Agent: A Discovery in History.* New York: Crown Publishers, 1954.

Hotchkiss, Jed. *Confederate Military History: Virginia.* Dayton, Ohio: Press of Morningside Bookshop, 1975.

Hume, Edgar Erskine. *Colonel Heros von Borcke: A Famous Prussian Volunteer in the Confederate States Army.* Charlottesville, Va.: The Historical Publishing Co., 1935.

Jefferson, Mary Armstrong. *Old Homes and Buildings of Amelia County, Virginia.* Berryville, Va.: Virginia Book Co., 1964.

Johnson, John Lipscomb. *The University Memorial Biographical Sketches.* Baltimore: Turnbull Brothers, 1871.

Jones, Virgil Carrington. *Ranger Mosby.* Chapel Hill, N.C.: The University of North Carolina Press, 1944.

————. *Gray Ghosts and Rebel Raiders.* McLean, Va.: EMP Publications, 1984.

Jordan, Ervin L., Jr. *Charlottesville and the University of Virginia in the Civil War.* Lynchburg, Va.: H. E. Howard, 1988.

Krick, Robert K. *Lee's Colonels.* Dayton, Ohio: Press of Morningside Bookshop, 1984.

————. *9th Virginia Cavalry.* Lynchburg, Va.: H. E. Howard, 1982.

McClellan, H. B. *I Rode With Jeb Stuart.* Bloomington, Ind.: Indiana University Press, 1958.

McDonald, William N. *A History of the Laurel Brigade.* Arlington: R. W. Beatty, Ltd., 1969.

McKinsey, Folger, and T. J. C. Williams. *History of Frederick County, Maryland.* Baltimore: Regional Publishing Company, 1979.

Mercer, Philip. *The Gallant Pelham.* Kennesaw, Ga.: Continental Book Company, 1958.

Milham, Charles G. *Gallant Pelham: American Extraordinary.* Gaithersburg, Md.: Butternut Press, 1985.

Musick, Michael P. *6th Virginia Cavalry.* Lynchburg, Va.: H. E. Howard, 1990.

Nanzig, Thomas P. *3rd Virginia Cavalry.* Lynchburg, Va.: H. E. Howard, 1989.

Neese, George M. *Three Years in the Confederate Horse Artillery.* Dayton, Ohio: Press of Morningside Bookshop, 1983.

Perrin, William Henry, ed. *History of Fayette County, Kentucky.* Chicago: O. L. Baskin & Co., Historical Publishers, 1882.

Phisterer, Frederick. *Statistical Record of the Armies of the United States.* New York: The Blue & The Gray Press, n.d.

Portrait and Biographical Record of the Sixth Congressional District—Maryland. New York: Chapman Publishing Company,1898.

Ramey, Emily G., and John K. Gott, eds. *The Years of Anguish: Fauquier County, Virginia 1861–1865.* Annandale, Va.: Bacon Race Books, 1965.

Richards, John R., comp. *Florida State Gazetteer.* New York: The South Publishing Company, 1886–87.

Robertson, Frank S. *Reminiscences of the Years 1861–1865.* Abingdon, Va.: Historical Society of Washington County,Virginia, 1986.

Scharf, J. Thomas. *History of Western Maryland.* Baltimore: Regional Publishing Company, 1968.

Scheel, Eugene M. *The Civil War in Fauquier County, Virginia.* Warrenton, 1985.

Scott, J. L. *36th and 37th Battalions Virginia Cavalry.* Lynchburg, Va.: H. E. Howard, 1986.

Scott, John. *Partisan Life with Col. John S. Mosby.* New York: Harpers & Brothers, 1867.

Sergent, Mary Elizabeth. *They Lie Forgotten.* Middletown, N.Y.: The Prior King Press, 1986.

Sigaud, Louis A. *Belle Boyd: Confederate Spy.* Richmond: The Dietz Press, 1944.

Smith, Gustavas W. *Confederate War Papers.* New York: Atlantic Publishing and Engraving Co., 1884.

Sommers, Richard J. *Richmond Redeemed: The Siege of Petersburg.* New York: Doubleday & Company, 1981.

Starr, Stephen Z. *Colonel Grenfell's Wars.* Baton Rouge, La., 1971.

Steitz, Don C. *Braxton Bragg: General of the Confederacy.* Columbia, S.C.: The State Company, 1924.

Stiles, Kenneth L. *4th Virginia Cavalry.* Lynchburg, Va.: H. E. Howard, 1985.

Swanberg, W. A. *First Blood: The Story of Fort Sumter.* New York: Charles Scribner's Sons, 1957.

Thomas, Emory M. *Bold Dragoon: The Life of J. E. B. Stuart.* New York: Harper & Row, Publishers, 1986.

Thomason, John W., Jr. *Jeb Stuart.* New York: Charles Scribner's Sons, 1930.

Thornrose: Beautiful Thornrose Cemetery. Staunton, Va., 1907.

Tucker, John Randolph. *A Tribute to the Memory of Maj. Lewis Frank Terrell.* N.p., n.d.

Vandiver, Frank. *Mighty Stonewall.* New York: McGraw-Hill Book Company, 1957.

Von Borcke, Heros. *Memoirs of the Confederate War.* Dayton, Ohio: Morningside House, 1985.
Wallace, Lee A., Jr. *A Guide to Virginia Military Organizations 1861–1865.* Lynchburg, Va.:
    H. E. Howard, 1986.
Warner, Ezra J. *Generals in Blue.* Baton Rouge, La.: Louisiana State University Press, 1964.
————. *Generals in Gray.* Baton Rouge, La.: Louisiana State University Press, 1959.
Williamson, James J. *Mosby's Rangers.* New York: Time-Life Books, 1981.
Wise, Jennings Cropper. *The Long Arm of Lee.* New York: Oxford University Press, 1959.
Wright, Stuart. *Colonel Heros von Borcke's Journal.* Palaemon Press Limited, 1981.

SOURCES OF PHOTOGRAPHS

Index